The Special Educator's Comprehensive Guide to 301 Diagnostic Tests

Revised and Expanded Edition

The Special Educator's Comprehensive Guide to 301 Diagnostic Tests

Revised and Expanded Edition

Roger Pierangelo, Ph.D.
George Giuliani, J.D., Psy.D.

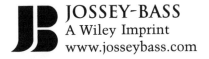

JOSSEY-BASS
A Wiley Imprint
www.josseybass.com

Published by Jossey-Bass
A Wiley Imprint
989 Market Street, San Francisco, CA 94103-1741   www.josseybass.com

Jossey-Bass books and products are available through most bookstores. To contact Jossey-Bass directly call our Customer Care Department within the U.S. at 800-956-7739, outside the U.S. at 317-572-3986, or fax 317-572-4002.

Jossey-Bass also publishes its books in a variety of electronic formats. Some content that appears in print may not be available in electronic books.

Library of Congress Cataloging-in-Publication Data
Pierangelo, Roger.
  The special educator's comprehensive guide to 301 diagnostic tests / by
Roger Pierangelo and George Giuliani.— Rev. and expanded ed.
      p. cm.
  Rev. ed. of: Special educator's complete guide to 109 diagnostic tests /
Roger Pierangelo, George Giuliani. 1998.
  Includes bibliographical references.
  ISBN-13: 978-0-7879-7813-6 (alk. paper)
  ISBN-10: 0-7879-7813-2 (alk. paper)
  1. Children with disabilities—Psychological testing. 2. Children with disabilities—Education—Ability testing. 3. Examinations—Interpretation. 4. Educational tests and measurements.
  I. Giuliani, George A., 1938- II. Pierangelo, Roger. Special educator's complete guide to 109 diagnostic tests. III. Title.
  LC4019.P53 2006
  371.9'04—dc22 $21.75
                                          2005025816

Printed in the United States of America
REVISED AND EXPANDED EDITION
PB Printing   10 9 8 7 6 5 4 3 2 1

About This Guide

The *Special Educator's Comprehensive Guide to 301 Diagnostic Tests* is the updated, detailed, and wide-ranging reference source from its predecessor, *Special Educator's Complete Guide to 109 Diagnostic Tests*. The *Guide* has been developed to provide those involved in the special education process with a detailed overview of the most frequently used tests for diagnosing suspected disabilities—ranging from intelligence, perception, and language to achievement, psychosocial behavior, and social maturity—from the early childhood years through adolescence.

Filled with practical tools, information, and suggestions, the *Guide* offers up-to-date guidance on gathering information and the parental role in the assessment process.

Furthermore, the *Guide* contains the following information designed to assist readers in selecting, understanding, and interpreting the wide range of tests available to them:

- A thorough explanation of the most commonly used diagnostic tests
- In-depth coverage of areas measured by each test
- Understanding a student's behavior during testing
- Reporting assessment test results to parents

Helpful and Unique Features

Most current books on test information do not deal with the practical, day-to-day needs of the special educator as a diagnostician. They explain the tests or cite statistical information, yet rarely include information on what everything means when examined as a whole.

The most commonly used measures found in this *Guide* offer special educators everything necessary to go from interpretation to remediation in one book. Every chapter of the *Guide* has been designed to make readers more knowledgeable concerning the often overwhelming process of special education testing and interpretation.

Other features of the *Guide* include:

- The developmental step-by-step approach takes readers through a variety of topics and procedures necessary for a realistic, complete awareness of children with disabilities.
- The easy-to-read format contains a wealth of information and proven suggestions from the authors' extensive experiences.
- Material is presented in such a way as to help readers use its content to provide students with the most appropriate education available in the least restrictive environment.
- Useful information can be applied immediately to the various experiences that special educators encounter in classrooms and in schools.

In Closing

From our experience, we know that most educational diagnosticians, teachers, and other special education professionals need some assistance in understanding the etiology (cause), nature, and meaning of the vast amount of diagnostic material available to them. With the proper tests and the proper interpretation, they can more rapidly and appropriately address many problems exhibited by students with special needs. Early diagnosis and intervention can mean all the difference in an individual's life.

Roger Pierangelo, Ph.D.
George Giuliani, J.D., Psy.D.

This book is dedicated to my wife, Jackie, and my two children, Jacqueline and Scott, who provide me with the love and purpose for undertaking projects that I hope will enhance the lives of others. My life has been blessed by their loving presence.

I also dedicate this book to my parents, who provided me with the secure and loving foundation from which to grow; my sister, Carol, who makes me smile and laugh; and my brother-in-law, George, who has always been a positive guiding light in my professional journey.

—R.P.

This book is dedicated to my wife, Anita, and two children, Collin and Brittany, who give me the greatest life imaginable. The long hours and many years it took to finish this book would never have been possible without the support of my loving wife. Her constant encouragement, understanding, and love provide me with the strength I need to accomplish my goals. I thank her with all my heart.

I also dedicate this book to my parents, who have given me support and guidance throughout my life. Their words of encouragement and guidance have made my professional journey a rewarding and successful experience.

—G.G.

Acknowledgments

In the course of writing this book, we have encountered many professional and outstanding sites. It has been our experience that those resources have contributed and continue to contribute enormous information, support, guidance, and education to parents, students, and professionals in the area of special education. Although we have accessed many worthwhile sites, we especially thank and acknowledge the National Dissemination Center for Children with Disabilities and the National Institutes of Health.

Roger Pierangelo: I extend thanks to the following: the faculty, administration, and staff in the Department of Graduate Special Education and Literacy at Long Island University; Ollie Simmons, for her friendship, loyalty, and great personality; the students and parents of the Herricks Public Schools I have worked with and known over the past thirty-five years; the late Bill Smyth, a truly gifted and "extraordinary ordinary" man; and Helen Firestone, for her influence on my career and tireless support of me.

George Giuliani: I extend sincere thanks to all of my colleagues at Hofstra University in the School of Education and Allied Human Services. I am especially grateful to those who have made my transition to Hofstra University such a smooth one, including James R. Johnson (former dean), Maureen Murphy (dean), Penelope J. Haile (associate dean), Daniel Sciarra (chairperson), Frank Bowe, Diane Schwartz (graduate program director of early childhood special education), Darra Pace, Gloria Wilson, Mary McDonald, Laurie Johnson, Joan Bloomgarden, Jamie Mitus, Estelle Gellman, Joseph Lechowicz, Holly Seirup, Adele Piombino, Marjorie Butler, Eve Byrne, Sherrie Basile, and Linda Cappa. I also thank my brother and sister, Roger and Claudia; mother-in-law, Ursula Jenkeleit; sisters-in-law, Karen and Cindy; and brothers-in-law, Robert and Bob. They have provided me with encouragement and reinforcement in all of my personal and professional endeavors.

The Authors

Roger Pierangelo is the co-Executive Director of the National Association of Special Education Teachers, vice president of the National Association of Parents with Children in Special Education, and co-executive director of American Academy of Special Education Professionals. He is a full-time associate professor in the Department of Special Education and Literacy at Long Island University. He has been an administrator of special education programs, served for eighteen years as a permanent member of committees on special education, has over thirty years of experience in the public school system as a regular education classroom teacher and school psychologist, and is a consultant to numerous private and public schools, the Parent-Teacher Association, and Special Education Parent-Teacher Association groups. He has also been an evaluator for the New York State Office of Vocational and Rehabilitative Services and a director of a private clinic. He is a New York State licensed clinical psychologist, certified school psychologist, Diplomate Fellow in Forensic Psychology, and a Diplomate Fellow in Child and Adolescent Psychology.

Dr. Pierangelo earned his B.S. from St. John's University, M.S. from Queens College, Professional Diploma from Queens College, Ph.D. from Yeshiva University, and Diplomate Fellow in Forensic Psychology from the International College of Professional Psychology. He is a member of the American Psychological Association, New York State Psychological Association, Nassau County Psychological Association, New York State Union of Teachers, and Phi Delta Kappa.

George Giuliani is the co-Executive Director of the American Academy of Special Education Professionals, National Association of Special Education Teachers, and president of the National Association of Parents with Children in Special Education. He is a full-time associate professor at Hofstra University's School of Education and Allied Human Services in the Department of Counseling, Research, Special Education, and Rehabilitation as the director of the special education program at the graduate school. He earned his B.A. from the College of the Holy Cross, M.S. from St. John's University, J.D. from City University Law School, and Psy.D. from Rutgers University, the Graduate School of Applied and Professional Psychology, and is a Diplomate Fellow in Forensic Psychology and a Diplomate Fellow in Child and

Adolescent Psychology. Dr. Giuliani is also a New York State licensed psychologist and certified school psychologist, and he has an extensive private practice focusing on children with special needs. He is a member of the American Psychological Association, New York State Psychological Association, the National Association of School Psychologists, Suffolk County Psychological Association, Psi Chi, and the Council for Exceptional Children.

Dr. Giuliani has been involved in early intervention for children with special needs and is a consultant for school districts and early childhood agencies. He has provided numerous workshops for parents and teachers on a variety of psychological and educational topics.

Dr. Roger Pierangelo is the author of *The Special Educator's Survival Guide, The Special Educator's Book of Lists,* and *301 Ways to Be a Loving Parent;* and coauthor with Dr. George Giuliani of *Special Educator's Complete Guide to 109 Diagnostic Tests; Assessment in Special Education: A Practical Approach; Transition Services in Special Education: A Practical Approach; Learning Disabilities: A Practical Approach to Foundations, Diagnosis, Assessment, and Teaching; Why Your Students Do What They Do—and What to Do When They Do It—Grades K–5; Why Your Students Do What They Do—and What to Do When They Do It—Grades 6–12; Creating Confident Children in the Classroom: The Use of Positive Restructuring,* and *What Every Teacher Should Know About Students with Special Needs;* and *The Big Book of Special Education Resources.*

Contents

Part One

Overview of Assessment

Chapter 1

Introduction to Assessment

Although children with disabilities have unique differences, the reality is that they may share many common features and characteristics. In particular, students with disabilities normally require some form of special education services. Before making a determination about special services offered to students with disabilities, a complete and comprehensive evaluation must be done (Pierangelo & Giuliani, 2006a).

According to the National Dissemination Center for Children with Disabilities (1999), assessment in educational settings serves five primary purposes:

- *Screening and identification:* To screen children and identify those who may be experiencing delays or learning problems
- *Eligibility and diagnosis:* To determine whether a child has a disability and is eligible for special education services and to diagnose the specific nature of the student's problems or disability
- *IEP development and placement:* To provide detailed information so that an individualized education program (IEP) may be developed and appropriate decisions may be made about the child's educational placement
- *Instructional planning:* To develop and plan instruction appropriate to the child's special needs
- *Evaluation:* To evaluate student progress

❖ Defining Assessment

Often special educators mistakenly use the terms *assessment* and *testing* interchangeably. Although these terms may appear to be synonymous, they are not. Testing is just one part of the assessment process (Pierangelo & Giuliani, 2006a). Assessment in special education involves gathering information about a student's strengths and needs in all areas of concern (Friend & Bursuck, 2006). A comprehensive assessment completed by school professionals may address any aspect of a student's educational functioning (Huefner, 2000).

❖ Purpose of Assessment

Following a referral for a suspected disability of a child and with written parental or guardian permission, an individual evaluation is conducted. This means that both formal and informal types of assessment will be given. The results of these comprehensive assessment measures will help determine the most practical educational goals and objectives for the student. Furthermore, this assessment will assist, among other information, in determining the least restrictive educational setting (Pierangelo & Giuliani, 2006a).

Assessment plays a critical role in the determination of six important decisions (Pierangelo & Giuliani, 2006a):

- *Evaluation decisions:* Information collected in the assessment process can provide detailed information on a student's strengths, weaknesses, and overall progress.
- *Diagnostic decisions:* Information collected in the assessment process can provide detailed information on the specific nature of the student's problems or disability.
- *Eligibility decisions:* Information collected in the assessment process can provide detailed information of whether a child is eligible for special education services.
- *IEP decisions:* Information collected in the assessment process can provide detailed information so that an IEP may be developed.
- *Educational placement decisions:* Information collected in the assessment process can provide detailed information so that appropriate decisions may be made about the child's educational placement.
- *Instructional planning decisions:* Information collected in the assessment process is critical in planning instruction appropriate to the child's special social, academic, physical, and management needs.

❖ Classifications Under IDEA 2004

The Individuals with Disabilities Education Improvement Act (IDEA 2004), Public Law (P.L.) 108–446, is the federal law that protects those in special education. Under IDEA 2004, there are thirteen separate categories of disabilities. Children are eligible to receive special education services and supports if they meet the eligibility requirements for at least one of the disabling conditions listed in P.L. 108–446 and if it is determined that they are in need of special education services (Pierangelo & Giuliani, 2006a).

IDEA 2004 states that the purpose of IDEA is:

(1) (A) to ensure that all children with disabilities have available to them a free appropriate public education that emphasizes special education and related services designed to meet their unique needs and prepare them for further education, employment, and independent living;

(B) to ensure that the rights of children with disabilities and parents of such children are protected; and

(C) to assist States, localities, educational service agencies, and Federal agencies to provide for the education of all children with disabilities;

(2) to assist States in the implementation of a statewide, comprehensive, coordinated, multidisciplinary, interagency system of early intervention services for infants and toddlers with disabilities and their families;

(3) to ensure that educators and parents have the necessary tools to improve educational results for children with disabilities by supporting system improvement activities; coordinated research and personnel preparation; coordinated technical assistance, dissemination, and support; and technology development and media services; and

(4) to assess, and ensure the effectiveness of, efforts to educate children with disabilities . . .

Under IDEA 2004, C.F.R. Section 300.8, the term *child with a disability* means a child evaluated in accordance with Sections 300.304–300.311 as having mental retardation, a hearing impairment including deafness, a speech or language impairment, a visual impairment including blindness, serious emotional disturbance (hereafter referred to as emotional disturbance), an orthopedic impairment, autism, traumatic brain injury, an other health impairment, a specific learning disability, deaf-blindness, or multiple disabilities, and who, by reason thereof, needs special education and related services.

The definitions of disabling conditions under IDEA 2004 are listed below:

- *Autism:* A developmental disability significantly affecting verbal and nonverbal communication and social interaction, generally evident before age three, that adversely affects a child's educational performance. Other characteristics often associated with autism are engagement in repetitive activities and stereotyped movements, resistance to environmental change or change in daily routines, and unusual responses to sensory experiences. The term does not apply if a child's educational performance is adversely affected because the child has an emotional disturbance.
- *Deafness:* A hearing impairment that is so severe that the child is impaired in processing linguistic information through hearing, with or without amplification, that adversely affects a child's educational performance.
- *Deaf-Blindness:* Concomitant hearing and visual impairments, the combination of which causes such severe communication and other developmental and educational problems that they cannot be accommodated in special education programs solely for children with deafness or children with blindness.
- *Emotional Disturbance:* A condition exhibiting one or more of the following characteristics over a long period of time and to a marked degree that adversely affects a child's educational performance: (A) An inability to learn that cannot be explained by intellectual, sensory, or health factors. (B) An inability to build or maintain satisfactory interpersonal relationships with peers and teachers. (C) Inappropriate types of behaviors or feelings under normal circumstances. (D) A general pervasive mood of unhappiness or depression. (E) A tendency to develop physical symptoms or fears associated with personal or school problems. (ii) The term includes schizophrenia. The term does not apply to children who are socially maladjusted, unless it is determined that they have an emotional disturbance.
- *Hearing Impairment:* An impairment in hearing, whether permanent or fluctuating, that adversely affects a child's performance but that is not included under the definition of deafness in this section.
- *Mental Retardation:* Significantly subaverage general intellectual functioning, existing concurrently with deficits in adaptive behavior and manifested during the developmental period, that adversely affects a child's performance.
- *Multiple Disabilities:* Concomitant impairments (such as mental retardation–blindness, mental retardation–orthopedic impairment, etc.) the combination of which causes such severe educational problems that the problems cannot be accommodated in special education programs solely for one of the impairments. The term does not include deaf-blindness.
- *Orthopedic Impairment*: A severe orthopedic impairment that adversely affects a child's educational performance. The term includes impairments caused by congenital anomaly (e.g., club foot, absence of some member), impairments caused by disease (e.g., poliomyelitis, bone tuberculosis), and impairments from other causes (e.g., cerebral palsy, amputations, and fractures or burns that cause contractures).
- *Other Health Impairment:* Having limited strength, vitality, or alertness due to chronic or acute health problems, such as a heart condition, tuberculosis, rheumatic fever,

nephritis, asthma, sickle cell anemia, hemophilia, epilepsy, lead poisoning, leukemia, or diabetes, that adversely affects a child's educational performance.

- *Specific Learning Disability:* A disorder in one or more of the basic psychological processes involved in understanding or in using language, spoken or written, which may manifest itself in an imperfect ability to listen, think, speak, read, write, spell, or do mathematical calculations. Such term includes conditions such as perceptual disabilities, brain injury, minimal brain dysfunction, dyslexia, and developmental aphasia. Such term does not include such learning problem that is primarily the result of visual, hearing, or motor disabilities; of mental retardation; of emotional disturbance; or of environmental, cultural or economic disadvantage.

  Under IDEA 2004, when determining whether a child has a specific disability, a local education agency shall not be required to take into consideration whether a child has a severe discrepancy between achievement and intellectual ability.

- *Speech or Language Impairment:* A communication disorder such as stuttering, impaired articulation, a language impairment, or a voice impairment that adversely affects a child's educational performance.

- *Traumatic Brain Injury:* An acquired injury to the brain caused by an external physical force, resulting in total or partial functional disability or psychosocial impairment or both, and that adversely affects a child's educational performance. The term applies to open or closed head injuries resulting in impairments in one or more areas, such as cognition; language; memory; attention; reasoning; abstract thinking; judgment; problem solving; sensory, perceptual, and motor abilities; psychosocial behavior; physical functions; information processing; and speech. The term does not apply to brain injuries that are congenital or degenerative or to brain injuries induced by birth trauma.

- *Visual Impairment:* An impairment in vision that, even with correction, adversely affects a child's educational performance. The term includes both partial and sight blindness.

❖ How Students Are Identified for Assessment

There are normally three ways in which a student may be identified for assessment of a suspected disability (Pierangelo & Giuliani, 2006a):

1. School personnel may suspect the presence of a learning or behavior problem and ask the student's parents for permission to evaluate the student individually. This may have resulted from a student's scoring far below his or her peers on some type of screening measure and thereby alerting the school to the possibility of a problem.

2. The child's teacher or teachers may observe serious symptoms in academic, social, emotional, or physical areas in the classroom that create concern.

3. The child's parents may notice or suspect symptoms that may need attention and bring their concerns to the attention of the school personnel.

❖ General Evaluation Provisions Under IDEA 2004

Under IDEA 2004, all evaluations must abide by the following requirements:

1. A child must be evaluated in all areas related to the suspected disability, including, if appropriate, health, vision, hearing, social and emotional functioning, general intelligence, academic performance, communicative status, and motor abilities. In addition, the evaluation must be sufficiently comprehensive to identify all of the child's special education and related services needs, whether or not they are commonly linked to the disability category in which the child is classified.

2. No single assessment procedure may be used as the sole criterion for determining whether a child has a disability and for determining an appropriate educational program for the child.

3. Evaluation materials must be technically sound and may assess the relative contribution of cognitive and behavioral factors, in addition to physical and developmental factors.

4. Evaluation materials and procedures must be appropriate to determine the nature and extent of a learning impairment and directly assist in identifying areas of educational need.

5. Evaluation materials and procedures must be validated for the specific purpose for which they are to be used.

6. Evaluation of a child who may have limited English proficiency should assess the child's proficiency in English as well as the child's native language to distinguish language proficiency from disability needs.

7. Evaluation materials and procedures used to assess a child with limited English proficiency must be selected and administered to ensure they measure a potential disability and need for special education rather than English language skills.

8. Evaluation materials and procedures must be provided in the language that most likely will yield accurate information on what the child knows and can do academically and functionally.

   The native language of the child is that language normally used by the child in the home and learning environment.

   For individuals with deafness, blindness, or no written language, it is the mode of communication normally used, such as sign language, Braille, or oral communication.

   A determination of "not feasible" is made when after reasonable effort, an individual cannot be located who is capable and willing at a reasonable cost to communicate in the child's primary language or communicate in the child's most frequent mode of communication.

   If a district determines that it is not feasible to conduct the evaluation in the child's primary language or other mode of communication, it must document its reasons and describe the alternatives used. Even when it is not feasible to assess the child in his or her native language or mode of communication, the group of qualified professionals and a parent of the child must still obtain and consider accurate and reliable information that will enable them to make an informed decision as to whether the child has a disability and the effects of the disability on the child's educational achievement.

9. Evaluation materials and procedures must be administered in adherence with the developer's instructions and by appropriately trained personnel. If an assessment is not conducted under standard conditions (pertaining, for example, to the qualifications of the test administrator or the method of test administration), this must be noted in the evaluation report.

10. All materials and procedures used for assessing and identifying children with disabilities must be selected and administered so as not to be biased in terms of race, gender, culture, or socioeconomic status.

11. Tests must be selected and administered so as best to ensure that when a test is administered to a child with impaired sensory, manual, or speaking skills, the test results accurately reflect the child's aptitude or achievement level, or whatever other factors the test purports to measure, rather than reflecting the child's impaired sensory, manual, or speaking skills (unless those skills are the factors that the test purports to measure).

12. Tests and other evaluation materials include those tailored to assess specific areas of educational need (including current classroom-based assessments and observations of

the teacher and related service providers, physical condition, social or cultural background, information provided by the parents, and adaptive behavior), and not merely those that are designed to provide a single general intelligence quotient.

13. Information obtained from all of these sources, including evaluations and information provided by the parents, must be documented and carefully considered.

14. A child shall not be determined to have a disability if the determinant factor is a lack of explicit and systematic instruction in essential components of reading (phonemic awareness, phonics, vocabulary development, reading fluency, including oral reading skills, and reading comprehension strategies), a lack of instruction in math, or limited English proficiency.

❖ Individuals Involved in the Assessment Process

Under IDEA 2004, an evaluation of a child with a suspected disability must be made by a multidisciplinary team or groups of persons including at least one teacher or specialist with knowledge in the area of the suspected disability. These professionals must use a variety of assessment tools and strategies to gather relevant functional and developmental information, including information provided by the parent, that will assist in determining whether a child has a disability as defined under federal law.

The members of the multidisciplinary team often include the following:

- Parents
- At least one regular education teacher of the child if he or she is, or may be, participating in the regular education environment
- At least one of the child's special education teachers or special education providers
- A representative of the public agency who is qualified to provide or supervise the provision of special education and who knows about the general curriculum (that is, the curriculum used by nondisabled students) and about available resources
- An individual who can interpret the instructional implications of the evaluation results
- Other individuals (invited at the parents' discretion or the discretion of the public agency) who have special knowledge or expertise regarding the child
- Representatives from any other agency that may be responsible for paying for or providing transition services (if the child is sixteen years old or, if appropriate, younger and will be planning for life after high school)
- The child, if appropriate (if transition services needs or transition services will be considered, the student must be invited to be part of the evaluation group)
- Other qualified professionals, as appropriate

❖ Components of a Comprehensive Assessment

An evaluation for special education should always be conducted on an individual basis. When completed, it is a comprehensive assessment of the child's abilities. According to the law, the comprehensive assessment on any child with a suspected disability must include assessment on every possible area of suspicion. This includes, where appropriate, evaluating a child's:

- Health
- Vision
- Hearing
- Social and emotional status
- General intelligence

- Academic performance
- Communicative status and motor abilities

The evaluation must be sufficiently comprehensive to identify all of the child's special education and related services needs, whether or not commonly linked to the disability category in which the child has been classified. Assessment tools and strategies that provide relevant information that directly assists persons in determining the educational needs of the child must be provided (Pierangelo & Giuliani, 2006a).

❖ Conclusion

A thorough and comprehensive assessment of a child can greatly enhance his or her educational experience. The assessment process has many steps and needs to be appropriately done. Furthermore, no one individual makes all of the decisions for a child's classification; it is done by a multidisciplinary team. Special educators have a professional responsibility to understand the laws, steps, and various assessment measures and procedures used in the special education process (Pierangelo & Giuliani, 2006a).

Chapter 2

The Special Education Process: How a Child Is Recommended for a Comprehensive Assessment

Special educators need to be very familiar with the process by which children are identified as having a disability in order to assist parents and students through the process. This special education process has a number of steps that must follow federal, state, and district guidelines, which have been created to protect the rights of students, parents, and school districts. Working together within these guidelines ensures a comprehensive assessment of a student and the proper special education services and modifications if required. When a student is having difficulty in school, professional staff typically make many attempts to resolve the problem. When these interventions do not work, a more extensive look at the student is required.

This chapter describes the information needed in order to guarantee that any child in special education is provided a comprehensive opportunity to clearly define his or her symptoms, problems, needs, learning styles, strengths and weaknesses, classroom placements, modifications, and so on. Although the specific stages of this process may vary from state to state, district to district, and even school to school, the steps outlined in this chapter encompass the concepts and information that should be used by any system.

There are two stages to the referral process. The first stage looks at potential high-risk children and determines the most suitable direction for that child. This direction can include a wide variety of options: change of program, consolidation of program, disciplinary actions, or parent counseling, for example. If the child study team, the local school committee assigned to monitor children with potential problems, determines that the child being reviewed fits the criteria for a suspected disability, the second stage begins: this is the start of the special education process.

This two-stage process has several steps. Each should be reviewed in terms of responsibilities, the legal procedures, parental rights and responsibilities, and implications for the student. This chapter goes through this process step by step.

Forms for the exhibits in this chapter can be found in Appendix B.

11

❖ Determining Whether There Is a Suspected Disability

Every staff member within a school should be trained to identify certain behaviors in children that may indicate a more serious problem. When such behaviors begin to interfere with the child's ability to function in school, the term used to indicate such a child is *high risk*.

The referral of a potential high-risk student can come from a variety of sources:

- The child's classroom teacher
- The special education teacher who identifies a potential problem
- The child's special teachers: art, music, and others
- The child's parents
- The school's support staff, such as a psychologist, speech and language therapist, or occupational therapist
- Outside professionals, such as the child's therapist or medical doctor
- The child
- Clergy
- Legal personnel such as police

When one of these sources feels a child needs to be reviewed as a potential high-risk student, a referral form is filled out and forwarded to a local school committee called the *child study team* (CST). Many schools are moving toward a team approach to the identification of potential high-risk students. This local school-based team may be called the child study team, school-based support team, pupil personnel team, or something else depending on the school district. The members of this team work as a single unit in determining the possible etiology (cause), contributing factors, educational status, prognosis (outcome), and recommendations for the referred student. The concept of bringing together many disciplines to help work on a case is the major objective of the CST. In this way, the school has many experts covering many fields and disciplines rather than a single individual trying to determine all of the factors.

❖ Membership of the CST

The child study team is usually made up of the following individuals:

- Administrator (usually the principal or assistant principal)
- School psychologist
- Nurse
- Classroom teacher
- Social worker
- Special education teacher
- Guidance counselor on the secondary level
- Reading teacher
- Speech/language teacher

The members of this team usually meet on a regular basis, once or twice a week depending on the caseload. This is a local school-based support team and should not be confused with the individualized education program (IEP) committee, which is a district-based team. The child study team does not have a parent member and is not required to do so, as is the IEP committee. A special education teacher will always be a sitting member of this committee. It will be up to the individual administrator to choose which special education teacher in the school will fill this position.

The school usually has a wealth of information about all children, distributed among a number of people and a number of records. Gathering this information after a referral has been initiated will provide a thorough picture of the child and his or her abilities and patterns. This information is usually gathered once a referral has been made and prior to the initial CST meeting. Gathering information will contribute to the overall picture of the child and assist each member of the CST in bringing certain information to the first meeting.

Administrator

This individual may bring prior knowledge or contact with the family or student, prior disciplinary or suspension information, and legal information that may have been communicated to the school by outside professionals. This information may have been obtained from prior conferences between previous teachers and parents and between administrators and parents that may be important in understanding the child's patterns and history.

School Psychologist

This psychologist may bring past psychological reports, information gained from observation, reports from therapists or outside mental health facilities, clinical interviews, or screening information. Besides this information, the school psychologist may bring prior teachers' reports. These comments written on report cards or in permanent record folders may provide a different view of the child under a different style of teaching. Successful years with positive comments may be a clue to the child's learning style and may provide information about the conditions under which the child responds best. If these reports or comments are not available, then someone should interview prior teachers to determine patterns of strengths and weaknesses. While certain information can be brought by several members, it is sometimes more likely that the school psychologist will bring group intelligence test information. This information is usually found in the permanent record folder. In some districts and on some tests, the term *school abilities index* has replaced the term *IQ* or *intelligence quotient*.

Nurse

This individual may bring past and present medical information, medical reports, medication information, screening results on eyesight and hearing, observation, and other medical screening information. This information will need to be investigated for indications of visual or hearing difficulties, prescribed medication that may have an effect on the child's behavior (such as antihistamines), and medical conditions in need of attention or that can be contributing to the child's situation.

Classroom Teacher

This individual may bring examples of class work, informal testing results, anecdotal records, observations of social interactions, academic levels, and parent intake information. He or she will also bring comments or reports of prior parent-teacher interviews. The classroom teacher usually brings attendance records that need to be reviewed for patterns of lateness or absence. If such patterns exist, the reasons should be investigated to rule out medical causes (hospital stays, illnesses), psychological causes (dysfunctional family patterns, school phobia), or social causes (peer rejection or isolation). The pattern of absences should also be reviewed. Two children both absent ten days a year can be absent for very different reasons. One child may have been out twice for five days each due to illness, while the other may have been out ten Mondays, possibly indicating a potential problem.

Classroom teachers should also bring nonstandardized assessment information. There may be times when teachers will assess students in their classroom using a variety of nonstandardized assessment measures, such as portfolios or informal reading inventories. Try to gather this material or ask the teacher to bring it to the initial meeting of the CST.

Social Worker

If a district has a social worker on staff, he or she may bring family history or information, history of outside agency involvement, observation, or experiences with the student in group interaction.

Special Education Teacher

This individual may bring past academic testing results, perceptual testing results, observations, prior special education services, outside educational test results and reports, copies of IEPs on students who have been involved in special education, and any screening results. This teacher may also be asked to bring standardized test score information on the child being discussed. These scores are usually in or on the permanent record folder found in the main office.

The entire permanent record folder on each child should always be brought to the meeting. Besides the previously mentioned information, this folder may contain teacher comments dating back to kindergarten, records from previous schools, individual reading test results, family information, and, most important, a history of the child's report card grades. This will be helpful in looking for patterns of strengths and weaknesses in academic, social, and behavioral areas over the years as well as number and types of schools attended. There are times when a child will be enrolled in several schools over several years. The reasons for the many moves should be investigated and may add to the child's adjustment difficulties.

Reading Teacher

This individual may bring observation information and past and recent reading diagnostic, screening, or standardized testing results.

Speech/Language Teacher

This individual may bring any past test results, outside test reports, observation if required, and screening results.

Classroom Observation

The law usually requires that a child who may be referred for special education be given a classroom observation. This observation may be required at some time in the process and often before the initial CST meeting. The special education teacher may be asked to do it. Observing children in different settings is a necessary part of the referral process and offers another perception of the child. A child who has been referred should be observed in a variety of settings, including the classroom, playground, gym, and lunchroom. It is very helpful to do this observation prior to the initial CST meeting.

Basic behaviors need to be observed: attention, focus, aggressiveness, compliance, flexibility, rigidity, oppositional behavior, shyness, controlling behavior, distractibility, impulsivity, social interaction, and so on. There are many types of prepared observation forms available. These forms usually fall into two categories: unstructured and structured.

An unstructured observation checklist (Exhibit 2.1) can be used to fill in any information that the special educator feels is important about a series of behaviors. Any of a number of general areas can and should be observed. This is an informal working scale for your own information. The spaces provided allow comments and notes that may shed some light on the child's overall pattern and severity of symptoms.

The structured type of observation form in Exhibit 2.2 defines in behavioral terms the specific target behaviors for observation.

Exhibit 2.1. Unstructured Observation Checklist

Name of Student Observed: **Observer:**

Date of Observation: **Place of Observation:**

Classroom   Playground   Lunchroom   Gym

Behaviors Observed

Impulsivity

Attention to task

Attention span

Conformity to rules

Social interaction with peers

Aggressiveness

Level of teacher assistance required

Frustration levels

Reaction to authority

Verbal interaction

Procrastination

Organizational skills

Developmental motor skills

Exhibit 2.2. Classroom Observation Form

Student's Name/ID Number _____

Date of Birth _____ Dominant Language _____

Dates of Observation _____ Length of Observation _____

Observer _____ Position _____

Classroom Observed _____ Location _____

Teacher's Name _____

Subject area being taught _____

TASK-INDIVIDUAL

A. When assigned a task, the student:

❏ Initiates task without need for teacher's verbal encouragement

❏ Requests help in order to start task

❏ Complains before getting started on a task

❏ Demands help in order to start a task

❏ Actively refuses to do task despite teacher's encouragement

❏ Passively retreats from task despite teacher's encouragement

B. While working on task, the student:

❏ Works independently

❏ Performs assigned task without complaint

❏ Needs teacher's verbal encouragement to keep working

❏ Needs teacher in close proximity to keep working

❏ Needs physical contact from teacher to keep working

❏ Seeks constant reassurance to keep working

❏ Is reluctant to have work inspected

❏ Belittles own work

C. At the end of the assigned time, the student:

❏ Completes task

❏ Takes pride in completed task

❏ Goes on to next task

❏ Refuses to complete task

SOCIAL INTERACTION

The student:

❏ Establishes a relationship with one or two peers

❏ Shares materials with peers

❏ Respects property of peers

Exhibit 2.2. *(continued)*

- ❏ Gives help to peers when needed
- ❏ Accepts help from peers when needed
- ❏ Establishes a relationship with most peers
- ❏ Teases or ridicules peers
- ❏ Expresses prejudiced attitudes toward peers
- ❏ Physically provokes peers
- ❏ Physically hurts peers
- ❏ Seeks to be attacked by peers
- ❏ Participates appropriately in group activities
- ❏ Postpones own needs for group objectives
- ❏ Withdraws from group
- ❏ Is overly assertive in group
- ❏ Disrupts group activities (for example, by calling out, using provocative language)
- ❏ Exhibits aggressive behavior within group not amenable to teacher intervention

RELATIONSHIP TO TEACHER

The student:

- ❏ Tries to meet teacher's expectations
- ❏ Functions adequately without constant teacher encouragement
- ❏ Interacts with teacher in nondemanding manner
- ❏ Responds to teacher without haggling
- ❏ Tests limits, tries to see how much teacher will allow
- ❏ Seeks special treatment from teacher
- ❏ Responds to teacher's criticism without fear
- ❏ Responds to teacher's criticism without verbal anger
- ❏ Responds to teacher's criticism without physical outbursts (for example, temper tantrums)
- ❏ Defies teacher's requirement
- ❏ Scorns or ridicules teacher's support
- ❏ Responds with anger when demands are thwarted by teacher
- ❏ Blames and accuses teacher ("doesn't help," "doesn't like me")
- ❏ Abuses teacher verbally (no apparent cause)
- ❏ Abuses teacher physically (no apparent cause)
- ❏ Requires close and constant supervision because behavioral controls are so limited

COMMENTS

Whatever the situation, the special education teacher should review the vast amount of available records in the school building and be ready to ask necessary questions pertaining to this information. In the area of observations, the following questions should be discussed by the team:

• *Is there a difference between the nature of behaviors in a structured setting such as a classroom and an unstructured setting such as a playground?* This factor may shed light on the child's need for a more structured environment in which to learn. Children who do not have well-developed internal control systems need a highly structured environment to maintain focus and appropriate behavior. Some children cannot shift between structured and unstructured and back again. They may not possess the internal monitor that regulates conformity and logical attendance to rules. These children may be more successful in a structured play setting set up by teachers during the lunch hour.

• *Does the child seem to respond to external boundaries?* This factor is important to the teacher since it is a monitor of potential learning style. If a child who lacks internal controls does conform to external boundaries such as time-out or teacher proximity during work time, then this factor needs to be taken into consideration when prescribing classroom management techniques. When the child conforms to such boundaries, then his or her behavior is a message for what works for this child.

• *What is the child's attention span during academic tasks?* Attention span at different ages is measured normally in minutes or hours. Special educators should become aware of the normal attention span for children of all ages and compare the child over several activities and days to see if a pattern of inattention is present. If the attention span is very short for someone of his or her age, then modifications to workload, such as shorter but more frequent assignments, may have to be included.

• *Does the child require constant teacher supervision or assistance?* A child who requires constant teacher supervision or assistance may be exhibiting a wide variety of possible symptomatic behavior that may be resulting from but not limited to attention deficit disorder, processing problems, emotional difficulties involving need for attention, need for control, high anxiety, internal stress, limited intellectual capacity, hearing problems, and others. All of these areas need to be checked, and a good evaluation should determine the root of such behavior. However, the key is always the frequency, intensity, and duration of such symptoms.

• *Does the child interact appropriately with peers?* Observing children at play can tell a great deal about them—for example, their self-esteem, tension levels, social maturity, and physical development. Social interaction is more common in children over the age of six or seven, while parallel play is still common in younger children. Appropriate social interaction provides insight into the child's own internal boundaries and organization. A child who always needs to control may be masking high levels of tension. The more controlling a child is, the more out of control he or she is feeling. A child who can appropriately conform to group rules, delay his or her needs for the good of the team, and conform to rules and various changes or inconsistencies in rules may be very self-assured and with a low anxiety level. The opposite is most always typical of children at risk. However, one should always consider developmental stages since certain behaviors, such as control, may be more typical at early ages.

• *Is the child a high- or low-status child?* Observing a child in different settings is an opportunity to see the social status of the child and its impact on his behavior. Low-status children, as often seen in children with learning disabilities, are more likely to feel insignificant and therefore fail to receive positive social cues that help reinforce feelings of self-esteem.

Guidance Counselor on the Secondary Level

This individual is very important on the secondary level since he or she represents all the child's teachers in communicating classroom progress, strengths, and weaknesses. Since it is not realistic on the secondary level for all seven or eight of the child's teachers to attend the CST meeting, the guidance counselor reviews the child's situation and progress with all the teachers prior to the meeting and then reports the results to the CST. He or she may also bring past report cards, schedules, standardized group test results, the permanent record folder, parent consultation information, aptitude testing results, observations, and past teacher comments.

Referral Forms

Regardless of the fact that special education teachers normally focus on children already classified, they can be part of the CST and therefore need to know what to do in order to get children with possible disabilities the services they require. They will be an integral part of this team and will offer the team guidance in exploring a child's potential for special education services. Although most referrals come from regular education personnel, the referral may be for a child with a suspected disability.

If an individual feels that a child should be reviewed by the CST, he or she is usually asked to fill out a referral form. This form may vary from school to school, district to district, and state to state. The major purpose of the form is to alert other school professionals that a student is exhibiting difficulties that may require further attention. These referral forms usually appear in two forms: open-ended and structured. Exhibit 2.3 shows an example of a completed open-ended referral form.

This type of referral form allows the individual filling out the form to include what he or she considers the most important issues about this child. However, the information given to the team may not be the type of information necessary for an overall indication of severity, history, and nature of the symptoms presented. Therefore, some schools or districts may use a more direct form called a *structured referral form*. This form takes the individual filling it out through a series of questions that more closely answer the information the team is seeking. In the example in Exhibit 2.4, the individual is guided through a series of questions that define the specific areas that the child study team sees as important. Room is also left at the end for any further comments that the individual feels are necessary to the understanding of the child.

Exhibit 2.3. Open-Ended Referral Form

Name: Matthew Jones   **Date of Referral:** November 3, 2005

Grade: 4

Age: 9–10

Teacher: Mrs. Brown

Date of Birth: January 2, 1996

Why are you referring this child?

Matthew is experiencing severe academic difficulties in the classroom. He procrastinates, is easily distracted, refuses to hand in work, has a short attention span, and has difficulty with social skills. The other children tolerate him but are losing patience. I have contacted the mother, and she has mentioned that these problems have been around for some time.

I have estimated his ability to be at least average and his academic performance is well below grade level in all areas.

He further exhibits low frustration tolerance, an unwillingness to attempt new concepts, self-criticism, and intolerance for those around him.

I am very concerned about Matthew's deterioration this year and would like some advice on how to handle the situation.

Has parent been notified of this referral? yes __X__ no _____

Administrator's signature _____ **date** _____

19

Exhibit 2.4. Referral to the Child Study Team

Student Name: Mary Williams

Grade Level: 3

Teacher Name: Mrs. Lacy

Parents' Names: Mary/John

Date of Referral: December 1, 2005

Date of Birth: 8/1/97

Chronological Age: 8–4

Phone: 555-8976

Please answer the following questions using behavioral terms.

What symptoms is the child exhibiting that are of concern at this time?

Mary is having a great deal of problems in my class. She exhibits numerous problems. She rarely hands in work; fails many tests, especially spelling and math; procrastinates; makes excuses; and has a great deal of difficulty handing in homework assignments.

What have you tried that has worked?

The only thing that seems to work is contacting her parents, but that is short-lived, and any noticeable changes last only for a day or two. Then Mary is right back to her patterns.

What have you tried that does not seem to work toward alleviating these symptoms?

I have attempted several things, including peer tutoring, limiting assignments, change of seat, parent conferences, and small group interventions all to see if she could accomplish anything, but nothing has worked.

What are the child's current academic levels of functioning?

From informal testing, I consider Mary to be low average in all academic skills and ability.

Any observable behavioral or physical limitations?

Mary does not seem to have any physical limitations.

What is the child's social behavior like?

Mary does not seem to avoid any social contact with the other children. She spends a great deal of her time with her friends.

Current performance estimates (below, on, or above grade level)

Reading: average   Math: below   Spelling: below

Have the parents been contacted? yes ___X___ no _____ If no, why not?

Further comments?

Parents are concerned. Not sure what to do next.

Initial Child Study Team Meeting

Once the referral is made and the available information gathered by all the members of the team, the initial child study team meeting is held. The team will try to review everything available on the child and make some recommendations as to its next step or direction on this case. When reviewing this information, the special educator may want to make sure that the team considers certain questions to help them decide the best options—for example:

• *Has this child ever been referred to the CST?* Prior referral may indicate a historical disturbance or long-term problem and therefore a more serious situation, especially if the same pattern exists. Situational disturbances with no prior problems usually have a better prognosis.

• *Do we have any prior psychological, educational, language, or other evaluations?* This information is important so that the child is not put through unnecessary testing. These reports also offer the team another perspective on the problem.

• *What are the comments from past teachers?* Never assume that the child is always the problem. Obtaining comments from past teachers may give a different picture and may also help pinpoint the changes that have led to the referral. A child who has had positive teacher feedback for the past four years and all of a sudden begins to deteriorate may have experienced something over the summer, experienced changes in the home, or may be having a personality conflict with the teacher.

• *Is anyone familiar with other family members?* Family patterns of behavior may help define contributing factors to the child's problem. They may also offer the team some experience on the best approach to take with this family.

• *What is going on at home?* Many symptoms in school may be the result of tension or problems emanating from the home. If they are interpreted as school-related problems, the true issue will be overlooked, and the team will be treating symptoms, not problems. Home issues affect every child, and some more than others. A brief conversation with the parents by the classroom teacher can possibly identify situational disturbances (brief but intense patterns of tension such as a loss of a job, death of a relative, or parental separation) that may be causing the child to have difficulty focusing or performing in school.

• *What does the developmental history look like?* A child's developmental history can be like a fingerprint in determining possible causes or influences that may be contributing to the problem. A thorough intake that covers all areas of a child's history is a crucial factor in the proper diagnosis of a child's problems. Information on developmental milestones, traumatic experiences, hospitalizations, or prior testing, for example, offers a closer look at the total child.

• *Are there any medical issues that might have an impact on this case?* These issues are crucial, and the existence of medical problems should always be determined first. Difficulties with hearing, eyesight, taking medication, or severe allergies, among others, may be significant contributors to poor performance and may be masked as "unmotivated," "lazy," "stubborn," and so on.

• *When was the last time the child's vision and hearing were checked?* These two factors should be ruled out immediately as having any influence on the presenting problem. If the child has not been evaluated in either area within at least one year or symptoms indicate possible visual or auditory involvement (for example, squinting, eye fatigue, failure to hear directions), then a retest is indicated.

• *Has anyone observed this child?* The observation should always be a piece of the contributing information presented to the CST. One member, usually the psychologist, social worker, guidance counselor, or special education teacher, should observe the child in a variety of situations prior to the first CST meeting. It is important for the team to know how this child functions in structured and unstructured settings.

- *Do we have samples of the child's class work?* Samples of class work over a period of time offer a clearer overview of the child's abilities and attitude toward class work. This also gives several team members an opportunity to observe possible academic symptoms that may first appear in written work.

- *Have the parents been notified of the teacher's concerns?* The team should not be the one to notify the parents that a problem may exist. It is the responsibility of the classroom teacher to alert the parents that he or she is concerned and would like a closer look by the CST. Parents do not have a legal right to refuse such a request since it is considered a normal school procedure. The parents should also be notified by the teacher that someone from the team will be in touch to gather more information and review any findings.

Options of the Child Study Team

This process of discussion on a specific child may take one or several meetings depending on the complications and needs of the case. Sometimes the CST may need further information not available at the time of the initial meeting—for example:

- *Educational screening:* This recommendation is chosen by the CST when a child's academic skill levels (reading, math, writing, and spelling) are unknown or inconsistent. A screening is not a formal evaluation but a series of short, brief measures that give the CST some basic academic knowledge on which to make other decisions.

- *Language screening:* This recommendation usually occurs when the child is experiencing significant delays in speech or language development, problems in articulation, or problems in receptive or expressive language. Some symptoms that might warrant such a screening to determine a direction are difficulty pronouncing words through grade 3, immature or delayed speech patterns, difficulty labeling thoughts or objects, or difficulty putting thoughts into words.

- *Intellectual screening:* This recommendation is used by the CST when the child's intellectual ability is unknown. An example of this brief type of intelligence screening is the Kaufman Brief Intelligence Test or the screening form of the Wechsler scales. This testing will be done by the school psychologist.

- *Parent intake:* This recommendation is used when family background information is missing or needs to be updated. The team may feel that this information may shed some light on the present situation. This intake may be assigned to any member of the CST. The next section provides more information about the parent intake.

Parent Intake and Interviews

A parent intake should be done with sensitivity and diplomacy. Although some questions may not be of concern to most parents, they may be perceived as intrusive by others. The questions should be specific enough to help in the diagnosis of the problem, but not so specific as to place the parent in a vulnerable and defensive position. There are four main areas usually covered in a parent intake:

Identifying data and family information: Confirmation of names, addresses, telephone numbers, and dates of birth; siblings' names, ages, and dates of birth; parents' occupations; other adults residing within the home; marital status of parents

Developmental history: Length of the labor and delivery of the child; type of delivery; complications if any at birth; approximate ages of critical stages (for example, walking and talking); hospital stays; illnesses other than normal ones; sleeping habits; eating habits; high fevers; most recent eye exam; most recent hearing exam; falls or injuries; traumatic experiences; medications; any prior developmental testing

Academic history: Number of schools attended, types of schools attended, adjustment to kindergarten, best school years, worst school year, best subject, worst subject, prior teacher reports and comments, and homework behavior

Social history: The child's groups or organizations, social behavior in a group situation, hobbies, areas of interest, circle of friends, and sports activities

This step in the referral process involves a complete social history, which can be regarded as a description of the family life situation. In some cases, this part of the process may not be possible to obtain because of a number of variables, such as parent's work restrictions, inability to obtain coverage for younger siblings, resistance, or apathy. However, if there is a parent intake, there are several things to consider before the meeting:

- Always make the parents feel comfortable and at ease by setting up a receptive environment. If possible, hold the meeting in a pleasant setting, use a round table (or any other table instead of a desk), and offer some type of refreshment to ease possible tension caused by the situation.
- Never view the parents as adversaries even if they are angry or hostile. Keep in mind that the anger or hostility is a defense because they may not know what they will be asked or have encountered a series of negative school meetings over the years. Since this may be an opportunity for parents to vent, listen to their concerns, do not get defensive, and be understanding without taking sides.
- Inform parents every step of the way as to the purpose of the meeting and the steps in the referral process. Reassure them that no recommendation will be made without their participation and permission.
- Be solution oriented, and offer realistic hope even if past experiences have resulted in frustration. Remind the parents that children can be more motivated, resilient, and successful at different developmental stages.
- Offer them a pad and pen so that they can write down information, terms, or notes on the meeting. Indicate that they should feel free to call anyone on the CST with any questions or concerns.
- Reassure the parents about the confidentiality of the information gathered. Identify the individuals on the team who will be seeing the information and the purpose for their review of the facts.
- Indicate to the parents the next step and who will be getting back to them with the results of the CST meetings.

Exhibit 2.5 is an example of a parent intake completed by the school social worker. Here, the intake was done with Jill Jones, the mother of the child.

Exhibit 2.5. Completed Parent Intake Form

Name of Client: Matthew Jones

Address: 12 Court Street

Phone: 555-7863

Date of Birth: 3/4/96

Age: 9–0

Siblings:

  Brothers (names and ages): Brian, 15

  Sisters (names and ages): Karen, 4

Mother's Name: Jill	**Father's name:** Ben
Mother's occupation: Medical technician	**Father's occupation:** Accountant

Referred by: Teacher

Grade: 4

School: Holland Avenue

Developmental History

Length of pregnancy: Full term, 22-hour labor

Type of delivery: Forceps

Complications: Apgar score 7, jaundice at birth

Long hospital stays: None

Falls or injuries: None

Allergies: Early food allergies, none recently

Medication: None at present

Early milestones (walking, talking, and toilet training): According to parent, Matthew was late in walking and talking in comparison to brother. He was toilet trained at 3. Parent added that he seemed to be slower than usual in learning things.

Traumatic experiences: None

Previous psychological evaluations or treatment (Please explain reasons and dates): None. However parent indicated that it was suggested by first-grade teacher but the teacher never followed through.

Any previous psychiatric hospitalizations? No

Sleep disturbances: Trouble falling asleep, somnambulism at age 5 but lasted only a few weeks. Talks a great deal in his sleep lately.

Eating disturbances: Picky eater; likes sweets

Last vision and hearing exams and results: Last eye test in school indicated 20/30. Last hearing test in school was inconclusive. Parent has not followed through on nurse's request for an outside evaluation.

Excessively high fevers: No

Childhood illnesses: Normal ones

Exhibit 2.5. *(continued)*

Academic History

Preschool experience: Matthew had difficulty adjusting to nursery school. The teacher considered him very immature, and his skills were well below those of his peers. He struggled through the year.

Kindergarten experience (adjustment, comments): Matthew's difficulties increased. According to the parent, he had problems with reading and social difficulties. His gross and fine motor skills were immature.

First grade through sixth grade (teacher's comments, traumatic experiences, strength areas, comments): According to past teachers Matthew struggled through the years. He was a nice boy and polite and at times tried hard. But in grades 2 and 3, his behavior and academics began to falter. Teachers always considered referral but felt he might grow out of it.

Subjects that presented the most difficulty: Reading, math, spelling

Subjects that were the least difficult: Science

Most recent report card grades (if applicable): Matthew has received mostly "Needs to Improve" on his report card.

Social History

Groups or organizations: Tried Boy Scouts but dropped out. Started Little League but became frustrated.

Social involvement as perceived by parent: Inconsistent. He does not seem to reach out to kids and lately spends a great deal of time alone.

Hobbies or interests: Baseball cards, science

Prereferral Strategy Plans

After analyzing all of the information presented at the meeting, the CST has to decide what to recommend. If this is the first time the student is being reviewed by the team, then prereferral strategies will be recommended to the teacher. These are techniques and suggestions to attempt to resolve the child's issues without the need for a more comprehensive assessment. The team, along with the teacher, will choose strategies and develop a prereferral strategy plan. This prereferral strategy plan as outlined in IDEA is an attempt to try every possible alternative prior to making a formal referral for assessment. The special educator will play a major role in the development of this plan since it will contain classroom suggestions for management, modifications, assessment, and accommodations.

Once the plan is developed by the members of the CST including the classroom teacher, the teacher collaborates with the support personnel assigned to assist him or her. This collaboration is accomplished through meetings and conferences between staff and classroom teacher or sometimes requires the direct participation and assistance of support personnel in the classroom. These techniques will be used to see if the child's progress can be enhanced and the issues resolved without putting the child and the family through a more formal evaluation process. The special educator may be called on to provide the teacher indirect collaboration (nonparticipation suggestions) or direct assistance involvement (working with the teacher in the classroom). Prereferral strategies can include a variety of intervention strategies (Pierangelo & Giuliani, 2006a):

- A team meeting with teachers.
- Parent interviews.
- Classroom management. There are times when the issue may not be the child but rather the teaching style of the classroom teacher, who may have unrealistic expectations or is critical or overly demanding. If that is the case, then help for the teacher can come in the form of classroom management techniques such as these:
  - Display daily class schedule with times so the student has a structured idea of the day ahead
  - Change the child's seating
  - Seat the student near good role models
  - Use peer tutors when appropriate
  - Limit number of directions
  - Simplify complex directions
  - Give verbal as well as written directions
  - Provide extra work time
  - Shorten assignments
  - Modify curriculum
  - Identify and address preferred learning styles
  - Provide manipulative materials
  - Provide examples of what is expected
  - Use color coding of materials to foster organizational skills
  - Develop a homework plan with parental support
  - Develop a behavior modification plan if necessary
  - Use lots of positive reinforcement
  - Use technology as an aid
- Special class for extra help.
- Remedial reading or math services.
- In-school counseling.
- Daily or weekly progress reports.
- A hearing test: symptoms that require this option:
  - The child frequently asks others to repeat what they have just said.
  - The child consistently misinterprets what he or she hears.
  - The child does not respond to auditory stimuli.
  - The child slurs speech, speaks in a monotone voice, or articulates poorly.
- Vision test: Symptoms that may require this option:
  - The child turns his or her head when looking at the board or other objects.
  - The child squints excessively.
  - The child rubs his or her eyes frequently.
  - The child holds books and materials close to the face or at unusual angles.
  - The child suffers frequent headaches.
  - The child avoids close work of any type.
  - The child covers an eye when reading.
  - The child consistently loses his or her place when reading.
- Disciplinary action.
- Medical exam.
- Change of program.

- Consolidation of program.
- Referral to Child Protective Services.
- Teacher-made tests.
- Further observation.
- Screening tests.

If after some time the teacher reports to the CST that the problems still exist despite the pre-referral strategies, then the CST must consider whether the child has a more serious suspected educational disability. The team will usually accomplish this by using the following criteria:

- The level of the discrepancy between the child's ability and performance
- The historical patterns of this discrepancy
- Behavioral manifestations of a suspected disability; for instance, in the case of a suspected learning disability, the following behaviors may be present:
  - Distractibility
  - Problems in attention
  - Problems in memory
  - Social difficulties
  - Gross motor coordination issues
  - Fine motor concerns

If these factors are present and the prereferral strategies were unsuccessful, then it is the responsibility of the CST to refer the child for a more formal assessment. This referral begins the second part of the special education process.

❖ Special Education Process: Assessment, Diagnosis, Classification, and Placement of a Child with a Suspected Disability

If the CST's prereferral strategies were unsuccessful and the issues still exist, a referral is made to the multidisciplinary team (MDT), which will be responsible for the formal assessment. Since this referral by the CST is for a formal assessment, it will require another referral form to be filled out. There is a strong possibility that either the special educator or the school psychologist, or both together, will be given this responsibility.

A formal referral to the MDT is nothing more than a form starting the special education process. A referral for more formal individualized evaluation and possible special education services is initiated by a written request by the CST. However, people other than those on the CST have the right under due process to initiate a formal referral for a child with a suspected disability. Depending on state regulations, these could include:

- The child's parent and advocate or another person who is in a parental relationship with the child
- A classroom teacher
- Any professional staff member of the public or private school district
- A judicial officer, that is, a representative of the court
- A student on his or her own behalf if he or she is eighteen years of age or older, or an *emancipated minor*—a person under the age of eighteen who has been given certain adult rights by the court
- The chief school officer of the state or his or her designee responsible for the welfare, education, or health of children

Regardless of who makes the referral, a referral form will be required. A referral from the CST should include a great deal of information to assist the MDT in its assessment. Furthermore, documentation as to why a possible disability exists, descriptions of attempts to remediate the child's behaviors (prereferral strategies), or performance prior to the referral should all be included. If the referral is not from the parent, the district must inform the parent in writing immediately that his or her child has been referred for assessment as a result of a suspected disability. The referral states that the child may have a disability that adversely affects educational performance. An important point to remember is that a referral to the MDT does not necessarily mean that the child has a disability. It signals that the child is having learning difficulties and that there is a concern that the problem may be due to a disability.

Membership of the Multidisciplinary Team

While specific state regulations may differ on the membership of the MDT, the members are usually drawn from individuals and professionals within the school and community. A special education teacher will be assigned as the member of the MDT who will be responsible for the educational and perhaps perceptual evaluations of the child. The law mandates that an individual who is an expert in the field of the suspected disability must be a member of the MDT. For instance, in the case of a suspected learning disability, the special educator will be considered the expert on the team in this area. It is important that this person be familiar with the professionals who might be asked to participate on this team in the evaluation of a child with a suspected disability. These may include but are not limited to (Pierangelo & Giuliani, 2006a):

- *School psychologist:* The school psychologist will administer individual intelligence tests, projective tests, and personality inventories and observe the student in a variety of settings.
- *School nurse:* The school nurse reviews all medical records, screens for vision and hearing, consults with outside physicians, and may refer the child to outside physicians if necessary.
- *Classroom teacher:* The teacher works with the local school-based CST to implement prereferral strategies and plans and implements, along with the special education team, classroom strategies that create an appropriate working environment for the student.
- *School social worker:* The social worker gathers and provides information concerning the family system. This may be accomplished through interviews, observations, conferences, and other means.
- *Special education teacher:* This individual consults with the parents and classroom teachers about prereferral recommendations, administers educational and perceptual tests, may be called on to observe the student in a variety of settings, may be involved in the screening of students with suspected disabilities, writes IEPs including goals and objectives, and recommends intervention strategies to teachers and parents.
- *Educational diagnostician:* The diagnostician administers a series of evaluations including norm-referenced and criterion-referenced tests, observes the student in a variety of settings, and makes educational recommendations that are applied to the IEP as goals and objectives.
- *Physical therapist:* The physical therapist is called on to evaluate a child who may be experiencing problems in gross motor functioning, living and self-help skills, and vocational skills necessary for the student to be able to function in certain settings. This professional may be used to screen, evaluate, provide direct services, or consult with the teacher, parent, or school.

- *Behavioral consultant:* This individual works closely with the team in providing direct services or consultation on issues involving behavioral and classroom management techniques and programs.
- *Speech/language clinician:* This professional screens for speech and language developmental problems, may be asked to provide a full evaluation on a suspected language disability, provides direct services, and consults with staff and parents.
- *Audiologist:* The audiologist evaluates a student's hearing for possible impairments and as a result of the findings may refer the student for medical consultation or treatment. He or she may also assist students and parents in obtaining equipment such as hearing aids to improve the child's ability to function in school.
- *Occupational therapist:* The occupational therapist evaluates a child who may be experiencing problems in fine motor skills and living and self-help skills. He or she may be used to screen; evaluate; provide direct services; consult with the teacher, parent, or school; and assist in obtaining the appropriate assistive technology or equipment for the student.
- *Guidance counselor:* This individual may provide aptitude test information or counseling services; work with the team on consolidating, changing, or developing a student's class schedule; and assist the child study team in developing prereferral strategies.
- *Parents:* The parents play an extremely important role on the MDT in providing input for the IEP; working closely with members of the team; and carrying out, assisting, or initiating academic or management programs within the child's home.

The role of the MDT is to work as a single unit in determining the possible cause, contributing behavioral factors, educational status, prognosis (outcome), and recommendations for a student with a suspected disability. The MDT's major objective is to bring together many disciplines and professional perspectives to help work on a case so that a single person is not required to determine and assimilate all of the factors that affect a particular child. The MDT is responsible for gathering all the necessary information on a child in order to determine the most effective and practical direction for his or her education. In many states, the MDT's findings are then reviewed by another committee (sometimes referred to as the IEP committee or committee on special education). Its role is to determine whether the findings of the MDT fall within the guidelines for classification as having an exceptionality and requiring special education services. In accomplishing this task, the team members employ several types of assessment and collect data from many sources.

Initial Referral to the MDT

When a suspected disability is determined and the referral is made by the CST, the team will be required to fill out a form like the one in Exhibit 2.6.

The initial referral to the MDT from the school staff alerts the chairperson of the MDT that the local school CST has made every attempt to resolve the student's difficulties prior to the formal referral. The form also informs the chairperson that the parent's rights have been followed. In other cases, a student's parent or guardian may initiate a referral to the MDT for suspicion of a disability under special education laws or Section 504 of the Rehabilitation Act. This form by the parent is sent to the appropriate special education administrator. Usually on the receipt of the parent's referral, the chairperson of the MDT will send to the parent or guardian an assessment plan and the parent's due process rights statement.

If a release for testing (assessment plan) is not secured at a separate meeting, usually at the initial parent intake, the chairperson of the MDT will mail one to the parent along with the letter indicating that a referral has been made. However, no formal evaluations may begin until the district has received signed permission from the parent or guardian.

Exhibit 2.6. Initial Referral to the MDT from the School Staff

To: Chairperson of the MDT

From: Sara Block   **School:** Baily Elementary   **Date:** 4/15/06

Name/Title: Chairperson of the child study team

The following student is being referred for suspicion of a disability:

Student Name: Ben Azziza   **Sex:** M   **Grade:** 4   **Ethnicity:** Hispanic

Parent/Guardian Name: Maria/Calo

Address: 10 Spring Street

City: Morris   **State:** NY   **Zip:** 11786

Telephone: 555-0987   **Date of Birth:** 3/2/96

Current Program Placement: Regular mainstream

Teacher (Elementary): Mrs. Stowe   **Guidance Counselor (Secondary):**

Reasons for Referral: Describe the specific reason and/or needs that indicate the suspicion of a disability. Specify why referral is considered appropriate and necessary.

Ben is being referred for a formal assessment as the result of a suspected learning disability. The school has attempted a variety of prereferral strategies but has been unable to change Ben's level of impaired performance. Although he is a bright boy and articulates appropriately, his written expression is well below average and continues to impair his performance. Ben also needs a great deal of encouragement and monitoring in the classroom. His performance still falls far below that of his classmates.

Describe recent attempts to remediate the pupil's performance prior to referral, including regular education interventions such as remedial reading and math, teaching modifications, behavior modifications, speech improvement, and parent conferences, and the results of those interventions.

The referral is considered necessary at this time because Ben continues to do poorly in school despite numerous interventions such as classroom modifications, parent training and conferences, portfolio assessment, observation, remedial reading and math intervention, and changes in teaching strategies and management. The results of these intervention strategies have been unsuccessful and have even added to Ben's sense of frustration and lack of confidence.

Do you have a signed Parent Assessment Plan? Yes __X__ No _____ (If yes, send copy attached)

Is there an attendance problem?   Yes __X__ No _____

Language spoken at home? English

Did student repeat a grade?   Yes _____ No __X__ If yes, when?

Is an interpreter needed?   Yes _____ No __X__ Deaf:

Is a bilingual assessment needed?   Yes _____ No __X__ If yes, what language?

Is student eligible to receive ESL (English as a Second Language) services? Yes _____ No __X__

If yes, how many years receiving ESL services? __NA__ If yes, determine how the student's educational, cultural, and experiential background were considered to determine if these factors are contributing to the student's learning or behavior problems.

Exhibit 2.6. *(continued)*

TEST SCORES WITHIN LAST YEAR
(Standardized Achievement, Regents Competency, etc.)

TEST NAME	AREA MEASURED	PERCENTILE SCORE	COMMENT
Wechsler Individual Achievement Test-2	Basic Reading	42	Screening
Wechsler Ind. Achievement Test-2	Reading Composition	10	Screening
Wechsler Ind. Achievement Test-2	Numerical Operations	22	Screening
Wechsler Ind. Achievement Test-2	Oral Expression	67	Screening
Wechsler Ind. Achievement Test-2	Written Expression	5	Screening
KBIT-Kaufman Brief Intelligence Test	Intelligence-2	57	

Has school staff informed parent/guardian of referral to CSE? Yes _X_ No____

By whom? School Psychologist

What was the reaction of the parent/guardian to the referral? Positive

To Be Completed by School Nurse—Medical Report Summary

Any medication?   Yes ____ No _X_   If yes, specify:

Health problems?   Yes ____ No _X_   If yes, specify:

Scoliosis screening: Positive ____   Negative _X_

Date of last physical: 8/05   **Vision results:** Normal   **Hearing results:** Normal

Relevant medical information: None

Nurse teacher signature:

Principal's signature:

To Be Completed by the Appropriate Administrator

Date received: **Signature:**

Chairperson:

Date Notice and Consent Sent to Parent/Guardian:

Parent Consent for Initial Evaluation Received:

Date Agreement to Withdraw Referral Received:

Projected Eligibility Meeting Date:

If eligible, projected date of implementation of services:

Projected Eligibility Board of Education meeting date:

Assessment Plans and Consent for Evaluation

This form can be obtained in several ways, but most of the time it is attached to the letter to the parents from the district office of special services indicating that their child has been referred for a formal evaluation. Because of legal requirements, this release is part of the assessment plan and must meet certain standards:

- Be in a language easily understood by the general public.
- Be provided in the primary language of the parent or other mode of communication used by the parent, unless to do so is clearly unfeasible.
- Explains the types of assessments to be conducted.
- States that no IEP will result from the assessment without the consent of the parent.
- No assessment shall be conducted unless the written consent of the parent is obtained prior to the assessment.
- The parent shall have at least fifteen days (this time period may vary from state to state) from the receipt of the proposed assessment plan to arrive at a decision. Assessment may begin immediately on receipt of the consent.
- The copy of the notice of parent rights shall include the right to electronically record the proceedings of the IEP committee meetings.
- The assessment shall be conducted by persons competent to perform the assessment, as determined by the school district, county office, or special education local plan area.
- Any psychological assessment of pupils must be conducted by a qualified school psychologist.
- Any health assessment of pupils shall be conducted only by a credentialed school nurse or physician who is trained and prepared to assess cultural and ethnic factors appropriate to the pupil being assessed.

Evaluation

Only when the parents have been informed of their rights, a release is obtained, and the assessment plan is signed can assessment begin. The MDT has several evaluation options from which to choose depending on the specializations of the members of the MDT. Keep in mind that a special educator will be doing the academic and perceptual evaluations, and this person's role on the MDT will be that of an academic diagnostician. The areas most often considered by the MDT to assess a child with a suspected disability follow.

Achievement Evaluation

Such an evaluation is frequently recommended when a child's academic skill levels (reading, math, writing, and spelling) are unknown or inconsistent and when his or her learning process shows gaps (for example, in memory and expression). The evaluation will determine if a discrepancy between intellectual potential and academic achievement required for the classification exists, and it will determine strengths and weaknesses in the child's academic and processing areas. The objectives of an academic evaluation are:

- To help determine the child's academic strengths and weaknesses.
- To help the teacher gear the materials to the learning capacity of the child. A child reading two years below grade level may require modified textbooks or greater explanations prior to a lesson.
- To develop a learning profile that can help the classroom teacher understand the best way to present information to the child and therefore increase his or her chances of success.

- Along with other information and test results, to help determine if the child's academic skills are suitable for a regular class or are so severe that he or she may require a more restrictive educational setting (an educational setting or situation best suited to the current needs of the student other than a full-time regular class placement, such as a resource room, self-contained class, or special school).

Whatever achievement battery (a *battery* is a group of tests) the special educator chooses, it should cover enough skill areas to make an adequate diagnosis of academic strengths and weaknesses.

Some symptoms that might suggest the recommendation for an academic evaluation follow:

- Consistently low test scores on group achievement tests
- Indications of delayed processing when faced with academic skills
- Labored handwriting after grade 3
- Poor word recall
- Poor decoding (word attack) skills
- Discrepancy between achievement and ability
- Consistently low achievement despite remediation

In most cases of a suspected disability, the academic evaluation is always a part of the formal evaluation.

Language Evaluation

This recommendation usually occurs when the child is experiencing significant delays in speech or language development, problems in articulation, or problems in receptive or expressive language. Some symptoms that might warrant such an evaluation follow:

- Difficulty pronouncing words through grade 3
- Immature or delayed speech patterns
- Difficulty labeling thoughts or objects
- Difficulty putting thoughts into words

Expressive and receptive language measures are normally administered by the speech and language therapist.

Psychological Evaluation

This recommendation is appropriate when the child's intellectual ability is unknown or there is a question about his or her ability to learn. It is useful when the CST suspects a potential learning, emotional, or intellectual problem. The psychological evaluation can rule out or rule in emotionality as a primary cause of a child's problem; ruling this factor out is necessary before the diagnosis of a learning disability can be made. Some symptoms that might signal the need for such an evaluation follow:

- High levels of tension and anxiety exhibited in behavior
- Aggressive behavior
- Lack of motivation or indications of low energy levels
- Patterns of denial
- Oppositional behavior
- Despondency
- Inconsistent academic performance, ranging from very low to very high

- History of inappropriate judgment
- Lack of impulse control
- Extreme and consistent attention-seeking behavior
- Pattern of provocative behavior

Objectives of the psychological assessment include:

- Determining the child's current overall levels of intellectual ability
- Determining the child's verbal intellectual ability
- Determining the child's nonlanguage intellectual ability
- Exploring indications of greater potential
- Finding possible patterns involving learning style (for example, verbal comprehension, concentration)
- Ascertaining possible influences of tension and anxiety on testing results
- Determining the child's intellectual ability to deal with current grade-level academic demands
- Exploring the influence of intellectual ability as a contributing factor to a child's past and existing school difficulties (for example, limited intellectual ability found in retardation)

As with the academic assessment, the psychological evaluation is a normal part of every referral for a suspected disability. Measures of an intellectual or psychological nature are usually administered by the school psychologist if the child is evaluated within the school building.

Perceptual Evaluation

A perceptual evaluation is suggested when the team suspects discrepancies in the child's ability to receive and process information. This assessment may focus on a number of perceptual areas—for example:

Auditory modality—The delivery of information through sound
Visual modality—The delivery of information through sight
Tactile modality—The delivery of information through touching
Kinesthetic modality—The delivery of information through movement
Reception—The initial receiving of information
Perception—The initial organization of information
Association or organization—Relating new information to other information and giving meaning to the information received
Memory—The storage or retrieval process that facilitates the associational process to give meaning to information or help in relating new concepts to other information that might have already been learned
Expression—The output of information through vocal, motoric, or written responses

The objectives of the perceptual assessment are:

- To help determine the child's stronger and weaker modality for learning. Some children are visual learners, some are auditory, and some learn best through any form of input. However, if a child is a strong visual learner in a class where the teacher relies on auditory lectures, then it is possible that his or her ability to process information may be hampered. The evaluation may give this information, which is useful when making practical recommendations to teachers about how best to provide information to assist the child's ability to learn.

• To help determine a child's stronger and weaker process areas. A child having problems in memory and expression will fall behind the rest of the class quickly. The longer these processing difficulties continue, the greater the chance is for secondary emotional problems (emotional problems resulting from continued frustration with the ability to learn) to develop.

• To develop a learning profile that can help the classroom teacher understand the best way to present information to the child and therefore increase his or her chances of success.

• Along with other information and test results, to help determine if the child's learning process deficits are suitable for a regular class or so severe that he or she may require a more restrictive educational setting (an educational setting or situation best suited to the needs of the student other than a full-time regular class placement, such as a resource room, self-contained class, or special school).

Tests that specifically measure areas of visual perception are normally administered by the special education teacher or psychologist.

Occupational Therapy Evaluation

The team may consider this evaluation when the child is exhibiting problems involving fine motor and upper body functions. Examples include abnormal movement patterns, sensory problems (sensitive to sound or visual changes, for example), hardship with daily living activities, organizational problems, attention span difficulties, equipment analysis, and interpersonal problems.

There are several nonstandarized forms of assessment that need to be considered when doing a comprehensive evaluation. The distinction between standardized and nonstandardized tests is that standardized tests have detailed procedures or administration, timing, scoring, and interpretation procedures that must be followed precisely to obtain valid and reliable results. Nonstandardized forms of assessment may include the following forms of assessment (Pierangelo & Giuliani 2006a).

Ecological Assessment

This basically involves directly observing and assessing the child in the many environments in which he or she routinely operates. The purpose is to probe how the different environments influence the student and his or her school performance.

Portfolio Assessment

A portfolio is "a purposeful collection of student works that exhibits the student's efforts, progress, and achievement in one or more areas. The collection must include student participation in selecting content, the criteria for selection, the criteria for judging merit, and evidence of student self-reflection" (Pierangelo & Giuliani, 2006a).

Authentic Assessment

Authentic assessment is a performance-based assessment technique that involves the application of knowledge to real-life activities, real-world settings, or a simulation of such a setting using real-life, real-world activities (Taylor, 2006).

Outcome-Based Assessment

Outcome-based assessment involves considering, teaching, and evaluating the skills that are important in real-life situations. Learning such skills will result in the student's becoming an effective adult.

Task Analysis

Task analysis is detailed; it involves breaking down a task into the basic sequential steps, component parts, or skills necessary to accomplish the task.

Learning Styles Assessment

Learning styles theory suggests that students may learn and problem-solve in different ways and that some ways are more natural for them than others. When they are taught or asked to perform in ways that deviate from their natural style, they are thought to learn or perform less well.

On completing the administration of tests and other evaluation measures (if they are determined to be needed), a committee on special education (sometimes referred to as the *IEP Team* or *CSE*) meets with the parents to determine whether or not the child is a "child with a disability," as defined by IDEA 2004 (see pages 5–6 of this book) and local policy, and whether the child needs (and is thus eligible for) special education and related services. Although a comprehensive multidisciplinary assessment is required under the law (IDEA 2004), this book will focus solely on the diagnostic standardized tests used in the assessment of a child with a suspected disability.

Part Two

301 Tests Used in Special Education

Chapter 3

Academic Achievement

One of the most important components in the evaluation of a suspected disability for special education services is the assessment of academic achievement (Pierangelo & Giuliani, 2006a). Most academic achievement measures assess a child in several areas of achievement in order to determine strengths and weaknesses:

• *Reading:* One of the major concerns of parents and teachers will be the child's skills in reading. Assessment of reading skills can be done either formally or informally (Taylor, 2006). These skill areas may include:

- Decoding/word recognition (words in isolation)
- Decoding/word recognition (words in context)
- Phonological awareness
- Fluency
- Silent reading comprehension
- Oral reading comprehension
- Reading rate

See Chapter Twenty-Three for details on reading and reading assessment measures.

• *Mathematics:* Numerical reasoning and calculation pose major problems for many students in special education. Students with learning disabilities perform lower than normally achieving children with every type of arithmetic problem at every grade level (Pierangelo & Giuliani, 2006b). Specific areas of mathematics that will need to be assessed may include but are not limited to:

- Mathematical operations
- Reasoning
- Computation
- Word problems
- Applications
- Time

- Money
- Geometry
- Algebra

See Chapter Seventeen for details on mathematics and mathematics assessment measures.

- *Written language*: Academic achievement tests that measure the area of written language often focus on spelling, handwriting, and written expression or composition. All of these skills will be instrumental to a child's success in school. Severe weaknesses in any of these areas will require serious modifications and accommodations to the child's daily school program. The impact of written language problems increases with a student's age because so many school assignments require written products (Smith, Polloway, Patton, & Dowdy, 2004). See Chapter Twenty-Six for details on written expression and written expression assessment measures.

It is important to remember that individual achievement tests (rather than group-administered tests) are preferred for assessment of school performance when making a determination for special education eligibility. When an evaluator is conducting an evaluation for identification or placement in special education, achievement tests should always be individually administered. There are many reasons that individually administered achievement tests are used (Pierangelo & Giuliani, 2006):

- They are designed to assess children at all ages and grade levels.
- They can assess the most basic skills of spelling, math, and reading.
- They allow the examiner to observe a child's test-taking strategies.
- They can focus on a specific area of concern.
- They can be given in oral, written, or gestural format.
- They allow the examiner to observe the child's behavior in a variety of situations.

Although assessment batteries typically include an individual measure of academic achievement, it is important to realize that standardized achievement tests may be inappropriate for use with immigrant or minority group children.

The assessment of academic achievement plays an essential role in the special education process. As Taylor (2006) notes, "Evaluation in this area is necessary to document that an education need exists (a requirement under the Individuals with Disabilities Education Improvement Act of 2004) and to help make eligibility decisions. More importantly, information in this area is used to assist in establishing relevant goals and objectives and to monitor progress in relation to those goals and objectives" (p. 281).

Basic Achievement Skills Inventory (BASI)

General Test Information

Author:	Achilles N. Bardos
Publisher:	Pearson Assessment
Address of Publisher:	5601 Green Valley Dr.
	Bloomington, MN 55437
Telephone Number:	1-800-627-7271
Fax Number:	1-800-632-9011
Web Site of Publisher:	www.pearsonassessments.com
Type of Test:	Academic achievement
Administration Time:	Comprehensive tests: 2 hours; survey test: 25 minutes each for math and verbal subtests
Type of Administration:	Individual
Ages/Grade Levels:	Grades 1 through 12 and post–high school; individuals 8 to 80 years

Purpose and Description of Test

The BASI is a versatile, multilevel, norm-referenced achievement test that helps measure math, reading, and language skills for children and adults.

Subtest Information

The comprehensive test is composed of six timed subtests:
- Vocabulary (10 minutes)
- Spelling (10 minutes)
- Language mechanics (10 minutes)
- Reading comprehension (30 minutes)
- Math computation (20 minutes)
- Math application (35 minutes)

Strengths of the Test

The BASI can help
- determine a child's or adult's academic strengths and weaknesses
- diagnose learning disabilities in reading, mathematics, and spelling
- design learning interventions
- estimate adequate yearly progress for No Child Left Behind reports

---

Brigance Comprehensive Inventory
of Basic Skills–Revised (CIBS-R)

General Test Information

Author:	Albert Brigance
Publisher:	Curriculum Associates
Address of Publisher:	153 Rangeway Road, North Billerica, MA 01862
Telephone Number:	1-800-225-0248
Fax Number:	1-800-366-1158
Web Site of Publisher:	www.curriculumassociates.com
Type of Test:	Academic achievement
Administration Time:	Varies
Type of Administration:	Individual
Ages/Grade Levels:	Pre-K through grade 9

Purpose and Description of Test

CIBS-R assesses various areas of academic achievement in students. The test is presented in a plastic ring binder that is designed to be laid open and placed between the examiner and the student. A separate student booklet provided for the student's answers is designed so that the skills range from easy to difficult; thus, the teacher can quickly ascertain the skills level the student has achieved.

Subtest Information

There are four subtest areas, including 154 pencil-and-paper or oral-response tests:

- *Readiness.* The skills assessed include color naming; visual discrimination of shapes, letters, and short words; copying designs; drawing shapes from memory; drawing a person; gross-motor coordination; recognition of body parts; following directional and verbal instructions; fine motor self-help skills; verbal fluency; sound articulation; personal knowledge; memory for sentences; counting; alphabet recitation; number naming and comprehension; letter naming; and writing name, numbers, and letters.
- *Reading.* This area evaluates word recognition, oral reading and comprehension, oral reading rate, word analysis (auditorily and while reading), meaning of prefixes, syllabication, and vocabulary.
- *Language Arts.* This area assesses cursive handwriting, grammar and mechanics, spelling, and reference skills.
- *Mathematics.* This area assesses rote counting, writing numerals in sequence, reading number words, ordinal concepts, numeral recognition, writing to dictation, counting in sets, roman numerals, fractions, decimals, measurement (money, time, calendar, linear and liquid/weight measurement, temperature), and two- and three-dimensional geometric concepts.

Strengths of the Test

- Assesses specific areas of educational need
- Facilitates development of performance goals
- Provides indicators of progress on specific skills
- Facilitates reporting to staff and parents
- Is normed in key skill areas for multidisciplinary or classroom-based administration
- Can be used for alternate assessment situations

Criterion Test of Basic Skills–Second Edition (CBS-2)

General Test Information

Authors:	James Evans, Kerth Lundell, and William Brown
Publisher:	Academic Therapy
Address of Publisher:	20 Commercial Boulevard, Novato, CA 94949
Telephone Number:	1-800-422-7249
Fax Number:	1-888-287-9975
Web Site of Publisher:	http://www.academictherapy.com
Type of Test:	Reading and math
Administration Time:	15 to 20 minutes
Type of Administration:	Individual
Ages/Grade Levels:	Ages 6 through 11

Purpose and Description of the Test

The CBS-2 is a standardized and criterion-referenced assessment of basic reading and math skills.

Subtest Information

The CBS-2 consists of a reading and a math subtest:

• *Reading:* Assesses basic word attack skills in the following areas: letter recognition, letter sounds, blending, sequencing, decoding of common spelling patterns and multisyllable words, and sight word recognition

• *Arithmetic:* Assesses skills in these areas: counting, number concepts and numerical recognition, addition, subtraction, multiplication, division, decimals, measurement, percents, geometric concepts, pre-algebra, and rounding and estimation

Strengths of the Test

• According to its publisher, "Skills are defined clearly and areas in need of remediation are easily identified."

Diagnostic Achievement Battery–Third Edition (DAB-3)

General Test Information

Author:	Phyllis Newcomer
Publisher:	PRO-ED
Address of Publisher:	8700 Shoal Creek Boulevard, Austin, TX 78757–6897
Telephone Number:	1-800-897-3202
Fax Number:	1-800-397-7633
Web Site of Publisher:	http://www.proedinc.com
Type of Test:	Academic achievement
Administration Time:	90 to 120 minutes
Type of Administration:	Individual
Ages/Grade Levels:	Ages 6–0 through 14–11

Purpose and Description of Test

The DAB-3 is a revision of one of the most popular and useful individual tests of school achievement ever made. It uses fourteen short subtests to identify a child's strengths and weaknesses across several areas of achievement.

Subtest Information

The DAB-3 subtests consist of:

Story Comprehension	Characteristics
Synonyms	Grammatic Completion
Alphabet/Word Knowledge	Reading Comprehension
Capitalization	Punctuation
Spelling	Contextual Language
Story Construction	Math Reasoning
Math Calculation	Phonemic Analysis (supplemental subtest, new to this edition of the DAB)

Scores from the subtests can be combined to form eight composites:

- Total Achievement
- Listening
- Speaking
- Reading
- Writing
- Mathematics
- Spoken Language
- Written Language

Strengths of the DAB-3

Many improvements were made in this updated edition of the DAB-3. These include:

- All-new normative data reflecting the changing population characteristics of the United States, collected from 1997 to 2000
- Several new validity studies, including correlations with the Wechsler Intelligence Scales for Children-III and the Stanford Achievement Test-Ninth Edition, as well as a confirmatory factor analysis confirming the model on which the DAB-3 is based
- Studies showing the absence of gender, ethnic, and disability bias improved scoring criteria for the written composition that includes contextual language and story construction
- Appealing and realistic color pictures
- Clear administration procedures

Diagnostic Achievement Test for
Adolescents–Second Edition (DATA-2)

General Test Information

Authors:	Phyllis Newcomer and Brian Bryant
Publisher:	PRO-ED
Address of Publisher:	8700 Shoal Creek Boulevard, Austin, TX 78757–6897
Telephone Number:	1-800-897-3202
Fax Number:	1-800-397-7633
Web Site of Publisher:	www.proedinc.com
Type of Test:	Academic achievement
Administration Time:	50 minutes
Type of Administration:	Individual
Ages/Grade Levels:	Grades 7 through 12

Purpose and Description of Test

The DATA-2, normed on more than two thousand adolescents, measures the spoken language ability and academic achievement levels of middle school and high school students.

Subtest Information

DATA-2 core subtests measure:

- Receptive Vocabulary
- Receptive Grammar
- Expressive Grammar
- Expressive Vocabulary
- Word Identification
- Reading Comprehension
- Math Calculations
- Math Problem Solving
- Spelling
- Writing Composition

Three supplemental subtests measure Science, Social Studies, and Reference Skills.

Strengths of the DATA-2

- The reliability and validity of DATA-2 are documented in the manual.
- The demographic characteristics of the normative sample approximate those of the nation as a whole.

Einstein Evaluation of School-Related Skills (E = MC^2)

General Test Information

Authors:	Ruth L. Gottesman, Jo Ann Doino-Ingersoll, and Frances M. Cerullo
Publisher:	Slosson Educational Publications
Address of Publisher:	P.O. Box 280, East Aurora, NY 14052
Telephone Number:	1-888-756-7766
Fax Number:	1-800-655-3840
Web Site of Publisher:	www.slosson.com
Type of Test:	Academic achievement
Administration Time:	7 to 10 minutes
Type of Administration:	Individual
Ages/Grade Levels:	Grades K through 5

Purpose and Description of Test

The Einstein was designed as a cross-validation system for school and home use, parent-teacher conferences, Head Start programs, and at-risk learning disability programs to ensure that "students are making the grade" in various subject areas (see Subtest Information).

Subtest Information

There are six levels of the Einstein, one for each grade from kindergarten through grade 5. Major skill areas underlying school achievement are measured. Areas tested include:

- *Language/cognition:* Measures the ability to define words, similarities, or complete analogies, at higher levels
- *Letter recognition:* Ability to recognize and name letters (kindergarten level only)
- *Word recognition:* Read words in isolation orally (except kindergarten level)
- *Oral reading:* Read passage orally (except kindergarten level)
- *Reading comprehension:* Grasp main idea, significant details from oral reading passage
- *Auditory memory:* Short-term memory, repeat series of numbers
- *Arithmetic:* Computation of standard number problems
- *Visual-motor integration:* Copy geometric pattern using hand-motor responses
- *Draw-a-person:* Human figure drawing, scored for detail

An acceptable performance score indicates that the child's performance on the Einstein is within normal range; scores falling below the norm indicate a high probability that a child may be at risk of experiencing school learning difficulties.

Strengths of the Test

- The test can be easily administered by a variety of professionals, including tutors who do not have specialized training in statistics, testing, or measurements. If the test is administered during the school year, the child's current level is administered. For summer months, the grade just completed is administered.
- A total of 1,781 children in both regular education and special education were used in the standardization sample.
- Cross-validation, .87 to .89, confirms correct decision-validity indexes using the Einstein pass-fail scoring criterion.
- Included is an extensive manual that provides the test description, administration, scoring, and interpretation.

Essential Skills Screener (ESS)

General Test Information

Authors:	Bradley T. Erford, Gary J. Vitali, Rose Mary Haas, and Rita R. Boykin
Publisher:	Slosson Educational Publications
Address of Publisher:	P.O. Box 280, East Aurora, NY 14052
Telephone Number:	1-888-756-7766
Fax Number:	1-800-655-3840
Web Site of Publisher:	www.slosson.com
Type of Test:	Academic achievement
Administration Time:	Varies
Type of Administration:	Individual and group
Ages/Grade Levels:	Preschool, ages 3 to 5; elementary, ages 6 to 8; upper elementary, ages 9 to 11

Purpose and Description of Test

A brief series of academic achievement screening tests, the ESS is used for identifying children at risk for school readiness or learning problems. The math and writing screeners can be group administered, often leading to efficient screening and scoring of an entire class in about an hour.

Subtest Information

Various tasks based on age level are performed on the ESS. These include:

- *Preschool Reading (RESS-P)*—letter identification, picture vocabulary, visual discrimination, visual figure-ground
- *Preschool Writing (WESS-P)*—form copying, letter and number copying, copying speed, name writing
- *Preschool Math (MESS-P)*—shapes, oral counting, quantities, numerals, equalities and inequalities, story problems
- *Elementary Reading (RESS-E)*—letter identification, consonant letter-sound association, digraphs, cluster sounds, sight-word vocabulary, oral reading, story retelling, inference
- *Elementary Writing (WESS-E)*—name writing, writing speed, spelling, sentence writing
- *Elementary Math (MESS-S)*—writing numerals, addition, subtraction, time, money, fractions, word problems
- *Upper Elementary Reading (RESS-U)*—sight-word vocabulary, digraphs, cluster sounds, oral reading, story retelling, inference
- *Upper Elementary Writing (WESS-U)*—writing speed, spelling, story composition
- *Upper Elementary Math (MESS-U)*—writing numerals, addition, subtraction, multiplication, division, time, money, fractions

Strengths of the Test

- The ESS was normed on 2,150 children ages 3 to 11 and provides both grade and age norms. Interpretation is simplified through the use of percentile ranks, performance ranges, and standard scores, with internal consistency in the high .80s to .90s. Concurrent validity studies show excellent validity at all age levels.

Hammill Multiability Achievement Test (HAMAT)

General Test Information

Authors:	Don Hammill, Wayne Hresko, Jerome Ammer, Mary Cronin, and Sally Quinby
Publisher:	PRO-ED
Address of Publisher:	8700 Shoal Creek Boulevard, Austin, TX 78757–6897
Telephone Number:	1-800-897-3202
Fax Number:	1-800-397-7633
Web Site of Publisher:	www.proedinc.com
Type of Test:	Academic achievement
Administration Time:	30 to 60 minutes
Type of Administration:	Individual
Ages/Grade Levels:	Ages 7–0 through 17–11

Purpose and Description of Test

The HAMAT is a popular, often-used, and content-driven achievement test. It is designed to be used by psychologists, educational diagnosticians, counselors, and other professionals concerned with the assessment of academic achievement.

Subtest Information

The HAMAT provides four subtests in the areas of Reading, Writing, Mathematics, and Facts.

- *The Reading Subtest* consists of a series of carefully constructed paragraphs, based on the cloze procedure. In the cloze procedure, words are selectively deleted from a paragraph. The student must select one word from a group of words to best complete a sentence. Reading skills measured: reading comprehension and word knowledge.
- *The Writing Subtest* requires the student to write sentences from dictation, stressing correctness. Writing skills measured: spelling, punctuation, and capitalization.
- *The Mathematics Subtest* measures the student's mastery of number facts and ability to complete mathematical calculations. Primary mathematics skill measured: calculation.
- *The Facts Subtest* requires the student to answer questions based on the content of social studies, science, history, and literature curricula. Primary knowledge measured: basic facts taught in school.

Strengths of the Test

- Internal consistency reliability coefficients (content sampling) all exceed or round to .90. Time sampling was investigated using the test-retest technique. Test-retest coefficients range from .83 to .94 for the subtests; the composite exceeds .94. The magnitude of the coefficients reported from all the reliability studies suggests that there is little error in the HAMAT and the examiners can have confidence in the results.
- Extensive evidence of the validity of HAMAT test scores is provided for content-description validity, criterion-prediction validity, and construct-identification validity.
- Many states require examiners to compute discrepancy scores between IQ and some achievement score as part of the process used to qualify individuals for services within the classification of learning disability. Because most states require the use of three methods to test the degree of underachievement, the HAMAT manual presents all methods used for calculating discrepancy scores. That means discrepancy scores can be calculated to make comparisons between HAMAT scores and the scores from virtually all of the popular tests of cognitive aptitude. In addition, the HAMAT was linked (co-normed) with the Hammill Multiability Intelligence Test to allow examiners to compute regression based discrepancy scores.

Kaufman Functional Academic Skills Test (K-FAST)

General Test Information

Authors:	Alan S. Kaufman and Nadeen L. Kaufman
Publisher:	AGS Publishing
Address of Publisher:	4201 Woodland Road, Circle Pines, MN 55014–1796
Telephone Number:	1-800-328-2560, 1-651-287-7220
Fax Number:	1-800-471-8457
Web Site of Publisher:	www.agsnet.com
Type of Test:	Norm referenced
Administration Time:	15 to 25 minutes
Type of Administration:	Individual
Ages/Grade Levels:	Ages 15 through 85+

Purpose and Description of Test

The K-FAST is a brief, individually administered test to determine performance in reading and mathematics as applied to daily life. Unlike adaptive behavior inventories that ask an informant to rate how a person functions, the K-FAST requires subjects to show they can perform the requested skill.

Subtest Information

The Arithmetic subtest contains twenty-five, and the Reading subtest contains twenty-nine items. In addition, there is a subtest. K-FAST reading and arithmetic tasks relate to everyday activities, such as understanding labels on drug containers, following directions in a recipe, budgeting monthly expenses, and making price comparisons among products.

Strengths of the Test

- Because the K-FAST can help assess a person's capacity to function effectively in society, it can be used by schools, adult education programs, clinics, hospitals, prisons, the military, senior care facilities, and other institutions.
- The K-FAST can be administered and scored by a variety of personnel, although results should be interpreted only by qualified professionals.
- Performance on the Arithmetic and Reading subtests and the Functional Academic Skills Composite can be interpreted using standard scores with a mean of 100 and a standard deviation of 15. The K-FAST was normed on a representative sample of 1,424 people. All items were checked for cultural bias.
- Several studies support the K-FAST's reliability and validity using both normal and clinical samples. Percentile ranks and descriptive categories are provided as additional aids to interpretation.
- The K-FAST was developed, field-tested, and standardized with the Kaufman Adolescent and Adult Intelligence Test, the Kaufman Brief Intelligence Test, and the Kaufman Short Neuropsychological Assessment Procedure. These four tests provide a range of cognitive assessment options. The K-FAST can be used to assess functional reading and mathematics skills that might be overlooked by more traditional ability tests.

Kaufman Test of Educational Achievement–Second Edition (KTEA-II)

General Test Information

Authors:	Alan S. Kaufman and Nadeen L. Kaufman
Publisher:	AGS Publishing
Address of Publisher:	4201 Woodland Road, Circle Pines, MN 55014–1796
Telephone Number:	1-800-328-2560, 1-651-287-7220
Fax Number:	1-800-471-8457
Web Site of Publisher:	www.agsnet.com
Type of Test:	Academic achievement
Administration Time:	Comprehensive Form—PreK–K: 30 minutes; grades 1 to 2: 50 minutes; grades 3+: 80 minutes. Brief Form: grades 4 to 6 to age 90: 20 to 30 minutes
Type of Administration:	Individual
Ages/Grade Levels:	Comprehensive Form: ages 4–6 through 25–0; Brief Form: ages 4–6 through 90+

Purpose and Description of Test

The KTEA-II is an individually administered battery that gives a flexible, thorough assessment of the key academic skills in reading, math, written language (new), and oral language (new).

Subtest Information

The KTEA-II consists of comprehensive form subtests and composites:

- Reading Composite
  - Letter and Word Recognition
  - Reading Comprehension
- Reading-Related Subtests
  - Phonological Awareness
  - Nonsense Word Decoding
  - Word Recognition Fluency
  - Decoding Fluency
  - Associational Fluency
  - Naming Facility
- Math Composite
  - Math Concepts and Applications
  - Math Computation
- Written Language Composite
  - Written Expression
  - Spelling
- Oral Language Composite
  - Listening Comprehension
  - Oral Expression
- Comprehensive Achievement Composite

The KTEA-II Brief Form has three subtests:

- *Reading*—word recognition and reading comprehension
- *Math*—computation and application problems
- *Written Expression*—written language and spelling

Strengths of the Test

- The test covers all achievement areas mandated by the Individuals with Disabilities Education Improvement Act (IDEA).
- The popular error analysis procedures from the original KTEA have been enhanced to offer additional in-depth information about a student's performance.
- With the expanded age range (ages 4–6 to 25–0), a thorough assessment can be made of preschoolers to adults using the Comprehensive Form.
- Alternate forms are provided to measure progress and response to intervention.
- The Written Expression and Oral Expression subtests use engaging stories and situations.
- Enhanced reading subtests measure skills from readiness through advanced levels.
- Useful comparisons can be made between reading and listening, and writing and speaking.
- Content coverage in math is enhanced with the addition of algebra and early numeracy items.
- The KTEA-II is easy to administer, score, and interpret. Redesigned and expanded, it covers all IDEA, Reading First, and National Council of Teachers of Mathematics achievement areas to ensure a comprehensive, research-based assessment.
- This instrument features alternate forms to help measure student progress or response to intervention and to adjust instruction based on performance.

Norris Educational Achievement Test (NEAT)

General Test Information

Authors:	Janet Switzer and Christian P. Gruber
Publisher:	Western Psychological Services
Address of Publisher:	12031 Wilshire Boulevard, Los Angeles, CA 90025–1251
Telephone Number:	1-800-648-8857 (United States and Canada only), 1-310-478-2061
Fax Number:	1-310-478-7838
Web Site of Publisher:	http://www.wpspublish.com
Type of Test:	Academic achievement
Administration Time:	30 minutes
Type of Administration:	Individual
Ages/Grade Levels:	Ages 4–0 to 17–11

Purpose and Description of Test

The NEAT gives school and clinical psychologists a standard assessment of basic educational abilities. It is the only major diagnostic achievement battery that offers all of the following features:

- Alternate forms
- Optional measures of written language as well as oral reading and comprehension
- Separate grade and age norms
- Tables identifying significant discrepancies between IQ and achievement
- A large standardization sample that is nationally representative in terms of parental education and ethnic composition

Subtest Information

Readiness Tests are used to assess children between 4 and 6 years of age, and Achievement Tests are used to evaluate examinees age 6 and older:

- Readiness Tests
  - Fine Motor Coordination
  - Math Concepts
  - Letters
- Achievement Tests
  - Word Recognition
  - Spelling
  - Arithmetic
- Supplemental Achievement Tests
  - Oral Reading and Comprehension
  - Written Language

Strengths of the Test

- Unlike other tests of its kind, NEAT makes it easy for the user to document discrepancies between IQ and achievement. The Technical Manual provides tables identifying critical differences between NEAT scores and the various Wechsler Intelligence Scales and Stanford-Binet scores. This information is highly useful in qualifying students for special education services.

- Standardized on a nationally representative sample of approximately 3,000 students, NEAT provides both grade and age norms. The Technical Manual gives complete information on the standardization sample, describing parental education, ethnic composition, geographical regions, gender, and urban-rural distribution. The test has undergone extensive analyses to ensure that it is unbiased when used with blacks, whites, and Hispanics. NEAT is valid for use in virtually any educational or clinical setting.
- Efficient and easy to use, this test is an excellent addition to any psychodiagnostic evaluation.
- The inclusion of Written Language and Oral Reading and Comprehension Tests gives users the option of assessing these skills without introducing additional instruments. Both of these supplemental tests are quick, efficient, and easy to score. The Written Language Test provides prototypical essays for every age and grade level. These serve as clear-cut, objective scoring guides.
- NEAT is available in two parallel forms (A and B), each separately normed and validated. This makes the test especially useful for individualized education program reviews, progress assessments, and other evaluations that involve retesting. The same test form is used from first grade through high school, making it easy to compare successive testings of a particular student over the course of his or her school career.
- The Readiness and Achievement Tests are included in one convenient test booklet. The student responds directly in the booklet. Because sections of the booklet can be removed, the examiner can score one test while the student works on another, a feature that saves considerable time.

Peabody Individual Achievement Test–Revised-Normative Update (PIAT-R/NU)

General Test Information

Author:	Frederick C. Markwardt Jr.
Publisher:	AGS Publishing
Address of Publisher:	4201 Woodland Road, Circle Pines, MN 55014–1796
Telephone Number:	1-800-328-2560, 1-651-287-7220
Fax Number:	1-800-471-8457
Web Site of Publisher:	www.agsnet.com
Type of Test:	Academic achievement
Administration Time:	60 minutes
Type of Administration:	Individual
Ages/Grade Levels:	Grades K to 12; ages 5–0 through 22–11

Purpose and Description of Test

The PIAT-R/NU is an efficient individual measure of academic achievement. Reading, mathematics, and spelling are assessed in a simple, nonthreatening format that requires only a pointing response for most items. This multiple-choice format makes the PIAT-R/NU ideal for assessing low-functioning individuals or those having limited expressive abilities.

Subtest Information

With PIAT-R/NU, only items within the student's range of difficulty are administered. The subtests measure:

- *General information.* This subtest has 100 open-ended questions that are presented orally. They measure the student's factual knowledge related to science, social studies, humanities, fine art, and recreation.
- *Reading Recognition.* There are 100 items. Items 1 through 16 are multiple choice and measure prereading skills. Items 17 through 100 measure decoding skills and require the student to read individually presented words orally.
- *Reading Comprehension.* This subtest consists of 82 items and measures the student's ability to draw meaning from printed sentences.
- *Spelling.* Items 1 through 15 are multiple-choice tasks that assess reading skills. Items 16 through 100 require the student to select from four possible choices the correct spelling of a word read orally by the examiner.
- *Written Expression.* This subtest has two levels. Level 1 consists of nineteen copying and dictation items that are arranged in order of ascending difficulty. In Level 2, the child is presented with one or two picture plates and given 20 minutes to write a story about the picture.
- *Mathematics.* In this subtest, the student is asked the question orally and must select the correct response from four choices. Questions cover topics ranging from numerical recognition to trigonometry.

PIAT-R/NU also provides a Written Language Composite, obtained by combining scores on the Spelling and Written Expression subtests, and a Total Reading score, a combination of scores from the Reading Recognition and Reading Comprehension subtests for overall indexes for written expression and reading achievement.

Strengths of the Test

- PIAT-R has NU norms. (*NU* means normative updates, that is, an update on the norms.) Based on a national sampling of over 3,000 people, it provides accurate score comparisons for reading decoding, reading comprehension, and math applications with the other achievement batteries with which it was co-normed: K-TEA/NU, KeyMath-R/NU, and WRMT-R/NU. Users gain added flexibility because they can substitute a subtest from a different battery if a subtest is spoiled or if additional diagnostic information is desired.
- The age range for the PIAT-R/NU has been extended to age 22–11 with the normative update.
- The simple multiple-choice format helps assess children with severe disabilities.
- Six subtests ensure a comprehensive assessment.
- Provides an ASSIST report. This report provides scores and a student performance narrative on each subtest and composite.

Wechsler Individual Achievement Test– Second Edition (WIAT-2)

General Test Information

Author:	David Wechsler
Publisher:	Harcourt Assessment (formerly known as the Psychological Corporation and Harcourt Educational)
Address of Publisher:	6277 Sea Harbor Drive, Orlando, FL 32887
Telephone Number:	1-800-211-8378
Fax Number:	1-800-232-1223
Web Site of Publisher:	www.harcourt.com
Type of Test:	Academic achievement
Administration Time:	30 to 75 minutes
Type of Administration:	Individual
Ages/Grade Levels:	Ages 4 to 85

Purpose and Description of Test

The WIAT-2 is one of the most often used comprehensive measures of academic achievement in schools.

Subtest Information

The WIAT-2 has nine subtests:

- *Word Reading:* Naming letters, phonological skills (working with sounds in words), and reading words aloud from lists. Only the accuracy of the pronunciation (not comprehension) is scored.
- *Pseudoword Decoding:* Reading nonsense words aloud from a list (phonetic word attack).
- *Reading Comprehension:* Matching words to pictures, reading sentences aloud, and orally answering oral questions about reading passages. Silent reading speed is also assessed.
- *Spelling:* Written spelling of dictated letters and sounds and words that are dictated and read in sentences.
- *Written Expression:* Writing letters and words as quickly as possible, writing sentences, and writing a paragraph or essay.
- *Numerical Operations:* Identifying and writing numbers, counting, and solving paper-and-pencil computation examples with only a few items for each computational skill.
- *Math Reasoning:* Counting, identifying shapes, and solving verbally framed word problems presented both orally and in writing or with illustrations. Paper and pencil are allowed.
- *Listening Comprehension:* Multiple-choice matching of pictures to spoken words or sentences and replying with one word to a picture and a dictated clue.
- *Oral Expression:* Repeating sentences, generating lists of specific kinds of words, describing pictured scenes, and describing pictured activities. The content of answers is scored, but the quality of spoken language is not for most items.

Strengths of the Test

- WIAT-2 is a comprehensive yet flexible measurement tool useful for achievement skills assessment, learning disability diagnosis, special education placement, curriculum planning, and clinical appraisal for preschool children to adults. New norms also allow the evaluation of and academic planning for college students with learning disabilities.
- WIAT-2 extends the age range down to 4 years and up to 85 years, including norms for two-year and four-year college students.
- In order to better assess both low- and high-functioning individuals, WIAT-2 includes more comprehensive items that provide a lower floor and a higher ceiling. Emerging academic skills are also addressed in reading, math, and written and oral language to target instructional needs of young children early and guide them to competency.
- With WIAT-2, users can choose which subtests to administer, engage examinees with interesting tasks that are instructionally relevant, quickly score the test manually or by computer, and develop plans with detailed skills analysis information.
- As with the earlier edition, WIAT-2 provides norm-referenced information about all seven areas required by the Individuals with Disabilities Education Improvement Act. This comprehensive battery includes a broad sample of curriculum content that exceeds IDEA requirements with nine subtests.
- WIAT-2 allows users to go beyond the correctness of a response and begin to examine how the individual solves problems and employs strategies and how this performance matches curricular expectations. Objective scoring guidelines, developed in consultation with leading reading and writing experts, are provided for the Written Expression subtest to evaluate the writing process as well as the product.
- WIAT-2 is the only achievement battery empirically linked with the Wechsler Intelligence Scale for Children–Third Edition (WISC-III), the Wechsler Preschool and Primary Scale of Intelligence Revised, and the Wechsler Adult Intelligence Scale-Third Edition, the most widely used intellectual ability tests. These relationships provide valid discrepancy scores to help make meaningful comparisons between achievement and ability and develop on-target intervention.

Wide Range Achievement Test–Fourth Edition (WRAT-4)

General Test Information

Author:	Gary S. Wilkinson
Publisher:	PAR
Address of Publisher:	16204 North Florida Avenue, Lutz, FL 33549
Telephone Number:	1-800-331-8378, ext. 361
Fax Number:	1-800-727-9329
Web Site of Publisher:	http://www.parinc.com
Type of Test:	Academic achievement
Administration Time:	15 to 25 minutes for individuals 5–7 years; approximately 35–45 minutes for individuals 8 years and older
Type of Administration:	Individual or group
Ages/Grade Levels:	Ages 5 through 95

Purpose and Description of Test

The latest edition of the Wide Range Achievement Test (WRAT-4) expands on this popular tool to enhance the study of the development of reading, spelling, and arithmetic codes.

Subtest Information

There are four subtests:

- *Word Reading*—a subtest involving decoding whereby the child is asked to recognize and rename letters and pronounce words in isolation
- *Spelling*—a subtest of written spelling whereby the child is asked to write his or her name, write letters, and write words from dictation
- *Math Computation*—a subtest of mathematical computation whereby the child is asked to count, read numbers, identify number symbols, solve oral problems, and perform written computation within a defined time limit
- *Sentence Comprehension*—a subtest measuring a student's ability to gain meaning from words and to comprehend ideas and information contained in sentences through the use of a modified cloze technique.

Strengths of the Test

The WRAT-4 can help

- Educators determine whether a learning disability is due to an inability to learn the codes necessary to acquire the skill or an inability to derive meaning from the codes
- Identify the level of coding performance on an absolute scale and in relation to age peers
- Diagnose learning disabilities in reading, spelling, and arithmetic when used in conjunction with a comprehensive test of general ability
- Measure the development of basic academic codes over time when intervention techniques are attempted
- Study the relationships between the coding aspects of reading and arithmetic and the behavioral disabilities of verbal and numerical comprehension and problem solving

Wide Range Achievement Test-Expanded (WRAT-E)

General Test Information

Author: Gary J. Robertson

Publisher: PAR

Address of Publisher: 16204 North Florida Avenue, Lutz, FL 33549

Telephone Number: 1-800-331-8378, ext. 361

Fax Number: 1-800-727-9329

Web Site of Publisher: http://www.parinc.com

Type of Test: Academic achievement

Administration Time: Approximately 1.5 to 2.0 hours

Type of Administration: Individual or group

Ages/Grade Levels: Child to adult

Purpose and Description of Test

The WRAT-E assesses the areas of reading comprehension, mathematics, listening comprehension, oral expression, and written language. A measure of nonverbal reasoning is also included. The WRAT-E includes both group-administered and individually administered formats.

Subtest Information and Strengths of the Test (Forms)

- WRAT-Expanded Group Assessment (Form G)
  - Designed to be administered by the classroom teacher or other testing professional in a small-group setting.
  - May be used to identify students needing a more in-depth assessment with the Individual Assessment (Form I).
  - Each subtest uses a multiple-choice format and is designed to be given within one classroom period.
  - Five levels are available: Level 1 (grade 2), Level 2 (grades 3–4), Level 3 (grades 5–6), Level 4 (grades 7–9), and Level 5 (grades 10–12).
  - Offers an optional content skills analysis.
  - Norms include age- and grade-based standard scores, percentile ranks, stanines, and grade equivalents.
- WRAT-Expanded Individual Assessment (Form I)
  - Designed to be administered individually.
  - The RM Module contains the Reading and Mathematics tests, which are presented in a specially designed flip book to facilitate test administration.
  - Both the Reading and Mathematics tests contain items covering a wide range of difficulty. The items administered are tailored to the ability of the student.
  - Future modules to be developed include Listening Comprehension, Oral Expression, Written Language, and a Primary Assessment.
- WRAT-Expanded Test Content
  - *Reading Comprehension:* Both Forms G and I assess reading comprehension with passages containing items that assess word meaning in context and literal and inferential reading skills. Passages include textbook, recreational, and functional reading selections.
  - *Mathematics:* Both Forms G and I assess understanding of concepts, computation, and problem solving. Content domains include numeration and number sense, operations, measurement, geometry, data analysis and interpretation, probability and discrete mathematics, and patterns and algebra.
  - *Nonverbal Reasoning:* Available in Form G only, this test measures the ability to reason with symbolic and figural content. It provides useful information about the reasoning ability of students who may have language disabilities that adversely affect their performance on verbal school achievement measures that depend on language facility. No reading is required.

Woodcock-Johnson Tests of Achievement-III (WJ-III)

General Test Information

Authors:	Richard W. Woodcock and Mary Bonner Johnson
Publisher:	Riverside Publishing
Address of Publisher:	425 Spring Lake Drive, Itasca, IL 60143–2079
Telephone Number:	1-800-323-9540
Fax Number:	1-630-467-7192
Web Site of Publisher:	www.riverpub.com
Type of Test:	Individual
Administration Time:	Part I, 60 to 90 minutes; Part II, 30 to 45 minutes; Part III, 15 to 30 minutes
Type of Administration:	Individual
Ages/Grade Levels:	Ages 3 through 80

Purpose and Description of Test

This is the first major individual instrument with measures of cognitive ability, academic achievement, and scholastic interest that are standardized on the same norming sample. A complex instrument with many facets and a wide range, it is an individual cognitive and achievement test.

Subtest Information

The following subtests make up the Standard Battery for the WJ-III:

- *Letter–Word Identification.* On the first test items, the student is shown a colored drawing and must match it to one of a series of smaller line drawings. Next, the student is shown a letter and must say its name. On more difficult items, the student is asked to pronounce real words.
- *Reading Fluency.* The task requires rapidly reading and comprehending simple sentences.
- *Story Recall.* The task requires listening to passages of gradually increasing length and complexity and then recalling the story elements.
- *Understanding Directions.* The task requires pointing to objects in a picture after listening to instructions that increase in linguistic complexity.
- *Passage Comprehension.* Early items present several colored drawings and a phrase that describes one of the drawings; the student points to the drawing corresponding to the phrase. Next, the student silently reads a passage of one or more sentences. In each passage, there is a blank space where one word has been omitted. The student's task is to say a word that correctly completes the sentence.
- *Calculation.* The student is given pages that contain computation problems and is asked to write the answer to each. Beginning items are simple number facts and basic operations. Also included are problems requiring manipulation of fractions and more advanced calculations using algebra, geometry, trigonometry, and calculus.
- *Applied Problems.* The student solves word problems. In the beginning items, the tester reads a question while the student looks at a drawing. On later items, the student is shown the word problem that the tester reads aloud. Answers are given orally on this subtest, but the student may use pencil and paper for computation.
- *Math Fluency.* The task requires rapid calculation of simple single-digit addition, subtraction, and multiplication of facts.

- *Writing Samples.* This subtest is made up of a series of brief writing prompts to which the student responds. Early items require only one-word answers. On later items, students must write a complete sentence. Prompts vary in specificity and complexity. For example, for some items, the student must write a sentence describing a drawing; in others, a phrase must be expanded.
- *Writing Fluency.* Students are given seven minutes to write sentences. They write to a series of prompts, each of which contains a drawing and three words. Sentences must describe the picture using the words provided.
- *Spelling.* Spelling measures the ability to spell dictated words.

The Extended Battery of the Achievement Tests includes the following subtests:

- *Word Attack.* The student is presented with nonsense words to read aloud. A pronunciation key is provided for the tester.
- *Reading Vocabulary.* The subtest is divided into two parts, Synonyms and Antonyms. The student reads a word aloud and then must supply either a word that means the same or one that has an opposite meaning.
- *Quantitative Concepts.* The student responds to oral questions concerning mathematics concepts. Items cover sample skills such as counting, understanding quantitative vocabulary, reading numerals, defining mathematical terms and symbols, and solving computational problems. Visuals accompany most test items.
- *Editing.* The student is shown a sentence or sentences with one error. After reading the passage silently, the student must locate the error and tell how to correct it. The tester may tell the student an occasional word but not an entire sentence. Like the Dictation subtest, this subtest contains items that assess punctuation and capitalization, spelling, and usage.
- *Punctuation and Capitalization.* Punctuation and Capitalization measures knowledge of punctuation and capitalization rules.
- *Story Recall-Delayed.* The task requires the student to recall, after a thirty-minute to eight-day delay, the story elements presented in the Story Recall Test.
- *Picture Vocabulary.* The task requires naming common to less familiar pictured objects.
- *Oral Comprehension.* The task requires listening to short passages and then supplying the missing final word.
- *Academic Knowledge.* The task involves answering questions about curricular knowledge in various areas of study.
- *Spelling of Sounds.* The task requires spelling nonwords that conform to English spelling rules.
- *Sound Awareness.* The task includes four measures of phonological awareness (rhyming, deletion, substitution, and reversal).

Strengths of the Test

- The strengths of the test are primarily in the originality of many tasks, the technical expertise and sophistication involved in the test construction, and the psychometric properties of the battery.
- This test is a multifaceted tool for assessing cognitive achievement and scholastic interests.
- The subtests show validity.
- The test is a useful measure for the assessment of school performance across a wide range of academic areas and ages.

Young Children's Achievement Test (YCAT)

General Test Information

Authors:	Wayne Hresko, Pamela Peak, Shelley Herron, and Deanna Bridges
Publisher:	PRO-ED
Address of Publisher:	8700 Shoal Creek Boulevard, Austin, TX 78757–6897
Telephone Number:	1-800-897-3202
Fax Number:	1-800-397-7633
Web Site of Publisher:	www.proedinc.com
Type of Test:	Norm referenced
Administration Time:	25 to 45 minutes
Type of Administration:	Individual
Ages/Grade Levels:	Ages 4–0 through 7–11

Purpose and Description of the Test

The YCAT represents a major improvement in the early identification of children at risk for school failure. It yields an overall Early Achievement standard score and individual subtest standard scores for General Information, Reading, Writing, Mathematics, and Spoken Language.

Subtest Information

The YCAT was designed with both the child and the examiner in mind. The individual subtests for General Information, Reading, Writing, Mathematics, and Spoken Language can be given independent of each other, leading to flexible testing sessions.

Strengths of the Test

- The YCAT was normed on 1,224 children representing thirty-two states and the District of Columbia. The information is clearly representative of the U.S. population as reported in the *2000 Statistical Abstract of the United States* (U.S. Census Bureau, 2000).
- Reliability was standardized using the coefficient alpha, test-retest, and interscorer procedures.
- Extensive evidence of the validity of YCAT test scores is proved for content-description validity, criterion-prediction validity, and construct-identification validity.
- The YCAT items were examined to ensure that little or no bias relative to gender, disability, race, socioeconomic level, or ethnic group existed. Differential item functioning techniques were used to examine items for potential bias.

Chapter 4

Anxiety and Depression

Emotional problems may impair a child's ability to work to his or her potential in school. Two of the most common emotional problems that impede learning are anxiety and depression.

Anxiety Disorders

Anxiety disorders are the most common mental health problems among children and adolescents (Turnbull et al., 2004). The symptoms that these children may experience include excessive fear, worry, and anxiety related to different situations. As many as 13 percent of youth and adolescents suffer from anxiety disorders. Surprisingly, only about a third of these children receive treatment (Jensen, 2005; Anxiety Disorders Association of America, 2002). According to the U.S. Department of Health and Human Services (1999), anxiety disorders that are not treated early can lead to:

- Repeated school absences or an inability to finish school
- Impaired relations with peers
- Low self-esteem
- Alcohol or other drug use
- Problems adjusting to work situations
- Anxiety disorder in adulthood

Many different anxiety disorders affect children and adolescents. These include (Jensen, 2005; American Psychiatric Association, 2000; Anxiety Disorders Association of America, 2002; U.S. Department of Health and Human Services, 1999):

Generalized Anxiety Disorder: The primary characteristic is unrealistic or excessive anxiety about a minimum of two or more circumstances directly related to the individual's life.

Separation Anxiety Disorder: The essential behavior required for a diagnosis of this disorder is a child's excessive anxiety and fear related to being separated from a significant individual. The excessive reaction is beyond what would be expected for the child's age and developmental level.

Phobias: Children with phobias may experience intense fear of reaction to a specific object or situation such as snakes, dogs, or heights. The level of fear is inappropriate to the situation and is recognized by the person as being irrational.

Obsessive Compulsive Disorder (OCD): Children with OCD may experience persistent, recurring thoughts (obsessions) that reflect exaggerated anxiety or fears. The obsessions may lead the person to perform a ritual or routine (compulsions).

Post-Traumatic Stress Disorder (PTSD): Symptoms experienced by children with PTSD include prolonged and recurrent emotional reactions after exposure to a traumatic event such as sexual or physical assault, unexpected death of a loved one, or a natural disaster, including flashbacks and nightmares, difficulty sleeping, irritability, and poor concentration.

Depression

Research suggests that the incidence of severe depression in children is estimated to be approximately 2 to 5 percent for elementary school children and 4 to 8 percent for adolescents (American Psychiatric Association, 2000). A depressive disorder is an illness that involves the body, mood, and thoughts. It affects the way a person eats and sleeps, the way one feels about oneself, and the way one thinks about things (National Institute of Mental Health, 2000). Major depression is one of the mental, emotional, and behavior disorders that can appear during childhood or adolescence. It affects a young person's thoughts, feelings, behavior, and body. Major depression in children and adolescents is serious; it is more than "the blues." It can lead to school failure, alcohol or other drug use, and even suicide (U.S. Department of Health and Human Services, 1999).

According to the National Institute of Mental Health (2000), the symptoms of depression in children and adolescence include:

- Persistent sad, anxious, or "empty" mood
- Feelings of hopelessness, pessimism
- Feelings of guilt, worthlessness, helplessness
- Loss of interest or pleasure in hobbies and activities that were once enjoyed
- Decreased energy, fatigue, being "slowed down"
- Difficulty concentrating, remembering, making decisions
- Insomnia, early-morning awakening, or oversleeping
- Appetite or weight loss or overeating and weight gain
- Thoughts of death or suicide, suicide attempts
- Restlessness, irritability
- Persistent physical symptoms that do not respond to treatment, such as headaches, digestive disorders, and chronic pain

Beck Anxiety Inventory (BAI)

General Test Information

Author:	Aaron T. Beck
Publisher:	Harcourt Assessment (formerly known as the Psychological Corporation and Harcourt Educational)
Address of Publisher:	6277 Sea Harbor Drive, Orlando, FL 32887
Telephone Number:	1-800-211-8378
Fax Number:	1-800-232-1223
Web Site of Publisher:	www.harcourt.com
Type of Test:	Anxiety inventory
Administration Time:	5 to 10 minutes
Type of Administration:	Individual
Ages/Grade Levels:	Adolescents and adults

Purpose and Description of Test

The purpose of the test is to screen for anxiety. Patients respond to twenty-one items rated on a scale from 0 to 3. Each item is descriptive of subjective, somatic, or panic-related symptoms of anxiety.

Strengths of the Test

- The BAI has been found to discriminate well between anxious and nonanxious diagnostic groups in a variety of clinical populations.
- Clinical validity: Data are reported on samples of patients who were diagnosed as having panic disorder with agoraphobia, panic disorder without agoraphobia, social phobia, obsessive-compulsive disorder, and generalized anxiety.

Beck Depression Inventory-II (BDI-II)

General Test Information

Authors:	Aaron T. Beck, Robert A. Steer, and Gregory K. Brown
Publisher:	Harcourt Assessment (formerly known as the Psychological Corporation and Harcourt Educational)
Address of Publisher:	6277 Sea Harbor Drive, Orlando, FL 32887
Telephone Number:	1-800-211-8378
Fax Number:	1-800-232-1223
Web Site of Publisher:	www.harcourt.com
Type of Test:	Depression inventory
Administration Time:	5 minutes
Type of Administration:	Individual
Ages/Grade Levels:	Ages 13 through 80

Purpose and Description of Test

The BDI-II, which is in line with the depression criteria of the *Diagnostic and Statistical Manual of Mental Health Disorders-Fourth Edition* (DSM-IV; American Psychiatric Association, 2000), is one of the leading inventories to assess depression in the United States. Like its predecessor, the BDI-II consists of twenty-one items to assess the intensity of depression in clinical and normal patients. Each item is a list of four statements arranged in increasing severity about a particular symptom of depression.

Strengths of the Test

- Items on the new scale replace items that dealt with symptoms of weight loss, changes in body image, and somatic preoccupation. Another item on the BDI-II that tapped work difficulty was revised to examine loss of energy. Also, sleep loss and appetite loss items were revised to assess both increases and decreases in sleep and appetite.
- Current DSM-IV guidelines require assessing depression symptoms over the preceding two weeks. The time frame for the response set in the new edition was changed from one week to two to comply.
- Improved clinical sensitivity. After testing original and new items on a large clinical sample ($N = 500$), test developers compared item-option characteristic curves. The new editions showed improved clinical sensitivity, with the reliability of the BDI-II (coefficient alpha = .92) higher than the BDI (coefficient alpha = .86).

Children's Depression Inventory (CDI)

General Test Information

Author:	Maria Kovacs
Publisher:	Multi-Health Systems (MHS)
Address of Publisher:	P.O. Box 950, North Tonawanda, NY 14120–0950
Telephone Number:	1-800-456-3003, 1-416-492-2627
Fax Number:	1-888-540-4484, 1-416-492-3343
Web Site of Publisher:	www.mhs.com
Type of Test:	Depression inventory
Administration Time:	Short, 5 minutes; Long, 15 minutes
Type of Administration:	Individual or group
Ages/Grade Levels:	Ages 6 to 17

Purpose and Description of Test

The CDI is a measure of depressive symptoms in children and adolescents. The CDI contains twenty-seven items, each of which consists of statements for each item. The individual is asked to select the statement that describes his or her feelings for the past two weeks.

Subtest Information

There are five subtests:

- Negative Mood
- Interpersonal Problems
- Ineffectiveness
- Anhedonia
- Negative Self-Esteem

Strengths of the Test

- The CDI is a reliable and well-tested symptom-oriented scale that discerns young people with the psychiatric diagnosis of major depressive or dysthymic disorder from those with other psychiatric conditions or those with no psychiatric condition.
- The CDI's sensitivity makes it an ideal instrument for measuring treatment progress, monitoring quality assurance, and meeting managed care requirements.

Children's Depression Rating Scale–Revised (CDRS-R)

General Test Information

Authors:	Elva O. Poznanski and Hartmut B. Mokros
Publisher:	Western Psychological Services
Address of Publisher:	12031 Wilshire Boulevard, Los Angeles, CA 90025–1251
Telephone Number:	1-800-648-8857 (United States and Canada only), 1-310-478-2061
Fax Number:	1-310-478-7838
Web Site of Publisher:	http://www.wpspublish.com
Type of Test:	Depression rating scale
Administration Time:	15 to 20 minutes
Type of Administration:	Individual
Ages/Grade Levels:	Ages 6 through 12; also successfully used with adolescents.

Purpose and Description of Test

The CDRS-R is used to diagnose depression and determine its severity. In clinical settings, it can be used to diagnose depression and monitor treatment response. In nonclinical contexts, such as schools and pediatric clinics, it can be used as a quick and economical screener, identifying children who need professional intervention.

Subtest Information

There are no subtests; however, the interviewer rates seventeen symptom areas, including those that serve as DSM-IV criteria for a diagnosis of depression:

Impaired schoolwork	Difficulty having fun	Social withdrawal
Appetite disturbance	Sleep disturbance	Excessive fatigue
Physical complaints	Irritability	Excessive guilt
Low self-esteem	Depressed feelings	Morbid ideation
Suicidal ideation	Excessive weeping	Depressed facial affect
Listless speech	Hypoactivity	

Strengths of the Test

- Unlike self-report inventories, the CDRS-R not only assesses depression but also takes the first step in the therapeutic process. A direct interview engages children who are isolated and withdrawn (as most depressed children are), bringing them into positive contact and interaction.

Depression and Anxiety in Youth Scale (DAYS)

General Test Information

Authors:	Phyllis Newcomer, Edna Barenbaum, and Brian Bryant
Publisher:	PRO-ED
Address of Publisher:	8700 Shoal Creek Boulevard, Austin, TX 78757–6897
Telephone Number:	1-800-897-3202
Fax Number:	1-800-397-7633
Web Site of Publisher:	www.proedinc.com
Type of Test:	Depression and anxiety
Administration Time:	10 minutes
Type of Administration:	Individual
Ages/Grade Levels:	Ages 6 to 19

Purpose and Description of Test

The DAYS is a unique battery of three norm-referenced scales useful in identifying major depressive disorder and overanxious disorders in children and adolescents. The primary theoretical frame of reference for the scales is the *Diagnostic and Statistical Manual of Mental Disorders-Fourth Edition-TR* (American Psychiatric Association, 2000), which presents a system for classifying a variety of anxiety and mood disorders in young people.

Subtest Information

The DAYS comprises three scales: Student Rating Scale (Scale S), the Teacher or Teacher Alternate Rating Scale (Scale T), and the Parent or Parent Alternate Rating Scale (Scale P). Each scale has been standardized and may be used independently or in conjunction with the other scales.

Strengths of the Test

- There were 5,000 typical learners in the norming sample.
- Norms have been developed for special education students classified as emotionally disturbed and learning disabled, as well as children and adolescents diagnosed as clinically depressed.

Multidimensional Anxiety Scale for Children (MASC)

General Test Information

Author:	John S. March
Publisher:	Multi-Health Systems (MHS)
Address of Publisher:	P.O. Box 950, North Tonawanda, NY 14120–0950
Telephone Number:	1-800-456-3003, 1-416-492-2627
Fax Number:	1-888-540-4484, 1-416-492-3343
Web Site of Publisher:	www.mhs.com
Type of Test:	Anxiety scale
Administration Time:	Short, 5 minutes; Long, 15 minutes
Type of Administration:	Individual
Ages/Grade Levels:	Ages 8 to 19

Purpose and Description of Test

The MASC is an assessment of the major dimensions of anxiety in children and adolescents.

Subtest Information

The MASC consists of thirty-nine items distributed across four basic scales (three of which have subscales):

- Physical Symptoms: Consists of two subscales: Somatic Symptoms and Tense Symptoms
- Harm Avoidance: Consists of two subscales: Perfectionism and Anxious Coping
- Social Anxiety: Consists of two subscales: Humiliation Fears and Performance Fears
- Separation/Panic

Strengths of the Test

- The MASC measures a cross-section of anxiety problems and can be used as a diagnostic aid.
- The scale provides a reliable and valid assessment that distinguishes between important anxiety symptoms and is sensitive to treatment-induced changes in symptom types and levels.
- Diverse case studies are provided in the technical manual to show application of the MASC in a number of situations and contexts and to clarify the use of MASC in actual practice.

Revised Children's Manifest Anxiety Scale (RCMAS)

General Test Information

Authors:	Cecil R. Reynolds and Bert O. Richmond
Publisher:	Western Psychological Services
Address of Publisher:	12031 Wilshire Boulevard, Los Angeles, CA 90025–1251
Telephone Number:	1-800-648-8857 (United States and Canada only), 1-310-478-2061
Fax Number:	1-310-478-7838
Web Site of Publisher:	http://www.wpspublish.com
Type of Test:	Anxiety self-report inventory
Administration Time:	10 minutes
Type of Administration:	Individual
Ages/Grade Levels:	Ages 6 to 19

Purpose and Description of Test

The RCMAS helps pinpoint the problems in a child's life. This brief self-report inventory measures the level and nature of anxiety in youth aged 6 to 19 years. Because anxiety is a good indicator of stress, RCMAS scores often lead the clinician to more basic problems. The scale is useful in evaluating children for academic stress, test anxiety, peer and family conflicts, and drug problems. Teachers find it an easy way to identify anxiety levels in the classroom, and parents find RCMAS data useful in helping their children adapt to anxiety-producing situations.

Subtest Information

The RCMAS is a thirty-seven-item self-report inventory that provides scores for Total Anxiety and four subscales:

- Worry/Oversensitivity
- Physiological Anxiety
- Social Concerns/Concentration
- Lie Scale

Strengths of the Test

- Sex-specific norms are provided for nearly 5,000 school-age children and adolescents, including those in special classes for gifted and learning disabled students.
- Separate norms based on black populations are available.
- A complete Spanish Language Kit is offered.

Reynolds Adolescent Depression Scale–Second Edition (RADS-2)

General Test Information

Author: William M. Reynolds

Publisher: PAR

Address of Publisher: 16204 North Florida Avenue, Lutz, FL 33549

Telephone Number: 1-800-331-8378, ext. 361

Fax Number: 1-800-727-9329

Web Site of Publisher: http://www.parinc.com

Type of Test: Depression scale

Administration Time: 5 to 10 minutes

Type of Administration: Individual or group administration

Ages/Grade Levels: Adolescents

Purpose and Description of Test

The RADS-2 screens and identifies adolescents with significant depressive symptoms within multistage school assessment programs or individual practice settings.

Subtest Information

The RADS-2 is a brief, thirty-item self-report measure with subscales that evaluate the current level of an adolescent's depressive symptomatology along four basic dimensions of depression: Dysphoric Mood, Anhedonia/Negative Affect, Negative Self-Evaluation, and Somatic Complaints. Interpretation of these four subscales is based on the nature of the depression domain and the item content of the subscale.

In addition, the RADS-2 yields a Depression Total score that represents the overall severity of depressive symptomatology. An empirically derived clinical cutoff score helps to identify adolescents who may be at risk for a depressive disorder or a related disorder. Data demonstrate the ability of this cutoff score to discriminate between adolescents with Major Depressive Disorder and an age- and gender-matched control group.

The six RADS-2 critical items alert clinicians that an adolescent (with a Depression Total score below the clinical cutoff) may be experiencing a significant level of depression.

Strengths of the Test

- The RADS-2 includes the following new features:

  - The text has been restandardized with a new school-based sample of 3,300 adolescents that was stratified to reflect the 2000 Census data for gender and ethnicity.
  - The expanded age range covers individuals ages 11 to 20 years.
  - Four factorially derived subscales reflect four basic domains of adolescent depression.
  - Updated normative tables provide standard (*T*) scores in addition to percentile ranks for the Depression Total scale and four subscales.
  - The new Professional Manual provides a comprehensive literature review.
  - Case studies illustrate expanded interpretation of subscale and Depression Total scale scores.
  - A carbonless, hand-scorable Test Booklet facilitates scoring and interpretation.

Comprehensive data are presented to demonstrate the reliability and validity of the RADS-2. Reliability data (internal consistency, test-retest, and standard errors of measurement) are presented for the Depression Total scale and the four subscales. Validity of the RADS-2 was examined from a number of perspectives: content validity, criterion-related validity, construct validity (convergent, discriminant, and factorial), and clinical validity. Reliability and validity studies included a school-based sample of over 9,000 adolescents and a clinical sample of 297 adolescents with *Diagnostic and Statistical Manual of Mental Disorders,* Third Edition Revised (American Psychiatric Association, 1987), or *Diagnostic and Statistical Manual of Mental Disorders,* Fourth Edition (American Psychiatric Association, 2000), who were evaluated in both school and clinical settings. Extensive documentation of reliability and validity evidence for the RADS collected by the author and other researchers over a twenty-year period is also presented.

The RADS-2 Professional Manual provides information regarding the development of the original RADS and the extensive research that led to development of the RADS-2. The RADS-2 restandardization sample included 3,300 adolescents, ages 11 to 20 years, from school settings in the United States and Canada. Normative data (*T*-scores and percentile ranks) are provided for the entire sample, as well as by gender, age group (11–13 years, 14–16 years, and 17–20 years), and gender for the three age groups. Each age group contained 1,100 participants; males and females were equally represented. The sample was ethnically diverse, reflecting the 2000 U.S. Census data. The manual also provides two case examples to illustrate appropriate interpretation of test results.

RADS-2 materials consist of the Professional Manual; the carbonless, hand-scorable Test Booklet; and the Summary/Profile Form. The RADS-2 items are written at a third-grade level and are worded in the present tense to elicit current symptom status. Symptom content is consistent with a wide range of expert systems and sources (for example, DSM-IV and the International Classification of Diseases-10).

Reynolds Child Depression Scale (RCDS)

General Test Information

Author:	William M. Reynolds
Publisher:	PAR
Address of Publisher:	16204 North Florida Avenue, Lutz, FL 33549
Telephone Number:	1-800-331-8378, ext. 361
Fax Number:	1-800-727-9329
Web Site of Publisher:	http://www.parinc.com
Type of Test:	Depression scale
Administration Time:	10 minutes
Type of Administration:	Individual or group administration
Ages/Grade Levels:	Grades 3 to 6

Purpose and Description of Test

The RCDS was developed to screen for depression in children and can be used in schools or in clinical settings for grades 3 to 6. It provides school and mental health professionals with a straightforward, easily administered measure for the evaluation of the severity of children's depressive symptoms. The RCDS can also be used in research on depression and related constructs.

Strengths of the Test

- The test is written at a second-grade level (items are read aloud to assist students in grades 3 and 4).
- Thirty items are rated on a four-point scale.
- The test is hand-scorable for individual or group administration.
- Reliability coefficients range from .87 to .91.
- The total sample alpha reliability is .90, and split-half reliability is .89.
- Validity has been consistently demonstrated in field testing since 1981.
- The Professional Manual provides basic information on the diagnosis and measurement of depression, a description of the RCDS and its development, normative information, and guidelines for interpretation.

Chapter 5

Aptitude

An aptitude test is a standardized test designed to predict an individual's ability to learn certain skills. Hammill (1998) notes that "aptitude is the ability that a person must possess to achieve some purpose. The purpose may be achievement in an academic subject, skill in independent living, success on the job, or proficiency in any other endeavor. For example, a person can be tested for musical talent, for probable success in school, for ability to do a particular job, and so forth" (p. 4).

Aptitude tests measure developed abilities, not necessarily innate abilities. They have a historical tie to the concept of innate mental abilities and the belief that such abilities can be defined and meaningfully measured (Atkinson, 2001). The development of these abilities begins at birth and continues through early adulthood and is influenced by both in-school and out-of-school experiences. Because these abilities are closely related to an individual's success in school in virtually all subjects, test results may be used in planning effective instructional programs. In combination with other relevant information about a student, scores on aptitude tests can be used to adapt instruction in ways that enhance the student's chances of success in learning.

Many authorities agree that intelligence tests are in fact best regarded as tests of scholastic aptitude or academic intelligence. According to Hammill (1998), "The choice of the word *aptitude* or *intelligence* in the title of most mental ability tests depends primarily on the personal preference of the author. The very same abilities that are measured for the purpose of predicting performance in these areas can be measured for the purpose of estimating an individual's intelligence. Aptitude and intelligence are closely related ideas. In discussions of such broad-based concepts as general life skills or overall school success, the two terms are virtually interchangeable" (p. 5).

Cognitive Abilities Test (CogAT)

General Test Information

Authors:	David F. Lohman and Elizabeth P. Hagen
Publisher:	Riverside Publishing
Address of Publisher:	425 Spring Lake Drive, Itasca, IL 60143–2079
Telephone Number:	1-800-323-9540
Fax Number:	1-630-467-7192
Web Site of Publisher:	www.riverpub.com
Type of Test:	Aptitude and abilities test
Administration Time:	Varies
Type of Administration:	Individual
Ages/Grade Levels:	Grades K to 12

Purpose and Description of Test

The CogAT is an integrated series of tests that provides information on the level of development of general and specific cognitive skills of students from kindergarten through grade 12. These abilities have substantial correlations with learning and problem solving both in and out of school. The primary purpose of CogAT is to provide a description of the student's cognitive resources for learning that teachers and other educators can use to help the student achieve instructional objectives.

Strengths of the Test

- The new edition of CogAT was developed under the same rigorous standards as the Iowa Tests. Its primary goal is to assess students' abilities in reasoning and problem solving; however, it can also provide predictive achievement scores when given with one of the Iowa Tests. Thus, students who would benefit from enrichment or intervention can be easily identified.

- Individual reports describe the level and pattern of each student's verbal, quantitative, and nonverbal reasoning abilities. Profile classifications are made dependable by a careful examination of the consistency of each student's responses to items within a subtest and across subtests within a battery. These profiles, when used with the related information in the CogAT Form 6 Interpretive Guide for Teachers and Counselors, can be the key to understanding how students learn.

- The new kindergarten test (Level K) measures the development of reasoning abilities that are critical for success in school. Results profile students' verbal, quantitative, and nonverbal reasoning abilities, allowing teachers to plan instructional interventions at a time when instruction can have the greatest impact on a child's long-term success in school.

- The items on CogAT have been designed to eliminate irrelevant sources of difficulty. Each item on the Multilevel Edition Verbal Battery has been reviewed for appropriateness of vocabulary level and sentence structure. All items have been reviewed to eliminate content that could be biased toward or offensive to any group of individuals. Empirical analyses were also made to eliminate items that had atypical patterns for particular cultural and social groups. Thus, an individual's score on CogAT primarily reflects her or his ability to discover relationships and demonstrate flexibility in thinking.

Detroit Tests of Learning Aptitude-4 (DTLA-4)

General Test Information

Author: Donald D. Hammill

Publisher: PRO-ED

Address of Publisher: 8700 Shoal Creek Boulevard, Austin, TX 78757–6897

Telephone Number: 1-800-897-3202

Fax Number: 1-800-397-7633

Web Site of Publisher: www.proedinc.com

Type of Test: Aptitude

Administration Time: 40 minutes to 2 hours

Type of Administration: Individual

Ages/Grade Levels: Ages 6 to 17

Purpose and Description of Test

The DTLA-4 is a popular test in schools for professionals interested in a thorough investigation of a person's cognitive functions. This test not only measures basic abilities, but also shows the effects of language, attention, and motor abilities on test performance.

Subtest Information

The latest edition of this test contains eleven subtests that are grouped into three domains. Within each domain are two subareas called composites. Listed below are the subtests included in each domain:

- Linguistic Domain

  Verbal Composite: Tests the student's knowledge of words and their use. The following subtests make up this composite:

Basic Information	Story Construction
Picture Fragments	Word Opposites
Reversed Letters	Word Sequences
Sentence Imitation	

  Nonverbal Composite: Does not involve reading, writing, or speech. The following subtests make up this composite:

Design Reproduction	Story Sequences
Design Sequences	Symbolic Relations

- Attentional Domain

  Attention-Enhanced Composite: Emphasizes concentration, attending, and short-term memory. The following tests make up this composite:

Design Reproduction	Sentence Imitation
Design Sequences	Story Sequences
Reversed Letters	Word Sequences

  Attention-Reduced Composite: Emphasizes long-term memory. The following subtests make up this composite:

Basic Information	Symbolic Relations
Picture Fragments	Word Opposites
Story Construction	

- Motoric Domain

  Motor-Enhanced Composite: Emphasizes complex manual dexterity. The following subtests make up this composite:

Design Reproduction	Reversed Letters
Design Sequences	Story Sequences

  Motor-Reduced Composite: The following subtests make up this composite:

Basic Information	Story Construction
Picture Fragments	Word Opposites
Sentence Imitation	Word Sequences

Strengths of the Test

- DTLA-4 was built with the American Psychological Association's standards for technical adequacy clearly in mind. The test was normed on 1,350 students residing in thirty-seven states. The demographic characteristics of the normative sample are representative of the U.S. population as a whole, as reported in the *1996 Statistical Abstract of the United States* (U.S. Census Bureau, 1996), with regard to gender, race, ethnicity, urban/rural residence, family income, educational attainment of parents, and geographical distribution. Norms are stratified by age.

- Reliability was investigated using estimates of content sampling, time sampling, and scorer differences. Internal consistency reliability coefficients (content sampling) generally exceed .80 for the subtests and .90 for the composites. Time sampling was investigated using the test-retest technique. Test-retest coefficients range from .71 to .96 for the subtests; those for the composites all exceed .90. Scorer reliability coefficients were all in the .90s.

- Evidence of the validity of DTLA-4 test scores is provided for content description validity, criterion prediction validity, and construct identification validity. Content description validity is demonstrated through careful documentation of subtest and item selection and analysis. A particularly powerful method for content description validity is the use of conventional item analysis procedures, which allow the identification of good items and the deletion of bad items. Criterion prediction validity is explored by comparing the results of DTLA-4 with those of other valid and reliable aptitude tests. Construct identification validity is demonstrated by showing the relationship between DTLA-4 and chronological age and tests of academic achievement. Furthermore, DTLA-4 subtests and composites intercorrelate and factor according to hypothesized constructs. Convincing evidence for validity is provided in the form of several confirmatory factor analyses.

- The DTLA-4 was built to minimize the effects of bias. Numerous steps were taken to detect and eliminate sources of cultural, gender, and racial bias. First, the effects of bias were controlled and minimized through the inclusion of minority and disability groups in the normative sample. Second, the examination of reliability and validity information was presented for all these subgroups.

- A particularly powerful element of content description validity is the demonstration of excellent internal consistency reliability for different racial, ethnic, and gender groups. The use of differential item functioning analysis reduces item bias during item selection. Delta score values were used to remove items that appeared to be biased against targeted groups. Finally, none of the subtests are timed.

Detroit Tests of Learning Aptitude-Primary–
Third Edition (DTLA-P:3)

General Test Information

Authors:	Donald D. Hammill and Brian R. Bryant
Publisher:	PRO-ED
Address of Publisher:	8700 Shoal Creek Boulevard, Austin, TX 78757–6897
Telephone Number:	1-800-897-3202
Fax Number:	1-800-397-7633
Web Site of Publisher:	www.proedinc.com
Type of Test:	Aptitude
Administration Time:	15 to 45 minutes
Type of Administration:	Individual
Ages/Grade Levels:	Ages 3–0 through 9–11

Purpose and Description of Test

The DTLA-P:3 is a quick, easily administered test for measuring the general aptitude of young children. It is particularly useful with low-functioning school-age children ages 3–0 through 9–11. It can be used to identify children with learning disabilities and mental retardation.

Subtest Information

This individually administered measure of abilities and deficiencies comprises thirteen subtests, measuring cognitive ability in areas such as language, attention, and motor abilities. Subtests include:

- Articulation
- Conceptual Matching
- Design Reproduction
- Digit Sequences
- Draw-A-Person
- Letter Sequences
- Motor Directions
- Object Sequences
- Oral Directions
- Picture Fragments
- Picture Identification
- Sentence Imitation
- Symbolic Relations

Strengths of the Test

Significant improvements over the previous editions have been made:

- All normative data are new and were collected between 2001 and 2003.
- Characteristics of the normative sample relative to socioeconomic factors, gender, and other critical demographics are the same as those reported in the *2001 Statistical Abstract of the United States* (U.S. Census Bureau, 2001) and are thereby representative of the U.S. population.
- The normative data have been stratified by age, geographical region, gender, race, ethnicity, socioeconomic status, and parent education.
- All pictures have been drawn in color to present a more appealing look to children.
- Pictures are presented to the child using an easel.

79

- Additional instructions have been provided for giving and scoring the digit sequences and design reproduction items.
- Interpretation sections have been expanded.
- Each item on the test has been reevaluated using both conventional item analysis to choose "good" statistical items and the newer differential item functioning analysis to find and eliminate biased items.
- Items have been validated by both exploratory and confirmatory factor analysis.
- Construct identification has been strengthened by including the studies of independent researchers.
- Evidence is provided to show that the test is reliable and valid for specific gender disability, ethnic, and racial groups and a general population.

Otis-Lennon School Ability Test–Eighth Edition (OLSAT-8)

General Test Information

Authors:	Arthur S. Otis and Roger T. Lennon
Publisher:	Harcourt Assessment (formerly known as the Psychological Corporation and Harcourt Educational)
Address of Publisher:	6277 Sea Harbor Drive, Orlando, FL 32887
Telephone Number:	1-800-211-8378
Fax Number:	1-800-232-1223
Web Site of Publisher:	www.harcourt.com
Type of Test:	Aptitude and abilities test
Administration Time:	A–C (grades K through 2), 75 minutes over two sessions; Levels D–G (grades 3 through 12), 60 minutes
Type of Administration:	Individual
Ages/Grade Levels:	Grades K through 12

Purpose and Description of Test

OLSAT-8 measures the cognitive abilities that relate to a student's ability to learn in school. By assessing a student's abstract thinking and reasoning abilities, OLSAT-8 supplies educators with information they can use to enhance the insight that traditional achievement tests provide.

Subtest Information

The test is broken down into five clusters:

- *Verbal Comprehension:* following directions, antonyms, sentence completion, and sentence arrangement
- *Verbal Reasoning:* logical selection, verbal analogies, verbal classification, and inference
- *Pictorial Reasoning:* picture classification, picture analogies, and picture series
- *Figural Reasoning:* figural classification, figural analogies, and figural series
- *Quantitative Reasoning* (given in Levels E–G): number series, numeric inference, and number matrix

Strengths of the Test

- When administered with the Stanford Achievement Test Series–Tenth Edition (Stanford-10), OLSAT-8 scores may also be used to relate a student's actual achievement with his or her school ability.
- OLSAT-8 assesses students' thinking skills and provides an understanding of a students' relative strengths and weaknesses in performing a variety of reasoning tasks. This information allows educators to design educational programs that will enhance students' strengths while supporting their learning needs.

Chapter 6

Attention Deficit-
Hyperactivity Disorder

All children may at some time have difficulty paying attention in school, act hyperactive, or exhibit impulsivity. However, children with Attention Deficit-Hyperactivity Disorder (ADHD) exhibit one or more of these behavioral traits on a consistent and intense basis. Children are diagnosed as having ADHD according to the criteria found in the *Diagnostic and Statistical Manual of Mental Disorders* (DSM-IV-TR) (American Psychiatric Association, 2000).

Three subtypes of ADHD are recognized by the American Psychiatric Association:

1. Predominantly hyperactive-impulsive type. These children do not show significant inattention. They often may:
   • Fidget and squirm
   • Get out of their chairs when they are not supposed to
   • Run around or climb constantly
   • Have trouble playing quietly
   • Talk too much
   • Blurt out answers before questions have been completed
   • Have trouble waiting their turn
   • Interrupt others who are talking
   • Butt in on the games others are playing
2. Predominantly inattentive type. These children do not show significant hyperactive-impulsive behavior. They often:
   • Do not pay close attention to details
   • Cannot stay focused on play or school work
   • Do not follow through on instructions or finish school work or chores
   • Cannot seem to organize tasks and activities
   • Get distracted easily
   • Lose things, such as toys, school work, and books
3. Combined type. These children display both inattentive and hyperactive-impulsive symptoms and have symptoms of both of the types described above. They have problems with paying attention, hyperactivity, and controlling their impulses.

ADHD is not a disability category recognized by the Individuals with Disabilities Education Improvement Act (IDEA); however, children with ADHD can receive Section 504 services or special education services under the IDEA classification of Other Health Impairment.

❖ How Do We Identify ADHD?

Components of a Comprehensive Evaluation

- Behavioral
- Educational
- Medical

A diagnosis of ADHD is multifaceted and includes behavioral, educational, and medical data gathering. One component of the diagnosis includes an examination of the child's history through comprehensive interviews with parents, teachers, and health care professionals. Interviewing these individuals determines the child's specific behavior characteristics, when the behavior began, duration of symptoms, whether the child displays the behavior in various settings, and coexisting conditions. The American Academy of Pediatrics (AAP) stresses that because a variety of psychological and developmental disorders frequently coexist in children who are being evaluated for ADHD, a thorough examination for any such coexisting condition should be an integral part of any evaluation (American Academy of Pediatrics, 2000).

Behavioral Evaluation

Specific questionnaires and rating scales are used to review and quantify the behavioral characteristics of ADHD. The AAP has developed clinical practice guidelines for the diagnosis and evaluation of children with ADHD and finds that such behavioral rating scales accurately distinguish between children with and without ADHD (American Academy of Pediatrics, 2000). Conversely, AAP recommends *not* using broadband rating scales or teacher global questionnaires in the diagnosis of children with ADHD. They suggest using ADHD-specific rating scales. You can view these evaluations options within this chapter.

As with all psychological tests, child-rating scales have a range of measurement error. Appropriate scales have satisfactory norms for the child's chronological age and ability levels. Collecting information about the child's ADHD symptoms from several different sources helps ensure that the information is accurate. Appropriate sources of information include the child's parents, teachers, and other diagnosticians such as psychologists, occupational therapists, speech therapists, social workers, and physicians. It is also important to review both the child's previous medical history as well as his or her school records (U.S. Department of Education, 2003).

Educational Evaluation

An educational evaluation assesses the extent to which a child's symptoms of ADHD impair his or her academic performance at school. The evaluation involves direct observations of the child in the classroom as well as a review of his or her academic productivity. Behaviors targeted for classroom observation may include the following:

- Problems of inattention, such as becoming easily distracted, making careless mistakes, or failing to finish assignments on time
- Problems of hyperactivity, such as fidgeting, getting out of an assigned seat, running around the classroom excessively, or striking out at a peer
- Problems of impulsivity, such as blurting out answers to the teacher's questions or interrupting the teacher or other students in the class
- More challenging behaviors, such as severe aggressive or disruptive behavior

Classroom observations are used to record how often the child exhibits various ADHD symptoms in the classroom. The frequency with which the child with ADHD exhibits these and other target behaviors are compared to norms for other children of the same age and gender. It is also important to compare the behavior of the child with ADHD to the behaviors of other children in his or her classroom. It is best to collect this information during two or three different observations across several days. Each observation typically lasts about twenty to thirty minutes. In order to receive special education and related services under Part B of IDEA, a child must be evaluated to determine (1) whether he or she has a disability and (2) whether he or she, because of the disability, needs special education and related services. The initial evaluation must be a full and individual evaluation that assesses the child in all areas related to the suspected disability and uses a variety of assessment tools and strategies (U.S. Department of Education, 2003).

Further, a child who has ADHD may be eligible for special education and related services because he or she also meets the criteria for at least one of the disability categories, such as specific learning disability or emotional disturbance. It is important to note that the assessment instruments and procedures used by educational personnel to evaluate other disabilities—such as learning disabilities—may not be appropriate for the evaluation of ADHD. A variety of assessment tools and strategies must be used to gather relevant functional and developmental information about the child. An educational evaluation also includes an assessment of the child's productivity in completing classwork and other academic assignments. It is important to collect information about both the percentage of work completed as well as the accuracy of the work. The productivity of the child with ADHD can be compared to the productivity of other children in the class.

Once the observations and testing are complete, a group of qualified professionals and the parents of the child will review the results and determine if the child has a disability and whether the child needs special education and related services. Using this information, the child's IEP team, which includes the child's parents, will develop an individualized education program that directly addresses the child's learning and behavior. If the child is recommended for evaluation and determined by the child's IEP team not to meet the eligibility requirements under IDEA, the child may be appropriate for evaluation under Section 504.

Medical Evaluation

A medical evaluation assesses whether the child is manifesting symptoms of ADHD, based on the following three objectives:

- To assess problems of inattention, impulsivity, and hyperactivity that the child is currently experiencing;
- To assess the severity of these problems; and
- To gather information about other disabilities that may be contributing to the child's ADHD symptoms.

Part B of IDEA does not necessarily require a school district to conduct a medical evaluation for the purpose of determining whether a child has ADHD. If a public agency believes that a medical evaluation by a licensed physician is needed as part of the evaluation to determine whether a child suspected of having ADHD meets the eligibility criteria of the OHI category, or any other disability category under Part B, the school district must ensure that this evaluation is conducted at no cost to the parents (OSEP Letter to Michel Williams, March 14, 1994, 21 IDELR 73).

In May 2000, the American Academy of Pediatrics (AAP) published a clinical practice guideline that provides recommendations for the assessment and diagnosis of school-aged children with ADHD. The guideline, developed by a committee composed of pediatricians and experts in the fields of neurology, psychology, child psychiatry, child development, and education, as well as experts in epidemiology and pediatrics, is intended for use by primary care clinicians who are involved in the identification and evaluation process. The recommendations are designed to provide a framework for diagnostic decision making. Medical evaluation for ADHD should be initiated by the primary care clinician. Questioning parents regarding school and behavioral issues, either directly or through a previsit questionnaire, may help alert physicians to possible ADHD. In diagnosing ADHD, physicians should use DSM-IV criteria. The assessment of ADHD should include information obtained directly from parents or caregivers, as well as a classroom teacher or other school professional, regarding the core symptoms of ADHD in various settings, the age of onset, duration of symptoms, and degree of functional impairment.

Evaluation of a child with ADHD should also include assessment of co-existing conditions such as learning and language problems, aggression, disruptive behavior, depression, or anxiety (U.S. Department of Education, 2003).

Attention Deficit Disorders Evaluation Scale–
Third Edition (ADDES-3)

General Test Information

Author:	Stephen B. McCarney
Publisher:	Hawthorne Educational Services
Address of Publisher:	800 Gray Oak Drive, Columbia, MO 65201
Telephone Number:	1-800-542-1673
Fax Number:	1-800-442-9509
Web Site of Publisher:	http://www.hes-inc.com
Type of Test:	ADHD
Administration Time:	Approximately 15 minutes
Type of Administration:	Individual
Ages/Grade Levels:	Ages 4 through 18

Purpose and Description of Test

The ADDES-3 enables educators, school and private psychologists, pediatricians, and other medical personnel to evaluate and diagnose Attention Deficit-Hyperactivity Disorder (ADHD) in children and youth from information provided by primary observers of the student's behavior.

Subtest Information

The ADDES-3 was developed from research in behavior disorders, learning disabilities, and ADHD; current literature in psychology, neurology, and education; and current practices in identification and diagnosis. Although there are no formal subtests on the ADDES-3, the subscales, Inattentive and Hyperactive-Impulsive, are based on the current subtypes of ADHD.

Strengths of the Test

- The scale is available in two versions: School Version, a reporting form for educators, and Home Version, a reporting form for parents. Internal consistency, test-retest, and interrater reliability; item and factor analysis; and content, diagnostic, criterion-related, and construct validity are documented and reported for the scale.
- The ADDES-3 is based on the American Psychiatric Association (2000) definition of ADHD and the criteria most widely accepted by educators and mental health professionals.
- The results provided by the scale are commensurate with criteria that educational, psychiatric, and pediatric professionals use to identify ADHD in children and youth.

Attention Deficit Disorders Evaluation Scale: Secondary-Age Student (ADDES-S)

General Test Information

Author:	Stephen B. McCarney
Publisher:	Hawthorne Educational Services
Address of Publisher:	800 Gray Oak Drive, Columbia, MO 65201
Telephone Number:	1-800-542-1673
Fax Number:	1-800-442-9509
Web Site of Publisher:	http://www.hes-inc.com
Type of Test:	ADHD
Administration Time:	Approximately 15 minutes
Type of Administration:	Individual
Ages/Grade Levels:	Ages 11–5 through 18–0

Purpose and Description of Test

The ADDES-S is based on the APA definition of Attention Deficit-Hyperactivity Disorder (DSM-IV-TR) and the criteria most widely accepted by educators and mental health providers. The School Version can be completed in approximately fifteen minutes and includes sixty items easily observed and documented by educational personnel. The Home Version can be completed by a parent or guardian in approximately twelve minutes and includes forty-six items representing behavior exhibited in and around the home environment. The Pre-Referral Attention Deficit Checklist provides a means of calling attention to the behavior for the purpose of early intervention before formal assessment of the student.

Subtest Information

The ADDES-2 consists of two subscales, Inattentive and Hyperactive-Impulsive. Both are based on the current recognized subtypes of ADHD.

Strengths of the Test

- The ADDES-S School Version was standardized on 1,280 students, including identified ADHD students.
- The standardization sample included students from nineteen states and represented all geographical regions of the United States.
- The ADDES-S was factor-analyzed to create the factor clusters (subscales).
- The Pre-Referral Attention Deficit Checklist provides a means of calling attention to the behavior for the purpose of early intervention before formal assessment of the student.
- The ADDES-2/DSM-IV Form provides a comparison of the behavioral characteristics from the ADDES-S to the ADHD criteria from the DSM-IV-TR.
- The Attention Deficit Disorders Intervention Manual: Secondary-Age Student includes individualized education program goals, objectives, and interventions for all sixty items on the School Version of the scale.
- The ADDES-S Quick Score computer program converts raw scores to standard and percentile scores and makes the scoring of both the ADDES-S School and ADDES-2 Home Version rating forms efficient and convenient.

Attention Deficit-Hyperactivity Disorder Test (ADHDT)

General Test Information

Author:	James E. Gilliam
Publisher:	PRO-ED
Address of Publisher:	8700 Shoal Creek Boulevard, Austin, TX 78757–6897
Telephone Number:	1-800-897-3202
Fax Number:	1-800-397-7633
Web Site of Publisher:	http://www.proedinc.com
Type of Test:	ADHD
Administration Time:	10 minutes
Type of Administration:	Individual
Ages/Grade Levels:	Ages 3 to 23

Purpose and Description of Test

The ADHDT is an effective instrument for identifying and evaluating attention deficit disorders.

Subtest Information

The ADHDT has three core subtests that represent the symptoms necessary for a diagnosis of ADHD:

- Hyperactivity
- Impulsivity
- Inattention

Strengths of the Test

- Normed in 1993 and 1994 on a representative national sample of more than 1,200 persons who were diagnosed with attention deficit disorders, these results constitute the most current norms available. Demographics of the standardization sample are reported in the manual by age, gender, geographical location, race, ethnicity, and socioeconomic status. Separate norms are available for males and females.
- Studies of internal consistency and test-retest reliability produced high (.90+) coefficients.
- Additional studies confirmed the test's content, construct, and criterion-related validity. Concurrent validity was established by correlating the ADHDT with other tests, including the Conners' Rating Scales, the Attention Deficit Disorders Evaluation Scale, and the ADD-H Comprehensive Teacher's Rating Scale. The results of these studies attest to the ADHDT's utility and effectiveness in the evaluation of ADHD.
- Extensive evidence of the statistical properties of the test is reported in the test manual.

Brown Attention-Deficit Disorder Scales: Child and Adolescent Versions (Brown ADD Scales for Children)

General Test Information

Author:	Thomas E. Brown
Publisher:	Harcourt Assessment (formerly known as the Psychological Corporation and Harcourt Educational)
Address of Publisher:	6277 Sea Harbor Drive, Orlando, FL 32887
Telephone Number:	1-800-211-8378
Fax Number:	1-800-232-1223
Web Site of Publisher:	www.harcourt.com
Type of Test:	ADHD
Administration Time:	10 to 20 minutes
Type of Administration:	Individual
Ages/Grade Levels:	Ages 3 through 12

Purpose and Description of Test

The Brown ADD Scales quickly screens for reliable indications of Attention Deficit Disorder. Based on Thomas Brown's model of cognitive impairment in children with ADD, the Brown ADDS Scales explore the executive cognitive functioning aspects of cognition associated with ADHD.

Subtest Information

The children's edition features six clusters frequently associated with ADHD that encompass problems in appropriately controlling behavior:

- Organizing, Prioritizing, and Activating to Work
- Focusing, Sustaining, and Shifting Attention to Tasks
- Regulating Alertness, Sustaining Effort, and Processing Speed
- Managing Frustration and Modulating Emotions
- Utilizing Working Memory and Accessing Recall
- Monitoring and Self-Regulating Action

Strengths of the Test

- Easy-to-understand parent and teacher questionnaires are available for the children's version, and self-report forms are provided for ages 8 through adult to obtain information that observers may overlook.
- The Brown ADD Scales allows users to gather and integrate important diagnostic information about an individual, with cluster and total scores used to arrive at a diagnostic decision. The Diagnostic Form helps users conduct a comprehensive evaluation, with a set of procedures for integrating a clinical history, a comorbidity screener, and a worksheet for integrating data from the Brown ADD Scales with standardized scores from other tests.

Children's Attention and Adjustment Survey (CAAS)

General Test Information

Authors:	Nadine Lambert and Jonathan Sandoval
Publisher:	AGS Publishing
Address of Publisher:	4201 Woodland Road, Circle Pines, MN 55014–1796
Telephone Number:	1-800-328-2560, 1-651-287-7220
Fax Number:	1-800-471-8457
Web Site of Publisher:	www.agsnet.com
Type of Test:	ADHD
Administration Time:	5 to 10 minutes per form
Type of Administration:	Individual
Ages/Grade Levels:	Ages 5–0 to 13–11

Purpose and Description of Test

The CAAS helps professionals assess specific behavior problems related to hyperactivity and attention problems. It is a brief survey for identifying behavior problems associated with ADHD in children. Two versions of the survey exist: The school form is completed by the child's teacher; the home form is completed by the child's parent.

Subtest Information

CAAS provides four scales for more precise intervention planning:

- Inattentiveness
- Impulsivity
- Hyperactivity
- Conduct Problems/Aggressiveness

Strengths of the Test

- According to its publisher, "School psychologists, mental health professionals, pediatricians, and other professionals appreciate the efficiency of CAAS's rating scale approach."

Conners' Rating Scales–Revised (CRS-R)

General Test Information

Author:	C. Keith Conners
Publisher:	Multi-Health Systems (MHS)
Address of Publisher:	P.O. Box 950, North Tonawanda, NY 14120–0950
Telephone Number:	1-800-456-3003, 1-416-492-2627
Fax Number:	1-888-540-4484, 1-416-492-3343
Web Site of Publisher:	www.mhs.com
Type of Test:	ADHD
Administration Time:	Long Version—15 to 20 minutes; Short Version—5 to 10 minutes
Type of Administration:	Individual
Ages/Grade Levels:	For the CRS-R: parents and teachers of children and adolescents ages 3 to 17; adolescent self-report, ages 12 to 17

Purpose and Description of Test

This instrument uses observer ratings and self-report ratings to help assess Attention Deficit-Hyperactivity Disorder (ADHD) and evaluate problem behavior in children and adolescents. Various CRS-R versions offer flexible administration options while also providing the ability to collect varying perspectives on a child's behavior from parents, teachers, caregivers, and the child or adolescent.

Subtest Information

There are three versions—Parent, Teacher, and Adolescent Self-Report—all of which also have a short and a long form. In addition, three screening tools offer the option of administering a twelve-item ADHD Index or the eighteen-item DSM-IV (American Psychiatric Association, 2000), Symptom Checklist, or both. These instruments also offer versions for parents, teachers, and adolescents. These forms measure a variety of behavioral characteristics grouped into several scales:

- Oppositional
- Cognitive Problems/Inattention
- Hyperactivity
- Anxious-Shy
- Perfectionism
- Social Problems
- Psychosomatic
- Conners' Global Index
- DSM-IV Symptom Subscales
- ADHD Index

Strengths of the Test

- Measures hyperactivity in children and adolescents through routine screening
- Provides a perspective of the child's behavior from those who interact with the child daily
- Establishes a base point prior to beginning therapy and monitoring treatment effectiveness and changes over time
- Provides valuable structured and normed information to support conclusions, diagnoses, and treatment decisions when the parent, teacher, and self-report scales are combined
- Long and short formats for the teacher, parent, and self-report scales
- Applicable to managed care situations through the quantification and measurement of a variety of behavior problems

Early Childhood Attention Deficit Disorder Evaluation Scale (ECADDES)

General Test Information

Author:	Stephen B. McCarney
Publisher:	Hawthorne Educational Services
Address of Publisher:	800 Gray Oak Drive, Columbia, MO 65201
Telephone Number:	1-800-542-1673
Fax Number:	1-800-442-9509
Web Site of Publisher:	http://www.hes-inc.com
Type of Test:	ADHD
Administration Time:	Approximately 15 minutes
Type of Administration:	Individual
Ages/Grade Levels:	Ages 24 through 83 months

Purpose and Description of Test

The ECADDES is based on the DSM-IV definition of Attention Deficit-Hyperactivity Disorder and the criteria most widely accepted by professionals (American Psychiatric Association, 2000).

Subtest Information

The subscales, Inattentive and Hyperactive-Impulsive, are based on the current subtypes of ADHD.

Strengths of the Test

- The standardization sample included children from thirty states and represented all geographical regions of the United States.
- The ECADDES was factor-analyzed to create the factor clusters (subscales).
- The ECADDES/DSM-IV Form provides a comparison of the behavioral characteristics from the ECADDES to the ADHD criteria from the DSM-IV-TR.
- The Early Childhood Attention Deficit Disorders Intervention Manual includes individualized education program goals, objectives, and interventions for all fifty-six items on the School Version of the scale.
- The Parent's Guide to Early Childhood Attention Deficit Disorders provides parents with specific, practical strategies to use in helping their child be more successful in the home environment.
- The ECADDES Quick Score computer program converts raw scores to standard and percentile scores and makes the scoring of both the School and Home Version rating forms efficient and convenient.
- The computer version of the Early Childhood Attention Deficit Disorders Intervention Manual provides an individualized printout of goals, objectives, and specific interventions selected for a student and implemented by teachers or personnel in the school environment.
- Spanish-language Home Version Rating Forms are available.

Scales for Diagnosing Attention Deficit-Hyperactivity Disorder (SCALES)

General Test Information

Authors:	Gail Ryser and Kathleen McConnell
Publisher:	PRO-ED
Address of Publisher:	8700 Shoal Creek Boulevard, Austin, TX 78757–6897
Telephone Number:	1-800-897-3202
Fax Number:	1-800-397-7633
Web Site of Publisher:	www.proedinc.com
Type of Test:	ADHD
Administration Time:	15 to 20 minutes
Type of Administration:	Individual
Ages/Grade Levels:	Ages 5 to 18

Purpose and Description of Test

The SCALES is a new assessment tool that accurately identifies and evaluates Attention Deficit/Hyperactivity Disorder in children.

Subtest Information

The SCALES is modeled after the guidelines for ADHD in the *Diagnostic and Statistical Manual of Mental Disorders-Fourth Edition-Text Revision* (American Psychiatric Association, 2000). Maintaining the internal coherency of those criteria, it evaluates the child's behavior using three subtests to measure inattention, hyperactivity, and impulsivity.

Strengths of the Test

- The SCALES was standardized using more than 3,000 children and is designed with two sets of norms: persons not identified with or not suspected of having ADHD and individuals already diagnosed with ADHD. It employs a four-point Likert scale to measure the extent to which the child's behavior interferes with his or her functioning within the school and home settings (0 indicating no interference and 4 representing consistent interference).
- Reliability and validity for the SCALES are strong. The average internal consistency coefficients across all ages ranged from .88 to .96.
- Criterion-prediction validity studies were conducted using both the Conners' Rating Scales and the Attention Deficit/Hyperactivity Disorder Test. Exploratory factor analysis confirms that the items on the rating scales accurately measure inattention and hyperactivity/impulsivity. The results of these studies attest to the SCALES's utility and effectiveness in the identification and evaluation of ADHD.

Spadafore Attention Deficit Hyperactivity Rating Scale (S-ADHD-RS)

General Test Information

Authors:	Gerald J. Spadafore and Sharon J. Spadafore
Publisher:	Academic Therapy
Address of Publisher:	20 Commercial Boulevard, Novato, CA 94949
Telephone Number:	1-800-422-7249
Fax Number:	1-888-287-9975
Web Site of Publisher:	http://www.academictherapy.com
Type of Test:	ADHD
Administration Time:	15 minutes
Type of Administration:	Individual
Ages/Grade Levels:	Ages 5 through 19

Purpose and Description of Test

The S-ADHD-RS provides quantification of a number of behaviors that are likely to indicate attention and/or hyperactivity disorders. The test kit contains the Manual, twenty-five Scoring Protocols, twenty-five Observation Forms, and twenty-five Medication Tracking Forms.

Subtest Information

The S-ADHD-RS consists of nine items (rated on a three-point scale) that yield an ADHD Index and fifty items (rated on a five-point scale) that yield three factors: Attention, Impulsivity/Hyperactivity, and Social Adjustment.

Strengths of the Test

- The S-ADHD-RS provides quantification of the severity of characteristics, not just the presence of them, and also provides a form to use when monitoring the effects (over time) of medications.
- The scoring protocol is easy to use.

Chapter 7

Auditory Processing

According to the National Institute on Deafness and Other Communication Disorders (2004), *auditory processing* is a term used to describe what happens when the brain recognizes and interprets sounds. It should be noted that auditory processing disorder (APD) goes by many other names. Sometimes it is referred to as *central auditory processing disorder* (CAPD). Other common names are *auditory perception problem, auditory comprehension deficit, central auditory dysfunction, central deafness,* and so-called *word deafness* (National Institute of Deafness and Other Communication Disorders, 2004). Despite normal hearing, children with APD often become confused and cannot comprehend what is being said when there is too much background noise. Furthermore, these children may have problems with word discrimination, following ongoing conversation in a crowd of people, and difficulty paying attention when others are talking.

According to Gertner (2005), "Children who present with APD have difficulty with some or all *listening activities.* They have particular problems when the activities occur in less than ideal listening environments. Hence, they may exhibit only mild problems with sound discrimination and they may make occasional errors when speaking on a one to one basis in a good (relatively quiet) environment . . . when the discussion topic is unfamiliar to them, or when they have to perform or remember several verbal tasks in a row. In addition, they often have weak phonemic systems (speech sound memories used in phonics, reading, and spelling). They also often appear as though they do not hear well. It is common for children with APD to say, 'what?' or 'huh?'"

According to the Auditory Verbal Center (2006), common indicators of APD are:

- Poor concentration
- Easily distracted
- Often misunderstands what is said
- Difficulty hearing in noise
- Difficulty following directions
- Short attention span
- Difficulty with reading, spelling, and/or language
- Low academic motivation

The exact cause of auditory processing disorder is unknown (National Institute on Deafness and Other Communication Disorders, 2004; Kaufman Children's Center, 2004), although several possible theories have been suggested, including genetic factors, early otitis media, lead poisoning, and other environmental factors. In children, auditory processing difficulty may be associated with conditions such as dyslexia, attention deficit disorder, autism, autism spectrum disorder, specific language impairment, pervasive developmental disorder, or developmental delay (National Institute on Deafness and Other Communication Disorders, 2004).

Auditory Processing Abilities Test (APAT)

General Test Information

Authors:	Deborah Ross-Swain and Nancy Long
Publisher:	Academic Therapy
Address of Publisher:	20 Commercial Boulevard, Novato, CA 94949
Telephone Number:	1-800-422-7249
Fax Number:	1-888-287-9975
Web Site of Publisher:	http://www.academictherapy.com
Type of Test:	Auditory processing
Administration Time:	45 minutes
Type of Administration:	Individual
Ages/Grade Levels:	Ages 5 through 12

Purpose and Description of the Test

The APAT assesses how well one understands what one hears.

Subtest Information

There are ten subtests on the APAT:

Phonemic Awareness	Word Sequences
Semantic Relationships	Sentence Memory
Cued Recall	Content Memory (Immediate and Delayed)
Complex Sentences	Sentence Absurdities
Following Directions	Passage Comprehension

Strengths of the Test

- This is a comprehensive assessment of auditory skills beyond hearing acuity (the realm of audiologists).
- The tasks are based on the latest theoretical and operational definitions of auditory functions and are designed to tap the skills necessary for understanding what is said in the classroom as well as at home.
- The normative sample is nationally stratified, and demographics match the 2000 U.S. Census.

Goldman-Fristoe-Woodcock Test of Auditory Discrimination

General Test Information

Authors:	Ronald Goldman, Macalyne Fristoe, and Richard W. Woodcock
Publisher:	AGS Publishing
Address of Publisher:	4201 Woodland Road, Circle Pines, MN 55014–1796
Telephone Number:	1-800-328-2560, 1-651-287-7220
Fax Number:	1-800-471-8457
Web Site of Publisher:	www.agsnet.com
Type of Test:	Auditory processing
Administration Time:	20 to 30 minutes
Type of Administration:	Individual
Ages/Grade Levels:	Ages 3 and older

Purpose and Description of Test

The Goldman-Fristoe-Woodcock Test of Auditory Discrimination is an individually adminis-tered test of the ability to discriminate speech sounds against two different backgrounds: quiet and noise. It is specifically designed to assess young children. Geared to children's vocabulary levels and limited attention spans, the test moves rapidly, as the child responds by pointing to appealing pictures of familiar objects. Writing and speaking are not required.

Subtest Information

- *Training Procedure.* During this time, the examinee is familiarized with the pictures and the names that are used on the two subtests.
- *Quiet Subtest.* The examinee is presented with individual words in the absence of any noise. This subtest provides a measure of auditory discrimination under ideal conditions.
- *Noise Subtest.* The examinee is presented with individual words in the presence of dis-tracting background noise on the tape. This subtest provides a measure of auditory discrimination under conditions similar to those encountered in everyday life.

Strengths of the Test

- Separate norms are provided for each subtest from ages 3–8 to 70 years and over.
- More reliability and validity data are given for this test than for most other discrimina-tion tests.
- The test is applicable to a wide age range.
- The test is easy to administer.
- The test manual provides clear instruction.

Inventory of Perceptual Skills (IPS)

General Test Information

Author: Donald R. O'Dell
Publisher: Stoelting Co.
Address of Publisher: 620 Wheat Lane, Lo Wood Dale, IL 60191
Telephone Number: 1-630-860-9700
Fax Number: 1-630-860-9775
Web Site of Publisher: http://www.stoeltingco.com
Type of Test: Auditory and visual perception
Administration Time: Approximately 15 minutes
Type of Administration: Individual
Ages/Grade Levels: Ages 5–0 to 10–11

Purpose and Description of Test

The IPS assesses visual and auditory perceptual skills and provides the structure for individual remedial programs. It assesses:

- Visual discrimination
- Visual memory
- Object recognition
- Visual-motor coordination
- Auditory discrimination
- Auditory memory
- Auditory sequencing
- Auditory blending

Strengths of the Test

- The IPS is easily administered by teachers, aides, or specialists. Once the test is scored and recorded on the Student Profile, a graphic comparison can be made of all the subtests. A score below the mean on any subtest indicates a weakness in that area.
- The Teacher's Manual contains many educational activities in visual and auditory perception. Games, exercises, and activities provide the teacher with a variety of approaches and materials to use with the student. The Student Workbook contains eighteen exercises to improve the areas in need of remediation.

Lindamood Auditory Conceptualization Test–Third Edition (LAC-3)

General Test Information

Authors:	Patricia C. Lindamood and Phyllis Lindamood
Publisher:	PRO-ED
Address of Publisher:	8700 Shoal Creek Boulevard, Austin, TX 78757–6897
Telephone Number:	1-800-897-3202
Fax Number:	1-800-397-7633
Web Site of Publisher:	www.proedinc.com
Type of Test:	Auditory processing
Administration Time:	20 to 30 minutes
Type of Administration:	Individual
Ages/Grade Levels:	Ages 5–0 to 18–11

Purpose and Description of Test

The LAC-3 measures an individual's ability to perceive and conceptualize speech sounds using a visual medium. Because of the importance of these auditory skills to reading, the results are helpful for speech/language pathologists, special educators, and reading specialists. The LAC-3 also measures the cognitive ability to distinguish and manipulate sounds, required for success in reading and spelling.

Subtest Information

There are no formal subtests, but the test is divided into four parts:

- *Precheck*—a five-item subtest designed to examine a child's knowledge of various concepts; for example, same/different, first/last
- *Category I, Part A*—a subtest consisting of ten items in which the student is asked to identify certain isolated sounds and determine whether they are the same or different
- *Category I, Part B*—requires the student to identify isolated sounds, sameness or difference, and their order
- *Category II*—consists of twelve items in which the student must change sound patterns when sounds are added, omitted, substituted, shifted, or repeated

Strengths of the Test

- Normative data—standard scores, percentile ranks, and age and grade equivalents—are provided for individuals between the ages of 5–0 and 18–11.
- The number of items in Category II has been increased from twelve to eighteen. The syllables have been extended from four phonemes to five. This category is now titled Tracking Phonemes (Monosyllables).
- Three new categories of items have been added that extend the test into the multisyllable level of processing. These subtests are titled Counting Syllables (Multisyllables), Tracking Syllables (Multisyllables), and Tracking Syllables and Phonemes (Multisyllables).
- All items on the test were evaluated using both conventional item analysis and the new differential item functioning analysis.
- Reliability coefficients are provided for subgroups of the normative sample (including African Americans, Hispanic Americans, gender groups) as well as for the entire normative sample.

- Many new validity studies have been conducted. Special attention has been devoted to showing that the test is valid for a wide variety of subgroups, as well as for the general population.
- Characteristics of the total normative sample relative to socioeconomic factors, gender, ethnicity, and other critical variables are the same as those reported in the *2001 Statistical Abstract of the United States* (U.S. Census Bureau, 2001) and therefore are representative of the current U.S. population.
- Studies showing the absence of gender, racial, linguistic, and ethnic bias have been added.
- An audio CD demonstrating correct pronunciation and administration of test items is provided with the complete test kit.

Test of Auditory Comprehension of Language–
Third Edition (TOAL-3)

General Test Information

Authors:	Don Hammill, Virginia Brown, Stephen Larson, and J. Lee Wiederholt
Publisher:	PRO-ED
Address of Publisher:	8700 Shoal Creek Boulevard, Austin, TX 78757–6897
Telephone Number:	1-800-897-3202
Fax Number:	1-800-397-7633
Web Site of Publisher:	www.proedinc.com
Type of Test:	Auditory comprehension
Administration Time:	Untimed; 1 to 3 hours
Type of Administration:	Individual or group
Ages/Grade Levels:	Ages 12–0 to 24–11

Purpose and Description of Test

The TOAL-3 assesses listening, speaking, reading, and writing skills. It is a revision of the popular Test of Adolescent Language originally published in 1981 and revised in 1987.

Subtest Information

The TOAL-3 consists of ten composite scores in the following areas:

- *Listening*—the ability to understand the spoken language of other people
- *Speaking*—the ability to express one's ideas orally
- *Reading*—the ability to comprehend written messages
- *Writing*—the ability to express thoughts in graphic form
- *Spoken Language*—the ability to listen and speak
- *Written Language*—the ability to read and write
- *Vocabulary*—the ability to understand and use words in communication
- *Grammar*—the ability to understand and generate syntactic (and morphological) structures
- *Receptive Language*—the ability to comprehend both written and spoken language
- *Expressive Language*—the ability to produce written and spoken language

Strengths of the Test

- There were more than 3,000 persons in twenty-two states and three Canadian provinces in the normative sample. It was representative of the U.S. population according to 1990 U.S. Census percentages for region, gender, race, and residence; the sample is stratified by age.
- Internal consistency, test-retest, and scores reliability were investigated. All reliability coefficients exceed .80. This indicates that test error was minimal and that TOAL-3 can be used with confidence.
- Content, criterion-related, and construct validity have been thoroughly studied. Correlations between TOAL-3 and other valid and reliable tests of language show a considerable relationship.
- TOAL-3 is related to IQ and age. Most important, the TOAL-3 scores distinguish dramatically between groups known to have language problems and those known to have normal language. Convincing evidence is also provided to show that TOAL-3 items are not biased with regard to race or gender.

- New features for TOAL-3:
  - Evidence for stability reliability is strengthened.
  - Additional criterion-related validity studies were reviewed to augment the previous research in this area. The results of these studies conducted by independent researchers have been included in the manual.
  - The provision of a factorial analysis has enhanced the construct validity of the test.
  - Studies showing the absence of racial and gender bias have been added.
  - The normative sample has been stratified to gender, residence, geographical region, and race.
  - Administration procedures, especially those pertaining to the use of basals and ceilings, have been rewritten for better clarity.
  - The test has been made more useful to professionals working in postsecondary settings by extending the normative data upward from 18 years to 24–11 years of age.

Test of Auditory Processing Skills–Third Edition (TAPS-3)

General Test Information

Authors:	Nancy A. Martin and Rick Brownell
Publisher:	Academic Therapy
Address of Publisher:	20 Commercial Boulevard, Novato, CA 94949
Telephone Number:	1-800-422-7249
Fax Number:	1-888-287-9975
Web Site of Publisher:	http://www.academictherapy.com
Type of Test:	Auditory processing
Administration Time:	45 to 60 minutes
Type of Administration:	Individual
Ages/Grade Levels:	Ages 4 through 18

Purpose and Description of Test

The TAPS-3 is a thorough reshaping of the Test of Auditory Perceptual Skills (previously authored by M. Gardner). The most obvious change is that there are no longer two levels of the test. The TAPS-3 measures what a person does with what is heard and is intended to be used along with other tests as part of a battery.

Subtest Information

The TAPS-3 consists of nine subtests:

- Word Discrimination
- Phonological Segmentation
- Phonological Blending
- Numbers Forward
- Numbers Reversed
- Word Memory
- Sentence Memory
- Auditory Comprehension
- Auditory Reasoning

In addition, an optional subtest, Auditory Figure-Ground, can be used to screen (not diagnose) possible problems with auditory attention.

Strengths of the Test

- This third edition marks the most extensive overhaul to date of TAPS, a well-known auditory skills assessment, with new subtests, new items, a new scoring scheme, new norms, and an optional subtest (Auditory Figure-Ground) to flag possible attention problems.
- It is designed to complement other auditory tests to provide a comprehensive assessment of auditory skills beyond hearing acuity. The tasks are based on the latest theoretical and operational definitions of auditory functions and are designed to tap the skills necessary for understanding what is said in the classroom as well as at home.
- The normative sample is nationally stratified and demographics match the 2000 U.S. Census.

The Listening Inventory (TLI)

General Test Information

Authors:	Donna Geffner and Deborah Ross-Swain
Publisher:	Academic Therapy
Address of Publisher:	20 Commercial Boulevard, Novato, CA 94949
Telephone Number:	1-800-422-7249
Fax Number:	1-888-287-9975
Web Site of Publisher:	http://www.academictherapy.com
Type of Test:	Listening comprehension inventory
Administration Time:	15 minutes
Type of Administration:	Individual
Ages/Grade Levels:	Ages 4 through 18

Purpose and Description of Test

The TLI is an informal inventory of 103 statements that uses a Likert-type scale to quantify frequency of observed listening behaviors. It is designed to help determine if a child should be assessed further for auditory problems.

Subtest Information

On the TLI, six areas are assessed and index scores are derived for each:

- Linguistic Organization
- Decoding/Language Mechanics
- Attention/Organization
- Sensory/Motor
- Social/Behavioral
- Auditory Processes

Strengths of the Test

- According to its publisher, "This provides a starting point for conversations between the speech-language professional and a child's parent/s and/or teacher when deciding whether to refer a student for further testing."
- TLI is broadly tuned to identify a wide variety of APD characteristics.
- TLI is a sensitive measure to identify those at risk for Auditory Processing Disorder (APD).

Wepman's Auditory Discrimination Test–Second Edition (ADT-2)

General Test Information

Authors:	Joseph M. Wepman and William M. Reynolds
Publisher:	Western Psychological Services
Address of Publisher:	12031 Wilshire Boulevard, Los Angeles, CA 90025–1251
Telephone Number:	1-800-648-8857 (United States and Canada only), 1-310-478-2061
Fax Number:	1-310-478-7838
Web Site of Publisher:	http://www.wpspublish.com
Type of Test:	Auditory processing
Administration Time:	5 minutes
Type of Administration:	Individual
Ages/Grade Levels:	Ages 4 to 8

Purpose and Description of Test

The ADT-2 is a quick, economical way to individually screen children for auditory discrimination and identify those who may have difficulty learning the phonics necessary for reading. Using a simple procedure, the ADT-2 assesses the child's ability to recognize the fine differences between phonemes used in English speech. The examiner reads aloud forty pairs of words, and the child indicates, verbally or gesturally, whether the words in each pair are the same or different.

Strengths of the Test

- Already used with millions of children, the ADT is an effective way to identify those who are slower than average in developing auditory discrimination.
- The test has a simple administration procedure.
- Because younger children are included in the norm sample, the ADT can be used for preschool and kindergarten screening as well as elementary school assessment.
- The test-retest reliability is high.
- The test is easy to score and interpret.

Chapter 8

Autism

The 2004 Individuals with Disabilities Education Improvement Act (C.F.R. Section 300.8) provides this definition of *autism*:

1. Autism means a developmental disability significantly affecting verbal and nonverbal communication and social interaction, generally evident before age 3, that adversely affects a child's educational performance. Other characteristics often associated with autism are engagement in repetitive activities and stereotyped movements, resistance to environmental change or change in daily routines, and unusual responses to sensory experiences.
    i. Autism does not apply if a child's educational performance is adversely affected primarily because the child has an emotional disturbance, as defined in paragraph I(4) of this section.
    ii. A child who manifests the characteristics of autism after age 3 could be identified as having autism if the criteria in paragraph I(1)(i) of this section are satisfied.

Although IDEA places all types of autism under one category, other forms of classification systems are also used. DSM IV-TR (American Psychiatric Association, 2000) defines five forms of autism under the heading of Pervasive Developmental Disorders: Autistic Disorder, Rett's Syndrome, Childhood Disintegrative Disorder, Asperger Syndrome, and Pervasive Developmental Disorder Not Otherwise Specified. Nevertheless, these disorders under DSM are more often referred to today as Autism Spectrum Disorder (ASD; Strock, 2004).

Although the classical form of autism can be readily distinguished from other forms of ASD, the terms *autism* and *ASD* are often used interchangeably. Indicators of autism spectrum disorder in young children include the following:

- Does not babble, point, or make meaningful gestures by 1 year of age
- Does not speak one word by 16 months
- Does not combine two words by 2 years

- Does not respond to name
- Loses language or social skills
- Poor eye contact
- Doesn't seem to know how to play with toys
- Excessively lines up toys or other objects
- Is attached to one particular toy or object
- Doesn't smile
- At times seems to be hearing impaired (Strock, 2004)

According to the Autism Society of America (2006):

There are no medical tests for diagnosing autism. An accurate diagnosis must be based on observation of the individual's communication, behavior, and developmental levels. However, because many of the behaviors associated with autism are shared by other disorders, various medical tests may be ordered to rule out or identify other possible causes of the symptoms being exhibited.

A brief observation in a single setting cannot present a true picture of an individual's abilities and behaviors. Parental (and other caregivers') input and developmental history are very important components of making an accurate diagnosis. At first glance, some persons with autism may appear to have mental retardation, a behavior disorder, problems with hearing, or even odd and eccentric behavior. To complicate matters further, these conditions can co-occur with autism. However, it is important to distinguish autism from other conditions, since an accurate diagnosis and early identification can provide the basis for building an appropriate and effective educational and treatment program (p. 1).

Asperger Syndrome Diagnostic Scale (ASDS)

General Test Information

Authors:	Brenda Myles, Stacey Bock, and Richard Simpson
Publisher:	PRO-ED
Address of Publisher:	8700 Shoal Creek Boulevard, Austin, TX 78757–6897
Telephone Number:	1-800-897-3202
Fax Number:	1-800-397-7633
Web Site of Publisher:	www.proedinc.com
Type of Test:	Autism/Asperger scale
Administration Time:	10 to 15 minutes
Type of Administration:	Individual
Ages/Grade Levels:	Ages 5 through 18

Purpose and Description of Test

The ASDS is a quick, easy-to-use rating scale that can help determine whether a child has Asperger syndrome. This instrument provides an AS Quotient that reveals the likelihood that an individual has Asperger syndrome. The fifty items that constitute the ASDS were drawn from five areas of behavior: cognitive, maladaptive, language, social, and sensorimotor. Diagnosis of Asperger syndrome is difficult because the characteristics of the disorder often resemble those of autism, behavior disorders, attention deficit-hyperactivity disorder, and learning disabilities.

Strengths of the Test

- Identifies persons who have Asperger syndrome
- Documents behavioral progress as a consequence of special intervention programs
- Targets goals for change and intervention on the student's individualized education program
- Measures Asperger syndrome for research purposes

Because the ASDS is based on observations, the test results are valid only when the rater knows the examinee well; that is, the examiner has had regular, sustained contact with the examinee for at least two weeks.

Autism Diagnostic Interview–Revised (ADI-R)

General Test Information

Authors:	Michael Rutter, Ann LeCouteur, and Catherine Lord
Publisher:	Western Psychological Services
Address of Publisher:	12031 Wilshire Boulevard, Los Angeles, CA 90025–1251
Telephone Number:	1-800-648-8857 (United States and Canada only), 1-310-478-2061
Fax Number:	1-310-478-7838
Web Site of Publisher:	http://www.wpspublish.com
Type of Test:	Autism/interview; not a test
Administration Time:	1.5 to 2.5 hours
Type of Administration:	Interview
Ages/Grade Levels:	Children and adults with mental age above 2 years

Purpose and Description of Test

Used in research for decades, this comprehensive interview provides a thorough assessment of individuals suspected of having autism or other autism spectrum disorders. The ADI-R has proven highly useful for formal diagnosis as well as treatment and educational planning.

To administer the ADI-R, an experienced clinical interviewer questions a parent or caretaker who is familiar with the developmental history and current behavior of the individual being evaluated. The interview can be used to assess both children and adults, as long as their mental ages are above 2–0.

Composed of ninety-three items, the ADI-R focuses on three functional domains:

- Language and communications
- Reciprocal social interactions
- Restricted, repetitive, and stereotyped behaviors and interests

Following highly standardized procedures, the interviewer records and codes the informant's responses. (Studies documented in the manual show high test-retest and interrater agreement. Interviewers can refer to the ADI-R training package to learn accurate coding procedures. It is recommended that users study the training materials before administering the ADI-R.) Results are scored and interpreted using a Diagnostic Algorithm, a Current Behavior Algorithm, or both, depending on the purpose of the evaluation.

Subtest Information

Although there are no subtests, the interview questions cover eight content areas:

- Overview of the subject's behavior
- The subject's background, including family, education, previous diagnoses, and medications
- Early development and developmental milestones
- Language acquisition and loss of language or other skills
- Current functioning in regard to language and communication
- Social development and play
- Interests and behaviors
- Clinically relevant behaviors, such as aggression, self-injury, and possible epileptic features

Strengths of the Test

- Because the ADI-R is an interview rather than a test and because it focuses on behaviors that are rare in nonaffected individuals, it provides categorical results rather than scales or norms.
- Results can be used to support a diagnosis of autism or determine the clinical needs of various groups in which a high rate of autism spectrum disorders might be expected (for example, individuals with severe language impairments or certain medical conditions, children with congenital blindness, and youngsters suffering from institutional deprivation).
- The ADI-R has proven highly effective in differentiating autism from other developmental disorders and in assessing syndrome boundaries, identifying new subgroups, and quantifying autistic symptomatology.

Autism Diagnostic Observation Schedule (ADOS)

General Test Information

Authors:	Catherine Lord, Michael Rutter, Pamela C. DiLavore, and Susan Risi
Publisher:	Western Psychological Services
Address of Publisher:	12031 Wilshire Boulevard, Los Angeles, CA 90025–1251
Telephone Number:	1-800-648-8857 (United States and Canada only), 1-310-478-2061
Fax Number:	1-310-478-7838
Web Site of Publisher:	http://www.wpspublish.com
Type of Test:	Autism
Administration Time:	35 to 40 minutes
Type of Administration:	Semistructured interview
Ages/Grade Levels:	Toddlers to adults

Purpose and Description of Test

This semistructured assessment can be used to evaluate almost anyone suspected of having autism—from toddlers to adults, from children with no speech to adults who are verbally fluent. The ADOS consists of various activities that allow the examiner to observe social and communication behaviors related to the diagnosis of pervasive developmental disorders. These activities provide interesting, standard contexts in which interaction can occur.

The ADOS consists of four modules, each requiring thirty-five to forty minutes to administer. The individual being evaluated is given just one module, depending on his or her expressive language level and chronological age. Following guidance provided in the manual, the examiner selects the appropriate module for each person. Module 1 is used with children who do not consistently use phrase speech, Module 2 with those who use phrase speech but are not verbally fluent, Module 3 with fluent children, and Module 4 with fluent adolescents and adults. The one group within the autism spectrum that the ADOS does not address is nonverbal adolescents and adults.

Modules 1 and 2 require the examiner and the child to move around the room. Modules 3 and 4, both of which involve more conversation, can be administered at a table.

Strengths of the Test

- Offering standardized materials and ratings, the ADOS presents a detailed picture of symptoms seen in individuals with autism spectrum disorder that is unaffected by language.

Childhood Autism Rating Scale (CARS)

General Test Information

Authors:	Eric Schopler, Robert J. Reichler, and Barbara Rochen Renner
Publisher:	Western Psychological Services
Address of Publisher:	12031 Wilshire Boulevard, Los Angeles, CA 90025–1251
Telephone Number:	1-800-648-8857 (United States and Canada only), 1-310-478-2061
Fax Number:	1-310-478-7838
Web Site of Publisher:	http://www.wpspublish.com
Type of Test:	Autism rating scale
Administration Time:	Untimed
Type of Administration:	Individual
Ages/Grade Levels:	Ages 2 and older

Purpose and Description of Test

This fifteen-item behavior rating scale helps to identify children with autism and distinguish them from developmentally handicapped children who are not autistic. In addition, it distinguishes mild-to-moderate from severe autism.

Strengths of the Test

- Brief, convenient, and suitable for use with any child over 2 years of age, the CARS helps clinicians and educators to recognize and classify autistic children.
- Developed over a fifteen-year period with more than 1,500 cases, CARS includes items drawn from five prominent systems for diagnosing autism. Each item covers a particular characteristic, ability, or behavior. After observing the child and examining relevant information from parent reports and other records, the examiner rates the child on each item. Using a seven-point scale, he or she indicates the degree to which the child's behavior deviates from that of a normal child of the same age.
- The product of long-term empirical research, CARS provides quantifiable ratings based on direct behavior observation. These ratings are an important element in the systematic diagnosis of autism.
- Two training videos, showing how to use and score the scale, are available, along with four videotapes covering the philosophy and teaching methods of North Carolina's TEACCH Program (Treatment and Education of Autistic and related Communication handicapped CHildren), where the CARS was developed.

Gilliam Autism Rating Scale (GARS)

General Test Information

Author:	James E. Gilliam
Publisher:	PRO-ED
Address of Publisher:	8700 Shoal Creek Boulevard, Austin, TX 78757–6897
Telephone Number:	1-800-897-3202
Fax Number:	1-800-397-7633
Web Site of Publisher:	www.proedinc.com
Type of Test:	Autism
Administration Time:	5 to 10 minutes
Type of Administration:	Individual
Ages/Grade Levels:	Ages 3 through 22

Purpose and Description of Test

Designed for use by teachers, parents, and professionals, the GARS helps to identify and diagnose autism in individuals ages 3 through 22 and to estimate the severity of the problem. Items on the GARS are based on the definitions of autism adopted by the Autism Society of America and the *Diagnostic and Statistical Manual of Mental Disorders,* Fourth Edition (American Psychiatric Association, 2000).

Subtest Information

The items are grouped into four subtests:

- Stereotyped Behaviors
- Communication
- Social Interaction
- Developmental Disturbances

The GARS has three core subtests that describe specific and measurable behaviors and an optional subtest (Developmental Disturbances) that allows parents to contribute data about their child's development during the first three years of life.

Strengths of the Test

- The test was normed on 1,092 representative subjects with autism from forty-five states, Puerto Rico, and Canada, and the validity and reliability of the instrument are high.
- The scale is easily completed by those who have knowledge of the subject's behavior or the greatest opportunity to observe him or her.
- The GARS has strong psychometric characteristics that were confirmed through studies of the test's reliability and validity.
- Coefficients of reliability (internal consistency, test-retest, and interscorer) for the subtests are all in the .80s and .90s. The GARS is the only test for autism that reports data for all three kinds of reliability.
- The validity of the GARS was demonstrated by confirming that (1) the items of the subtests are representative of the characteristics of autism, (2) the subtests are strongly related to each other and to performance on other tests that screen for autism, and (3) the GARS performance discriminates persons with autism from persons with other severe behavioral disorders such as emotional disturbance, mental retardation, speech and language disorders, and other multidisabling conditions.

Krug Asperger's Disorder Index (KADI)

General Test Information

Authors:	David A. Krug and Joel R. Arick
Publisher:	PRO-ED
Address of Publisher:	8700 Shoal Creek Boulevard, Austin, TX 78757–6897
Telephone Number:	1-800-897-3202
Fax Number:	1-800-397-7633
Web Site of Publisher:	www.proedinc.com
Type of Test:	Autism/Asperger's
Administration Time:	15 to 20 minutes
Type of Administration:	Individual
Ages/Grade Levels:	Ages 6 to 22

Purpose and Description of Test

The KADI is a highly sensitive test to identify individuals with Asperger's disorder. It enables professionals to accurately distinguish individuals with Asperger's disorder from individuals with other forms of high-functioning autism.

Strengths of the Test

- Information associated with the KADI can be used to help assess a student's educational needs.
- The KADI is also a prescreening scale that immediately identifies individuals who do not have Asperger's disorder.
- The KADI is easy to administer.
- The manual provides evidence that the KADI produces a high degree of reliability across all three types of reliability and that the test user can have high confidence in the results.

Psychoeducational Profile–Third Edition (PEP-3)

General Test Information

Authors:	Eric Schopler, Margaret D. Lansing, Robert Reichler, and Lee M. Marcus
Publisher:	PRO-ED
Address of Publisher:	8700 Shoal Creek Boulevard, Austin, TX 78757–6897
Telephone Number:	1-800-897-3202
Fax Number:	1-800-397-7633
Web Site of Publisher:	www.proedinc.com
Type of Test:	Autism
Administration Time:	45 minutes to 1.5 hours
Type of Administration:	Individual
Ages/Grade Levels:	Ages 6 months through 7 years

Purpose and Description of Test

The PEP-3 is a revision of the popular instrument that has been used for more than twenty years to assess the skills and behaviors of children with autism and communicative disabilities who function between the ages of 6 months and 7 years. The profile resulting from the PEP-3 graphically charts uneven and idiosyncratic development, emerging skills, and autistic behavioral characteristics. This test meets the need for an assessment tool to assist in the educational programming for young children (ages 3 through 5) with disabilities and is particularly useful in planning for older students' individualized education programs.

Strengths of the Test

- The PEP-3 now includes a Caregiver Report, which has been shown to help orient teachers to a student's developmental inconsistencies. This report uses parent input and is completed prior to the administration of the assessment. The form asks the parent or caregiver to estimate the child's developmental level compared with typical children.
- The PEP-3 includes data that identify special learning strengths and teachable skills. Also, the third edition is improved by offering normative data from both a group of children in the autism spectrum and a comparison group of children without autism. It is the only test to date that provides data for within-group comparison to children in the autism spectrum.
- Improvements to the PEP-3:
  - The function domains have been revised to reflect current research and clinical concerns, especially in the area of social and communication functions.
  - All of the toys and materials needed to administer the test (except food, drink, and a light switch) are now included with the test.
  - New items and subtests have been added; obsolete ones were deleted.
  - Normative data were collected from 2002 to 2003 with large national samples of children in the autism spectrum and of typical children ranging from 2 to 7½ years of age. These are the first normative data provided for comparison of a child's PEP results with children of either comparison group.

- Reliability coefficients have been computed by age for subgroups within the normative sample (males; females; and white, black, and Hispanic Americans). Validity evidence is provided for children in the autism spectrum for all areas measured by the test.
- The scoring has been quantified as 0, 1, and 2. Each score is clearly defined, improving the accuracy of statistical comparisons. At the same time, the flexibility of the previous system, using pass, emerge, and fail, has been maintained.
- The Caregiver Report includes current developmental levels, diagnostic categories, and degree of problem and three subtests: Problem Behaviors, Personal Self-Care, and Adaptive Behavior. It provides teachers and other professionals with information needed for a more thorough and complete planning for each child.

Social Communication Questionnaire (SCQ)

General Test Information

Authors:	Michael Rutter, Anthony Bailey, and Catherine Lord
Publisher:	Western Psychological Services
Address of Publisher:	12031 Wilshire Boulevard, Los Angeles, CA 90025–1251
Telephone Number:	1-800-648-8857 (United States and Canada only), 1-310-478-2061
Fax Number:	1-310-478-7838
Web Site of Publisher:	http://www.wpspublish.com
Type of Test:	Autism
Administration Time:	10 minutes
Type of Administration:	Individual
Ages/Grade Levels:	Age 4 and older as long as the subject's mental age exceeds 2 years

Purpose and Description of Test

This brief instrument helps evaluate communication skills and social functioning in children who may have autism or autism spectrum disorders. The SCQ is a cost-effective way to determine whether an individual should be referred for a complete diagnostic evaluation.

Strengths of the Test

- The Lifetime Form focuses on the child's entire developmental history, providing a total score that is interpreted in relation to specific cutoff points. This score identifies individuals who may have autism and should be referred for a more complete evaluation—with the Autism Diagnostic Interview-Revised (ADI-R) or the Autism Diagnostic Observation Schedule, for example. SCQ content parallels that of the ADI-R, and the agreement between SCQ and ADI-R scores is high and substantially unaffected by age, gender, language level, and performance IQ. This indicates that the SCQ is a valid screener, providing a reasonable picture of symptom severity.

- Moving from developmental history to current status, the Current Form looks at the child's behavior over the most recent three-month period. It produces results that can be helpful in treatment planning, educational intervention, and measurement of change over time.

- In addition to its screening and educational applications, the SCQ can be used to compare symptom levels across various groups—children with developmental language disorders, for example, or youngsters with medical conditions typically associated with autism spectrum disorders.

- Because the SCQ is brief, quick, easily administered, and relatively inexpensive, it allows clinicians and educators to routinely screen children for autism spectrum disorders. This in turn permits early intervention.

Social Responsiveness Scale (SRS)

General Test Information

Author:	John N. Constantino
Publisher:	Western Psychological Services
Address of Publisher:	12031 Wilshire Boulevard, Los Angeles, CA 90025–1251
Telephone Number:	1-800-648-8857 (United States and Canada only), 1-310-478-2061
Fax Number:	1-310-478-7838
Web Site of Publisher:	http://www.wpspublish.com
Type of Test:	Autism
Administration Time:	15 to 20 minutes
Type of Administration:	Individual
Ages/Grade Levels:	Ages 4 to 18

Purpose and Description of Test

The SRS measures the severity of autism spectrum symptoms as they occur in natural social settings. It provides a clear picture of a child's social impairments, assessing social awareness, social information processing, capacity for reciprocal social communication, social anxiety and avoidance, and autistic preoccupations and traits.

Strengths of the Test

- Sensitive and reliable across a wide range of symptom severity, the SRS can be used as a screener in clinical or educational settings, an aid to clinical diagnosis, or a measure of response to intervention. Scores are particularly helpful in identifying Autism, Asperger's Disorder, Pervasive Developmental Disorder Not Otherwise Specified (PDD-NOS), and Schizoid Personality Disorder of Childhood. In addition, the scale can alert clinicians to subthreshold autistic symptoms that may be relevant in evaluating children with a wide variety of psychological problems.

- The SRS has a major advantage over other instruments used to assess autism spectrum conditions. Rather than providing a yes or no decision about the presence of a symptom or a given disorder, the SRS measures impairment on a quantitative scale across a wide range of severity—which is consistent with recent research indicating that autism is best conceptualized as a spectrum condition rather than an all-or-nothing diagnosis. This is important because even mild degrees of impairment can have significant adverse effects on social functioning. For the most common (and often the most subtle) autism spectrum conditions, no previous instrument has demonstrated the ability to reliably measure the severity of social impairment.

- The SRS is also helpful in qualifying a child for mental health or special education services. Diagnosing the milder autism spectrum conditions (including PDD-NOS, Asperger's Disorder, or higher-functioning Autistic Disorder) can be difficult, particularly when information comes from different settings or sources. The SRS provides a quantitative score for autistic social impairment that allows comparisons across settings and against norms established with different raters. Mental health professionals who make diagnostic or screening decisions can use the score to achieve consensus about where a given child falls within the range of impairment encompassed by autism spectrum conditions.

- Standardization is based on a sample of more than 1,600 children (4 through 18 years of age) from the general population. Norms are separated by rater (parent or teacher) and gender of the child rated.
- The brevity of the SRS makes it highly useful for screening, special education, and clinical applications. Its quantitative nature makes it ideal for measuring response to intervention over time, and its reliance on naturalistic observations of parents and teachers makes it easy to use in clinical, research, and educational settings. It is crucial in such settings to distinguish the presence of autism spectrum conditions from other child psychiatric conditions, and the SRS is ideally suited for this purpose because it captures the type of social impairment that is characteristic of autism spectrum conditions in children as young as 4 years old.

Chapter 9

Behavioral Disorders

Children with behavioral disorders are characterized primarily by behavior that falls significantly beyond the norms of their cultural and age group on two dimensions: externalizing and internalizing. Both patterns of abnormal behavior have adverse effects on children's academic achievement and social relationships (Heward, 2006).

Externalizing disorders, sometimes referred to as undercontrolled disorders, are characterized by aggressiveness, temper tantrums, acting out, and noncompliant behaviors (Gargiulo, 2004). Other externalizing behaviors include, but are not limited to (Heward, 2006):

- Getting out of seat
- Yelling, talking out, and cursing
- Disturbing peers
- Hitting or fighting
- Complaining
- Stealing
- Arguing
- Lying
- Destroying property

Two frequently cited externalizing behavioral disorders are conduct disorder and oppositional defiant disorder. According to the U.S. Department of Health and Human Services (2005), children with conduct disorder repeatedly violate the personal or property rights of others and the basic expectations of society. A diagnosis of conduct disorder is likely when symptoms continue for six months or longer. Conduct disorder is known as a disruptive behavior disorder because of its impact on children and their families, neighbors, and schools.

Oppositional defiant disorder may be a precursor of conduct disorder. A child is diagnosed with oppositional defiant disorder when he or she shows signs of being hostile and defiant for at least six months. Oppositional defiant disorder may start as early as the preschool years, while conduct disorder generally appears when children are older. Oppositional defiant disorder and conduct disorder are not co-occurring conditions (U.S. Department of Health and Human Services, 2005).

Internalizing disorders, sometimes referred to as overcontrolled disorders, are characterized by social withdrawal, depression, and anxiety. Children with internalizing behavioral disorders have the opposite problem of those with externalizing behaviors: they often have too little social interaction with others and often appear withdrawn and lacking social skills needed to make friends and have fun. Children and youth with internalizing disorders are far less likely to be identified by their teachers and families because they do not create the chaos that often characterizes children and youth with externalizing disorders (Gargiulo, 2004).

Other internalizing behaviors include:

- Exhibiting sadness, depression, and feelings of worthlessness
- Decreased interest in activities that were previously of interest
- Suddenly cries or cries frequently
- Cannot get mind off certain thoughts, ideas, or situations

Behavioral and Emotional Rating Scale–Second Edition (BERS-2)

General Test Information

Author:	Michael H. Epstein
Publisher:	PRO-ED
Address of Publisher:	8700 Shoal Creek Boulevard, Austin, TX 78757–6897
Telephone Number:	1-800-897-3202
Fax Number:	1-800-397-7633
Web Site of Publisher:	www.proedinc.com
Type of Test:	Behavior problem rating scale
Administration Time:	Approximately 10 minutes
Type of Administration:	Individual
Ages/Grade Levels:	Ages 5–0 through 18–11

Purpose and Description of Test

Designed for use in schools, mental health clinics, juvenile justice settings, and child welfare agencies, the BERS-2 helps to measure the personal strengths and competencies of children.

Subtest Information

The BERS-2 is a multimodal assessment system that measures the child's behavior from three perspectives: the child (Youth Rating Scale), parent (Parent Rating Scale), and teacher or other professional (Teacher Rating Scale). It measures several aspects of a child's strength: interpersonal strength, involvement with family, intrapersonal strength, school functioning, affective strength, and career strength.

Strengths of the Test

- The BERS-2 can identify children's individual behavior and emotional strengths and the areas in which individual strengths need to be developed. The BERS-2 has been widely adopted by local, state, and federal agencies to evaluate the outcomes of services. It has been used in several national studies of children with and without disabilities.
- All of the BERS-2 scales were normed on representative samples of children without disabilities, and the BERS-2 Teacher Rating Scale was normed on children with emotional and behavioral disorders. Demographics of the standardization samples are reported in the manual by age, gender, geographical location, race, ethnicity, and socioeconomic status. Separate norms are available on the teacher rating scale for children diagnosed with emotional and behavioral disorders.
- The internal consistency reliability of the BERS-2 subtests was established with children without disabilities and with children who were emotionally disturbed. Coefficients exceeded .80 for each subtest and .95 for the overall score. Over fifteen studies have confirmed the BERS's content, construct, and criterion-related validity.

Behavior Dimensions Scale (BDS)

General Test Information

Author:	Stephen B. McCarney
Publisher:	Hawthorne Educational Services
Address of Publisher:	800 Gray Oak Drive, Columbia, MO 65201
Telephone Number:	1-800-542-1673
Fax Number:	1-800-442-9509
Web Site of Publisher:	http://www.hes-inc.com
Type of Test:	Behavioral assessment
Administration Time:	20 to 30 minutes
Type of Administration:	Individual
Ages/Grade Levels:	Ages 5–0 through 18–11

Purpose and Description of Test

The BDS is based on the American Psychiatric Association's DSM-IV criteria (2000) and definition of each behavior disorder. The School Version can be completed in approximately twenty minutes and includes 104 items easily observed and documented by educational personnel. The Home Version can be completed by a parent or guardian in approximately thirty minutes and includes 108 items representing behaviors exhibited in and around the home environment.

Subtest Information

The scale provides an assessment of those dimensions of behavior that most interfere with success in the educational, home, and community environments of children and adolescents:

- Attention Deficit-Hyperactivity Disorder
- Oppositional Defiant Disorder
- Conduct Disorder
- Avoidant Personality Disorder
- Generalized Anxiety Disorder
- Major Depressive Episode

Strengths of the Test

- The BDS School Version was standardized on 4,323 students. The standardization sample included students from twenty-two states and represented all geographical regions of the United States.
- The BDS was factor-analyzed to create the factor clusters (subscales).
- The BDS School Version provides separate norms for male and female students 5 through 15 years of age.
- The BDS Home Version provides separate norms for male and female children 3 through 18 years of age.
- The Behavior Dimensions Intervention Manual includes individualized education program goals, objectives, and interventions for all ninety-nine items on the School Version of the scale.
- The BDS Quick Score computer program converts raw scores to standard and percentile scores and makes the scoring of the School and Home Versions efficient and convenient.
- Spanish-language Home Version Rating Forms are available.

Behavior Disorders Identification Scale–Second Edition (BDIS-2)

General Test Information

Authors:	Stephen B. McCarney and Tamara J. Arthaud
Publisher:	Hawthorne Educational Services
Address of Publisher:	800 Gray Oak Drive, Columbia, MO 65201
Telephone Number:	1-800-542-1673
Fax Number:	1-800-442-9509
Web Site of Publisher:	http://www.hes-inc.com
Type of Test:	Behavioral assessment
Administration Time:	The School Version can be completed in approximately 20 minutes; the Home Version can be completed by a parent or guardian in approximately 15 minutes
Type of Administration:	Individual
Ages/Grade Levels:	Ages 5–0 through 18–11

Purpose and Description of Test

The BDIS-2 is based on the federal definition of emotional disturbance according to the Individuals with Disabilities Education Improvement Act. The eighty-three items in the School Version are easily observed and documented by educational personnel. The seventy-three items in the Home Version, which can be completed by a parent or guardian, include behavior exhibited in and around the home environment.

Subtest Information

The BDIS-2 subscales are:

- Learning Problems
- Interpersonal Relations
- Inappropriate Behavior
- Unhappiness/Depression
- Physical Symptoms/Fears

Strengths of the Test

- The Pre-Referral Behavior Checklist provides a means of calling attention to the student's behavior for the purpose of early intervention, before formal assessment.
- The Teacher's Guide to Behavioral Interventions (TGBI) contains individualized education program (IEP) goals, objectives, and interventions for all eighty-three items on the School Version of the scale and twenty-seven additional behavior problems common in the educational environment.
- The Intervention Strategies Documentation Form provides a written record to place in the student's file, documenting problem areas and interventions implemented.
- The BDIS-2 Quick Score computer program converts raw scores to standard and percentile scores and makes the scoring of both the School and Home Version rating forms efficient and convenient.
- The computer version of the TGBI provides an individualized printout of goals, objectives, and interventions chosen for each student's specific behavior problems for the development of the student's IEP.
- Spanish-language Home Version Rating Forms are available.

Behavior Evaluation Scale–Third Edition: Long (BES-3:L)

General Test Information

Authors:	Stephen B. McCarney and Tamara J. Arthaud
Publisher:	Hawthorne Educational Services
Address of Publisher:	800 Gray Oak Drive, Columbia, MO 65201
Telephone Number:	1-800-542-1673
Fax Number:	1-800-442-9509
Web Site of Publisher:	http://www.hes-inc.com
Type of Test:	Behavioral assessment
Administration Time:	Approximately 20 minutes
Type of Administration:	Individual
Ages/Grade Levels:	Ages 4 to 19

Purpose and Description of Test

The BES-3:L provides results that assist school personnel in making decisions about eligibility, placement, and programming for students with behavior problems who have been referred for evaluation. The scale yields relevant behavioral information about students regardless of handicapping conditions and therefore may be used with students who have learning disabilities, mental retardation, physical impairments, and other handicapping conditions.

Subtest Information

The BES-3 is based on the Individuals with Disabilities Education Improvement Act definition of emotional disturbance/behavioral disorders, which makes it particularly useful in the assessment of students who are suspected of having behavior disorders. The BES-3 was factor-analyzed to create the following factor clusters (subscales):

- Learning Problems
- Interpersonal Difficulties
- Inappropriate Behavior
- Unhappiness/Depression
- Physical Symptoms/Fears

Strengths of the Test

- The BES-3 School Version was standardized on 5,124 students ages 4 through 19 years old. The BES-3 Home Version was standardized on 4,643 students ages 4 through 19 years old. The standardization population included students from twenty-nine states, represented all geographical regions of the United States, and closely approximated the demographic characteristics of the United States in the year 2000.
- The BES-3 provides norms based on age and grade for males and females (K–12). Internal consistency, item and factor analysis, standard errors or measurement, and test-retest reliability are reported. Content, criterion-related, concurrent, and construct validity are reported.
- The BES-3:L School Version can be completed in approximately twenty minutes and contains seventy-six items easily observed and documented by educational personnel.
- The BES-3:L Home Version can be completed by a parent or guardian in approximately twenty minutes and contains seventy-three items representing behaviors exhibited in and around the home environment.

- The Behavior Evaluation Scale: Long Pre-Referral Checklist provides a means of calling attention to the behavior for the purpose of early intervention before formal assessment of the student.
- The BES:L Intervention Manual (2005) provides individualized education program goals, objectives, and interventions for all seventy-six items on the School Version of the scale. The manual was designed to serve as a guide for program development for any student in need of behavior improvement.
- The Intervention Strategies Documentation Form provides a written record to place in the student's file, documenting problem areas and interventions implemented.
- The Parent's Guide provides parents with specific, practical strategies to use in helping the child be more successful in the home environment.
- The BES-3:L Quick Score computer program converts raw scores to standard and percentile scores and makes the scoring of both the School and Home Version rating efficient and convenient.

Behavior Evaluation Scale–Third Edition: Short (BES-3:S)

General Test Information

Authors:	Stephen B. McCarney and Tamara J. Arthaud
Publisher:	Hawthorne Educational Services
Address of Publisher:	800 Gray Oak Drive, Columbia, MO 65201
Telephone Number:	1-800-542-1673
Fax Number:	1-800-442-9509
Web Site of Publisher:	http://www.hes-inc.com
Type of Test:	Behavioral assessment
Administration Time:	Approximately 15 minutes
Type of Administration:	Individual
Ages/Grade Levels:	Ages 4 through 19

Purpose and Description of Test

The BES-3:S provides results that assist school personnel in making decisions about eligibility, placement, and programming for students with behavior problems who have been referred for evaluation. The scale yields relevant behavioral information about students regardless of handicapping conditions, and therefore may be used with students who have learning disabilities, mental retardation, physical impairments, and other handicapping conditions.

Subtest Information

The BES-3 is based on the Individuals with Disabilities Education Improvement Act definition of emotional disturbance/behavioral disorders, which makes it particularly useful in the assessment of students who are suspected of having behavior disorders. The BES-3 was factor-analyzed to create the following factor clusters (subscales):

- Learning Problems
- Interpersonal Difficulties
- Inappropriate Behavior
- Unhappiness/Depression
- Physical Symptoms/Fears

Strengths of the Test

- The BES-3 School Version was standardized on 5,124 students ages 4 through 19 years old. The BES-3 Home Version was standardized on 4,643 students ages 4 through 19 years old. The standardization population included students from twenty-nine states, represented all geographical regions of the United States, and closely approximated the demographic characteristics of the United States in the year 2000.
- The BES-3 provides norms based on age and grade for males and females (grades K–12). Internal consistency, item and factor analysis, standard errors or measurement, and test-retest reliability are reported. Content, criterion-related, concurrent, and construct validity are reported.
- The BES-3:S School Version can be completed in approximately fifteen minutes and contains fifty-four items easily observed and documented by educational personnel.
- The BES-3:S Home Version can be completed by a parent or guardian in approximately fifteen minutes and contains fifty-two items representing behaviors exhibited in and around the home environment.

- The Behavior Evaluation Scale: Short Pre-Referral Checklist provides a means of calling attention to the behavior for the purpose of early intervention, before formal assessment of the student.
- The BES:S Intervention Manual (2005) includes individualized education program goals, objectives, and interventions for all fifty-four items on the School Version of the scale. The manual was designed to serve as a guide for program development for any student in need of behavior improvement.
- The Intervention Strategies Documentation Form provides a written record to place in the student's file, documenting problem areas and interventions implemented.
- The Parent's Guide provides parents with specific, practical strategies to use in helping the child be more successful in the home environment.
- The BES-3:S Quick Score computer program converts raw scores to standard and percentile scores and makes the scoring of both the School and Home Version rating forms efficient and convenient.

Behavior Rating Profile–Second Edition (BRP-2)

General Test Information

Authors:	Linda Brown and Donald D. Hammill
Publisher:	PRO-ED
Address of Publisher:	8700 Shoal Creek Boulevard, Austin, TX 78757–6897
Telephone Number:	1-800-897-3202
Fax Number of Publisher:	1-800-397-7633
Web Site of Publisher:	www.proedinc.com
Type of Test:	Behavioral assessment
Administration Time:	20 minutes
Type of Administration:	Individual
Ages/Grade Levels:	Ages 6–6 to 18–6

Purpose and Description of Test

The BRP-2 identifies students whose behavior is perceived to be deviant, the settings in which behavior problems are prominent, and the persons whose perceptions of a student's behavior are different from those of other respondents. The responses allow examiners to test different diagnostic hypotheses when confronted with reports of problem behavior. The BRP-2 is a unique battery of six instruments that provide different evaluations of a student's behavior at home, at school, and in interpersonal relationships from the varied perspectives of parents, teachers, peers, and the target students themselves.

Strengths of the Test

- The BRP-2 components were all normed individually on large, representative populations. The Student Rating Scales normative group included 2,682 students residing in twenty-six states. The Parent Rating Scales were completed by 1,948 parents in nineteen states, and the Teacher Rating Scales were normed on a group of 1,452 teachers from twenty-six states.
- The internal consistency reliability of the BRP-2 components was established with normal subjects and with groups of students who were learning disabled and emotionally disturbed. Coefficients generally exceed .80 at all ages. Stability reliability coefficients are also reported.
- Extensive evidence of validity is reported in the manual.
- Correlations between the BRP-2 components and other measures of behavior are reported.

Burks' Behavior Rating Scales (BBRS)

General Test Information

Author:	Harold F. Burks
Publisher:	Western Psychological Services
Address of Publisher:	12031 Wilshire Boulevard, Los Angeles, CA 90025–1251
Telephone Number:	1-800-648-8857 (United States and Canada only), 1-310-478-2061
Fax Number:	1-310-478-7838
Web Site of Publisher:	http://www.wpspublish.com
Type of Test:	Behavioral assessment
Administration Time:	15 minutes
Type of Administration:	Individual
Ages/Grade Levels:	Grades 1 through 9; Preschool and Kindergarten Edition also available for ages 3 to 6

Purpose and Description of Test

The BBRS helps diagnose and treat children with behavior problems. Administered and scored in minutes, these scales identify the nature and severity of pathological symptoms in first-through ninth-grade children. A Preschool and Kindergarten Edition is available for use with 3- to 6-year-olds.

Subtest Information

The BBRS gives a profile of scores covering nineteen problem behaviors:

Excessive self-blame
Excessive withdrawal
Poor ego strength
Poor coordination
Poor academics
Poor impulse control
Poor sense of identity
Poor anger control
Excessive aggressiveness
Poor social conformity

Excessive anxiety
Excessive dependency
Poor physical strength
Poor intellectuality
Poor attention
Poor reality contact
Excessive suffering
Excessive sense of persecution
Excessive resistance

Strengths of the Test

BBRS scores can be used to:

- Pinpoint personality areas that require further evaluation or treatment
- Identify behaviors that may interfere with school functioning
- Identify children who will (or will not) benefit from special education
- Provide parents with information that is concrete, specific, and easy to understand

Conduct Disorder Scale (CDS)

General Test Information

Author: James E. Gilliam

Publisher: PRO-ED

Address of Publisher: 8700 Shoal Creek Boulevard, Austin, TX 78757–6897

Telephone Number: 1-800-897-3202

Fax Number: 1-800-397-7633

Web Site of Publisher: www.proedinc.com

Type of Test: Behavioral assessment

Administration Time: 5 to 10 minutes

Type of Administration: Individual

Ages/Grade Levels: Ages 5 to 22

Purpose and Description of Test

The CDS is an efficient and effective instrument for evaluating students exhibiting severe behavior problems who may have conduct disorder. It is the only test of its kind that provides standard scores for use in identifying students with this disorder.

Subtest Information

The forty items on the CDS describe the specific diagnostic behaviors characteristic of persons with conduct disorder. These items comprise four subscales representing the core symptom clusters necessary for the diagnosis of this disorder:

- Aggressive Conduct
- Non-Aggressive Conduct
- Deceitfulness and Theft
- Rule Violations

Strengths of the Test

- Forty items in a behavioral checklist format are easily rated using objective frequency-based ratings.
- A detailed interview form, derived from DSM-IV-TR diagnostic criteria (American Psychiatric Association, 2000), is provided to document infrequent but serious behavior problems that are indicative of persons who have conduct disorder.
- The test was standardized on 1,040 persons representing the following diagnostic groups: normal, gifted and talented, mentally retarded, with attention deficit/hyperactivity disorder, emotionally disturbed, learning disabled, physically handicapped, and persons with conduct disorder.
- Norms were developed based on 644 representative individuals with conduct disorder.
- Standard scores and percentiles are provided. The Conduct Disorder Quotient, derived based on information from all four subscales, is an interpretation guide provided for determining the likelihood that a participant has conduct disorder and the severity of the disorder.

Disruptive Behavior Rating Scale (DBRS)

General Test Information

Author: Bradley T. Erford
Publisher: Slosson Educational Publications
Address of Publisher: P.O. Box 280, East Aurora, NY 14052
Telephone Number: 1-888-756-7766
Fax Number: 1-800-655-3840
Web Site of Publisher: www.slosson.com
Type of Test: Behavioral assessment
Administration Time: Approximately 7 minutes
Type of Administration: Individual or group administration
Ages/Grade Levels: Ages 5–0 to 10–11

Purpose and Description of Test

A brief fifty-item inventory, the DBRS identifies common behavior problems such as attention deficit disorder (ADD), attention deficit disorder with hyperactivity (ADHD), oppositional disorders, and antisocial conduct problems, as reported by mother, father, or teacher.

Strengths of the Test

- Unlike other rating scales, the wording of the teacher and parent versions is nearly identical, thus allowing legitimate comparisons between their responses. Scale items were specifically written to allow direct teacher transfer to behavior-modification plans, individualized education programs (IEPs), or Section 504 plans. The DBRS facilitates decisions for student placement, especially with regard to least restrictive instructional settings.
- The DBRS provides separate norms for teacher, mother, and father responses. Normative data were obtained from teachers of 1,766 children, mothers of 1,399 children, and fathers of 1,252 children for boys and girls 5 to 10 years of age. Internal consistency and test-retest reliabilities are generally in the high .80s to mid-.90s. Normative data convert to raw scores yielding *T*-scores, percentile ranks, as well as standard error of measurement and critical item determination.
- Easy-to-use computer software aids scoring. The computer-generated report quickly calculates a summary statistics table, *T*-scores, percentile ranks, and interpretation ranges. It also identifies critical items of importance. Features are separate norms for teacher, mother, and father responses.
- Facilitates IEP, Section 504, or behavior-modification plans.
- Excellent reliability and validity studies.
- Identifies common behavior problems such as ADD and ADHD (distractibility, impulsive-hyperactivity, anti-social conduct).

Emotional and Behavior Problem Scale–Second Edition (EBPS-2)

General Test Information

Authors:	Stephen B. McCarney and Tamara J. Arthaud
Publisher:	Hawthorne Educational Services
Address of Publisher:	800 Gray Oak Drive, Columbia, MO 65201
Telephone Number:	1-800-542-1673
Fax Number:	1-800-442-9509
Web Site of Publisher:	http://www.hes-inc.com
Type of Test:	Behavioral assessment
Administration Time:	Approximately 15 minutes
Type of Administration:	Individual
Ages/Grade Levels:	Ages 5–0 to 18–11

Purpose and Description of Test

The EBPS-2 is a comprehensive assessment measure of emotional and behavioral problems in children and adolescents.

Subtest Information

Two interpretations of the items on the scale are provided:

- The Theoretical Interpretation is based on the federal definition of emotional disturbance according to the 2004 Individuals with Disabilities Education Improvement Act. The EBPS-2 Theoretical Interpretation subscales are Learning Problems, Interpersonal Relations, Inappropriate Behavior, Unhappiness/Depression, and Physical Symptoms/Fears.
- The EBPS-2 Empirical Interpretation subscales are Social Aggression/Conduct Disorder, Social-Emotional Withdrawal/Depression, Learning/Comprehension Disorder, Avoidance/Unresponsiveness, and Aggressive/Self-Destructive.

Strengths of the Test

- The EBPS-2 School Version was standardized on 3,986 students from twenty states representing all geographical regions of the United States.
- The EBPS-2 School and Home Versions provide separate norms for male and female students 5 through 18 years of age.
- The EBPS-2 School and Home Versions can be completed in approximately fifteen minutes and contain fifty-eight items easily observed and documented by educational personnel and the parent or guardian.
- The Emotional and Behavior Problem Scale individualized education program (IEP) and Intervention Manual include IEP goals, objectives, and interventions for all fifty-eight items on the scale.
- The EBPS-2 Quick Score computer program converts raw scores to standard and percentile scores and makes scoring efficient and convenient.
- The computer version of the Emotional and Behavior Problem Scale IEP and Intervention Manual provides an individualized printout of goals, objectives, and intervention strategies chosen for each student's specific behavior problem.

Preschool and Kindergarten Behavioral Scales–
Second Edition (PKBS-2)

General Test Information

Author:	Kenneth W. Merrell
Publisher:	PRO-ED
Address of Publisher:	8700 Shoal Creek Boulevard, Austin, TX 78757–6897
Telephone Number:	1-800-897-3202
Fax Number:	1-800-397-7633
Web Site of Publisher:	www.proedinc.com
Type of Test:	Behavioral assessment
Administration Time:	Approximately 12 minutes
Type of Administration:	Individual
Ages/Grade Levels:	Ages 3 to 6

Purpose and Description of Test

The PKBS-2 is a behavior rating scale. With seventy-six items on two separate scales, it provides an integrated and functional appraisal of the social skills and problem behaviors of young children.

Subtest Information

The Social Skills scale contains thirty-four items on three subscales:

- Social Cooperation
- Social Interaction
- Social Independence

The Problem Behavior scale has forty-two items on two subscales:

- Externalizing Problems
- Internalizing Problems

In addition, five supplementary problem behavior subscales are available for optional use.

Strengths of the Test

- The PKBS-2 was standardized with a nationwide sample of ratings of 3,317 children ages 3 through 6. Ethnicity, socioeconomic status, and special education classification of the standardization sample are very similar to those characteristics of the U.S. population based on the 2000 Census.
- Internal consistency reliability ranges from .96 to .97 for the two scale totals and from .81 to .95 for the subscales.
- A wide variety of reliability and validity evidence in support of the PKBS-2 is included in the Examiner's Manual.

School Social Skills (S3)

General Test Information

Authors:	Laura Brown, Donald Black, and John Downs
Publisher:	Slosson Educational Publications
Address of Publisher:	P.O. Box 280, East Aurora, NY 14052
Telephone Number:	1-888-756-7766
Fax Number:	1-800-655-3840
Web Site of Publisher:	www.slosson.com
Type of Test:	Social/behavioral assessment (in schools)
Administration Time:	10 minutes
Type of Administration:	Individual
Ages/Grade Levels:	Grades 1 to 12

Purpose and Description of Test

The S3 is designed to assist school personnel, specifically classroom teachers, in identifying student deficits in school-related social behaviors. The forty-item scale of observable prosocial skills has been socially validated and determined to be important for student school success in the areas of adult relations (twelve items), peer relations (sixteen items), school rules (six items), and classroom behaviors (six items).

Strengths of the Test

- The S3 is a criterion-referenced instrument that yields knowledge of a student's social strengths and deficiencies. Ratings are done on a six-point Likert scale, over the previous months' observations, and test-retest and the interrater reliability data indicate the S3 has comparable reliability with residential, special education, and regular education students.
- A comprehensive manual accompanies the Rating Scale Form and provides conditions under which the forty skills should be used.

Social Behavior Assessment Inventory (SBAI)

General Test Information

Authors:	Thomas M. Stephens and Kevin D. Arnold
Publisher:	PAR
Address of Publisher:	16204 North Florida Avenue, Lutz, FL 33549
Telephone Number:	1-800-331-8378, ext. 361
Fax Number:	1-800-727-9329
Web Site of Publisher:	http://www.parinc.com
Type of Test:	Social behavioral assessment
Administration Time:	30 to 45 minutes
Type of Administration:	Individual
Ages/Grade Levels:	Grades K to 9

Purpose and Description of Test

The SBAI measures the level of social behaviors exhibited by children and adolescents in classroom settings (grades K–9). It was designed as a companion instrument to Social Skills in the Classroom. The SBAI consists of 136 items that describe social skills commonly observed in the classroom. A teacher or other individual (such as a counselor or parent) who has observed a student's behavior rates each item on a four-point scale describing both the presence and level of the behaviors that the student exhibits.

Subtest Information

The SBAI consists of four behavior scales:

- Environmental
- Interpersonal
- Self-Related
- Task-Related

Strengths of the Test

- Results from the four behavior scales and thirty subscales can be used to develop social skills instructional strategies.
- It is appropriate for special education classes or any other classroom where behavior problems may exist.

Social-Emotional Dimension Scale–Second Edition (SEDS-2)

General Test Information

Authors:	Jerry B. Hutton and Timothy G. Roberts
Publisher:	PRO-ED
Address of Publisher:	8700 Shoal Creek Boulevard, Austin, TX 78757–6897
Telephone Number:	1-800-897-3202
Fax Number:	1-800-397-7633
Web Site of Publisher:	www.proedinc.com
Type of Test:	Behavioral assessment
Administration Time:	20 to 30 minutes
Type of Administration:	Individual
Ages/Grade Levels:	Ages 6–0 through 18–11

Purpose and Description of Test

The SEDS-2 provides school personnel such as teachers, counselors, educational diagnosticians, and psychologists with a means for rating student behavior problems that may interfere with academic functioning. It is a highly structured, norm-referenced rating scale that is useful for identifying students who are at risk for problematic behaviors.

Strengths of the Test

- The absence of racial and ethnic bias has been demonstrated.
- Reliability coefficients are provided for subgroups of the sample (for example, gender, race, ethnicity, and age), as well as for the entire normative sample.
- New validity studies show the relationship of test scores to similar measures and the ability of the test to discriminate between students with and without emotional disabilities.
- Outside experts helped select items.
- The number of items in the scale was increased from thirty-two to seventy-four, providing a greater range of behavioral assessment. In addition, the scoring criteria are expanded and allow more choices in rating frequency of the behaviors.
- Reliability and validity studies are included for the new subscales, as well as for the composite scores.
- The SEDS-2 includes a fifteen-item screener and a structured interview form for functional assessment of behavior.
- Behavioral descriptors have been added to assist the examiner in rating behaviors on each item.

Social Skills Rating System (SSRS)

General Test Information

Authors:	Frank M. Gresham and Stephen N. Elliott
Publisher:	AGS Publishing
Address of Publisher:	4201 Woodland Road, Circle Pines, MN 55014–1796
Telephone Number:	1-800-328-2560, 1-651-287-7220
Fax Number:	1-800-471-8457
Web Site of Publisher:	www.agsnet.com
Type of Test:	Social/behavioral assessment
Administration Time:	10 to 25 minutes for each questionnaire
Type of Administration:	Individual
Ages/Grade Levels:	Ages 3 to 18; Student Self Report can be used in grades 3 to 12

Purpose and Description of Test

The SSRS is a nationally standardized series of questionnaires that obtain information on the social behaviors of children and adolescents from teachers, parents, and the students themselves. The SSRS can be used to:

- Assess children who have problems with behavior and interpersonal skills
- Detect the problems behind children's shyness, trouble initiating conversation, and difficulty making friends
- Select behaviors for treatment and assist in planning intervention

Subtest Information

Examiners can select from three rating forms—teacher, parent, and student—or use all three for a comprehensive picture across school, home, and community settings. Items on each scale are rated according to perceived frequency and importance, a feature unique to the SSRS.

The Social Skills Scale measures positive social behaviors:

- Cooperation
- Empathy
- Assertion
- Self-Control
- Responsibility

The Problem Behaviors Scale measures behaviors that can interfere with the development of positive social skills. It assesses behavior in three subscales:

- Externalizing Problems, such as aggressive acts and poor temper control
- Internalizing Problems, such as sadness and anxiety
- Hyperactivity, such as fidgeting and impulsive acts

The Academic Competence Scale provides a quick estimate of academic functioning. Teachers rate reading and mathematics performance, general cognitive functioning, as well as motivation and parental support.

Strengths of the Test

- The test provides a comprehensive picture of social behaviors.
- Three rating forms offer flexibility.
- Appropriate interventions can be planned quickly.
- The Social Skills Rating System allows the examiner to obtain a fuller picture of social behaviors from teachers, parents, and even students themselves and evaluate a broad range of socially validated behaviors that affect teacher-student relationships, peer acceptance, academic performance, and more.

Student Behavior Survey (SBS)

General Test Information

Authors:	David Lachar, Sabine A. Wingenfeld, Rex B. Kline, and Christian P. Gruber
Publisher:	Western Psychological Services
Address of Publisher:	12031 Wilshire Boulevard, Los Angeles, CA 90025–1251
Telephone Number:	1-800-648-8857 (United States and Canada only), 1-310-478-2061
Fax Number:	1-310-478-7838
Web Site of Publisher:	http://www.wpspublish.com
Type of Test:	Behavioral assessment
Administration Time:	15 minutes
Type of Administration:	Individual
Ages/Grade Levels:	Ages 5 through 18 (grades K to 12)

Purpose and Description of Test

The SBS assesses achievement, academic and social skills, parent cooperation, and emotional and behavioral adjustment. It documents the presence and severity of specific classroom behaviors required to establish disruptive behavior diagnoses. It also provides a comprehensive description of the student, reflecting academic achievement, adjustment problems, and behavioral assets needed for classroom success. By offering an efficient way to quantify classroom observations, the SBS facilitates communication between school and clinician.

Subtest Information

The SBS consists of the following subtests:

- Academic Resources
- Academic Performance
- Academic Habits
- Social Skills
- Parent Participation
- Adjustment Problems
- Health Concerns
- Emotional Distress
- Unusual Behavior
- Social Problems
- Verbal Aggression
- Physical Aggression
- Behavior Problems
- Disruptive Behavior
- Attention Deficit-Hyperactivity
- Oppositional Defiant
- Conduct Problems

Strengths of the Test

- The SBS, a rating scale from the author of the Personality Inventory for Children–Second Edition (PIC-2) and the Personality Inventory for Youth (PIY), joins these other highly regarded instruments to give a comprehensive evaluation of student adjustment. The PIC-2 supplies the parents' view of the child, the PIY adds the student's self-report, and now the SBS provides the teacher's perspective.
- The SBS manual provides extensive interpretive guidance, including discussion of clinically relevant score elevations and associated behaviors. Case studies are also included, some using the SBS alone to measure student adjustment and some using the SBS in conjunction with other instruments, such as the PIC-2 and PIY. These case studies illustrate the test's value in educational, clinical, neuropsychological, and forensic applications.
- In the course of test development, the SBS was used to rate more than 4,000 students. Over half of these ratings involved concurrent administration of other instruments, providing significant independent evidence supporting use of the SBS. Standardization was based on teacher ratings of more than 2,500 students (K–12, evenly distributed by grade and gender) from twenty-two school districts in twelve states spanning the United States. This sample closely reflects census figures in regard to ethnicity and socioeconomic status. In addition, SBS ratings were collected on more than 1,300 students referred for behavioral or academic problems in special education, clinical, and juvenile justice settings.

Chapter 10

Deaf and Hearing Impairments

Under the Individuals with Disabilities Education Improvement Act (IDEA) of 2004, hearing impairment and deafness are two of the categories under which children with disabilities may be eligible for special education and related services programming. While the term *hearing impairment* is often used to describe a wide range of hearing losses, including deafness, the regulations for IDEA define hearing loss and deafness separately (National Dissemination Center for Children with Disabilities, 2004c). A *hearing impairment* is defined by IDEA as "an impairment in hearing, whether permanent or fluctuating, that adversely affects a child's educational performance" (C.F.R. 300.7(c)(5)). *Deafness* is defined as "a hearing impairment that is so severe that the child is impaired in processing linguistic information through hearing, with or without amplification" (C.F.R. 300.7(c)(3)).

The U.S. Department of Education (2004) reports that, during the 2003–2004 school year, 71,118 students aged 6 to 21 (or 1.2 percent of all students with disabilities) received special education services under the category of "hearing impairment." However, the number of children with hearing loss and deafness is undoubtedly higher, since many of these students may have other disabilities as well and may be served under other categories (Holden-Pitt & Diaz, 1998). Also, these figures represent only students who receive special services; a number of students with hearing loss who could benefit from additional services do not receive them (U.S. Department of Education, 2004).

Impairments in hearing can occur in either or both areas and may exist in one or both ears. Hearing loss is generally described as slight, mild, moderate, severe, or profound, depending on how well a person can hear the intensities or frequencies most greatly associated with speech. Generally only children whose hearing loss is greater than 90 decibels are considered deaf for the purposes of educational placement (Hardman, Drew, & Egan, 2005).

According to the National Dissemination Center for Children with Disabilities (2004c), there are four types of hearing loss:

- Conductive hearing losses, which are due to the effects of diseases or obstructions in the outer or middle ear (the conduction pathways for sound to reach the inner ear). These losses usually affect all frequencies of hearing evenly and do not result in severe losses. A person with a conductive hearing loss usually is able to use a hearing aid well or can be helped medically or surgically.

- Sensorineural hearing losses, which result from damage to the delicate sensory hair cells of the inner ear or the nerves that supply it. These hearing losses can range from mild to profound. They often affect the ability to hear certain frequencies more than others. Thus, even with amplification to increase the sound level, a person with a sensorineural hearing loss may perceive distorted sounds, sometimes making the successful use of a hearing aid impossible.
- Mixed hearing losses, which refer to a combination of conductive and sensorineural loss, that is, a problem occurs in both the outer or middle and the inner ear.
- Central hearing losses, which result from damage or impairment to the nerves or nuclei of the central nervous system, either in the pathways to the brain or in the brain itself.

For babies who are born deaf or with a hearing impairment, the earliest possible detection and intervention are crucial. Currently, a child's hearing loss is usually diagnosed between the ages of 14 months and 3 years, resulting in the loss of a significant window of opportunity for acquiring language, whether spoken or signed. A delayed diagnosis can also affect a child's social skills. The research strongly suggests that children with a hearing loss must receive early intervention as soon as possible if they are to learn the language skills necessary for reading and other academic subjects as they approach the school years (Calderon & Naidu, 2000).

Students with hearing impairments go through a different social development from that of children who can hear (Easterbrooks, 1999). Delayed language development may lead to more limited opportunities for social interaction.

Hearing loss or deafness does not affect a person's intellectual capacity or ability to learn (Moores, 2001; Schirmer, 2000; National Dissemination Center for Children with Disabilities, 2004c). However, children who are either hard of hearing or deaf generally require some form of special education services in order to receive an adequate education (U.S. Department of Education, 2004). Such services may include:

- Regular speech, language, and auditory training from a specialist
- Amplification systems
- Services of an interpreter for students who use sign language
- Favorable seating in the class to facilitate lip reading
- Captioned films and videos
- Assistance of a note taker, who takes notes for the student with a hearing loss, so that the student can fully attend to instruction
- Instruction for the teacher and peers in alternate communication methods, such as sign language
- Counseling

Speech and language skills are the areas of development most severely affected for individuals with hearing losses, particularly for those who are born deaf. Their speech develops at a slower rate than that of their peers, thereby leading to a greater risk for social isolation and emotional difficulties (Kaland & Salvatore, 2003).

The educational achievement of students with hearing loss may be significantly delayed compared to that of students who can hear. Low achievement is characteristic of students who are deaf (National Dissemination Center for Children with Disabilities, 2004c; Schirmer, 2000). They average three to four years below their age-appropriate grade levels. Reading is the academic area that gives these students the greatest difficulties (Kuntz & Hessler, 1998).

Auditory Perception Test for the Hearing Impaired (APT/HI)

General Test Information

Authors:	Susan G. Allen and Thomas S. Serwatka
Publisher:	Psychological and Educational Publications
Address of Publisher:	P.O. Box 520, Hydesville, CA 95547–0520
Telephone Number:	1-800-523-5775
Fax Number:	1-800-447-0907
Web Site of Publisher:	http://www.psych-edpublications.com/
Type of Test:	Deaf and hearing impairment
Administration Time:	30 minutes
Type of Administration:	Individual
Ages/Grade Levels:	Ages 5–0 and older

Purpose and Description of Test

The test is designed to assess the building-block processes used to decode speech. It allows specific analysis of the individual's ability to decode phonemes in isolation and in the context of words and sentences. It consists of a manual, plates, and record forms.

Strengths of the Test

- Although designed specifically for the hearing impaired, the test can also be used with children who have other auditory processing deficits.
- The test analyzes auditory decoding skills at the most basic level.

Carolina Picture Vocabulary Test (CPVT)

General Test Information

Authors:	Thomas Layton and David Holmes
Publisher:	PRO-ED
Address of Publisher:	8700 Shoal Creek Boulevard, Austin, TX 78757–6897
Telephone Number:	1-800-897-3202
Fax Number:	1-800-397-7633
Web Site of Publisher:	www.proedinc.com
Type of Test:	Deaf and hearing impairment
Administration Time:	10 to 15 minutes
Type of Administration:	Individual
Ages/Grade Levels:	Ages 4–0 to 11–6

Purpose and Description of Test

The CPVT is a norm-referenced, validated, individually administered, receptive sign vocabulary test for children between the ages of 4 and 11½ who are deaf or hearing impaired. The CPVT consists of 130 items with suggested basal and ceiling levels.

Strengths of the Test

- The population used in the standardization research ($N = 767$) was based on a nationwide sample of children who use manual signs as their primary means of communication. Stratification of the sample was based on geographical region, educational facility, parental occupation, gender, race, age, grade, etiology, age of onset of hearing impairment, number of years of signing, IQ, and threshold of hearing loss in the better ear.

Hiskey-Nebraska Test of Learning Aptitude

General Test Information

Author:	Marshall S. Hiskey
Publisher:	PRO-ED
Address of Publisher:	8700 Shoal Creek Boulevard, Austin, TX 78757–6897
Telephone Number:	1-800-897-3202
Fax Number:	1-800-397-7633
Web Site of Publisher:	www.proedinc.com
Type of Test:	Deaf and hearing impairment
Administration Time:	Approximately 60 minutes
Type of Administration:	Individual
Ages/Grade Levels:	Ages 2 to 18

Purpose and Description of Test

The test is designed as a nonverbal measure of mental ability that has been found helpful in the intellectual assessment of a variety of language-handicapped children and youth. The test is a performance scale that can be administered entirely using pantomimed instructions and requires no verbal response from the subject. The scale consists of a series of performance tasks that are organized in ascending order of difficulty within subscales.

Subtest Information

The test has the following subtests:

- *Memory Colored Objects.* The child is required to perform memory tasks using colored objects.
- *Bead Stringing.* The child is required to put beads on a string.
- *Pictorial Associations.* The child has to decide what various pictures look like.
- *Block Building.* The child is required to build with blocks.
- *Memory for Digits.* The child is given groups of numbers and asked to repeat them.
- *Completion of Drawings.* The child is required to finish a picture that is not completed.
- *Pictorial Identification.* The child has to say what the picture is that is being shown.
- *Visual Attention Span.* The child must focus on an object for a set period of time.
- *Puzzle Blocks.* The child is required to arrange the blocks into a picture that is shown.
- *Pictorial Analogies.* The child is required to compare two pictures and pick a picture that goes with the third picture.

Strengths of the Test

- The test is easy to administer.
- The test results are reported as a learning quotient rather than pure IQ, which may be easier for parents to understand.
- It is the only test of learning standardized on individuals who are deaf.

Leiter International Performance Scale–Revised

General Test Information

Authors:	Russel Graydon Leiter and Grace Arthur
Publisher:	Stoelting Co.
Address of Publisher:	620 Wheat Lane, Lo Wood Dale, IL 60191
Telephone Number:	1-630-860-9700
Fax Number:	1-630-860-9775
Web Site of Publisher:	http://www.stoeltingco.com
Type of Test:	Deaf and hearing impairment
Administration Time:	30 to 60 minutes
Type of Administration:	Individual
Ages/Grade Levels:	Ages 2 to 21

Purpose and Description of Test

The test is designed as a totally nonverbal intelligence and cognitive abilities test. It therefore does not require the child to read or write any materials or need any spoken words from the examiner or the child. It is presented in a gamelike administration by having the child match the full-color response cards with corresponding illustrations on the easel display.

Subtest Information

The Leiter International Performance Scale-Revised contains twenty subtests, which are combined to create numerous composites that measure both general intelligence and discrete ability areas. The test consists of two batteries measuring a variety of skills: the Visualization and Reasoning Battery and the Attention and Memory Battery.

In the Visualization and Reasoning Battery, the following reasoning skills are measured:

- Classification
- Repeated patterns
- Sequential order
- Design analogies

The battery measures these visualization skills:

- Matching
- Picture context
- Figure ground
- Paper folding
- Form completion
- Figure rotation

In the Attention and Memory Battery, the following memory skills are measured:

- Memory span (forward)
- Associative memory
- Memory span (reversed)
- Associative delayed memory
- Spatial memory
- Immediate recognition
- Visual coding
- Delayed recognition

The attention skills measured in this battery are:

- Attention sustained
- Attention divided

Strengths of the Test

- Because of its nonverbal approach, the scale is a useful instrument and has made possible the testing of many children who could not be properly evaluated by the Stanford-Binet or Wechsler Intelligence Scale for Children (WISC).
- The test has a high correlation (.84) with the WISC-III Full Scale IQ.
- The extensive age range measured by the test, ages 2 to 17, allows the use of one test throughout a child's school career, which facilitates comparisons of performance over time.
- Because the test is nonverbal, there is no dominant language bias as found on other IQ tests.

Rhode Island Test of Language Structure (RITLS)

General Test Information

Authors:	Elizabeth Engen and Trygg Engen
Publisher:	PRO-ED
Address of Publisher:	8700 Shoal Creek Boulevard, Austin, TX 78757–6897
Telephone Number:	1-800-897-3202
Fax Number:	1-800-397-7633
Web Site of Publisher:	www.proedinc.com
Type of Test:	Deaf and hearing impairment
Administration Time:	30 minutes
Type of Administration:	Individual
Ages/Grade Levels:	Ages 3 to 20 with hearing impairments and ages 3 to 6 without hearing impairments

Purpose and Description of Test

The RITLS provides a measure of English language development and assessment data. It is designed primarily for use with children who are hearing impaired but also is useful in other areas where language development is of concern, including mental retardation, learning disability, and bilingual programs. The RITLS focuses on syntax, unlike other tests, which test morphology.

Subtest Information

This test measures syntax-response errors for twenty sentence types, both simple and complex. The sentence elements tests are:

- Relative and adverbial clauses
- Subject and other complements
- Reversible and nonreversible passives
- Datives
- Deletions
- Negations
- Conjunctives
- Embedded imperatives

Strengths of the Test

- Norms were developed from 513 children with hearing impairments and 283 children without hearing impairments.
- Reliability and validity are high.
- The test includes hearing-impaired individuals as part of the standardized group, which adds to the effectiveness of generalizability.
- The test is useful in areas in which level of language development is of concern; for example, mental retardation, learning disability, and bilingual programs.
- The RITLS is easy to administer, score, and interpret.
- A variety of syntactic structures are included in the test.

Test of Early Reading Ability—Deaf or Hard of Hearing (TERA-D/HH)

General Test Information

Authors:	D. Kim Reid, Wayne Hresko, Don Hammill, and Susan Wiltshire
Publisher:	PRO-ED
Address of Publisher:	8700 Shoal Creek Boulevard, Austin, TX 78757–6897
Telephone Number:	1-800-897-3202
Fax Number:	1-800-397-7633
Web Site of Publisher:	www.proedinc.com
Type of Test:	Deaf and hearing impairment
Administration Time:	20 to 30 minutes
Type of Administration:	Individual
Ages/Grade Levels:	Ages 3 to 13

Purpose and Description of Test

This is the only individually administered test of reading designed for children with moderate to profound sensory hearing loss (ranging from 41 to beyond 91 decibels, corrected). TERA-D/HH is also the only individually administered reading test designed for children younger than age 8 who are deaf or hard of hearing. It has equivalent forms and taps the child's ability to construct meaning, knowledge of the alphabet and its functions, and awareness of print conventions.

Subtest Information

Three aspects of early reading behavior are addressed:

- *Constructing meaning from print.* The construction of meaning encompasses a child's ability to read frequently encountered signs, logos, and words; relate words to one another; and understand the contextual nature of written discourse.
- *Knowledge of the alphabet.* This aspect is defined as letter and word decoding (either orally or through sign).
- *Understanding print conventions.* This aspect evaluates the child's awareness of text orientation and organization (for example, book handling, the spatial orientation of print on a page, and the ability to uncover textual or print errors).

Strengths of the Test

- TERA-D/HH was standardized on a national sample of more than 1,000 students from twenty states who were deaf or hard of hearing.
- Normative data are given for every six-month interval from age 3–0 through 13–11. Internal consistency and test-retest reliability are reported in the manual. In all instances, coefficients approach or exceed .90.
- Validity coefficients for TERA-D/HH compared with other reading, language, intelligence, and achievement tests frequently used with students who are deaf or hard of hearing also are reported in the manual.

Chapter 11

Emotional Disturbance

Under the Individuals with Disabilities Education Improvement Act (IDEA), an emotional disturbance is defined as (C.F.R. Section 300.8)

A condition exhibiting one or more of the following characteristics over a long period of time and to a marked degree that adversely affects a child's educational performance—

(A) An inability to learn that cannot be explained by intellectual, sensory, or health factors.

(B) An inability to build or maintain satisfactory interpersonal relationships with peers and teachers.

(C) Inappropriate types of behavior or feelings under normal circumstances.

(D) A general pervasive mood of unhappiness or depression.

(E) A tendency to develop physical symptoms or fears associated with personal or school problems.

Emotional disturbance includes schizophrenia but does not apply to children who are socially maladjusted unless it is determined that they have an emotional disturbance.

There is significant controversy to the definition and language used to describe a child with an emotional disturbance. However, there is general agreement on the following three factors related to behavioral problems of students with emotional disturbances (Jensen, 2005):

- The behavior problem is extreme. It is not just a little more serious than the usual problems that children experience.
- The behavior problem is chronic. It seems to be resistant to intervention and is not a stage or phase.
- The behavior problem is in direct opposition to the accepted social, cultural, and moral values of society.

Problematic to the definition of emotional disturbance is that much of the language interpretation in the definition is left to the interpretation of the reader. In addition, interpretation of the criteria can vary from one school district to another and from state to state (Heward, 2006).

The U.S. Department of Education (2002) reports that 473,663 children and youth with an emotional disturbance were provided special education and related services in the public schools in the 2001–2002 school year. Research suggests that boys outnumber girls in the classification of emotional disturbance by about five to one (Heward, 2006; Jensen, 2005).

According to the National Dissemination Center for Children with Disabilities (2004c), the following characteristics and behaviors are seen in children who have emotional disturbances:

- Aggression or self-injurious behavior (acting out, fighting)
- Hyperactivity (short attention span, impulsiveness)
- Immaturity (inappropriate crying, temper tantrums, poor coping skills)
- Learning difficulties (academically performing below grade level)
- Withdrawal (failure to initiate interaction with others; retreat from exchanges of social interaction; excessive fear or anxiety)

It is important to note that the school's responsibility is to provide services for children with emotional disturbances when their problems are so severe that they cannot succeed in school without special education. Such children may or may not have an outside mental health diagnosis; rather, their emotional and behavioral needs in school determine their eligibility for special education.

BarOn Emotional Quotient Inventory: Youth Version (BarOn EQ-i:YV)

General Test Information

Authors:	Reuven BarOn and James D. A. Parker
Publisher:	Multi-Health Systems
Address of Publisher:	P.O. Box 950, North Tonawanda, NY 14120–0950
Telephone Number:	1-800-456-3003, 1-416-492-2627
Fax Number:	1-888-540-4484, 1-416-492-3343
Web Site of Publisher:	www.mhs.com
Type of Test:	Social and emotional development
Administration Time:	Short, 10 minutes; Long, 30 minutes
Type of Administration:	Individual
Ages/Grade Levels:	Ages 7 to 18

Purpose and Description of Test

The BarOn EQ-i:YV assesses the level of emotional and social functioning in children and adolescents.

Subtest Information

The BarOn EQ-i:YV consists of seven subtests:

- Interpersonal
- Intrapersonal
- Adaptability
- Stress Management
- General Mood
- Positive Impression
- Inconsistency Index

Strengths of the Test

- The BarOn EQ-i:YV identifies strong and weak areas rather than just weak areas, so that strong areas can be used to their full potential and weak areas can be further developed.
- It has a large normative base (approximately 10,000) and a correction factor to adjust for positive response bias.

Beck Youth Inventories of Emotional and Social Impairment

General Test Information

Authors:	Judith S. Beck and Aaron T. Beck, with John Jolly
Publisher:	Harcourt Assessment (formerly known as the Psychological Corporation and Harcourt Educational)
Address of Publisher:	6277 Sea Harbor Drive, Orlando, FL 32887
Telephone Number:	1-800-211-8378
Fax Number:	1-800-232-1223
Web Site of Publisher:	www.harcourt.com
Type of Test:	Emotional and social development
Administration Time:	5 to 10 minutes
Type of Administration:	Individual
Ages/Grade Levels:	Ages 7 through 14

Purpose and Description of Test

The Beck Youth Inventories of Emotional and Social Impairment evaluate children's emotional and social impairment. Five self-report inventories can be used separately or in combination to assess symptoms of depression, anxiety, anger, disruptive behavior, and self-concept. Each inventory contains twenty statements about thoughts, feelings, and behaviors associated with emotional and social impairment in youth. Children describe how frequently the statement has been true for them during the past two weeks, including the day of test administration. The following instruments measure a child's emotional and social impairment in five areas:

- *Beck Depression Inventory for Youth.* In line with the depression criteria of the *Diagnostic and Statistical Manual of Mental Health Disorders,* Fourth Edition (American Psychiatric Association, 2000), this inventory allows early identification of symptoms of depression. It includes items related to a child's negative thoughts about self, life and the future, feelings of sadness and guilt, and sleep disturbance.
- *Beck Anxiety Inventory for Youth.* This inventory reflects children's specific worries about school performance, the future, negative reactions of others, fears including loss of control, and physiological symptoms associated with anxiety.
- *Beck Anger Inventory for Youth.* This inventory valuates a child's thoughts of being treated unfairly by others and feelings of anger and hatred.
- *Beck Disruptive Behavior Inventory for Youth.* This inventory identifies thoughts and behaviors associated with conduct disorder and oppositional-defiant behavior.
- *Beck Self-Concept Inventory for Youth.* This taps cognitions of competence, potency, and positive self-worth.

Strengths of the Test

- Using the same principles as the widely used Beck Depression Inventory–II and other adult Beck Inventories for anxiety, hopelessness, and suicide ideation, the Beck Youth Inventories focus on children's self-perceived behavior, cognitions, and feelings.
- Items are written at a second-grade reading level, with language that is easy to understand for self-reporting. The inventories may be administered orally to those who have difficulty reading at this level. Items have been selected from statements made by children seen in various treatment settings.
- Consistent with Individuals with Disabilities Education Improvement Act legislation requirements, the Beck Youth Inventories are intended for screening for emotional and social difficulties that may impair a child's ability to function in school settings. These inventories are useful in planning and monitoring educational placement as well as in clinical treatment settings. For children who are classified as emotionally disturbed or are emotionally volatile, the inventories may be used for routine monitoring.
- Norms allow comparison with responses of children within age and gender groups that are ethnically and socioeconomically representative of the U.S. population.

Bell Relationship Inventory for Adolescents (BRIA)

General Test Information

Author: Morris D. Bell

Publisher: Western Psychological Services

Address of Publisher: 12031 Wilshire Boulevard, Los Angeles, CA 90025–1251

Telephone Number: 1-800-648-8857 (United States and Canada only), 1-310-478-2061

Fax Number: 1-310-478-7838

Web Site of Publisher: http://www.wpspublish.com

Type of Test: Emotional disturbance

Administration Time: 10 to 15 minutes

Type of Administration: Individual or group

Ages/Grade Levels: Adolescents

Purpose and Description of Test

The BRIA offers a quick and convenient way to evaluate psychological disturbance and inter-personal relationship problems in adolescents. This brief self-report inventory is an alternative to time-consuming projective tests that often require specialized training for evaluators.

Subtest Information

The BRIA assesses only object relations, not reality testing. Its fifty items measure the adolescent's ability to maintain a stable sense of identity and appropriate emotional bonds with others. Four scales parallel those on the Bell Object Relations and Reality Testing Inventory Form, and a fifth scale, with new items written specifically for adolescents, focuses on healthy relationships:

- *Alienation*—Lack of trust, difficulty with intimacy, feelings of alienation
- *Insecure Attachment*—Sensitivity to rejection, fears of separation and abandonment
- *Egocentricity*—Lack of empathy, self-protectiveness, tendency to control and exploit
- *Social Incompetence*—Social discomfort, shyness, difficulty making friends
- *Positive Attachment*—Satisfaction with current relationships with peers and parents

Strengths of the Test

- In clinical or school settings, the BRIA can be used to identify preteens and teens who are likely to experience psychological disturbance and difficulty with interpersonal relationships.
- The inventory may be especially helpful in assessing youngsters with nonverbal learning disability, Asperger syndrome, or other conditions in which interpersonal connections are problematic.
- By revealing deficits in object relations, the BRIA can help distinguish among conduct disorder, borderline personality disorder, mood disorders, and psychosis.
- The Positive Attachment Scale can inform treatment planning by uncovering feelings of support or affection that might serve to moderate difficulties indicated by pathological scores on the other scales.

Differential Test of Conduct and Emotional Problems (DT/CEP)

General Test Information

Authors:	Edward J. Kelly; edited by Gary J. Vitali
Publisher:	Slosson Educational Publications
Address of Publisher:	P.O. Box 280, East Aurora, NY 14052
Telephone Number:	1-888-756-7766
Fax Number:	1-800-655-3840
Web Site of Publisher:	www.slosson.com
Type of Test:	Assessment of emotional disturbance
Administration Time:	15 to 20 minutes
Type of Administration:	Individual or group
Ages/Grade Levels:	Grades K to 12

Purpose and Description of Test

The DT/CEP is designed to address one of the most critical new challenges in education and juvenile care: accurate identification of nonhandicapped children and adults with conduct problems.

Subtest Information

The DT/CEP differentiates among three critical populations:

- Conduct disorder (socially maladjusted)
- Emotionally disturbed
- Noninvolved

Strengths of the Test

- The autonomous conduct problem and emotional disturbance scales make the DT/CEP ideal for mass screenings in both educational and private settings.
- This instrument can be reliably administered by paraprofessionals because of its user-friendly design and detailed manual, allowing psychologists and counselors more time with disordered populations. The DT/CEP is designed to be statistically accountable as well as practical, and it generates relevant information for individualized education program meetings, parental or professional staffing, and, especially, educational placement decisions.
- User-friendly procedures emphasize simple but effective screening identification, verification, and diagnostic steps to facilitate more accountable placement and programming for students with conduct problems or emotional disturbances. The comprehensive manual clearly describes administration and scoring criteria and presents nine case studies that illustrate test use and related procedural uses.
- The DT/CEP scales were standardized on 2,367 public school children in grades K–12. The standardization sample approximates the current U.S. census with respect to sex, race, and ethnic group percentages. The DT/CEP has internal consistency correlations of .81 and .92.
- Extensive validation research, including discriminate function analysis, indicates the DT/CEP can be used as a predictive instrument of behavior.

Draw-A-Person Screening Procedures for Emotional Disturbance (DAP:SPED)

General Test Information

Authors: Jack Naglieri, Timothy McNeish, and Achilles Bardos
Publisher: PRO-ED
Address of Publisher: 8700 Shoal Creek Boulevard, Austin, TX 78757–6897
Telephone Number: 1-800-897-3202
Fax Number: 1-800-397-7633
Web Site of Publisher: www.proedinc.com
Type of Test: Emotional disturbance
Administration Time: 15 minutes
Type of Administration: Individual or group
Ages/Grade Levels: Ages 6 to 17

Purpose and Description of Test

DAP:SPED helps identify children and adolescents ages 6 to 17 years who have emotional problems and require further evaluation. It has items that are used to rate the drawings of a man, a woman, and the self. The items were based on an exhaustive review of the literature on human figure drawings, and the test was written to be fast to score.

Subtest Information

There are no subtests. The DAP:SPED scoring system is composed of two types of criteria or items. With the first type, eight dimensions of each drawing are scored; a separate template for each age group is provided. With the second type, each drawing is rated according to forty-seven specific items. Cutoff scores are divided into three categories: additional assessment is not indicated, additional assessment is indicated, and additional assessment is strongly indicated.

Strengths of the Test

- The DAP:SPED was normed on a nationwide sample of 2,260 students representative of the nation as a whole with regard to gender, race, ethnicity, geographical region, and socioeconomic status.
- The test reliability is relatively high.
- The test manual provides a clear description of the scoring system. The record form is clear and efficient.
- The test is psychometrically sound as well as easily and objectively quantified.

Scale for Assessing Emotional Disturbance (SAED)

General Test Information

Authors:	Michael H. Epstein and Douglas Cullinan
Publisher:	PRO-ED
Address of Publisher:	8700 Shoal Creek Boulevard, Austin, TX 78757–6897
Telephone Number:	1-800-897-3202
Fax Number:	1-800-397-7633
Web Site of Publisher:	http://www.proedinc.com
Type of Test:	Assessment of emotional disturbance
Administration Time:	10 minutes
Type of Administration:	Individual
Ages/Grade Levels:	Ages 5 to 18

Purpose and Description of Test

The SAED helps identify children and adolescents who qualify for the federal special education category Emotional Disturbance (ED). Information from the SAED is useful in understanding the emotional and behavioral disorders of children, identifying students who may meet the criteria for the ED education disability category, selecting appropriate education goals for an individualized education program, and periodically evaluating student progress toward desired outcomes.

Subtest Information

The SAED contains fifty-two items that measure seven areas of child functioning:

- Inability to learn
- Relationship problems
- Inappropriate behavior
- Unhappiness or depression
- Physical symptoms or fears
- Social maladjustment
- Overall competence

Strengths of the Test

- The SAED was normed on a nationally representative sample of 2,266 students without disabilities and 1,371 students with ED. Demographics of the standardization sample are reported in the manual by age, gender, geographical location, race, and ethnicity. Separate norms are reported for students of elementary, middle, and high school age with and without ED.
- The internal consistency reliability of the SAED subtests was established with students with and without ED. Coefficients exceeded .75 for each subtest and .90 for the overall SAED score.
- Additional studies confirmed the SAED's concurrent validity, construct validity, test-retest reliability, and interrater reliability.

Chapter 12

English as a Second Language and Bilingual Education

The term *exceptional children* often includes children classified under the 2004 Individuals with Disabilities Education Improvement Act (IDEA) as having a classified disability, students identified as having a documented disability and in need of only modifications or accommodations, and students with special educational needs. This last category includes students who are not entitled to special education services unless it can be shown that they have concomitant factors that require special education services. The children who often fall into this category may include gifted, slow learners, and children with cultural and linguistic differences. However, if a student with special needs is referred for a suspected disability, then it is imperative that the assessment measures used are not culturally or linguistically biased. As a result, the assessment of students with diverse cultural and linguistic differences (CLD) has become one of special education's major issues. These students are disproportionately represented in special education, a fact that leads us to examine an assessment process that is difficult at best. There is a shortage of personnel qualified to assess culturally and linguistically diverse students (Flores, Lopez, & DeLeon, 2000).

If a student with a diverse cultural or linguistic background is found to have a suspected disability, then the same process required under IDEA for a comprehensive assessment should be followed.

In recognition of these difficulties, a number of solutions and best practices are suggested (Burnette, 2000):

- *Convening a full, multidisciplinary assessment team.* Parents, educators, and assessors are part of any assessment team. Other integral members of the team include interpreters, bilingual educators, and a person who is familiar with the student's culture and language.
- *Using prereferral strategies and interventions.* If a student is having difficulties, information should be gathered to determine whether these difficulties stem from language or cultural differences, a lack of opportunity to learn, or a disability.

- *Determining the language to be used in testing.* Assessment of language dominance and proficiency should be completed before further testing is conducted for students whose home language is other than English.
- *Conducting a tailored, appropriate assessment of the child and environment.* Ideally, nonbiased, appropriate instruments should be combined with other sources of information (observations, interviews) from a variety of environments (school, home, community) to produce a multidimensional assessment.

IDEA requires that a member of the multidisciplinary team that will do the comprehensive assessment be an expert in the area of the suspected disability. In the case of a student with a diverse cultural or linguistic background, it would also be an advantage to have someone who is familiar with the student's culture and language.

This person can be a valuable source of information about the culture and the student, as well as providing a key to understanding the results of test data and other aspects of the assessment process. If the child being evaluated is bilingual, it is recommended that the team also include a bilingual educator (McLean, 2000).

Once a student from a diverse cultural or linguistic background is thought to have a suspected disability, a language proficiency assessment should be given serious consideration. If the child is able to fully understand the English language, then the assessment team may consider administering all the evaluations in English. However, if the student is unable to fully or adequately understand English, then the student will need to be tested in his or her native language. Furthermore, under IDEA 2004 (20 U.S.C. 1414(b) (1)-(3), 1412 (a)(6)(B), and 20 U.S.C. 1414(c)):

Evaluation materials and procedures used to assess a child with limited English proficiency must be selected and administered to ensure they measure a potential disability and need for special education, rather than English language skills.

Evaluation materials and procedures must be provided in the language that most likely will yield accurate information on what the child knows and can do academically and functionally.

The native language of the child is that language normally used by the child in the home/learning environment.

In the case of a student with a diverse cultural or linguistic background formal standardized evaluations should be considered as only one source of assessment. The team should consider curriculum based assessment, interviews, observations, portfolio assessments, etc. Further, the team will have to make sure that a thorough background history intake is obtained from the parents in order to see if similar patterns existed in the child's prior school (if applicable) and prior country (if applicable). Such patterns of academic, social, intellectual or psychological difficulties may add to the possibility of a documented disability.

The Bilingual Verbal Ability Tests (BVAT)

General Test Information

Authors:	Ana F. Muñoz-Sandoval, Jim Cummins, Criselda G. Alvarado, and Mary L. Ruef
Publisher:	Riverside Publishing
Address of Publisher:	425 Spring Lake Drive, Itasca, IL 60143–2079
Telephone Number:	1-800-323-9540
Fax Number:	1-630-467-7192
Web Site of Publisher:	www.riverpub.com
Type of Test:	Bilingual/English as a Second Language
Administration Time:	Untimed
Type of Administration:	Individual
Ages/Grade Levels:	5 years to Adult

Purpose and Description of Test

The BVAT is intended for measuring bilingual verbal ability or the unique combination of cognitive and academic language abilities possessed by bilingual individuals in English and another language. The need for this test is based in the reality that bilingual persons know some things in one language, some things in the other language, and some things in both languages. Traditional procedures allow the person's ability to be measured in only one language, usually the one considered to be dominant. Examiners intuitively know that these individuals know more than they can show on these monolingual approaches.

Strengths of the Test

- Provides assessment in eighteen languages plus English
- Includes two new languages: Hmong and Navajo
- Creates a fairer prediction of ability for gifted and special education evaluations
- Assesses the combined knowledge of a bilingual individual
- Includes a scoring and reporting software program

Expressive One-Word Picture Vocabulary Test– Spanish Bilingual Edition

General Test Information

Author:	Rick Brownell
Publisher:	Academic Therapy
Address of Publisher:	20 Commercial Boulevard, Novato, CA 94949
Telephone Number:	1-800-422-7249
Fax Number:	1-888-287-9975
Web Site of Publisher:	http://www.academictherapy.com
Type of Test:	Bilingual/English as a Second Language
Administration Time:	20 minutes
Type of Administration:	Individual
Ages/Grade Levels:	Ages 4 through 12

Purpose and Description of Test

This edition offers an assessment of expressive vocabularies of individuals who are bilingual in Spanish and English. By permitting examinees to respond in both languages, this test assesses total acquired vocabulary.

Strengths of the Test

- This is one of the few standardized vocabulary tests normed on a Spanish-bilingual sample; it includes provisions for dialectical differences.
- It is co-normed with the Receptive One-Word Picture Vocabulary Test–Spanish Bilingual Edition (2001).
- The normative sample is nationally stratified, and demographics match the U.S. Census.

Receptive One-Word Picture Vocabulary Test–
Spanish Bilingual Edition (ROWPVT-SBE)

General Test Information

Author:	Rick Brownell
Publisher:	Academic Therapy
Address of Publisher:	20 Commercial Boulevard, Novato, CA 94949
Telephone Number:	1-800-422-7249
Fax Number:	1-888-287-9975
Web Site of Publisher:	http://www.academictherapy.com
Type of Test:	Bilingual/English as a Second Language
Administration Time:	20 minutes
Type of Administration:	Individual
Ages/Grade Levels:	Ages 4 through 12

Purpose and Description of Test

This edition offers an assessment of receptive vocabularies of individuals who are bilingual in Spanish and English. By permitting examinees to respond in both languages, this test assesses total acquired vocabulary.

Strengths of the Test

- This is one of the few standardized vocabulary tests normed on a Spanish-bilingual sample.
- Includes provisions for dialectical differences.
- Co-normed with the Expressive One-Word Picture Vocabulary Test–Spanish Bilingual Edition (2001).
- The normative sample is nationally stratified, and demographics match the U.S. Census.

Test de Vocabulario en Imagenes Peabody (TVIP)

General Test Information

Authors:	Lloyd M. Dunn, Delia E. Lugo, Eligio R. Padilla, and Leota M. Dunn
Publisher:	AGS Publishing
Address of Publisher:	4201 Woodland Road, Circle Pines, MN 55014–1796
Telephone Number:	1-800-328-2560, 1-651-287-7220
Fax Number:	1-800-471-8457
Web Site of Publisher:	www.agsnet.com
Type of Test:	Bilingual/English as a Second Language
Administration Time:	10 to 15 minutes
Type of Administration:	Individual
Ages/Grade Levels:	Ages 2–6 through 17–11

Purpose and Description of Test

Based on the popular Peabody Picture Vocabulary Test–Third Edition, TVIP contains 125 translated items to assess the vocabulary of Spanish-speaking and bilingual students. Items were carefully selected through rigorous item analysis for their universality and appropriateness to Spanish-speaking communities.

TVIP is easy to administer and score and does not require reading, verbal, or written responses. To administer an item, the examiner shows a plate in the test easel and says a corresponding stimulus word. The student responds by pointing to one of the pictures. The manual is available in English and Spanish. Norms are available for combined and separate Mexican and Puerto Rican standardization samples.

Strengths of the Test

- Evaluating the language development of Spanish-speaking preschool children
- Screening Spanish-speaking children entering kindergarten or first grade
- Determining the more effective language of instruction for bilingual children
- Evaluating the Spanish vocabulary of older students

Chapter 13

Gifted and Talented

Sidney P. Marland Jr., former U.S. commissioner of education, stated in his report to Congress (Marland, 1972), "Gifted and talented children are those identified by professionally qualified persons who by virtue of outstanding abilities are capable of high performance. These are children who require differentiated educational programs and/or services beyond those normally provided by the regular school program in order to realize their contribution to self and society."

The most recent federal definition of giftedness is included in the Jacob K. Javits Gifted and Talented Students Education Act of 1988, reauthorized in 1994:

Children and youth with outstanding talent who perform or show the potential for performing at remarkably high levels of accomplishment when compared with others of their age, experience, or environment. These children and youth exhibit high performance capability in intellectual, creative, and/or artistic areas, possess an unusual leadership capacity, or excel in specific academic fields. They require services or activities not ordinarily provided by schools. Outstanding talents are present in children and youth from all cultural groups, across all economic strata, and in all areas of human endeavor.

Upon examination of the Marland and Javits definitions, Friend (2005) notes that "based on these definitions, giftedness is evidence of advanced development across intellectual areas, within a specific academic or arts-related area, or unusual organizational power to bring about desired results. Talent sometimes is defined as extraordinary ability in a specific area, but it is also now used interchangeably with giftedness" (p. 576).

The estimates of the prevalence of giftedness vary considerably due to the fact that each state determines its own definition of what constitutes its meaning. Currently, anywhere from 2 to 22 percent of students may be served in programs for students who are gifted and talented. On average, school districts serve 12 percent of students under the label of gifted, regardless of whether they receive state funding for programs (Council of State Directors, 2001, cited in Friend, 2005).

Using a broad definition of giftedness, a school system could expect to identify 10 to 15 percent or more of its student population as gifted and talented. A brief description of each area of giftedness or talent as defined by the Office of Gifted and Talented is useful for understanding this definition (Education Commission of the States, 2004).

Gifted and talented education in the United States is entirely in the purview of the states. According to the Education Commission of the States (2004), there is no federal legislation mandating states to provide special services to gifted and talented students. Therefore, states are free to establish their own programs and definitions of gifted and talented students. These definitions are important as a guide to the state department in formulating programs, for identification of gifted students in local districts, and on judicial review of gifted determinations.

Gifted and talented students (Gargiulo, 2004; Friend, 2005; Heward, 2006):

- Demonstrate exceptional critical thinking skills or problem-solving ability
- Frequently ask in-depth, probing questions
- Have a keen sense of humor
- Have an excellent memory
- Have special talents; for example, in technology, the arts, or science
- Have superior insight and the ability to draw inferences or is intuitive
- Have superior leadership and interpersonal skills
- Have unusual or advanced interests
- Are advanced readers in English or their home language
- Are creative or imaginative; for example, they produce many ideas or are highly original
- Are highly motivated, particularly in self-selected tasks
- Are independent—and may prefer to work alone
- Learn rapidly and quickly grasp new concepts
- May demonstrate a high degree of social responsibility or moral reasoning
- Possess a large, advanced vocabulary

Creativity Assessment Packet (CAP)

General Test Information

Author:	Frank Williams
Publisher:	PRO-ED
Address of Publisher:	8700 Shoal Creek Boulevard, Austin, TX 78757–6897
Telephone Number:	1-800-897-3202
Fax Number:	1-800-397-7633
Web Site of Publisher:	www.proedinc.com
Type of Test:	Gifted and talented
Administration Time:	Untimed
Type of Administration:	Group
Ages/Grade Levels:	Ages 6 through 18

Purpose and Description of Test

The CAP measures the cognitive thought factors of fluency, flexibility, elaboration, originality, vocabulary, and comprehension. CAP is a test packet consisting of two group-administered instruments for children: the Test of Divergent Thinking (Forms A and B) and the Test of Divergent Feeling. A third instrument, the Williams Scale, is a rating instrument for teachers and parents of the same tested factors among children.

Strengths of the Test

- The three instruments can be used to evaluate, screen, and identify the most important factors of creativity found in some degree among children.

Gifted and Talented Evaluation Scales (GATES)

General Test Information

Authors:	James Gilliam, Betsy Carpenter, and Janis Christensen
Publisher:	PRO-ED
Address of Publisher:	8700 Shoal Creek Boulevard, Austin, TX 78757–6897
Telephone Number:	1-800-897-3202
Fax Number:	1-800-397-7633
Web Site of Publisher:	www.proedinc.com
Type of Test:	Gifted and talented
Administration Time:	5 to 10 minutes
Type of Administration:	Individual
Ages/Grade Levels:	Ages 5 to 18

Purpose and Description of Test

The GATES is an innovative, quick approach for identifying students ages 5 to 18 who are gifted and talented. Based on the most current federal and state definitions, the GATES is a norm-referenced instrument that assesses the characteristics, skills, and talents of gifted students.

Strengths of the Test

- The GATES was normed in 1995 on a representative national sample of over 1,000 persons who were identified as gifted and talented. Characteristics of the normative group approximate those for the 1990 Census relative to gender, geographical location, race, ethnicity, and socioeconomic status.

Screening Assessment for Gifted Elementary and Middle School Students–Second Edition (SAGES-2)

General Test Information

Authors:	Susan Johnsen and Anne Corn
Publisher:	PRO-ED
Address of Publisher:	8700 Shoal Creek Boulevard, Austin, TX 78757–6897
Telephone Number:	1-800-897-3202
Fax Number:	1-800-397-7633
Web Site of Publisher:	www.proedinc.com
Type of Test:	Gifted and talented
Administration Time:	20 minutes
Type of Administration:	Individual or group
Ages/Grade Levels:	Ages 5-0 to 14–11

Purpose and Description of Test

The SAGES-2 is helpful in identifying gifted students in kindergarten through eighth grade.

Subtest Information

The SAGES-2 has three subtests that sample aspects of two of the most commonly used areas for identifying gifted students: aptitude and achievement. Aptitude is measured in the Reasoning subtest: the student is asked to solve analogical problems by identifying relationships among pictures and figures. The other two subtests assess achievement. On one of these subtests, the child answers questions about language arts and social studies, and on the other, about mathematics and science. The student selects answers from a series of pictures, symbols, or words. The subtests can be used to examine the relationships between aptitude and achievement.

Strengths of the Test

- Several important improvements to the technical characteristics of the initial SAGES have been made. First, test-retest studies were added. Second, each item on the test was evaluated using both classical item analyses and item response theories to choose good statistical items. Third, differential item functioning analyses were performed on three dichotomous groups in order to find and eliminate adversely biased items. Finally, several new validity studies were conducted with special attention devoted to demonstrating that the test proves valid for a wide variety of subgroups as well as for a general population.
- The reliability coefficients for the test are high, ranging from .77 to .95. Ninety-seven percent of these reach or exceed .80, and 74 percent reach or exceed .90. Test-retest studies show that the SAGES-2 is stable over time. The potential bias of every item on the test on the basis of gender and ethnic group was studied. Forty-four items were eliminated from the final version.
- Extensive validity data are reported, documenting the test's relationship to the Wechsler Intelligence Scale for Children-III, Otis-Lennon School Ability Test, Stanford Achievement Test, and Gifted and Talented Evaluation Scales, and its efficiency in discriminating groups appropriately.

Test of Mathematical Abilities for Gifted Students (TOMAGS)

General Test Information

Authors:	Gail R. Ryser and Susan K. Johnsen
Publisher:	PRO-ED
Address of Publisher:	8700 Shoal Creek Boulevard, Austin, TX 78757–6897
Telephone Number:	1-800-897-3202
Fax Number:	1-800-397-7633
Web Site of Publisher:	www.proedinc.com
Type of Test:	Gifted and talented
Administration Time:	Untimed; 30 to 60 minutes
Type of Administration:	Individual or group
Ages/Grade Levels:	Grades K to 6

Purpose and Description of Test

The Primary Level (grades K–3) and the Intermediate Level (grades 4–6) of this standardized, norm-referenced test are used to identify children gifted in mathematics. The TOMAGS measures students' ability to use mathematical reasoning and mathematical problem solving. It provides one composite score and can be interpreted using two sets of national norms: one sample consisting of children who are identified as gifted in mathematics and one sample consisting of "normal" children. Therefore, the TOMAGS can be used to identify students who excel in mathematical abilities, measure the degree of mathematical abilities among gifted students, or evaluate gifted educational programs.

Strengths of the Test

- The TOMAGS has reliability coefficients above .80 at one-year age intervals. Content validity is addressed, and several criterion-referenced studies favorably compare the TOMAGS to other measures of quantitative reasoning ability, including the Cognitive Abilities Test. Several strong construct validity studies support using the TOMAGS as an identification measure for mathematical giftedness.
- The TOMAGS was written to reflect the National Council of Teachers of Mathematics curriculum and evaluation standards.

Chapter 14

Infants, Toddlers, and Preschoolers

Early intervention (EI) is a system of coordinated services that promotes the child's growth and development and enhances the capacity of the family to meet the child's needs during the critical early years. Research shows that participation in family-centered early intervention services during the first years of life has substantial positive effects on the cognitive development, social adjustment, and overall development of children with developmental disabilities. If a state chooses to provide comprehensive early intervention services to infants and toddlers and their families, it can receive federal funds under the early intervention provisions of the 2004 Individuals with Disabilities Education Improvement Act (IDEA).

Under Part C of IDEA, states *must provide* services to any child "under 3 years of age who needs early intervention services" (20 U.S.C. §1432(5)(A)) because the child:

(i)   is experiencing developmental delays, as measured by appropriate diagnostic instruments and procedures in one or more of the areas of cognitive development, physical development, communication development, social or emotional development, and adaptive development; or

(ii) has a diagnosed physical or mental condition which has a high probability of resulting in developmental delay (20 U.S.C. §1432(5)(A)).

Part C of IDEA authorizes the creation of early intervention programs for infants and toddlers with disabilities and provides federal assistance for states to maintain and implement statewide systems of services for eligible children, aged birth through 2 years, and their families (Shackelford, 2006).

In 1986, Congress created a nationwide incentive for states to implement coordinated systems of early intervention services for infants and toddlers with disabilities and their families by adding Part C to IDEA. (An infant or toddler is defined as someone from birth to 36 months of age.) This is a federal law that provides financial assistance to states for the purpose of providing services to infants and toddlers (age birth through age 2) with disabilities. The purpose of these services is to enhance the development of infants and toddlers with disabilities and to minimize their potential for developmental delay. The ultimate goal of the program is to maximize the child's potential for independent living as an adult (National Dissemination Center for Children with Disabilities, 2005).

Each year since 1987, the state lead agency has received federal funds by submitting an application to the U.S. Department of Education, which ensures that the state will implement the early intervention system in compliance with statutory and regulatory requirements.

The focus of early intervention services is to increase the capacity of families to care for their children with disabilities and potential delays. The services are provided through a coordinated network of service providers. The services are driven by the needs of the family and the child and are documented through an individualized family service plan (IFSP).

❖ Eligibility Criteria for Early Intervention Services

Referral to early intervention services can be based on objective criteria, screening tests, or clinical suspicion. Under IDEA (Part C), individual states retain the right to determine eligibility criteria for early intervention services; some require referral within a certain time period.

Two eligibility criteria are typical of most states: birth to 3 years of age and developmental delay or deficit in one or more of these areas: (1) cognitive development (for example, limited interest in environment, play, and learning); (2) physical and motor development, including vision and hearing (for example, hypertonia, dystonia, asymmetry); (3) communication development (for example, limited sound use, limited response to speech); (4) emotional-social development (for example, impaired attachment, self-injurious behavior); and (5) adaptive development (for example, feeding difficulties). While most states require children to demonstrate one or more of these types of deficits, some states permit enrolling children who are at risk for delays or disabilities due to environmental factors.

❖ Evaluation of Infants and Toddlers for Early Intervention Services

According to the California Department of Education (2001), the following concepts represent the preferred practices in early childhood evaluation and assessment:

- A collaborative evaluation and assessment process includes families as providers of information and as team members.
- A transdisciplinary team knowledgeable in all areas of child development, including typical and atypical development and family systems, conducts the assessments. As part of the assessment team, families are given the opportunity to learn about the procedures, observations of the professionals, and interpretations of the data. The result of the assessment is a coordinated intervention plan.
- The evaluation and assessment team looks at the child in the context of the family, culture, and community, interpreting information about the child in the child's environment.
- The assessment team considers the reliability and validity of the various procedures for the child and the family when choosing observation strategies and assessment measures.
- The evaluation or assessment team designs procedures to obtain appropriate information for determining a child's eligibility for programs and his or her progress and for planning intervention strategies.
- The team provides a written report that communicates the results and recommendations in lay terms without jargon to parents and program providers. Personnel who assess children from ages birth to 5 years should adopt a philosophy about assessment practices.

If a child does not have a diagnosed medical condition known to result in delay, the child may receive a screening to determine whether a full evaluation should be conducted. Screenings may involve interviews, tests, or simple evaluations that are used to identify risk factors or indicators and are not as comprehensive as evaluations. The parents may be referred to a screening site in the community to begin this process. The screenings are provided at no cost to families.

All children suspected of having a developmental delay are entitled to receive an evaluation to determine eligibility for Part C services and an assessment to determine what specific services must be provided. Evaluations usually involve the administration of a research-based test done by a licensed professional and are designed to determine the child's abilities and needs. The child must be evaluated and show a delay in one or more of the developmental areas to be eligible for Part C services.

❖ Service Coordinators

When a child's needs are assessed and the child is found eligible for services, a service coordinator is assigned to the family. This person should have a background in early childhood development and methods for helping young children who may have developmental delays. The service coordinator should know the policies for early intervention programs and services in the state. This person can help parents locate other services in their community, such as recreation, child care, or family support groups. The service coordinator will work with the family as long as the baby is receiving early intervention services. After the child is 2 years old, the service coordinator will help the family move on to programs for children ages 3 through 5.

❖ Types of Services

Early intervention services can include special instruction; occupational, physical, speech, and language therapies; and psychological services. They can also include training and other services the family needs to support the child's development. All necessary services must be provided without cost to the family. Whenever possible, EI services must be provided in the child's natural environment, that is, the child's home, the day care center, or another community setting. A separate, specialized facility can be used only if the child's needs require such a restrictive setting.

❖ Determination of Services

The decision is made at a meeting of an individualized family service plan (IFSP) team. Required team members include the parents and anyone else the parents invite; the service coordinator; a person who was involved with the evaluation of the child; and, as appropriate, persons who will be involved in providing services to the child or family. The team develops an IFSP for the child and family.

❖ Individualized Family Service Plan

The family and the service coordinator work with other professionals, as appropriate, to develop an IFSP. The guiding principal of the IFSP is that the family is a child's greatest resource and that the child's needs are closely tied to the needs of the family. The best way to support children and meet their needs is to support and build on the individual strengths of their family. The IFSP is thus a whole family plan, with the parents as the most important part of the team. Involvement of other team members depends on what the child needs. These other team members could come from several agencies and may include medical people, therapists, child development specialists, and social workers.

The IFSP describes the child's development levels, family information (with parents' concurrence), the major outcomes expected to be achieved for the child and family, the services the child will be receiving, when and where he or she will receive these services, and the steps to be taken to support his or her transition to another program. The IFSP also identifies the service coordinator. The IFSP may identify services the family may be interested in, such as financial information or information about raising a child with a disability.

The evaluation of a child and the initial IFSP must all be completed within forty-five calendar days of the parents' contact requesting services. In an emergency and with the parent's permission, services can begin before the full evaluation is completed.

Part C of IDEA does not require that all services be provided at no cost to families. Several early intervention services, however, must be provided at no cost to the family. These include evaluations or assessments, the development of the IFSP, and service coordination for eligible children and their families.

Some early intervention programs provide services at no charge to families. Other early intervention programs charge families on a sliding-fee scale. The law says that no family shall be denied needed services because it cannot afford them.

❖ Transition Services for Infants and Toddlers

The purpose of transition services is to ensure that children continue to receive services and support as they move within and between service delivery systems. There are two types of transitions that can be addressed by the IFSP.

First are transitions within the early intervention program. These can include transitions between service providers or service settings. For example, support and planning would be required to move smoothly from a program designed for infants to a program for toddlers. The physical environment in the toddler setting differs significantly from that in the infant setting to support the developmental goals of toddlers, who are more mobile and expected to explore their environment.

The other type of transition takes place when the child moves from early intervention services to a variety of preschool settings. When the child with disabilities nears the age of 3, he or she must be considered for services beyond EI services, which include special education preschool programs (under Part B of the IDEA), Head Start programs, and public and private preschool programs.

Special education preschool programs are available to children with disabilities who are 3 to 5 years old. If the child is eligible for preschool special education services, he or she must have an IEP in place by age 3. All services provided under the program must be free to the parents. If a child is not eligible for special education preschool, Head Start or public or private preschool programs should be considered.

With the permission of the parents, the IFSP will contain steps to be taken to support the transition of a child from EI services to preschool services. A written transition plan must be developed before the child's third birthday. This plan outlines the steps, services, and supports necessary to support the child's transition from early intervention services to preschool or other appropriate settings.

In most states, the person responsible for ensuring the completion of the transition plan is the service coordinator. The service coordinator must inform the child's local school district that the child is nearing the third birthday and must, with the permission of the family, schedule a meeting with the family, other team members, and the local school district representative. The purpose of the meeting is to discuss what is needed to determine whether the child is eligible for special education preschool services. A representative of the child's local school district must attend this transition planning conference. In general, this meeting must be held at least 120 days before the child's third birthday. At this meeting, team members review existing evaluations, assessments, and progress reports. If the team determines that it is likely that the child will be eligible for special education preschool services, a multifactored evaluation will be completed to determine the areas of documented disability or deficit. The IEP is developed from this evaluation.

Basic School Skills Inventory–Third Edition (BSSI-3)

General Test Information

Authors:	Don Hammill, James Leigh, Nils Pearson, and Taddy Maddox
Publisher:	PRO-ED
Address of Publisher:	8700 Shoal Creek Boulevard, Austin, TX 78757–6897
Telephone Number:	1-800-897-3202
Fax Number:	1-800-397-7633
Web Site of Publisher:	www.proedinc.com
Type of Test:	Early childhood
Administration Time:	5 to 8 minutes
Type of Administration:	Individual
Ages/Grade Levels:	Age 4–0 to 6–11

Purpose and Description of Test

The BSSI-3 is used to locate children who are at high risk for school failure, need more in-depth assessment, and should be referred for additional study.

Subtest Information

There are six areas of assessment on the BSSI-3:

- *Daily Living Skills*—basic knowledge and skills typically required for participation in day-to-day activities in school
- *Spoken Language*—ability to communicate orally
- *Reading*—knowledge of print in the form of letters, words, sentences, and paragraphs
- *Writing*—abilities and skills directly involved in writing letters, words, sentences, and paragraphs
- *Mathematics*—knowledge of numerical concepts and arithmetic operations involved in beginning mathematics
- *Classroom Behavior*—attentiveness, cooperation, attitude, socialization, and work habits

Strengths of the Test

- Using a four-point Likert-type scale that ranges from "does not perform" to "performance indicates mastery," the BSSI-3 provides a quick teacher rating scale of early abilities.
- Standard scores, percentiles, and age and grade equivalents are reported for each scale. Reliability coefficients are in the .90s for each scale.

Battelle Developmental Inventory–Second Edition (BDI-2)

General Test Information

Author:	Jean Newborg
Publisher:	Riverside Publishing
Address of Publisher:	425 Spring Lake Drive, Itasca, IL 60143–2079
Telephone Number:	1-800-323-9540
Fax Number:	1-630-467-7192
Web Site of Publisher:	www.riverpub.com
Type of Test:	Early childhood
Administration Time:	Complete: 1 to 2 hours; screening test: 10 to 30 minutes
Type of Administration:	Individual
Ages/Grade Levels:	Birth to age 7–11

Purpose and Description of Test

The BDI-2 is used for screening, diagnosis, and evaluation of early development. This instrument may be used by a team of professionals or an individual service provider. It can be administered to children with various handicapping conditions by using stated modifications. This instrument is based on the concept of milestones. That is, a child typically develops by attaining critical skills or behaviors in a certain sequence, and the acquisition of each skill generally depends on the acquisition of the preceding skills.

Subtest Information

The test consists of five subtests:

- *Personal–Social Domain*—measures coping skills, self-concept, expressions of feelings, and adult interaction
- *Adaptive Domain*—measures attention, eating skills, dressing skills, personal responsibility, and toileting
- *Motor Domain*—measures muscle control, body coordination, locomotion, fine muscle skills, and perceptual-motor skills
- *Communication Domain*—measures receptive and expressive communication
- *Cognitive Domain*—measures memory, reasoning skills, perceptual discrimination, academic skills, and conceptual development

Strengths of the Test

The BDI-2 is ideal for the following uses:

- Identification of children with disabilities
- Speech/language impairments and delays
- Social/emotional developmental delays
- Cognitive delays and mental retardation
- Motoric impairments and delays
- Learning disabilities
- Hearing impairment and deafness
- Other health impairments
- Evaluation of groups of children with disabilities in early education programs
- Assessment of the typically developing child
- Assessment (screening) for school readiness
- Program evaluation for accountability

New features of the BDI-2 include:

- New colorful items
- Child-friendly manipulatives at all ages
- New comprehensive norms, sensitive to the rapid development of children
- Clear, comprehensive scripted interview items, with follow-up probes designed to provide complete information on the child's development
- Choice of computer- or hand-scored processing
- Personal digital assistant electronic record form, which reduces administration time and improves accuracy of assessment
- Flexible administration, which allows use by a team of professionals
- Expanded range of items in all domains to measure development from birth to age 7–11
- Web-based scoring option for all reports
- A wide range of reports to choose from
- Useful for Head Start assessment mandates
- Matching all areas as required by IDEA

Bayley Infant Neurodevelopmental Screener (BINS)

General Test Information

Author:	Glen P. Aylward
Publisher:	Harcourt Assessment (formerly known as the Psychological Corporation and Harcourt Educational)
Address of Publisher:	6277 Sea Harbor Drive, Orlando, FL 32887
Telephone Number:	1-800-211-8378
Fax Number:	1-800-232-1223
Web Site of Publisher:	www.harcourt.com
Type of Test:	Early childhood
Administration Time:	10 to 15 minutes
Type of Administration:	Individual
Ages/Grade Levels:	Ages 3 through 24 months

Purpose and Description of Test

BINS quickly screens infants ages 3 through 24 months at risk for neurological impairment or developmental delay. It reliably assesses basic neurological functions, auditory and visual receptive functions, verbal and motor expressive functions, and cognitive processes. Item sets contain eleven to thirteen items selected from the Bayley Scales of Infant Development–Second Edition (BSID–II) and neurological assessments. The items were chosen for their ability to discriminate between a nonclinical and clinical sample of infants. Three classifications of risk status (low, moderate, and high) are delimited by two cut scores, allowing the examiner to select the cut score according to his or her criteria for detecting impairment or delay.

Strengths of the Test

- The nonclinical sample is demographically representative of the U.S. infant population according to the infant's sex, race/ethnicity, region of the country, and parents' level of education. The clinical sample represents infants from neonatal intensive care unit follow-up clinics who were born prematurely, asphyxiated at birth, or have experienced intraventricular hemorrhage, apnea, patent ductus arteriosus, or seizures.
- Test-retest reliability ranges from .71 to .84 across ages, interrater reliability ranges from .79 to .96, and internal consistency reliability ranges from .73 to .85. A validation study with BSID–II shows 80 to 88 percent classification agreement for infants who are developmentally delayed.

Bayley Scales of Infant Development–
Second Edition (BSID–II)

General Test Information

Author:	Nancy Bayley
Publisher:	Harcourt Assessment (formerly known as the Psychological Corporation and Harcourt Educational)
Address of Publisher:	6277 Sea Harbor Drive, Orlando, FL 32887
Telephone Number:	1-800-211-8378
Fax Number:	1-800-232-1223
Web Site of Publisher:	www.harcourt.com
Type of Test:	Early childhood
Administration Time:	Under 14 months: 25 to 35 minutes; over 15 months: up to 60 minutes
Type of Administration:	Individual
Ages/Grade Levels:	Ages 1 through 42 months

Purpose and Description of Test

BSID–II offers a standardized assessment of cognitive and motor development for children ages 1 through 42 months.

Subtest Information

BSID–II retains the broad content coverage that characterized the original scales and has three scales:

- *Mental Scale:* Yields a normalized standard score, the Mental Development Index, which evaluates a variety of abilities: sensory/perceptual acuities, discriminations, and response; acquisition of object constancy; memory, learning, and problem solving; vocalization and beginning of verbal communication; basis of abstract thinking; habituation; mental mapping; complex language; and mathematical concept formation
- *Motor Scale:* Assesses degree of body control, large muscle coordination, finer manipulatory skills of the hands and fingers, dynamic movement, dynamic praxis, postural imitation, and stereognosis
- *Behavior Rating Scale:* Provides information that should be used to supplement information gained from the Mental and Motor scales. The thirty-item scale rates the child's relevant test-taking behaviors and measures the following factors: attention/arousal, orientation/engagement, emotional regulation, and motor quality.

Strengths of the Test

- BSID–II incorporates technical soundness, expanded content coverage, enhanced clinical validity, and brighter stimulus materials. It reflects current norms and allows diagnostic assessment at an earlier age than other tests provide for to help lead to needed intervention.
- BSID–II was renormed on a stratified random sample of 1,700 children (850 boys and 850 girls) ages 1 to 42 months, grouped at one-month to three-month intervals on the variables of age, sex, region, race/ethnicity, and parental education. Now, a child's performance can be more accurately compared to a contemporary reference group.
- BSID–II includes information about clinical samples. Data are provided in the manual for the following groups: children who were born prematurely, have the HIV antibody, were prenatally drug exposed, were asphyxiated at birth, are developmentally delayed, have frequent otitis media, are autistic, or have Down syndrome.
- More than 100 new items were created to apply to the expanded age range. The Behavior Rating Scale (formerly the Infant Behavior Record) also was revised in structure and content to reflect more relevant dimensions of test-taking behavior.

185

Birth to Three Assessment and Intervention System–Second Edition (BTAIS-2)

General Test Information

Authors:	Jerome J. Ammer and Tina Bangs
Publisher:	PRO-ED
Address of Publisher:	8700 Shoal Creek Boulevard, Austin, TX 78757–6897
Telephone Number:	1-800-897-3202
Fax Number:	1-800-397-7633
Web Site of Publisher:	www.proedinc.com
Type of Test:	Early childhood
Administration Time:	15 minutes
Type of Administration:	Individual
Ages/Grade Levels:	Birth to age 3

Purpose and Description of Test

The BTAIS-2 has been completely revised and updated to provide examiners with an integrated, three-component system for screening, assessing, and intervening with children. It contains eighty-five items for identifying problems in the following areas:

- Language comprehension
- Language expression
- Nonverbal thinking
- Social/personal development
- Motor development

Strengths of the Test

- The Manual for Teaching Developmental Abilities sets out a series of activities that are appropriate for enhancing skills and strengthening areas identified by the assessments as weak. The manual presents a step-by-step treatment guide for professionals participating in the care of developmentally delayed young children.

Boehm–3 Preschool

General Test Information

Author:	Ann E. Boehm
Publisher:	Harcourt Assessment (formerly known as the Psychological Corporation and Harcourt Educational)
Address of Publisher:	6277 Sea Harbor Drive, Orlando, FL 32887
Telephone Number:	1-800-211-8378
Fax Number:	1-800-232-1223
Web Site of Publisher:	www.harcourt.com
Type of Test:	Early childhood
Administration Time:	20 to 30 minutes
Type of Administration:	Individual
Ages/Grade Levels:	Ages 3–0 through 5–11

Purpose and Description of Test

The Boehm–3 Preschool individually evaluates basic concept comprehension. By helping to identify children who lack understanding of basic relational concepts, it can provide early intervention, increasing their chance of success in school.

Strengths of the Test

- Measures concepts relevant to preschool and early childhood curriculum.
- Quick and easy to administer and score.
- Children respond favorably to the colorful stimulus materials.
- Standardized and normed on a nationally representative sample of children.
- Each concept is tested twice to determine the child's understanding of it across contexts.
- Includes curriculum-based test summary, an observation and intervention planning tool, a parent report form, and suggestions for modifying and adapting administration directions and testing materials for children with differing abilities.

Boehm Test of Basic Concepts–Third Edition (Boehm-3)

General Test Information

Author:	Ann E. Boehm
Publisher:	Harcourt Assessment (formerly known as the Psychological Corporation and Harcourt Educational)
Address of Publisher:	6277 Sea Harbor Drive, Orlando, FL 32887
Telephone Number:	1-800-211-8378
Fax Number:	1-800-232-1223
Web Site of Publisher:	www.harcourt.com
Type of Test:	Basic concepts measure
Administration Time:	30 to 45 minutes
Type of Administration:	Group administered in a classroom setting
Ages/Grade Levels:	Ages 5–0 through 7–11; grades K to 2

Purpose and Description of Test

The Boehm-3 evaluates basic concepts essential for school success. It identifies students who may be at risk for learning difficulty and may need a referral for additional testing. The test consists of fifty concept items in two test booklets, Booklet 1 and Booklet 2, to facilitate administration in two sessions to children in grades K through 2. The test has two alternate forms, C and D. The examiner reads the questions, and the student marks the correct response directly in the test booklet. The test materials include individual student test booklets and the examiner's manual.

Strengths of the Test

- The new edition helps measure fifty basic concepts most frequently occurring in the kindergarten, first-, and second-grade curriculum.
- Two parallel forms, E and F, enable the examiner to conduct pre- and posttesting to help determine if the student's comprehension of the concept is consistent across multiple contexts. The results can be used to demonstrate progress as a result of teaching or intervention.
- Includes tools to aid in complying with Individuals with Disabilities Education Improvement Act guidelines.

Bracken Basic Concept Scale–Revised

General Test Information

Author:	Bruce A. Bracken
Publisher:	Harcourt Assessment (formerly known as the Psychological Corporation and Harcourt Educational)
Address of Publisher:	6277 Sea Harbor Drive, Orlando, FL 32887
Telephone Number:	1-800-211-8378
Fax Number:	1-800-232-1223
Web Site of Publisher:	www.harcourt.com
Type of Test:	Early childhood
Administration Time:	20 to 40 minutes
Type of Administration:	Individual
Ages/Grade Levels:	Ages 2–6 to 7–11

Purpose and Description of Test

The Bracken Basic Concept Scale–Revised measures a child's comprehension of 308 foundational and functionally relevant education concepts. This test measures eleven diagnostic subtest areas. Items are multiple choice, and the child is shown four monochrome pictures and asked to identify the picture that depicts a particular concept. The test contains an examiner's manual, a diagnostic stimulus manual, diagnostic record forms, one Screening Test Form A, and one Screening Test Form B.

Subtest Information

The Bracken Basic Concept Scale–Revised has the following subtests:

- *Color Identification.* Children are tested on their knowledge of colors.
- *Letter Identification.* Children are tested on their knowledge of letters.
- *Numbers/Counting.* Children are required to tell how many items they see and recognize numbers.
- *Comparisons.* Children are required to make comparisons.
- *Shapes.* Children are tested regarding their ability to recognize different shapes.
- *Direction/Position.* Children are tested on their ability to distinguish between different directions and positions.
- *Social/Emotional.* This subtest determines children's social and emotional development.
- *Size.* This subtest determines children's ability to differentiate sizes.
- *Texture/Material.* Children are given objects of different texture and must identify them.
- *Quantity.* Children are tested on their ability to distinguish amounts.
- *Time/Sequence.* Children are given numbers and asked to tell the missing number or the number that comes next.

Strengths of the Test

- One of the major strengths is the detailed and well-organized examiner's manual.
- The test administration procedures are fairly well planned and coordinated.
- The test is a comprehensive test of basic concept identification for young children.
- The test can be used for norm-referenced, criterion-referenced, or curriculum-based purposes.
- A criterion-referenced record form is available in Spanish.

Bracken School Readiness Assessment

General Test Information

Author:	Bruce A. Bracken
Publisher:	Harcourt Assessment (formerly known as the Psychological Corporation and Harcourt Educational)
Address of Publisher:	6277 Sea Harbor Drive, Orlando, FL 32887
Telephone Number:	1-800-211-8378
Fax Number:	1-800-232-1223
Web Site of Publisher:	www.harcourt.com
Type of Test:	Early childhood/school readiness
Administration Time:	10 to 15 minutes
Type of Administration:	Individual
Ages/Grade Levels:	Ages 2–6 through 7–11

Purpose and Description of Test

The Bracken School Readiness Assessment tests assess a child's concept knowledge and receptive language skills for school readiness.

Subtest Information

The tests have these subtests:

- *Color/Letter Identification.* Children are tested on their knowledge of colors and letters.
- *Numbers/Counting.* Children are required to tell how many items they see and recognize numbers.
- *Comparisons.* Children are required to compare things.
- *Shapes.* Children are tested regarding their ability to recognize different shapes.
- *Sizes.* Children are tested on their ability to differentiate sizes.

Strengths of the Test

- Short administration time and national normative scores make this assessment time- and cost-effective.
- A low age range (to 2½ years) allows testing of a wide range of young learners.
- Information on how to develop local norms is provided, helping to establish local criteria for identifying at-risk children.

CELF Preschool–Second Edition

General Test Information

Authors:	Elisabeth H. Wiig, Wayne A. Secord, and Eleanor Semel
Publisher:	Harcourt Assessment (formerly known as the Psychological Corporation and Harcourt Educational)
Address of Publisher:	6277 Sea Harbor Drive, Orlando, FL 32887
Telephone Number:	1-800-211-8378
Fax Number:	1-800-232-1223
Web Site of Publisher:	www.harcourt.com
Type of Test:	Early childhood/speech and language
Administration Time:	15 to 20 minutes
Type of Administration:	Individual
Ages/Grade Levels:	Ages 3 through 6

Purpose and Description of Test

The CELF Preschool assesses the language skills of preschool children bound for the classroom.

Subtest Information

There are eight subtests:

- Sentence Structure
- Word Structure
- Expressive Vocabulary
- Following Directions
- Recalling Sentences
- Basic Concepts
- Word Classes
- Phonological Awareness

Strengths of the Test

- Specifically designed for preschool-aged children who are bound for the classroom
- Provides a variety of subtests to comprehensively measure language skills needed in an academic-oriented setting
- Includes a preliteracy scale, a phonological awareness subtest, and a pragmatics profile that helps to describe the child's language use at school or at home
- Meets current Individuals with Disabilities Education Improvement Act guidelines

Cognitive Abilities Scale–Second Edition (CAS-2)

General Test Information

Authors:	Sharon Bradley-Johnson and C. Merle Johnson
Publisher:	PRO-ED
Address of Publisher:	8700 Shoal Creek Boulevard, Austin, TX 78757–6897
Telephone Number:	1-800-897-3202
Fax Number:	1-800-397-7633
Web Site of Publisher:	http://www.proedinc.com
Type of Test:	Early childhood/cognitive development
Administration Time:	20 to 30 minutes
Type of Administration	Individual
Ages/Grade Levels:	Infants, toddlers, and preschoolers

Purpose and Description of Test

The CAS-2 provides norm-referenced results useful in identifying children who have delays in cognitive development. It is used with infants, toddlers, and preschoolers who are shy, have unintelligible speech, or are unwilling or unable to vocalize or talk.

Subtest Information

The items on the CAS-2 are divided into three sections:

- Exploration of Objects
- Communication with Others
- Initiation and Imitation

The Preschool Form contains eighty-eight items divided into five sections:

- Oral Language
- Reading
- Math
- Writing
- Enabling Behaviors

Strengths of the Test

- The CAS-2 was normed on 1,106 children from twenty-seven states. Characteristics of the normative group approximate those projected for the year 2000 in the *1997 Statistical Abstract of the United States* (U.S. Census Bureau, 1997) with regard to gender, geographical region, occupation of parents, race, ethnicity, and urban/rural residence.
- The reliability of the CAS-2 was studied extensively, including internal consistency and interscorer reliability.
- Test-retest reliability data are provided for each one-year age interval.
- Content validity is addressed in detail for each item on the test. Concurrent and construct validity are also addressed. Evidence is presented in the manual to show that items contain little or no bias for the groups studied. Predictive validity has been examined over approximately five years for the Preschool Form, showing that results are predictive of later performance on both intelligence and achievement measures.
- One popular facet of the CAS that was retained for the new edition is *Mikey's Favorite Things,* a small black-and-white illustrated book that children read from during the assessment and then take home as a coloring book.

Columbia Mental Maturity Scale (CMMS)

General Test Information

Authors:	Bessie B. Burgemeister, Lucille Hollander Blurn, and Irving Lorge
Publisher:	Harcourt Assessment (formerly known as the Psychological Corporation and Harcourt Educational)
Address of Publisher:	6277 Sea Harbor Drive, Orlando, FL 32887
Telephone Number:	1-800-211-8378
Fax Number:	1-800-232-1223
Web Site of Publisher:	www.harcourt.com
Type of Test:	Early childhood/perceptual test
Administration Time:	15 to 30 minutes
Type of Administration:	Individual
Ages/Grade Levels:	Ages 3–5 to 10–0

Purpose and Description of Test

The CMMS is an individual-type scale that requires perceptual discrimination involving color, shape, size, use, number, kind, missing parts, and symbolic material. Items are printed on ninety-two six- by nineteen-inch cards arranged in a series of eight overlapping levels. The child responds by selecting the picture in each series that is different from or unrelated to the others.

Subtest Information

There are no formal subtests on this scale; rather, it is a ninety-two-item test of general reasoning abilities.

Strengths of the Test

- Most children enjoy taking this test.
- The test can be administered relatively quickly.
- A trained examiner can get quality judgments of the child and his or her method of attacking problems.

DABERON-2 Screen for School Readiness

General Test Information

Authors:	Virginia Danzer, Mary Frances Gerber, and Theresa Lyons, with Judith Voress
Publisher:	PRO-ED
Address of Publisher:	8700 Shoal Creek Boulevard, Austin, TX 78757–6897
Telephone Number:	1-800-897-3202
Fax Number:	1-800-397-7633
Web Site of Publisher:	www.proedinc.com
Type of Test:	School readiness
Administration Time:	20 to 40 minutes
Type of Administration:	Individual
Ages/Grade Levels:	Ages 4 to 6

Purpose and Description of Test

The DABERON-2 provides a standardized assessment of school readiness in children ages 4 to 6, including those with learning or behavior problems who are functioning at the early elementary level. The Learning Readiness Equivalency Age score may be used to identify children at risk for school failure. Knowledge of body parts, color and number concepts, gross motor development, categorization, and other developmental abilities are assessed.

Strengths of the Test

- The text was standardized on a national sample of more than 1,000 children.
- The test can help identify instructional objectives and develop individualized education programs.

DeGangi-Berk Test of Sensory Integration (TSI)

General Test Information

Authors:	Georgia A. DeGangi and Ronald A. Berk
Publisher:	Western Psychological Services
Address of Publisher:	12031 Wilshire Boulevard, Los Angeles, CA 90025–1251
Telephone Number:	1-800-648-8857 (United States and Canada only), 1-310-478-2061
Fax Number:	1-310-478-7838
Web Site of Publisher:	http://www.wpspublish.com
Type of Test:	Early childhood/occupational therapy
Administration Time:	30 minutes
Type of Administration:	Individual
Ages/Grade Levels:	Ages 3 to 5

Purpose and Description of Test

The thirty-six test items require the child to perform specific tasks or respond to various stimuli. It consists of design sheets, protocol booklets, and a manual. Other test materials (for example, a stopwatch, scooter board, and hula hoop) must be supplied by the examiner.

Subtest Information

The test measures the child's ability on three clinically significant subdomains:

- Postural control
- Bilateral motor integration
- Reflex integration

These vestibular-based functions are essential to the development of motor skills, visual-spatial and language abilities, hand dominance, and motor planning.

Strengths of the Test

- The test effectively differentiates normal from developmentally delayed children.
- When used as the basis for screening decisions, the test's total scores demonstrate a high accuracy rate.
- The TSI effectively differentiates normal and developmentally delayed children. When used as the basis for screening decisions, total scores demonstrate an 81 percent accuracy rate, with a false-normal error rate of only 9 percent.

Developmental Activities Screening Inventory–Second Edition (DASI-II)

General Test Information

Authors:	Rebecca Fewell and Mary Beth Langley
Publisher:	PRO-ED
Address of Publisher:	8700 Shoal Creek Boulevard, Austin, TX 78757–6897
Telephone Number:	1-800-897-3202
Fax Number:	1-800-397-7633
Web Site of Publisher:	www.proedinc.com
Type of Test:	Early childhood/developmental
Type of Administration:	Individualized
Ages/Grade Levels:	Birth to age 60 months

Purpose and Description of Test

The DASI-II is a revised edition of the popular Developmental Activities Screening Inventory. It is designed to provide early detection of developmental disabilities in children functioning between the ages of birth and 60 months, although the lowest scorable age is 1 month.

Strengths of the Test

- Developmental skills assessed by DASI-II cover fifteen skills categories, including sensory intactness, means-end relationships, causality, memory, seriation, and reasoning.
- Activities are simply constructed and clearly defined.
- The test provides suggestions for adaptations for administering items to children with visual impairments.

Developmental Assessment of Young Children (DAYC)

General Test Information

Authors: Judith K. Voress and Taddy Maddox
Publisher: PRO-ED
Address of Publisher: 8700 Shoal Creek Boulevard, Austin, TX 78757–6897
Telephone Number: 1-800-897-3202
Fax Number: 1-800-397-7633
Web Site of Publisher: www.proedinc.com
Type of Test: Early childhood
Administration Time: 10 to 20 minutes
Type of Administration: Individual
Ages/Grade Levels: Birth through age 5–11

Purpose and Description of Test

The DAYC is used to identify children birth through age 5–11 with possible delays in the domains of cognition, communication, social-emotional development, physical development, and adaptive behavior. The format allows the examiner to obtain information about a child's abilities through observation, interview of caregivers, and direct assessment. He or she will be able to identify infants and young children who may benefit from early intervention. The DAYC may also be used in arena assessment so that each discipline can use the evaluation tool independently.

Subtest Information

The five subtests can be administered separately or as a comprehensive battery to individual children:

- Cognition
- Communication
- Social-Emotional Development
- Physical Development
- Adaptive Behavior

Strengths of the Test

- The DAYC was normed on a national sample of 1,269 individuals, broken into twenty-three age groups.
- The reliability of the DAYC has been studied, and evidence relating to content-sampling and test-retest time sampling reliability is provided. Reliability coefficients range from .90 to .99. Standard error of measure ranges from 1.5 to 4.74, with the majority smaller than 3.0.
- Reliabilities for children identified as environmentally at risk and biologically at risk are .98 and .99. Compared to Battelle Screening, criterion-referenced validity, construct validity, and content-description validity are provided.

Developmental Observation Checklist System (DOCS)

General Test Information

Authors:	Wayne Hresko, Shirley Miguel, Rita Sherbenou, and Steve Burton
Publisher:	PRO-ED
Address of Publisher:	8700 Shoal Creek Boulevard, Austin, TX 78757–6897
Telephone Number:	1-800-897-3202
Fax Number:	1-800-397-7633
Web Site of Publisher:	www.proedinc.com
Type of Test:	Early childhood
Administration Time:	10 to 15 minutes
Type of Administration:	Individual
Ages/Grade Levels:	Birth to age 6

Purpose and Description of Test

DOCS is a three-part inventory/checklist system for the assessment of young children with respect to general development, adjustment behavior, and parent stress and support.

Subtest Information

The general development component measures the areas of language, motor, social, and cognitive development.

Strengths of the Test

- DOCS was normed on more than 1,400 children from birth to age 6 from more than thirty states. Characteristics of the normative group approximate those for 1990 Census data relative to gender, geographical region, race/ethnicity, and urban/rural residence.
- Internal consistency reliability scores approximate .90 for all ages.
- Family involvement, as mandated by federal law, is addressed by the parent-report nature of the DOCS questionnaire.
- Substantial construct validity, content validity, and criterion-related validity is offered.

Developmental Profile II (DP-II)

General Test Information

Author:	Gerald Alpern, Thomas Boll, and Marsha Shearer
Publisher:	Western Psychological Services
Address of Publisher:	12031 Wilshire Boulevard, Los Angeles, CA 90025–1251
Telephone Number:	1-800-648-8857 (United States and Canada only), 1-310-478-2061
Fax Number:	1-310-478-7838
Web Site of Publisher:	http://www.wpspublish.com
Type of Test:	Early childhood/developmental
Administration Time:	20 to 40 minutes
Type of Administration:	Individual
Ages/Grade Levels:	Infancy through age 9–6 years

Purpose and Description of Test

The DP-II allows examiners to spot advanced or delayed development in any of the five areas covered (see subtest information). The test contains 186 items, each describing a particular skill. These items are typically answered by the parent or a therapist who is familiar with the child. The respondent indicates whether the child has mastered the skill in question.

Subtest Information

The test assesses development in five areas, generating the following scale scores:

- *Physical Age*—Large and small muscle coordination, strength, stamina, flexibility, and sequential motor skills
- *Self-Help Age*—Ability to cope independently with the environment—to eat, dress, work, and take care of self and others
- *Social Age*—Interpersonal abilities, emotional needs, and manner in which the child relates to friends, relatives, and various adults
- *Academic Age*—Intellectual abilities and skills prerequisite to academic achievement, plus an IQ equivalency score
- *Communication Age*—Expressive and receptive communication skills, including written, spoken, and gestural language

Strengths of the Test

- The DP-II allows the examiner to quickly compare a child's development to that of other children who are the same age.
- Using the DP-II, an examiner can do in twenty to forty minutes what in the past has required expensive and time-consuming examinations by a variety of child development specialists.
- Because basals and ceilings are used, the examiner does not have to administer all 186 items.
- Each scale has its own norms; therefore, it is not necessary for the examiner to administer all five scales.

Developmental Tasks for Kindergarten Readiness–
Second Edition (DTKR-II)

General Test Information

Authors:	Walter Lesiak and Judi Lesiak
Publisher:	PRO-ED
Address of Publisher:	8700 Shoal Creek Boulevard, Austin, TX 78757–6897
Telephone Number:	1-800-897-3202
Fax Number:	1-800-397-7633
Web Site of Publisher:	www.proedinc.com
Type of Test:	School readiness
Administration Time:	20 to 30 minutes
Type of Administration:	Individual
Ages/Grade Levels:	Students entering kindergarten

Purpose and Description of Test

The DTKR-II provides objective data on a child's skills and abilities as they relate to successful performance in kindergarten. It can be used for both screening and diagnostic-prescriptive purposes.

Strengths of the Test

- The DTKR-II was normed on 2,521 prekindergarten children (1,273 males and 1,248 females). Reliability was determined using internal consistency, interrater agreement, and test-retest reliability. Test-retest reliability ranges from .82 to .97. The composite score reliability is .93.
- Predictive validity data are available in the manual.
- The result can be used by school personnel to plan remedial instructional programs and to make adjustments in the kindergarten curriculum when a child enters school.

Early Childhood Behavior Scale (ECBS)

General Test Information

Author:	Stephen B. McCarney
Publisher:	Hawthorne Educational Services
Address of Publisher:	800 Gray Oak Drive, Columbia, MO 65201
Telephone Number:	1-800-542-1673
Fax Number:	1-800-442-9509
Web Site of Publisher:	http://www.hes-inc.com
Type of Test:	Early childhood/behavior
Administration Time:	Approximately 15 minutes
Type of Administration:	Individual
Ages/Grade Levels:	Ages 36 through 71 months

Purpose and Description of Test

The ECBS is based on the federal definition of emotional disturbance (Individuals with Disabilities Education Improvement Act) and the most recently approved definition developed by the National Mental Health and Special Education Coalition of ED/BD. The ECBS can be completed in approximately fifteen minutes and contains fifty-three items easily observed and documented by educational personnel.

Subtest Information

The ECBS subscales—Academic Progress, Social Relationships, and Personal Adjustment—were developed using behaviors appropriate for children 36 through 71 months in preschool and kindergarten settings.

Strengths of the Test

- The ECBS provides separate norms for male and female children.
- The Pre-Referral Early Childhood Behavior Checklist provides a means of calling attention to behavior for the purpose of early intervention before formal assessment of the child.
- The Early Childhood Behavior Intervention Manual includes individualized education program goals, objectives, and interventions for all items on the scale.
- The ECBS Quick Score computer program converts raw scores to standard and percentile scores and makes scoring efficient and convenient.

Early Screening Profiles (ESP)

General Test Information

Authors:	Patti Harrison, Alan Kaufman, Nadeen Kaufman, Robert Bruininks, John Rynders, Steven Ilmer, Sara Sparrow, and Domenic Cicchetti
Publisher:	AGS Publishing
Address of Publisher:	4201 Woodland Road, Circle Pines, MN 55014–1796
Telephone Number:	1-800-328-2560, 1-651-287-7220
Fax Number:	1-800-471-8457
Web Site of Publisher:	www.agsnet.com
Type of Test:	Early childhood
Administration Time:	15 to 40 minutes
Type of Administration:	Individual
Ages/Grade Levels:	Ages 2–0 through 6–11

Purpose and Description of Test

ESP is a comprehensive yet brief multidimensional screening instrument for children that uses multiple domains, settings, and sources to measure cognitive, language, motor, self-help, and social development. It also surveys the child's articulation, home environment, health history, and test behavior.

Subtest Information

The ESP contains three profiles:
- The Cognitive/Language Profile is administered individually to the child. Tasks assess reasoning skills, visual organization and discrimination, receptive and expressive vocabulary, and basic school skills. The profile can be separated into cognitive (nonverbal) and language (verbal) subscales, a useful feature for screening children with limited English proficiency, language difficulties, or hearing problems.
- The Motor Profile, also individually administered, assesses gross and fine motor skills, such as walking a straight line, imitating arm and leg movements, tracing mazes, and drawing shapes.
- The Self-Help/Social Profile is a questionnaire completed by the child's parent, teacher, day care provider, or a combination of them. It assesses the child's typical performance in the areas of communication, daily living skills, socialization, and motor skills.

The ESP also contains four surveys:

- The Articulation Survey measures the child's ability to pronounce twenty words selected to test common articulation problems in the initial, medial, and final positions of words.
- The Home Survey is completed by the parent and asks nonintrusive questions about the child's home environment.
- The Health History Survey, also completed by the child's parent, is a brief checklist of any health problems the child has had.
- The Behavior Survey is used by the examiner to rate the child's behavior during administration of the Cognitive/Language and Motor Profiles. The child is rated in categories such as attention span, frustration tolerance, and response style.

Strengths of the Test

- The result is an ecologically valid assessment that provides a wealth of practical information to help make accurate screening decisions and plan intervention strategies for children and their families.
- Professionals and paraprofessionals in educational, medical, or community settings will appreciate ESP's clear directions, simple scoring system, and test items that appeal to the very young. These qualities, coupled with straightforward parent and teacher questionnaires, make ESP efficient and easy to use.
- The three basic components, called *profiles,* are supplemented by four surveys. Examiners can administer all of the profiles and surveys or just the ones needed. For most children, the profiles can be administered in less than thirty minutes. The surveys require an additional fifteen to twenty minutes.
- A national sample of 1,149 children, ages 2–0 through 6–11, was tested. The sample was stratified by sex, geographical region, parent education level, and racial/ethnic group.
- ESP is compatible with instruments that can be used for more detailed follow-up assessment, such as the Kaufman Assessment Battery for Children (K-ABC), Vineland Adaptive Behavior Scales, and Bruininks-Oseretsky Test of Motor Proficiency.
- ESP's three basic components, the profiles, are supplemented by four surveys. For most children, the total time needed for the three profiles is under thirty minutes. The surveys, completed by a parent, teacher, or screening examiner, require an additional fifteen minutes.
- ESP has a number of other strengths:
  - Is an excellent predictor of later development and school achievement.
  - Meets federal guidelines and mandates.
  - Can be administered by paraprofessionals, allowing professionals to focus on children identified as needing more comprehensive assessment.
  - Represents the first nationally standardized screener to provide users with a manual that reports the results of predictive, concurrent, and construct validity studies conducted during the two-year period between standardization and test publication. The manual also includes information regarding internal consistency, immediate and delayed test-retest reliability, and standard error of measurement.
  - Is backed by extensive research. A representative national standardization sample allows appropriate comparisons of children with others the same age in the United States. The scoring system also provides simple determination of local norms.
  - Links directly to many other diagnostic tools, such as the K-ABC, Vineland Adaptive Behavior Scales, and Bruininks-Oseretsky Test of Motor Proficiency.

Infant/Toddler Symptom Checklist:
A Screening Tool for Parents

General Test Information

Authors:	Georgia A. DeGangi, Susan Poisson, Ruth Z. Sickel, and Andrea Santman Wiener; developed by the Reginald S. Lourie Center for Infants and Young Children
Publisher:	Harcourt Assessment (formerly known as the Psychological Corporation and Harcourt Educational)
Address of Publisher:	6277 Sea Harbor Drive, Orlando, FL 32887
Telephone Number:	1-800-211-8378
Fax Number:	1-800-232-1223
Web Site of Publisher:	www.harcourt.com
Type of Test:	Early childhood
Administration Time:	10 minutes
Type of Administration:	Individual
Ages/Grade Levels:	Ages 7 to 30 months

Purpose and Description of Test

The Infant/Toddler Symptom Checklist screens for regulatory and sensory disorders.

Strengths of the Test

- The Infant/Toddler Symptom Checklist can be helpful in the determination of whether a child may have a predisposition toward developing sensory integrative disorders; attention deficits; or emotional, behavioral, or learning difficulties.

Kaufman Developmental Scale (KDS)

General Test Information

Author:	Harvey Kaufman
Publisher:	Stoelting Co.
Address of Publisher:	620 Wheat Lane, Lo Wood Dale, IL 60191
Telephone Number:	1-630-860-9700
Fax Number:	1-630-860-9775
Web Site of Publisher:	http://www.stoeltingco.com
Type of Test:	Early childhood/developmental
Administration Time:	Untimed; approximately 30 minutes
Type of Administration:	Individual
Ages/Grade Levels:	Infant through age 9 and mentally retarded persons at any age

Purpose and Description of Test

The KDS is both an assessment tool and a curricular and programming tool for normal children through age 9 and persons with mental retardation at any age. It consists of 270 behavioral evaluation items representing maturational levels. All items assessed are samples of behaviors that can be taught, thus stressing the use of the KDS in developing teaching objectives.

Subtest Information

The behavioral items are divided into six basic developmental modalities:

- Gross Motor
- Fine Motor
- Receptive
- Expressive
- Personal Behavior
- Receptive Interpersonal Behavior

The modalities are further divided into six developmental stages to allow immediate visual scrutiny of developmental progress:

- Infancy
- Early Childhood
- Play Age
- Receptive Middle Childhood
- Early Adolescence
- Late Adolescence and Beyond

Strengths of the Test

- Evaluation Booklets (not included with complete set) list KDS items by developmental modality and afford an opportunity to evaluate and assess developmental gains through color coding or the empirical method.

Kaufman Infant and Preschool Scale (KIPS)

General Test Information

Author:	Harvey Kaufman
Publisher:	Stoelting Co.
Address of Publisher:	620 Wheat Lane, Lo Wood Dale, IL 60191
Telephone Number:	1-630-860-9700
Fax Number:	1-630-860-9775
Web Site of Publisher:	http://www.stoeltingco.com
Type of Test:	Early childhood
Administration Time:	Untimed; approximately 30 minutes
Type of Administration:	Individual
Ages/Grade Levels:	Ages 1 month to 4 years and individuals with delays

Purpose and Description of Test

The KIPS measures early, high-level cognitive thinking and indicates possible need for intervention. All items are "maturational prototypes," which can be taught to enhance maturation. It is based on the formulation that early high-level cognitive functioning can be assessed and stimulated through tasks devoid of motor or self-help skills.

Strengths of the Test

- Scores provided include an Overall Functioning Age and Quotient. Based on a child's performance on the scale, the manual suggests the types of activities and general experiences a child may need for effective general adaptive behavior.

Kaufman Survey of Early Academic and Language Skills (K-SEALS)

General Test Information

Authors:	Alan S. Kaufman and Nadeen L. Kaufman
Publisher:	AGS Publishing
Address of Publisher:	4201 Woodland Road, Circle Pines, MN 55014–1796
Telephone Number:	1-800-328-2560, 1-651-287-7220
Fax Number:	1-800-471-8457
Web Site of Publisher:	www.agsnet.com
Type of Test:	Early childhood/academic
Administration Time:	15 to 25 minutes
Type of Administration:	Individual
Ages/Grade Levels:	Ages 3–0 to 6–11

Purpose and Description of Test

K-SEALS is used in preschools, kindergartens, elementary schools, speech and language clinics, medical agencies, and other settings in which young children are assessed. It is valuable in a variety of situations: testing school readiness, identifying gifted children, evaluating program effectiveness, and researching children's early development.

Subtest Information

K-SEALS consists of three subtests:

- *Vocabulary Subtest.* The child identifies, by gesture or name, pictures of objects or actions and points to or names objects based on verbal descriptions of their attributes.
- *Numbers, Letters, and Words.* The child selects or names numbers, letters, or words; counts; indicates knowledge of number concepts ("smallest," "half"); and solves number problems.
- *Articulation Survey.* The child pronounces the names of common objects or actions and is assessed for correctness of pronunciation.

Strengths of the Test

- The K-SEALS ensures reliable, valid scores, as well as test-retest stability over long and short intervals.
- High-quality norms and reliability coefficients offer confidence in the scores of young children. Results like these make the K-SEALS a valuable tool for program planning and evaluation.
- K-SEALS is standardized on a national sample of 1,000. The sample was controlled for age, gender, race, geographical region, community size, socioeconomic status, and parent education.

Kindergarten Readiness Test (KRT)

General Test Information

Authors:	Sue Larson and Gary J. Vitali
Publisher:	Slosson Educational Publications
Address of Publisher:	P.O. Box 280, East Aurora, NY 14052
Telephone Number:	1-888-756-7766
Fax Number:	1-800-655-3840
Web Site of Publisher:	www.slosson.com
Type of Test:	School readiness
Administration Time:	15 minutes
Type of Administration:	Individual
Ages/Grade Levels:	Ages 4 to 6

Purpose and Description of Test

The KRT was designed for professionals and parents concerned with whether a child is ready to begin school. The testing needs and concerns of parents, early educators, psychologists, speech/language pathologists, and public school administrators were incorporated into the test rationale. According to its publisher, "The KRT consolidates critical areas of various developmental tests into one single form, thereby making identification of school readiness more efficient and valid." The KRT targets and screens key developmental traits across a broad range of skills necessary to begin school:

- Reasoning
- Language
- Auditory and visual attention
- Numbers
- Fine motor skills
- Other cognitive and sensory-perception areas

Strengths of the Test

- Using state-of-the-art child development theories and test design, the KRT is sensitive to current state and federal laws regulating school readiness.
- Test booklet and additional forms are designed to enhance parent conferences or inter-professional presentations by graphically depicting individual strengths, as well as weaknesses, in a concise manner. The KRT has been used effectively to identify possible handicapping conditions at an early age. Also, it greatly facilitates writing developmental objective programs for teachers or parents.
- Tasks are presented in a sequential developmental-maturational format.
- Appropriate for school, preschool, and clinical settings.
- Comprehensive and user-friendly manual, test booklets, and stimulus materials.
- Thorough reliability and validity section.
- Assesses key areas proven to be critical for school readiness and consolidates information validly on one form.
- Can be reliably administered by specialists, teachers, or paraprofessionals.

McCarthy Scales of Children's Abilities

General Test Information

Author: Dorothea McCarthy

Publisher: Harcourt Assessment (formerly known as the Psychological Corporation and Harcourt Educational)

Address of Publisher: 6277 Sea Harbor Drive, Orlando, FL 32887

Telephone Number: 1-800-211-8378

Fax Number: 1-800-232-1223

Web Site of Publisher: www.harcourt.com

Type of Test: Early childhood/intelligence

Administration Time: 45 to 60 minutes

Type of Administration: Individual

Ages/Grade Levels: Ages 2–4 to 8–7

Purpose and Description of Test

The McCarthy Scales of Children's Abilities assesses cognitive and motor development. The test consists of eighteen tests grouped into six scales: Verbal, Perceptual-Performance, Quantitative, Composite (General Cognitive), Memory, and Motor.

Subtest Information

The test consists of six scales comprising eighteen subtests. Some subtests fall into more than one scale. Listed below are each scale and the corresponding subtests measuring that skill:

- *Verbal Scale.* This scale consists of five subtests:
  - *Pictorial Memory.* The child is required to recall names of objects pictured on cards.
  - *Word Knowledge.* In Part One, the child is required to point to pictures of common objects named by the examiner. In Part Two, the child is required to give oral definitions of words.
  - *Verbal Memory.* In Part One, the child is required to repeat word series and sentences. In Part Two, the child is required to retell a story read by the examiner.
  - *Verbal Fluency.* The child is required to name as many articles as possible in a category within twenty seconds.
  - *Opposite Analogies.* The child is required to complete sentences by providing opposites.
- *Perceptual Performance Scale.* This scale consists of seven subtests:
  - *Block Building.* The child is required to copy block structures built by the examiner.
  - *Puzzle Solving.* The child is required to assemble picture puzzles of common animals or foods.
  - *Tapping Sequence.* The child is required to imitate sequences of notes on a xylophone, as demonstrated by the examiner.
  - *Right–Left Orientation.* The child is required to demonstrate knowledge of right and left.
  - *Draw-a-Design.* The child is required to draw geometrical designs as presented in a model.
  - *Draw-a-Child.* The child is required to draw a picture of a child of the same sex.
  - *Conceptual Grouping.* The child is required to classify blocks on the basis of size, color, and shape.

209

- *Quantitative Scale.* This scale consists of three subtests:
  - *Number Questions.* The child is required to answer orally presented questions involving number information or basic arithmetical computation.
  - *Numerical Memory.* In Part One, the child is required to repeat a series of digits exactly as presented by the examiner. In Part Two, the child is required to repeat a digit series in exact reverse order.
  - *Counting and Sorting.* The child is required to count blocks and sort them into equal groups.
- *Motor Scale.* This scale consists of three subtests:
  - *Leg Coordination.* The child is required to perform motor tasks that involve lower extremities such as walking backward or standing on one foot.
  - *Arm Coordination.* In Part One, the child is required to bounce a ball. In Part Two, the child is required to catch a beanbag, and in Part Three, the child is required to throw a beanbag at a target.
  - *Imitative Action.* The child is required to copy simple movements such as folding hands or looking through a tube.
- *General Cognitive.* This scale consists of eighteen subtests from many of the measures shown previously. (Refer to the four prior scales for a complete explanation of the subtests):

Pictorial Memory	Draw-a-Design
Word Knowledge	Draw-a-Child
Verbal Memory	Conceptual Grouping
Verbal Fluency	Number Questions
Opposite Analogies	Numerical Memory
Block Building	Counting and Sorting
Puzzle Solving	Leg Coordination
Tapping Sequence	Arm Coordination
Right–Left Orientation	Imitative Action

- *Memory.* This scale consists of four subtests (refer to the first four scales for a complete explanation of these subtests):

Pictorial Memory	Verbal Memory
Tapping Sequence	Numerical Memory

Strengths of the Test

- The test's technical manual contains elaborate information about the standardization process, norm tables, and guidelines for administration and interpretation.
- The test creates a framework within which the child being tested can function comfortably.
- Reliability and validity are good determinants of achievement for children in school.
- The manual is well written and easy to read.

Metropolitan Readiness Test–Sixth Edition (MRT-6)

General Test Information

Author:	J. R. Nurss
Publisher:	Harcourt Assessment (formerly known as the Psychological Corporation and Harcourt Educational)
Address of Publisher:	6277 Sea Harbor Drive, Orlando, FL 32887
Telephone Number:	1-800-211-8378
Fax Number:	1-800-232-1223
Web Site of Publisher:	www.harcourt.com
Type of Test:	Early childhood/school readiness
Administration Time:	85 to 100 minutes in four sessions
Type of Administration:	Individual
Ages/Grade Levels:	4 to 7 years; pre-K through grade 1

Purpose and Description of Test

The MRT-6 assesses literacy development in children from preschool to the first grade. It is the oldest and most widely used readiness test. It provides a reliable measure to validate and expand on what teachers know about the children in their classrooms.

Subtest Information

The MRT-6 assesses five areas:

- Visual discrimination
- Beginning consonants
- Sound-letter correspondence
- Story comprehension
- Quantitative concepts and reasoning

Strengths of the Test

- The MRT-6 is a comprehensive and diagnostic tool.
- It includes a conference report that explains the purpose and the results of the MRT-6 in a convenient format for teachers to use when conferring with parents (Venn, 2000).
- The MRT-6 has a colorful easel format that children appear to enjoy.
- The MRT-6 provides excellent standardization.

Mullen Scales of Early Learning

General Test Information

Author:	Eileen M. Mullen
Publisher:	AGS Publishing
Address of Publisher:	4201 Woodland Road, Circle Pines, MN 55014–1796
Telephone Number:	1-800-328-2560, 1-651-287-7220
Fax Number:	1-800-471-8457
Web Site of Publisher:	www.agsnet.com
Type of Test:	Early childhood
Administration Time:	15 minutes (age 1 year); 25 to 35 minutes (age 3 years); 40 to 60 minutes (age 5 years)
Type of Administration:	Individual
Ages/Grade Levels:	Birth to age 68 months

Purpose and Description of Test

The Mullen Scales of Early Learning is a developmentally integrated system that assesses language, motor, and perceptual abilities.

Subtest Information

The test consists of five scales:

- Gross Motor
- Visual Reception
- Fine Motor
- Expressive Language
- Receptive Language

Strengths of the Test

- Excellent standardization and reliability data
- Easy profile analysis
- An array of stimulating manipulatives and materials
- An Item Administration Booklet for administering and scoring items
- Scale scores and an Early Learning Composite
- Identifies a child's strengths and weaknesses
- Assesses early intellectual development and readiness for school
- Provides a foundation for successful interventions
- Produces a baseline for tracking the effectiveness of teaching methods and interactions

Pre-Kindergarten Screen (PKS)

General Test Information

Authors: Raymond E. Webster and Angela Matthews
Publisher: Academic Therapy
Address of Publisher: 20 Commercial Boulevard, Novato, CA 94949
Telephone Number: 1-800-422-7249
Fax of Publisher: 1-888-287-9975
Web Site of Publisher: http://www.academictherapy.com
Type of Test: School readiness
Administration Time: 10 minutes
Type of Administration: Individual
Ages/Grade Levels: Ages 4–0 through 5–11

Purpose and Description of Test

The PKS was developed for use prior to kindergarten entry. It identifies 4- and 5-year-old children who, when compared to their peers, lack the skills needed for later academic success. Among the skills assessed are fine- and gross-motor development, understanding of verbal directions, visual perception and discrimination, rudimentary letter and number identification, and impulse control.

Subtest Information

Areas assessed on the PKS include:

- Fine and gross motor skills
- Visual-spatial skills
- Elementary color and number concepts
- Letter identification
- Impulse control

Strengths of the Test

- According to its publisher, "Pilot studies show that the PKS reliably identified children who, without early intervention, lacked the skills necessary for primary grade success."

Preschool Evaluation Scale (PES)

General Test Information

Authors:	Stephen B. McCarney and Paul Anderson
Publisher:	Hawthorne Educational Services
Address of Publisher:	800 Gray Oak Drive, Columbia, MO 65201
Telephone Number:	1-800-542-1673
Fax Number:	1-800-442-9509
Web Site of Publisher:	http://www.hes-inc.com
Type of Test:	Early childhood/developmental delays
Administration Time:	Untimed
Type of Administration:	Individual
Ages/Grade Levels:	Birth through age 72 months

Purpose and Description of Test

The PES was developed to provide educators, diagnosticians, pediatricians, and psychologists with a measure of child development from birth through 72 months. The PES may be used to contribute to the early identification of students with developmental delays for the purpose of implementing an intervention plan for remediation. It is based on the most commonly recognized domains of child development identified in the federal definition of developmental delays (P.L. 99–457).

Subtest Information

Each subscale is associated with one of the developmental domains:

- Large muscle skills
- Small muscle skills
- Cognitive thinking
- Expressive language skills
- Social/emotional
- Self-help skills

Strengths of the Test

- Internal consistency, test-retest, and interrater reliability; item analysis; and content, criterion-related, diagnostic, and construct validity are documented and reported for the scale.
- The PES is completed by a child care professional in the child's home or while other screening activities are taking place.
- The PES can be completed without requiring additional time on the part of screening or diagnostic personnel.

Preschool Language Assessment Instrument–
Second Edition (PLAI-2)

General Test Information

Authors:	Marion Blank, Susan A. Rose, and Laura J. Berlin
Publisher:	PRO-ED
Address of Publisher:	8700 Shoal Creek Boulevard, Austin, TX 78757–6897
Telephone Number:	1-800-897-3202
Fax Number:	1-800-397-7633
Web Site of Publisher:	www.proedinc.com
Type of Test:	Early childhood/language
Administration Time:	30 minutes
Type of Administration:	Individual
Ages/Grade Levels:	Ages 3–0 to 5–11

Purpose and Description of Test

The PLAI-2 is a revision of a classic test that assesses children's abilities to meet the demand of classroom discourse. It tells how effectively a child integrates cognitive, linguistic, and pragmatic components to deal with the full range of adult-child exchange.

Subtest Information

Of the six subtests, four assess levels of abstraction, and two assess modes of response. These are measured through items requiring:

- *Matching*—the close linking of verbal and perceptual information (for example, "What is this?" or "Find me the . . .")
- *Analysis*—the identification or combining of perceptual components (for example, "How are these different?" "What is happening in this picture?")
- *Reordering*—the reduction or restructuring of salient perceptual cues (for example, "Which one is NOT a . . . ?" "How are these [different objects] the same?")
- *Reasoning*—the prediction of events and the justification of ideas (for example, "What will happen if . . . ?" "How do you know that . . . ?")
- *Receptive Mode*—a nonverbal response
- *Expressive Mode*—a verbal response

Strengths of the Test

- Permits early identification of children with language and communication difficulties that might impede current or later classroom performance
- Serves as a guide for structuring teaching or therapy to match preschoolers' levels of functioning

Preschool Language Scale–Fourth Edition (PLS-4)

General Test Information

Authors:	Irla Lee Zimmerman, Violette G. Steiner, and Roberta Evatt Pond
Publisher:	Harcourt Assessment (formerly known as the Psychological Corporation and Harcourt Educational)
Address of Publisher:	6277 Sea Harbor Drive, Orlando, FL 32887
Telephone Number:	1-800-211-8378
Fax Number:	1-800-232-1223
Web Site of Publisher:	www.harcourt.com
Type of Test:	Early childhood/speech and language
Administration Time:	20 to 45 minutes
Type of Administration:	Individual
Ages/Grade Levels:	Birth through age 6–11

Purpose and Description of Test

The PLS-4 provides an accurate picture of children's receptive and expressive language skills from birth to age 6, appropriate for children with and without disabilities. For children from birth to age 3, the test includes items targeting interaction, attention, and vocal and gestural behaviors to assess language skills.

Subtest Information

The test has two scales:

- *Auditory Comprehension Scale.* The scale requires nonverbal responses such as pointing to a picture that the examiner has named.
- *Expressive Communication Scale.* Items are presented that require the child to name or explain the items. The difficulty varies depending on the child's developmental level at the time of testing.

The items on the test assess the following areas in both the receptive and expressive modes:

Vocabulary	Morphology
Concepts of quality	Syntax
Concepts of quantity	Integrative thinking skills
Space and time	

Strengths of the Test

- This test may be useful to a preschool teacher who wishes to identify a pattern of strengths and weaknesses in a child's conceptual and auditory abilities.
- The test offers a comprehensive assessment of receptive and expressive language in young children.
- The test meets general federal and state guidelines, including the Individuals with Disabilities Education Improvement Act , for evaluating preschoolers for special services.
- The test is a good screening measure for qualification in early intervention programs such as Head Start, Even Start, or Title I programs.
- A separately developed Spanish PLS-4 test, with separate norms, provides an accurate instrument to assess young Spanish speakers.

Screening Kit of Language Development (SKOLD)

General Test Information

Authors:	Lynn S. Bliss and Doris V. Allen
Publisher:	Slosson Educational Publications
Address of Publisher:	P.O. Box 280, East Aurora, NY 14052
Telephone Number:	1-888-756-7766
Fax Number:	1-800-655-3840
Web Site of Publisher:	www.slosson.com
Type of Test:	Early childhood/language
Administration Time:	15 minutes
Type of Administration:	Individual
Ages/Grade Levels:	Ages 2–6 to 4–11 and developmentally delayed older children

Purpose and Description of Test

Designed for early identification of language disorders and delays, the SKOLD may be administered by speech pathologists and preschool specialists.

Subtest Information

The SKOLD assesses preschool language development in six areas:

- Vocabulary
- Comprehension
- Story completion
- Individual and paired sentence repetition with pictures
- Individual sentence repetition without pictures
- Comprehension of commands

Strengths of the Test

- The SKOLD has stimulus materials and scoring guidelines containing 135 illustrations (over 90 in full color).
- The SKOLD facilitates individualized education programs and individual program plans.

Test of Kindergarten/First Grade Readiness Skills (TKFGRS)

General Test Information

Author:	Karen Gardner Codding
Publisher:	Slosson Educational Publications
Address of Publisher:	P.O. Box 280, East Aurora, NY 14052
Telephone Number:	1-888-756-7766
Fax Number:	1-800-655-3840
Web Site of Publisher:	www.slosson.com
Type of Test:	School readiness
Administration Time:	20 minutes
Type of Administration:	Individual
Ages/Grade Levels:	Ages 3–6 to 7–11

Purpose and Description of Test

The TKFGRS is a standardized test to evaluate the child's basic skills in reading: letter, phonetic, and word identification and story comprehension; spelling: letter and word recognition; and arithmetic: number and time identification, written computation, and verbal word problems.

Strengths of the Test

- The test may be given by principals, elementary school teachers, psychologists, counselors, admissions personnel, resource specialists, and other professionals to assess a child's academic readiness for kindergarten or first grade.
- Directions for the examiner as well as for the child are concise and easy to understand. Scoring is simple, with the results given in age equivalents, standard scores, percentiles, and stanines. The test shows strengths and weaknesses in the areas of reading, spelling, and arithmetic.

Vineland Adaptive Behavior Scales–Second Edition (VABS-2)

General Test Information

Authors:	Sara S. Sparrow, Domenic V. Cicchetti, and David A. Balla
Publisher:	AGS Publishing
Address of Publisher:	4201 Woodland Road, Circle Pines, MN 55014–1796
Telephone Number:	1-800-328-2560, 1-651-287-7220
Fax Number:	1-800-471-8457
Web Site of Publisher:	www.agsnet.com
Type of Test:	Early childhood/delays
Administration Time:	Survey interview and parent or other caregiver rating forms: 20 to 60 minutes
Type of Administration:	Individual
Ages/Grade Levels:	Survey Interview Form, Parent/Caregiver Rating Form, and Expanded Interview Form: birth through age 90; Teacher Rating Form: ages 3–0 through 21–11

Purpose and Description of Test

The VABS-2 is used to identify individuals who have mental retardation, developmental delays, brain injuries, or other impairments.

Subtest Information

All VABS-2 forms aid in diagnosing and classifying mental retardation and other disorders, such as autism, Asperger syndrome, and developmental delays. As with the current Vineland, the content and scales of VBAS-2 were organized within a three-domain structure: Communication, Daily Living, and Socialization. This structure corresponds to the three broad domains of adaptive functioning recognized by the American Association of Mental Retardation: Conceptual, Practical, and Social. In addition, VBAS-2 offers the Motor Skills Domain and the optional Maladaptive Behavior Index to provide in-depth information about children.

Strengths of the Test

- Addresses special needs populations, such as individuals with mental retardation, autism spectrum disorder, and attention deficit/hyperactivity disorder
- Updated with new norms, an expanded age range, and improved items
- Useful for diagnosis, qualification for special programs, progress reporting, program and treatment planning, and research
- Semistructured interview format focuses discussion and gathers in-depth information
- More flexibility with four forms:
  - The Survey Interview, which provides a targeted assessment of adaptive behavior. The examiner administers the survey to a parent or caregiver using a semistructured interview format. This approach gathers in-depth information with its open-ended questions and promotes rapport between the interviewer and respondent.
  - The Parent/Caregiver Rating Form, which covers the same content as the Survey Interview but uses a rating scale format. This alternative approach works when time or access is limited.
  - The Expanded Interview, which yields a more comprehensive assessment of adaptive behavior using the semistructured interview format. At the same time, it helps the examiner prepare an educational or treatment program. The Expanded Interview can also serve as a follow-up to obtain more information about deficits suggested by the Survey Interview.
  - The Teacher Rating Form, which assesses adaptive behavior of a student in the classroom. Similar to the previous Vineland Classroom Edition, this form uses a questionnaire format completed by the teacher.

Vulpe Assessment Battery–Revised (VAB-R)

General Test Information

Author:	Shirley German Vulpe; edited by Gary J. Vitali
Publisher:	Slosson Educational Publications
Address of Publisher:	P.O. Box 280, East Aurora, NY 14052
Telephone Number:	1-888-756-7766
Fax Number:	1-800-655-3840
Web Site of Publisher:	www.slosson.com
Type of Test:	Early childhood
Administration Time:	Untimed
Type of Administration:	Individual or group
Ages/Grade Levels:	Most appropriate for developmental ages: birth to age 6

Purpose and Description of Test

The VAB-R is a comprehensive, process-oriented, criterion-referenced assessment that emphasizes children's functional abilities. It is appropriate for children with atypical developmental patterns related to medical or social conditions that affect their developmental potential. The VAB-R provides a systematic interactive method to gather information for early intervention for those who may be at risk of educational failure. It provides an assessment and analysis of several key developmental domains to identify current competencies and develop individualized education or treatment or therapy plans. Each developmental scale can be used individually or collectively to form a battery.

Strengths of the Test

- Independent assessment scales.
- Nondiscriminatory assessment regardless of the child's challenges in biological, psychological, or social behavior.
- Includes a training packet used to establish interrater agreement and reliability.
- Uses familiar toys and equipment from the natural environment.
- Appropriate for educators, therapists, and parents.
- Perfect for multidisciplinary use with young children who have challenges or developmental delays, or known disorders that compromise activities of daily living or school readiness skills. This product was designed for modern realities in terms of caseloads and time restrictions.
- A good tool for Head Start, public or private preschools, and similar programs responsible for children.
- Comprehensive and user-friendly manual.
- Useful, relevant, and current with respect to school-based mandates.

Chapter 15

Intelligence

The question of what constitutes intelligence and how to describe it has challenged educators, psychologists, and thinkers through the years (Gargiulo, 2004). Even today, there is considerable disagreement among professionals as to the meaning of this term and the best way to measure intelligence. There are numerous theories as to what constitutes intelligence, as well as the nature-nurture controversy surrounding its origin. Issues related to the definition of *intelligence* and the fairness of using measures of intelligence also become less of concern if one knows the purpose for which the test is being used. Intelligence tests are most helpful (and probably most appropriate) when they are used to determine specific skills, abilities, and knowledge that the child either has or does not have and when such information is combined with other evaluation data and then directly applied to school programming for that child.

Intellectual assessments are often criticized because of their highly verbal nature and reflection of middle-class Anglo standards. Yet despite the criticisms and concerns about IQ tests, IQ testing does a good job of predicting how well a student does in school—in other words, his or her potential for academic success. Still, educators should not overrely on a single predictor of performance in the classroom. An IQ score should be only one piece of the diagnostic puzzle.

Two major types of intelligence tests are used with children: those administered to individuals and those administered to groups. Individual measures are used when assessing a student for a suspected disability.

The two main individual intelligence tests are the Stanford-Binet Intelligence Test and the Wechsler tests: WPPSI-III for children ages 2 to 7, WISC-IV for children ages 6 to 16, and WAIS-III for adults (over the age of 16).

These individual intelligence tests allow the examiner a one-on-one consultation with the child. The tests have various verbal and nonverbal subtests that can be combined to give a series of cognitive scores, and also valuable separate subtest scores and measures based on the behavioral responses of the child to the test items.

The other type of intelligence test is one that is often used by schools because it can be administered to large groups. Group-administered intelligence tests present a series of different problems and can be used in other mass testing situations such as the military. Examples of group tests are the Multidimensional Aptitude Battery, the Cognitive Abilities Test, and the Scholastic Assessment Tests.

There are a number of skills that an intelligence test appears to measure, including social judgment, level of thinking, language skill, perceptual organization, processing speed, and spatial abilities. In addition, several areas of the individual intelligence test appear to be affected by experience, training, and intact verbal abilities.

According to Taylor (2006), "Individual intelligence testing, until recently, has been a crucial, even mandatory component in the formal assessment process. It is still required to determine eligibility for special education in the vast majority of states" (p. 179).

Beta III

General Test Information

Author:	Written by Harcourt Assessment
Publisher:	Harcourt Assessment (formerly known as the Psychological Corporation and Harcourt Educational)
Address of Publisher:	6277 Sea Harbor Drive, Orlando, FL 32887
Telephone Number:	1-800-211-8378
Fax Number:	1-800-232-1223
Web Site of Publisher:	www.harcourt.com
Type of Test:	Intelligence
Administration Time:	30 minutes
Type of Administration:	Individual
Ages/Grade Levels:	Ages 16 through 89

Purpose and Description of Test

The BETA III is a quick measure of nonverbal intellectual abilities.

Subtest Information

There are five subtests on the BETA III:

- Coding
- Picture Completion
- Clerical Checking
- Picture Absurdities
- Matrix Reasoning (a measure of fluid reasoning that is new to Beta III)

Strengths of the Test

- Extensive reliability and validity studies were conducted with Beta III. The norm sample consisted of 1,260 adults. Validation data were collected using individuals with mental retardation and more than 400 prison inmates.
- The standardization sample was stratified by age, gender, race/ethnicity, educational level, and geographical region according to 1997 Census data.

Comprehensive Test of Nonverbal Intelligence (CTONI)

General Test Information

Authors: Donald D. Hammill, Nils A. Pearson, and Lee Wiederholt
Publisher: PRO-ED
Address of Publisher: 8700 Shoal Creek Boulevard, Austin, TX 78757–6897
Telephone Number: 1-800-897-3202
Fax Number: 1-800-397-7633
Web Site of Publisher: www.proedinc.com
Type of Test: Intelligence
Administration Time: 60 minutes
Type of Administration: Individual
Ages/Grade Levels: Ages 6 to 18

Purpose and Description of Test

The CTONI is a seemingly unbiased test that measures six types of nonverbal reasoning ability. No oral responses, reading, writing, or object manipulation are involved.

Subtest Information

The subtests require students to look at a group of pictures or designs and solve problems involving analogies, categorizations, and sequences. Individuals indicate their answer by pointing to alternative choices. There are six subtests arranged according to the following three abilities:

- *Analogical reasoning.* The two subtests are Pictorial Analogies and Geometric Analogies. They identify the ability to recognize a fourth object that bears the same relation to the third as the second does to the first.
- *Categorical classification.* The two subtests are Pictorial Categories and Geometric Categories. Categorical classification assesses the ability to understand the common attributes by which objects are grouped.
- *Sequential reasoning.* The two subtests are Pictorial Sequences and Geometric Sequences. Sequential reasoning assesses the ability to understand the successive relationship of objects.

Strengths of the Test

- The reliability of the CTONI has been studied extensively, and evidence relating to content sampling, time sampling, and interscorer reliability is provided. The reliability coefficients are all .80 or greater, indicating a high level of test reliability.
- Evidence of content, criterion-related, and construct validity is reported. The CTONI has attempted to detect and eliminate sources of cultural, gender, racial, and linguistic bias.
- The normative sample is representative relative to gender, race, social class, language spoken in the home, and disability.
- Convincing evidence is presented in the manual to show that the CTONI items contain little or no bias for the groups studied.

Das-Naglieri Cognitive Assessment System (CAS)

General Test Information

Authors:	Jack A. Naglieri and J. P. Das
Publisher:	Riverside Publishing
Address of Publisher:	425 Spring Lake Drive, Itasca, IL 60143–2079
Telephone Number:	1-800-323-9540
Fax Number:	1-630-467-7192
Web Site of Publisher:	www.riverpub.com
Type of Test:	Intelligence
Administration Time:	Varies based on administration battery
Type of Administration:	Individual
Ages/Grade Levels:	Ages 5–0 to 17–11

Purpose and Description of Test

The CAS is an assessment battery designed to evaluate cognitive processing. It was developed to integrate theoretical and applied areas of psychological knowledge using a theory of cognitive processing and tests designed to measure those processes. More specifically, the CAS was developed to evaluate planning, attention, simultaneous, and successive cognitive processes of individuals.

Subtest Information

There are thirteen subtests on the CAS, organized as follows:
- Planning
  - *Matching Number.* Find the two that are the same.
  - *Planned Codes.* Fill in symbols matched to letters.
  - *Planned Connections.* Connect a series in sequence.
- Attention
  - *Expressive Attention.* Suppress visual image to verbalize the correct response.
  - *Visual Selective Attention.* Underline numbers that match the stimulus.
  - *Receptive Attention.* Underline pairs that match.
- Simultaneous
  - *Matrices.* Select one of six options that best completes matrix.
  - *Simultaneous Verbal.* Choose the picture (one of six) that answers a verbal question.
  - *Figure Memory.* View a stimulus for five seconds, and find and trace it in the embedded figure.
- Successive
  - *Word Series.* Repeat a string of words in order.
  - *Sentence Repetition.* Repeat sentences that have syntax but reduced meaning.
  - *Sentence Questions.* Answer questions about statements.
  - *Speech Rate.* Repeat a series of words ten times fast.

Strengths of the Test

- Measures planning and attention important for evaluation of attention deficits and brain injuries
- Predicts achievement and provides an ability-achievement discrepancy procedure
- Facilitates the identification of attention deficit-hyperactivity disorders, traumatic brain injury, learning disabilities, mental retardation, and giftedness

Differential Ability Scales (DAS)

General Test Information

Author:	Colin D. Elliott
Publisher:	Harcourt Assessment (formerly known as the Psychological Corporation and Harcourt Educational)
Address of Publisher:	6277 Sea Harbor Drive, Orlando, FL 32887
Telephone Number:	1-800-211-8378
Fax Number:	1-800-232-1223
Web Site of Publisher:	www.harcourt.com
Type of Test:	Intelligence
Administration Time:	Full cognitive battery: 45 to 65 minutes; achievement tests: 15 to 25 minutes
Type of Administration:	Individual
Ages/Grade Levels:	Preschool Level: ages 2–6 through 5–11; School Age Level: ages 6–0 to 17–11

Purpose and Description of Test

The DAS yields overall cognitive ability and achievement scores and provides a reliable measure of specific abilities. It assesses the multidimensional nature of abilities in children and adolescents.

Subtest Information

DAS comprises seventeen cognitive and three achievement subtests. Achievement subtests are Basic Number Skills, Spelling, and Word Reading. In addition to obtaining a General Conceptual Ability score for a child, the examiner can obtain cluster scores, including Verbal and Nonverbal Ability for the Preschool subtests and Verbal, Nonverbal Reasoning, and Spatial Ability for the School Age subtests. For language-impaired and non-English-speaking children, a special nonverbal composite may be obtained. The examiner can also assess distinct, interpretable abilities with subtests and items appropriate for a child's age and ability level. Harder or easier sets of items can be administered to children expected to be of unusually high or low ability.

Strengths of the Test

- The DAS norm sample contained 3,475 children, stratified by age, sex, race/ethnicity, parent education, geographical region, and educational preschool enrollment.
- The sample included exceptional children such as those with learning disabilities, speech and language impairments, educable mental retardation, gifted performance, or emotional disturbance and those with mild visual, hearing, or motor impairment. Up-to-date methods of bias analysis were applied to the performance of large samples of African American and Hispanic children to identify and eliminate biased items.
- All subtests for younger children start with items easy enough to measure low ability. Subtests within both the Preschool and School Age batteries were also normed on the adjoining age years (most Preschool subtests through age 7 and School Age subtests down to age 5). Thus, average- to below-average-ability 6- and 7-year-old children may take the Preschool subtests, and average to above-average 5-year-old children may take the School Age subtests. The battery also offers out-of-level testing for older children of low ability and younger children of high ability.

Draw-A-Person Intellectual Ability Test for Children, Adolescents, and Adults (DAP:IQ)

General Test Information

Authors:	Cecil R. Reynolds and Julie Hickman
Publisher:	PRO-ED
Address of Publisher:	8700 Shoal Creek Boulevard, Austin, TX 78757–6897
Telephone Number:	1-800-897-3202
Fax Number:	1-800-397-7633
Web Site of Publisher:	www.proedinc.com
Type of Test:	Intelligence
Administration Time:	10 to 12 minutes
Type of Administration:	Individual or group
Ages/Grade Levels:	Ages 4–0 to 89–11

Purpose and Description of Test

The DAP:IQ provides a common set of scoring criteria to estimate intellectual ability from a human figure drawing.

Strengths of the Test

- Standardized instructions for the task are easy to derive.
- Drawings are collected in a rapid, efficient manner.
- Few people are hesitant to do the drawing once they are assured that their artistic ability is not being evaluated.
- Drawings can be obtained in even the most challenging of clinical situations, such as the assessment of autistic or severely hyperactive children or nonreading or non-English-speaking clients.
- Scoring criteria have less cultural specificity than most other intelligence tests, verbal or nonverbal (culture reduced).
- The only materials needed to give and score the DAP:IQ are the test manual, the Administration/Scoring Form, and a sharpened pencil.

Goodenough-Harris Drawing Test

General Test Information

Authors:	Florence L. Goodenough and Dale B. Harris
Publisher:	Harcourt Assessment (formerly known as the Psychological Corporation and Harcourt Educational)
Address of Publisher:	6277 Sea Harbor Drive, Orlando, FL 32887
Telephone Number:	1-800-211-8378
Fax Number:	1-800-232-1223
Web Site of Publisher:	www.harcourt.com
Type of Test:	Intelligence
Administration Time:	Untimed; approximately 10 to 15 minutes
Type of Administration:	Individual or group
Ages/Grade Levels:	Ages 3 through 15

Purpose and Description of Test

The Goodenough-Harris Drawing Test is a nonverbal assessment of mental maturity. It includes Harris's restandardization of the Goodenough Draw-a-Man Test, a standardization of a similar Draw-a-Woman Scale, and an experimental Self-Drawing Scale.

Subtest Information

The Goodenough-Harris Drawing Test is composed of two scales: Draw a Man and Draw a Woman. Performance may be scored by a short, holistic method with Quality Scale Cards or by a more detailed method. Each drawing may also be scored for the presence of up to seventy-three characteristics.

Strengths of the Test

- The test's reliability is relatively high.
- The test manual provides a clear description of the scoring system. The record form is clear and efficient.
- The test is psychometrically sound, as well as easily and objectively quantified.
- It is a popular test because of its ease in administration.

Kaufman Assessment Battery for Children–Second Edition (KABC-II)

General Test Information

Authors:	Alan S. Kaufman and Nadeen L. Kaufman
Publisher:	AGS Publishing
Address of Publisher:	4201 Woodland Road, Circle Pines, MN 55014–1796
Telephone Number:	1-800-328-2560, 1-651-287-7220
Fax Number:	1-800-471-8457
Web Site of Publisher:	www.agsnet.com
Type of Test:	Intelligence
Administration Time:	25 to 55 minutes (core battery, Luria model); 35 to 70 minutes (core battery, Cattell-Horn-Carroll model)
Type of Administration:	Individual
Ages/Grade Levels:	Ages 3 to 18

Purpose and Description of Test

This individually administered intelligence test was developed in an effort to minimize the influence of language and acquired facts and skills on the measurement of a child's intellectual ability.

Subtest Information

The intelligence test contains ten subtests:

- *Face Recognition.* This test requires the child to choose from a group photo the one or two faces that were exposed briefly.
- *Gestalt Closure.* This test requires the child to name an object or scene from a partially constructed inkblot.
- *Hand Movements.* The child is required to perform a series of hand movements presented by the examiner.
- *Magic Windows.* This test requires the child to identify a picture that the examiner exposes slowly through a window; only a small part is shown.
- *Matrix Analogies.* This test requires the child to choose a meaningful picture or abstract design that best completes a visual analogy.
- *Number Recall.* The child is required to repeat a series of digits in the same sequence as presented by the examiner.
- *Photo Series.* This test requires the child to place photographs of an event in the proper order.
- *Spatial Memory.* This test requires the child to recall the placement of a picture on a page that was briefly exposed.
- *Triangles.* This test requires the child to assemble several identical triangles into an abstract pattern.
- *Word Order.* The child is required to touch a series of silhouettes of objects in the same order as presented verbally by the examiner.

Strengths of the Test

- The new, optional Knowledge/Crystallized Ability scale means that one test can be used with all children.
- An expanded age range allows using one test for preschool, elementary, and high school children.
- There is full co-norming with the new Kaufman Test of Educational Achievement–Second Edition, for in-depth ability and achievement comparisons.
- Extensively redesigned and updated, this test provides detailed, accurate information with much flexibility. Like the original KABC, the second edition more fairly assesses children of different backgrounds and with diverse problems, with small score differences between ethnic groups.
- Subtests are designed to minimize verbal instructions and responses. This gives in-depth data with less filtering due to language.
- The examiner can choose the Cattell-Horn-Carroll model for children from a mainstream cultural and language background. Or if Crystallized Ability would not be a fair indicator of the child's cognitive ability, the examiner may choose the Luria model, which excludes verbal ability. The same subtests can be administered on four or five ability scales with the results interpreted based on the chosen model. Either approach gives a global score that is highly valid and shows small differences among ethnic groups in comparison with other comprehensive ability batteries. In addition, a nonverbal option allows assessing a child whose verbal skills are significantly limited.

Kaufman Adolescent and Adult Intelligence Test (KAIT)

General Test Information

Authors:	Alan S. Kaufman and Nadeen L. Kaufman
Publisher:	AGS Publishing
Address of Publisher:	4201 Woodland Road, Circle Pines, MN 55014–1796
Telephone Number:	1-800-328-2560, 1-651-287-7220
Fax Number:	1-800-471-8457
Web Site of Publisher:	www.agsnet.com
Type of Test:	Intelligence
Administration Time:	Core Battery, 60 minutes; Expanded Battery, 90 minutes
Type of Administration:	Individual
Ages/Grade Levels:	Ages 11 through 85+

Purpose and Description of Test

The KAIT is a multisubtest battery that covers the age range from 11 years to 85+ and is based on the Cattell-Horn model of fluid/crystallized intelligence.

Subtest Information

The Core Battery can be used as part of a psychoeducational evaluation or a neuropsychological, vocational, or clinical battery. It has two scales:

- Crystallized Scale
  - *Auditory Comprehension:* Listening to a recording of (or examiner reading aloud) a news story and then answering literal and inferential questions about the story
  - *Double Meanings:* Studying two sets of word clues and then thinking of a word with two different meanings that fits both sets of clues
  - *Definitions:* Integrating two types of clues—a word with some of its letters missing and an oral clue about the word's meaning—to identify the word
- Fluid Scale
  - *Rebus Learning:* Learning the word or concept that is represented by a rebus (that is, a picture that stands for a word), and then "reading" phrases and sentences composed of these rebuses
  - *Mystery Codes:* Cracking a code that is used to identify a set of pictures and then applying this code to a new set of pictures
  - *Logical Steps:* Attending to logical premises presented both visually and orally and then using these to solve a problem

The examiner can add one or more of four additional subtests to the Core Battery to administer the Expanded Battery. These subtests permit comparison of immediate versus delayed memory. The Expanded Battery is especially useful for clinical and neuropsychological assessment. These subtests include:

- *Memory for Block Designs:* Studying a printed design that is briefly exposed and then constructing the design using six cubes and a form board (also serves as an alternate subtest for the Core Battery Fluid Scale)
- *Famous Faces:* Naming people of current or historical fame based on their photographs and a verbal clue (also serves as an alternate subtest for the Core Battery Crystallized Scale)

- *Rebus Recall:* "Reading" phrases and sentences composed of rebuses that were learned earlier during the administration of Rebus Learning
- *Auditory Recall:* Answering literal and inferential questions about news stories that were heard during the administration of Auditory Comprehension

Strengths of the Test

- Internal Consistency Reliability
  - Core Battery Subtests: .87 to .93
  - Expanded Battery Subtests: .71 to .92
  - Crystallized Scale: .95
  - Fluid Scale: .95
  - Composite Intelligence: .97
- Test-Retest Reliability
  - Core Battery Subtests: .72 to .95
  - Expanded Battery Subtests: .63 to .84
  - Crystallized Scale: .94
  - Fluid Scale: .87
  - Composite Intelligence: .94
- The two-factor structure (Crystallized and Fluid) is based on exploratory and confirmatory factor analyses described in the manual. Joint factor analyses with the Wechsler Adult Intelligence Scale-R and Wechsler Intelligence Scale for Children-R ($N = 461$) indicate that the KAIT Crystallized and Wechsler Verbal scales are similar ($r = .81$) but the KAIT Fluid and Wechsler Performance scales represent distinct factors ($r = .70$). The KAIT Composite IQ correlates highly with the Wechsler FSIQ (.84) and the Stanford-Binet (4th edition) Composite (.87).

Kaufman Brief Intelligence Test–Second Edition (KBIT-2)

General Test Information

Authors:	Alan S. Kaufman and Nadeen L. Kaufman
Publisher:	AGS Publishing
Address of Publisher:	4201 Woodland Road, Circle Pines, MN 55014–1796
Telephone Number:	1-800-328-2560, 1-651-287-7220
Fax Number:	1-800-471-8457
Web Site of Publisher:	www.agsnet.com
Type of Test:	Intelligence
Administration Time:	Approximately 20 minutes
Type of Administration:	Individual
Ages/Grade Levels:	Ages 4 through 90

Purpose and Description of Test

The KBIT-2 is a brief, individually administered screener of verbal and nonverbal ability. Like its predecessor, KBIT-2 can be used in a variety of situations. Examiners can:

- Obtain a quick estimate of intelligence
- Estimate an individual's verbal versus nonverbal intelligence
- Reevaluate the intellectual status of a child or adult who previously received thorough cognitive assessment
- Screen to identify students who may benefit from enrichment or gifted programs
- Identify high-risk children

Subtest Information

KBIT-2 measures two distinct cognitive abilities through two scales: Crystallized and Fluid:

- The Crystallized (Verbal) Scale contains two item types: Verbal Knowledge and Riddles.
- The Fluid (Nonverbal) Scale is a matrices subtest.

Strengths of the Test

- Features the new Crystallized (Verbal) Scale
- Measures verbal and nonverbal intelligence quickly
- Is easy to administer and score
- Useful for a variety of purposes
- Provides valid and reliable results

Matrix Analogies Test–Expanded Form (MAT-Expanded Form)

General Test Information

Author:	Jack A. Naglieri
Publisher:	Harcourt Assessment (formerly known as the Psychological Corporation and Harcourt Educational)
Address of Publisher:	6277 Sea Harbor Drive, Orlando, FL 32887
Telephone Number:	1-800-211-8378
Fax Number:	1-800-232-1223
Web Site of Publisher:	www.harcourt.com
Type of Test:	Intelligence
Administration Time:	20 to 25 minutes
Type of Administration:	Individual
Ages/Grade Levels:	Ages 5 through 17

Purpose and Description of Test

The MAT-Expanded Form assesses nonverbal reasoning abilities with an in-depth measure. It can help to assess children and young adults with special needs and abilities, or can be used as part of a comprehensive testing battery. Directions are brief and can be communicated non-verbally if necessary.

Strengths of the Test

- The MAT-Expanded Form is especially appropriate for assessing the abilities of children with learning disabilities, mental retardation, hearing or language impairments, physical disabilities, ability to speak in more than one language, and ability to perform at the gifted level. The colors (blue, yellow, black, and white) used in the stimulus materials reduce the influence of impaired color vision. The matrix design of the stimulus items requires minimal verbal comprehension and no verbal response.
- Norms are based on a large, representative sample of individuals ages 5 to 17 years living in the United States.
- Items are organized into four groups determined by factor analysis prior to standardization: Pattern Completion, Reasoning by Analogy, Serial Reasoning, and Spatial Visualization.

Pictorial Test of Intelligence–Second Edition (PTI-2)

General Test Information

Author: Joseph L. French
Publisher: PRO-ED
Address of Publisher: 8700 Shoal Creek Boulevard, Austin, TX 78757–6897
Telephone Number: 1-800-897-3202
Fax Number: 1-800-397-7633
Web Site of Publisher: www.proedinc.com
Type of Test: Standardized
Administration Time: 15 to 30 minutes
Type of Administration: Individual
Ages/Grade Levels: Ages 3 to 8

Purpose and Description of Test

The PTI-2, a revision of the Pictorial Test of Intelligence (French, 1964), is a test of general intelligence for both normal and disabled children.

Subtest Information

There are three subtest areas on the PTI-2:

- *Verbal Abstractions*—requires the examinee to identify pictures that (1) represent the meaning of a spoken word, (2) represent the meaning of a spoken definition of a word, and (3) are different in form or function from a set of pictures
- *Form Discrimination*—requires the examinee to match forms, differentiate among similar shapes, identify unfinished pictures, find embedded shapes, and reason about abstract shapes and patterns
- *Quantitative Concepts*—samples an examinee's recognition of size, comprehension of number symbols, ability to count, and ability to solve simple arithmetic problems

Strengths of the Test

- Standardized on 972 persons from seventeen states, the data are representative of the current population of the United States as reported in the *1997 Statistical Abstract of the United States* (U.S. Census Bureau, 1997) for the entire school-age population.
- Coefficient alphas for Verbal Abstractions, Form Discrimination, Quantitative Concepts, and Pictorial Intelligence Quotient are .89, .88, .88, and .94, respectively. Evidence of validity of the PTI-2 test scores is proven for content-description validity, criterion-prediction validity, and construct-identification validity.
- The PTI-2 items were developed to be fair with diverse groups. The items were examined to ensure that little or no bias relative to gender, race, or ethnicity exists. Differential item functioning techniques were used to examine items for potential bias. The PTI-2 is especially helpful when used with children who have difficulty with fine motor skills or a speech/language problem. The test has been normed so that it can be used with children with cortical disorders or other conditions affecting speech or motor coordination. Respondents do not need to use expressive language, but they do need near-normal vision and hearing. No items are timed.

Porteus Maze

General Test Information

Author:	Stanley D. Porteus
Publisher:	Harcourt Assessment (formerly known as the Psychological Corporation and Harcourt Educational)
Address of Publisher:	6277 Sea Harbor Drive, Orlando, FL 32887
Telephone Number:	1-800-211-8378
Fax Number:	1-800-232-1223
Web Site of Publisher:	www.harcourt.com
Type of Test:	Intelligence
Administration Time:	Untimed
Type of Administration:	Individual
Ages/Grade Levels:	3 years through adult

Purpose and Description of Test

The Porteus Maze series is a brief, nonverbal test of mental ability that yields information useful in assessing a person's ability to plan and change problem-solving approaches.

Strengths of the Test

- This cognitive measure has a variety of applications, including programs for those who are verbally impaired, anthropological research, and studies of the effects of drugs and neurosurgery.
- The series is based on extensive research with various populations and is relatively culture free.

Reynolds Intellectual Screening Test (RIST)

General Test Information

Authors:	Cecil R. Reynolds and Randy Kamphaus
Publisher:	PRO-ED
Address of Publisher:	8700 Shoal Creek Boulevard, Austin, TX 78757–6897
Telephone Number:	1-800-897-3202
Fax Number:	1-800-397-7633
Web Site of Publisher:	www.proedinc.com
Type of Test:	Intelligence
Administration Time:	10 to 12 minutes
Type of Administration:	Individual
Ages/Grade Levels:	Ages 3 to 94

Purpose and Description of Test

Derived from the Reynolds Intellectual Assessment Scales (RIAS), this brief screening measure helps identify individuals who need a more comprehensive intellectual assessment or to document the continuing presence of intellectual deficits. The RIST serves as a quick screener at reevaluation or follow-up when a full intellectual assessment may not be warranted.

Subtest Information

The RIST consists of two RIAS subtests: Guess What (a verbal subtest) and Odd-Item Out (a nonverbal subtest). Both have good psychometric properties and good factor-analytic and criterion-related validity evidence, and both are efficiently administered and scored. The examiner presents the two RIST subtests to the client, beginning with the age-based subtest item, and then records the response on the RIST Record Form. Item administration continues until the end rule criterion for each subtest is met.

Strengths of the Test

- The RIST was administered to 507 individuals representing fifteen clinical groups. Individuals diagnosed with mental retardation or dementia had mean RIST Index scores in the mid-70s, well below the normal population mean. Thus, the RIST can effectively differentiate between individuals with and without intellectual impairment.
- For the RIST Index, the median reliability coefficient is .95, and test-retest reliability is .84. The RIST Index is highly correlated with the Wechsler Intelligence Scale for Children-III and the Wechsler Individual Achievement Test.
- Evidence supports the RIST as an appropriate screening instrument for intelligence.

Slosson Full-Range Intelligence Test (S-FRIT)

General Test Information

Authors:	Bob Algozzine, Ronald C. Eaves, Lester Mann, and H. Robert Vance
Publisher:	Slosson Educational Publications
Address of Publisher:	P.O. Box 280, East Aurora, NY 14052
Telephone Number:	1-888-756-7766
Fax Number:	1-800-655-3840
Web Site of Publisher:	www.slosson.com
Type of Test:	Intelligence
Administration Time:	25 to 45 minutes
Type of Administration:	Individual
Ages/Grade Levels:	Ages 5 through adult

Purpose and Description of Test

The S-FRIT is a reliable, individual screen that gives a balanced measure of verbal/perform-ance/memory cognitive assessments. It differentially screens nonverbal from verbal abilities even when language skills are limited. It is intended to supplement the use of more extensive cognitive assessment instruments, such as the Wechsler Intelligence Scale for Children-III, Kaufman Assessment Battery for Children, and the Stanford-Binet Intelligence Scale–IV, to facilitate screening in charting cognitive progress. The test can be given by regular or special education teachers, psychologists, counselors, or other personnel who have taken basic courses in statistics tests or measurements.

Subtest Information

There are no subtests on the S-FRIT; however, when testing is completed, the examiner quickly gets a picture of the individual's mental abilities in the following areas:

- Verbal skills
- Quantitative
- Recall memory
- Abstract performance
- Reasoning

The Brief Score Form has a unique color coding system that tabulates standard scores in sec-onds. It also separates the index items and the Full-Range Intelligence Quotient. The examiner can test for the Best Global Index using specific questions that correlate highest with the S-FRIT total score. The Rapid Cognitive Index may be given using only half of the test items to deter-mine verbal, abstract, quantitative, or memory subdomains in approximately fifteen minutes.

Strengths of the Test

- The S-FRIT was standardized on a representative sample of 1,500 individuals across thirty-seven states. Internal consistency reliability for median values ranges from .96 to .98, the mean is 100, and the standard deviation is 16.
- The standard error of measurement at age 10 is 2.77. The criterion validity studies indicate a correlation between the Full Scale WISC-R IQ and the Full Range S-FRIT IQ to be .89.
- The S-FRIT Computer Report produces a two-page report printing the standard scores, percentiles, *t*-scores, Best *g* Index, Rapid Cognitive Index, and subdomain scores. In addition, the S-FRIT CR compares the S-FRIT total standard score with any achieve-ment test having standard scores using the achievement-ability discrepancy procedure.

Slosson Intelligence Test–Primary (SIT-P)

General Test Information

Authors:	Bradley T. Erford, Gary J. Vitali, and Steven W. Slosson
Publisher:	Slosson Educational Publications
Address of Publisher:	P.O. Box 280, East Aurora, NY 14052
Telephone Number:	1-888-756-7766
Fax Number:	1-800-655-3840
Web Site of Publisher:	www.slosson.com
Type of Test:	Intelligence
Administration Time:	10 to 25 minutes (shorter time for younger children)
Type of Administration:	Individual
Ages/Grade Levels:	Ages 2–0 to 7–11

Purpose and Description of Test

The SIT-P is a new, brief, standardized screening test of children's intelligence. It is not just a lower extension of the Slosson Intelligence Test and Slosson Intelligence Test–Revised, but includes both verbal and performance items to give a balanced measure of a child's cognitive ability. It was designed to facilitate the screening identification of children at risk of educational failure, provide a quick estimate of mental ability, and identify children who may be appropriate candidates for deeper testing services. The SIT-P can be easily administered by professionals and paraprofessionals with appropriate training and supervision. Appropriate settings include schools, clinics, and organizations whose interests include estimating an individual's cognitive ability.

Subtest Information

There are no subtests on the SIT-P; however, a wide range of verbal/perceptual speed/block design/visual-motor/performance items yields two scaled Verbal and Performance standard scores that combined form a total standard score, to quickly give the administrator an overall picture of a young person's cognitive abilities.

Strengths of the Test

- The SIT-P was standardized on a sample of 825 children and anchored to the Stanford-Binet Intelligence Scale–Fourth Edition. Reliabilities are excellent (.90+ for full scale scores), and validity comparisons with other intelligence tests such as the Wechsler Intelligence Scale for Children-III, the Stanford-Binet Intelligence Scale–Fourth Edition, and the Slosson Intelligence Test–Revised warrant the use of the SIT-P as a quick, reliable measure of intelligence for children with a mean of 100 and a standard deviation of 15.
- Scoring is simple: one point is awarded for each acceptable response. There are two separate scoring forms: Lower Level (ages 2–0 to 3–11) and Upper Level (ages 4–0 to 7–11). Block design and motor abilities are integrated within nonverbal/performance items (90 items), with the perceptual motor speed being the target vehicle for the point of entry.
- Test forms are user friendly, and stimulus materials are appropriate for children from diverse environments. The complete kit contains a comprehensive manual, including test items with directions for scoring, norms tables, and technical information; a picture book with twenty-five plates; eight one-inch blocks with patterns; and two sets of scoring forms and response booklets, one for ages 2–0 to 3–11 and the other for ages 4–0 to 7–11, which include the perceptual motor speed and visual-motor integration items.

Slosson Intelligence Test–Revised (SIT-R3)

General Test Information

Authors:	Richard L. Slosson; revised by Charles L. Nicholson and Terry L. Hibpshman
Publisher:	Slosson Educational Publications
Address of Publisher:	P.O. Box 280, East Aurora, NY 14052
Telephone Number:	1-888-756-7766
Fax Number:	1-800-655-3840
Web Site of Publisher:	www.slosson.com
Type of Test:	Intelligence
Administration Time:	10 to 20 minutes
Type of Administration:	Individual
Ages/Grade Levels:	Ages 4 to 65

Purpose and Description of Test

This newly revised edition remains a quick and reliable individual screening test of crystallized verbal intelligence. It is a multidimensional assessment tool that can be used for general education testing populations and also for most special testing populations. It is designed for use by teachers, psychologists, guidance counselors, special educators, learning disability instructors, and others who need to evaluate an individual's mental ability.

Subtest Information

Although there are no subtests on the SIT-R3, the cognitive areas of measurement assessed are:

- Vocabulary (thirty-three items)
- General information (twenty-nine items)
- Similarities and differences (thirty items)
- Comprehension (thirty-three items)
- Quantitative (thirty-four items)
- Auditory memory (twenty-eight items)

Strengths of the Test

- The SIT-R3 has been especially constructed so any professional who has taken an introductory course in tests and measurements can easily administer this quick screening instrument.
- The SIT-R3 correlated .827 with the Wechsler Intelligence Scale for Children (WISC-R), Verbal VIQ, even though the SIT-R3 does not cover Fluid performance. The calibrated norms reflect a high .828 correlation between the SIT-R3 TSS and the WISC-III Full Scale Intelligence Quotient. The 1998 calibrated norms were formulated to keep the mean of the SIT-R3 at 100, SD = 16, with a total standard score range of 36 through 165.
- The calibrated norms tables divide the chronological age every three months, which is a refinement over earlier norms tables and reestablishes the age 18+ ceiling level, applicable for adults through age 65. The SIT-R3 is appropriate for Title Fund programs.
- The test has been nationally restandardized and developed with the American Psychological Association criteria in mind. Multiple statistical procedures were used to ensure no significant gender or racial bias. Every item on the test was reevaluated using classical item analysis to choose good statistical items and new differential item functioning analysis to find and eliminate biased items.

- The SIT-R3 Computer Report aids educators in determining expected achievement and finding levels of ability or weakness. It scores and prints an individual three-page report using the TSS and computes the Severe Discrepancy Level to determine learning disabilities under federal guidelines.
- The SIT-R3 is appropriate for the United States and other English-speaking countries. Quantitative reasoning questions were designed to be administered to populations that use metric or standard references, using language common to both.

Stanford-Binet Intelligence Scales–Fifth Edition (SB5)

General Test Information

Author:	Gaile Roid
Publisher:	Riverside Publishing
Address of Publisher:	425 Spring Lake Drive, Itasca, IL 60143–2079
Telephone Number:	1-800-323-9540
Fax Number:	1-630-467-7192
Web Site of Publisher:	www.riverpub.com
Type of Test:	Intelligence
Administration Time:	45 to 60 minutes
Type of Administration:	Individual
Ages/Grade Levels:	Ages 2 to 90+

Purpose and Description of Test

The SB5 is an individually administered assessment of intelligence and cognitive abilities.

Subtest Information

The SB5 consists of five factors covering ten domains (subtests):

- Fluid Reasoning
  - Nonverbal Fluid Reasoning
  - Verbal Fluid Reasoning
- Knowledge
  - Nonverbal Knowledge
  - Verbal Knowledge
- Quantitative Reasoning
  - Nonverbal Quantitative Reasoning
  - Verbal Quantitative Reasoning
- Visual-Spatial Processing
  - Nonverbal Visual-Spatial Processing
  - Verbal Visual-Spatial Processing
- Working Memory
  - Nonverbal Working Memory
  - Verbal Working Memory

After the individual completes both Routing Tests, the examiner administers all nonverbal subtests, followed by all verbal subtests.

Strengths of the Test

- A wide variety of items requiring nonverbal performance by examinees; ideal for assessing individuals with limited English, deafness, or communication disorders
- Comprehensive measurement of five factors—Fluid Reasoning, Knowledge, Quantitative Reasoning, Visual-Spatial Processing, and Working Memory—providing a broad assessment of individual intelligence
- Ability to compare verbal and nonverbal performance, which is useful in evaluating learning disabilities
- Greater diagnostic and clinical relevance of tasks, such as verbal and nonverbal assessment of working memory

- Includes Full Scale IQ, Verbal and Nonverbal IQ, and Composite Indices spanning five dimensions with a standard score mean of 100 and a standard deviation of 15
- Includes subtest scores with a mean of 10 and a standard deviation of 3
- Extensive high-end items, many adapted from previous Stanford-Binet editions and designed to measure the highest level of gifted performance
- Improved low-end items for better measurement of young children, low-functioning older children, and adults with mental retardation
- Enhanced memory tasks provide a comprehensive assessment for adults and the elderly
- Co-normed with measures of visual-motor perception and test-taking behavior
- Scorable by hand or with computer software
- Enhanced artwork and manipulatives that are colorful and child friendly
- Helps identify special needs
- In addition to the concurrent validity studies, numerous studies of individuals with special needs or areas of disability have been conducted in order to best reflect the changes in the Individuals with Disabilities Education Improvement Act and use multiple criteria for identifying children in need of special services. Substantial efforts have been taken to ensure the SB5 will help identify and adequately describe individuals who fall into the following categories:
  - Learning disabilities
  - Gifted and talented
  - Mental retardation
  - Attention deficit-hyperactivity disorder
  - Speech and language delays
  - Traumatic brain injury
  - Autism

Swanson Cognitive Processing Test (S-CPT)

General Test Information

Author:	H. Lee Swanson
Publisher:	PRO-ED
Address of Publisher:	8700 Shoal Creek Boulevard, Austin, TX 78757–6897
Telephone Number:	1-800-897-3202
Fax Number:	1-800-397-7633
Web Site of Publisher:	www.proedinc.com
Type of Test:	Intelligence
Administration Time:	2 hours
Type of Administration:	Individual
Ages/Grade Levels:	Ages 5 to adult

Purpose and Description of Test

The S-CPT measures different aspects of intellectual abilities and information processing potential.

Subtest Information

The S-CPT has eleven subtests. This test battery can be administered in an abbreviated form (five subtests) or in a complete form under traditional or interactive testing conditions.

Strengths of the Test

- The test was individually administered to 1,611 children and adults (ages 4–5 to 78–6) in ten U.S. states and two Canadian provinces. The sample closely matches the 1990 U.S. Census figures for ethnicity, gender, region, and community size. The total coefficient alpha score (sum of scores across subtests for initial gain and maintenance) for the SCPT is highly reliable (r = .989). The results on composite and component scores indicate that the majority of scores range from .82 to .95, with 64 percent (16 of 25) of the reliabilities at .90 or greater.
- High construct and criterion-related validity coefficients are reported.

Test of Nonverbal Intelligence–Third Edition (TONI-3)

General Test Information

Authors:	L. Brown, R. J. Serbenou, and S. K. Johnsen
Publisher:	PRO-ED
Address of Publisher:	8700 Shoal Creek Boulevard, Austin, TX 78757–6897
Telephone Number:	1-800-897-3202
Fax Number:	1-800-397-7633
Web Site of Publisher:	www.proedinc.com
Type of Test:	Intelligence
Administration Time:	15 to 20 minutes
Type of Administration:	Individual
Ages/Grade Levels:	Ages 5 to 89–11

Purpose and Description of Test

The TONI-3 is designed to measure the nonverbal intelligence of students who are bilingual, speak a language other than English, or are socially or economically disadvantaged, deaf, language disordered, motor impaired, or neurologically impaired. The test requires no reading, writing, speaking, or listening on the part of the test subject. It is completely nonverbal and largely motor free, requiring only a point, nod, or other symbolic gesture to indicate response choices.

Subtest Information

There are no subtests on the TONI-3. Each form of the TONI-3 contains fifty items arranged from easy to difficult.

Strengths of the Test

- This language-free format makes the TONI-3 ideal for evaluating subjects who have previously been difficult to test with any degree of confidence or precision. It is particularly well suited for individuals who are known or believed to have disorders of communication or thinking, such as aphasia, dyslexia, language disabilities, learning disabilities, speech problems, specific academic deficits, and similar conditions, that may be the result of mental retardation, deafness, developmental disabilities, autism, cerebral palsy, stroke, disease, head injury, or other neurological impairment. The format also accommodates the needs of subjects who do not read or write English well due to disability or lack of exposure to the English language and U.S. culture.
- Meets the highest psychometric standards for norms, reliability, and validity.
- Is language free, requiring no reading, writing, or listening.
- Is culturally reduced, using novel abstract and figural content.
- Is motor reduced, with only a meaningful gesture required in response.
- Is quick to score, requiring less than fifteen minutes to administer and score.
- Is appropriate for use with children, adolescents, and older adults ages 6 through 89.
- Has two equivalent forms suitable for test-retest and pre- and posttesting situations.
- Provides detailed directions for administering, scoring, and interpreting the test in the manual.
- Has a twenty-year body of reliability.

Wechsler Preschool Primary Scales of Intelligence-III (WPPSI-III); Wechsler Intelligence Scale for Children-IV (WISC-IV); Wechsler Adult Intelligence Scale-III (WAIS-III)

General Test Information

Author:	David Wechsler
Publisher:	Harcourt Assessment (formerly known as the Psychological Corporation and Harcourt Educational)
Address of Publisher:	6277 Sea Harbor Drive, Orlando, FL 32887
Telephone Number:	1-800-211-8378
Fax Number:	1-800-232-1223
Web Site of Publisher:	www.harcourt.com
Type of Test:	Intelligence
Administration Time:	60 to 75 minutes
Type of Administration:	Individual
Ages/Grade Levels:	The three tests are designed for ages 4 to adult. The age ranges for the three Wechsler tests are: WPPSI-III: ages 4–0 to 6–11; WISC-III: ages 6–0 to 16–11; WAIS-III: ages 17–0 and older

Purpose and Description of Test

The test comprises two areas of assessment: Verbal and Performance. The verbal areas are considered auditory/vocal tasks (auditory input and vocal output), and the performance areas are visual/vocal and visual/motor tasks (visual input and vocal or motoric output).

Subtest Information

The three Wechsler Scales consist of twenty-one possible subtests. Unless otherwise noted, all subtests are contained in each scale:

- *Animal House*—Measures the ability to associate meaning with symbol, visual-motor dexterity, flexibility, and speed in learning tasks (part of the WPPSI-III only).
- *Arithmetic*—Measures mental alertness, concentration, attention, arithmetic reasoning, reaction to time pressure, and practical knowledge of computational facts. This is the only subtest directly related to the school curriculum and is greatly affected by anxiety.
- *Block Design*—Measures ability to perceive, analyze, synthesize, and reproduce abstract forms; visual-motor coordination; spatial relationships; general ability to plan and organize.
- *Cancellation*—Measures processing speed using random and structured animal target forms (foils are common nonanimal objects). This subtest is part of the WISC-IV only.
- *Coding*—Measures the ability to associate meaning with symbols, visual-motor dexterity (pencil manipulation), flexibility, and speed in learning tasks (part of the WISC-IV only).
- *Comprehension*—Measures social judgment, commonsense reasoning based on experience, and practical intelligence.
- *Digit Span*—Measures attention, concentration, immediate auditory memory, auditory attention, and behavior in a learning situation. This subtest correlates poorly with general intelligence.
- *Digit Symbol*—Measures the ability to associate meaning with symbol, visual-motor dexterity (pencil manipulation), flexibility, and speed in learning tasks (part of the WAIS-III only).

- *Geometric Design*—Measures a child's pencil control and visual-motor coordination, speed and accuracy, and planning capability (part of the WPPSI-III only).
- *Information*—Measures general information acquired from experience and education, remote verbal memory, understanding, and associative thinking. The socioeconomic background and reading ability of the student may influence the subtest score.
- *Letter-Number Sequencing*—Measures working memory (adapted from WAIS–III). The child is presented a mixed series of numbers and letters and repeats the numbers first (in numerical order) and then the letters (in alphabetical order). This subtest is part of the WISC-IV only.
- *Matrix Reasoning*—Measures fluid reasoning a (highly reliable subtest on WAIS–III and WPPSI–III). The child is presented with a partially filled grid and asked to select the item that properly completes the matrix.
- *Mazes*—Measures the ability to formulate and execute a visual-motor plan, pencil control and visual-motor coordination, speed and accuracy, and planning capability (part of the WPPSI-III and WISC-IV only).
- *Object Assembly*—Measures immediate perception of a total configuration, part–whole relationships, and visual-motor-spatial coordination (part of the WAIS-III only).
- *Picture Arrangement*—Measures visual perception, logical sequencing of events, attention to detail, and ability to see cause–effect relationships (part of the WISC-III and WAIS-III only).
- *Picture Completion*—Measures visual alertness to surroundings, remote visual memory, attention to detail, and ability to isolate essential from nonessential detail.
- *Picture Concepts*—Measures fluid reasoning, perceptual organization, and categorization (requires categorical reasoning without a verbal response). From each of two or three rows of objects, the child selects objects that go together based on an underlying concept (part of the WISC-IV only).
- *Sentences*—Measures attention, concentration, immediate auditory memory, auditory attention, and behavior in a learning situation (part of the WPPSI-III only).
- *Similarities*—Measures abstract and concrete reasoning, logical thought processes, associative thinking, and remote memory.
- *Symbol Search*—Measures visual discrimination (part of the WISC-III only).
- *Vocabulary*—Measures a child's understanding of spoken words, learning ability, general range of ideas, verbal information acquired from experience and education, and kind and quality of expressive language. This subtest is relatively unaffected by emotional disturbance but is highly susceptible to cultural background and level of education. It is also the best single measure of intelligence in the entire battery.
- *Word Reasoning*—Measures reasoning with verbal material; the child identifies the underlying concept given successive clues (part of the WISC-IV only).

In order to make interpretation more clinically meaningful, the dual IQ and index structure from WISC–III has been replaced with a single system of four composite scores (consistent with the Four Index Scores in WISC–III) and the Full Scale IQ. This new system helps the examiner better understand a child's needs in relation to contemporary theory and research in cognitive information processing. In the following list of the indexes, an asterisk means that the subtest is not included in the index total score:

- Verbal Comprehension Index
  - Similarities
  - Vocabulary
  - Comprehension

- *Information
- *Word Reasoning
- Perceptual Reasoning Index
  - Block Design
  - Picture Concepts
  - Matrix Reasoning
  - *Picture Completion
- Working Memory Index
  - Digit Span
  - Letter-Number Sequencing
  - *Arithmetic
- Processing Speed Index
  - Coding
  - Symbol Search
  - *Cancellation

Strengths of the Test

- This is the fourth generation of the most widely used children's intellectual ability assessment. While maintaining the integrity of the Wechsler tradition, the WISC–IV builds on contemporary approaches in cognitive psychology and intellectual assessment to provide a new, powerful, and efficient tool to help develop and support clinical judgments.
- Understanding of learning disabilities and attentional disorders has greatly expanded since the publication of the WISC–III.
- The WISC–IV's modern artwork is colorful and engaging and incorporates recent changes in clothing, technology, and demographics. Instructions to both the examiner and the child are improved to make the WISC–IV more user friendly.
- The WISC–IV is designed to meet several goals:
  - Expand and strengthen clinical utility to support decision making
  - Develop the four Index Scores as the primary interpretive structure
  - Improve the assessment of fluid reasoning, working memory, and processing speed
  - Improve subtest reliabilities, floors, and ceilings from WISC–III
  - Link to the Wechsler Individual Achievement Test–Second Edition and to measures of memory (Children's Memory Scale), adaptive behavior (Adaptive Behavior Assessment System), emotional intelligence (BarOn EQ), and giftedness (Gifted Rating Scale)

Chapter 16

Learning Disabilities

The definition for a specific learning disability cited in the 2004 Individuals with Disabilities Education Improvement Act (IDEA) is (C.F.R. Section 300.8):

A disorder in one or more of the basic psychological processes involved in understanding or in using language, spoken or written, which may manifest itself in an imperfect ability to listen, think, speak, read, write, spell, or do mathematical calculations. Such term includes conditions such as perceptual disabilities, brain injury, minimal brain dysfunction, dyslexia, and developmental aphasia. Such term does not include a learning problem that is primarily the result of visual, hearing, or motor disabilities; of mental retardation; of emotional disturbance; or of environmental, cultural or economic disadvantage.

Under IDEA 2004, when determining whether a child has a specific disability, a local education agency shall not be required to take into consideration whether a child has a severe discrepancy between achievement and intellectual ability (C.F.R. Section 300.307).

Learning disabilities (LD) vary from person to person. One person with LD may not have the same kind of learning problems as another person with LD. One may have trouble with reading and writing, another with understanding math, and another in each of these areas, as well as with understanding what people are saying.

Researchers think that learning disabilities are caused by differences in how a person's brain works and how it processes information. Children with learning disabilities usually have average or above-average intelligence. Their brains just process information differently (National Dissemination Center for Children with Disabilities, 2004e).

Interestingly, there is no clear and widely accepted definition of *learning disabilities*. Because of the multidisciplinary nature of the field, there is ongoing debate on the issue of definition, and there are currently at least twelve definitions that appear in the professional literature. There are several technical definitions offered by various health and education sources. Overall, most experts agree that (cited in Pierangelo & Giuliani, 2006b):

- Individuals with learning disabilities have difficulties with academic achievement and progress.
- Discrepancies exist between a person's potential for learning and what he or she actually learns.
- Individuals with learning disabilities show an uneven pattern of development (language development, physical development, academic development, or perceptual development).
- Learning problems are not due to environmental disadvantage.
- Learning problems are not due to mental retardation or emotional disturbance.
- Learning disabilities can affect one's ability to read, write, speak, spell, compute math, and reason and also affect a person's attention, memory, coordination, social skills, and emotional maturity.
- Individuals with learning disabilities have normal intelligence, and sometimes even giftedness.
- Individuals with learning disabilities have differing capabilities, with difficulties in certain academic areas but not in others.
- Learning disabilities affect either input (the brain's ability to process incoming information) or output (the person's ability to use information in practical skills, such as reading, math, and spelling).

As many as one in every five people in the United States has a learning disability. Almost 3 million children (ages 6 through 21) have some form of a learning disability and receive special education services in school. In fact, over half of all children who receive special education have a learning disability (U.S. Department of Education, 2002).

According to the Child Development Institute (2005) children with learning disabilities exhibit a wide range of symptoms (previously mentioned). Learning disabilities typically affect five general areas:

- *Spoken language:* delays, disorders, and deviations in listening and speaking
- *Written language:* difficulties with reading, writing, and spelling
- *Arithmetic:* difficulty in performing arithmetic operations or in understanding basic concepts
- *Reasoning:* difficulty in organizing and integrating thoughts
- *Memory:* difficulty in remembering information and instructions

If a child has unexpected problems learning to read, write, listen, speak, or do math, teachers and parents may want to investigate. The same is true if the child is struggling to do any one of these skills. The child may need to be evaluated to see if he or she has a learning disability (National Dissemination Center for Children with Disabilities, 2004a).

A learning disability usually has a history that can be traced to a child's early years in school. Many schools use kindergarten screening programs to identify high-risk children. It is normally at this stage that some signs of a potential problem may be noticed. As the child progresses through school and the work demands increase, the symptoms of a possible learning disability may become more apparent. Once these symptoms are recognized, the child is usually referred to the child study team, a local school-based team, to determine whether a suspected disability exists. If the study team suspects that the student has a disability, a referral is made to the multidisciplinary team for a comprehensive assessment. This assessment will cover many areas, including reading, writing, spelling, math, and perceptual, cognitive, psychological and social skills. Other areas of information will be gathered as well from the classroom teacher, parent, and the student.

If the comprehensive assessment indicates the presence of a learning disability, the child will receive special education services and supports. In most cases these services and supports can be maintained in the regular education setting through resource room, inclusion, or special education classes.

Analytic Learning Disability Assessment (ALDA)

General Test Information

Authors:	Thomas D. Gnagey and Patricia A. Gnagey
Publisher:	Slosson Educational Publications
Address of Publisher:	P.O. Box 280, East Aurora, NY 14052
Telephone Number:	1-888-756-7766
Fax Number:	1-800-655-3840
Web Site of Publisher:	www.slosson.com
Type of Test:	Assessment of Learning Disabilities
Administration Time:	75 minutes
Type of Administration:	Individual
Ages/Grade Levels:	Kindergarten to high school (most reliable for ages 8 to 14)

Purpose and Description of Test

The ALDA was designed specifically to match the student's unique learning style with the most effective method of learning. It tests the seventy-seven skills that underlie the basic school subjects. Each subtest taps a discrete learning process called a unit skill. Each neuropsychological unit skill is a small, practically functional skill unit of brain processing, such as sound blending and visual figure-ground discrimination.

Subtest Information

The ALDA analyzes reading, spelling, math computation, and handwriting into the several diverse ways that, according to recent neuropsychological research, a student's brain seems to be able to go about learning each. It matches the strengths and weaknesses of the student's underlying skills with that student's most appropriate learning method for each school subject: eleven reading methods, twenty-three spelling methods, six math computation methods, and eight handwriting methods. The learning methods are ranked in order, with the most effective and efficient being numbered one and the higher numbers being the most time-consuming.

Strengths of the Test

- The results are quickly transformed onto the accompanying multipage Recommendation Pamphlet, creating an individualized teaching plan providing specific procedures and methods for the students. The beginning section of the pamphlet is devoted to how the student can function best in the general classroom no matter what the activity or subject. It proceeds to the specific recommendations for each subject area. Often these recommendations fit into established classroom procedures. The special education teacher can take the results of each subtest and know where to begin remedial work, as well as have an indication of just how strong or weak each skill is at that time.

Dyslexia Early Screening Test–Second Edition (DEST-2)

General Test Information

Authors:	Rod Nicolson and Angela Fawcett
Publisher:	Harcourt Assessment (formerly known as the Psychological Corporation and Harcourt Educational)
Address of Publisher:	6277 Sea Harbor Drive, Orlando, FL 32887
Telephone Number:	1-800-211-8378
Fax Number:	1-800-232-1223
Web Site of Publisher:	www.harcourt.com
Type of Test:	Assessment of learning disabilities
Administration Time:	30 minutes
Type of Administration:	Individual
Ages/Grade Levels:	Ages 4–6 to 6–5

Purpose and Description of Test

The DEST-2 profiles strengths and weaknesses often associated with dyslexia.

Subtest Information

The ten diagnostic subtests cover the range of skills known to be affected in dyslexia:

- *Rapid Naming*—Measures the time it takes to name a page full of outline drawings
- *Bead Threading*—Assesses hand and eye coordination
- *Phonological Discrimination*—Assesses the ability to hear the sounds in words
- *Postural Stability*—Provides an accurate index of balance ability
- *Rhyme Detection*—Assesses the ability to tell whether words rhyme and to determine the first letter sound
- *Digit Span-Forward*—Provides an index of a child's working memory
- *Digit Naming*—Checks whether the child is able to name the digits from 1 to 9
- *Letter Naming*—Determines if a child can name lowercase letters
- *Sound Order*—Determines if a child can discriminate the order of two sounds presented close together
- *Shape Copying*—Assesses the quality of pencil control when copying simple shapes

Strengths of the Test

- The battery contains screening tests of attainment and ability. These determine whether a young child is experiencing difficulty in areas known to be affected in dyslexia. An at-risk score for dyslexia determines whether further in-depth testing should be undertaken. A profile of skills provides valuable information that can be used to guide in-school support.

Dyslexia Screening Instrument

General Test Information

Authors:	Kathryn B. Coon, Mary Jo Polk, and Melissa McCoy Waguespack
Publisher:	Harcourt Assessment (formerly known as the Psychological Corporation and Harcourt Educational)
Address of Publisher:	6277 Sea Harbor Drive, Orlando, FL 32887
Telephone Number:	1-800-211-8378
Fax Number:	1-800-232-1223
Web Site of Publisher:	www.harcourt.com
Type of Test:	Assessment of Learning Disabilities
Administration Time:	20 minutes
Type of Administration:	Individual
Ages/Grade Levels:	Grades 1 through 12; ages 6 through 21

Purpose and Description of Test

The Dyslexia Screening Instrument helps identify students at risk for dyslexia. Designed for clients who have reading, spelling, writing, or language processing problems, it consists of thirty-three statements to be rated by the classroom teacher using a five-point scale.

Strengths of the Test

- Practical and efficient, this instrument measures a cluster of characteristics associated with dyslexia and discriminates between those who have the cluster and those who do not.
- The Dyslexia Screening Instrument helps meet the requirements of Section 504 of the Rehabilitation Act of 1973, the Individuals with Disabilities Education Improvement Act, and state guidelines.
- Rating scores are entered into the scoring program software, and within two minutes the examiner obtains a pass, fail, or inconclusive classification.

Learning Disabilities Diagnostic Inventory (LDDI)

General Test Information

Authors:	Don Hammill and Brian Bryant
Publisher:	PRO-ED
Address of Publisher:	8700 Shoal Creek Boulevard, Austin, TX 78757–6897
Telephone Number:	1-800-897-3202
Fax Number:	1-800-397-7633
Web Site of Publisher:	www.proedinc.com
Type of Test:	Assessment of learning disabilities
Administration Time:	10 to 20 minutes
Type of Administration:	Individual
Ages/Grade Levels:	Ages 8–0 to 17–11

Purpose and Description of Test

The LDDI is a rating scale designed to identify intrinsic processing disorders and learning disabilities in students. It was designed for the single purpose of helping professionals identify learning disabilities in individuals. It is not an ability or achievement measure; it will not tell how well or how poorly students read, write, speak, and so forth. Instead, it will identify the extent to which students' skill patterns in a particular area are consistent with individuals known to have a learning disability in that area (for example, dyslexia, dysgraphia). Thus, using the LDDI shifts the diagnostic emphasis away from interpreting norm-referenced ability test scores and toward studying an individual's skill patterns, especially patterns that are indicative of people who are known to have specific learning disabilities.

Subtest Information

The LDDI is composed of six independent scales, one for each of the areas listed in the definition by the U.S. Office of Education and the National Joint Committee on Learning Disabilities:

- Listening
- Speaking
- Reading
- Writing
- Mathematics
- Reasoning

Strengths of the Test

- The LDDI was built with the American Psychological Association's standards for technical adequacy clearly in mind. The test was normed on 2,152 students with learning disabilities residing in forty-three states and the District of Columbia. The demographic characteristics of the normative sample are representative of the population of students who have learning disabilities in the United States as a whole with regard to gender, race, ethnicity, urban/rural residence, family income, educational attainment of parents, and geographical distribution. The sample characteristics were stratified by age and keyed to the demographic characteristics reported in the *1996 Statistical Abstract of the United States* (U.S. Census Bureau, 1996).

- The LDDI was built to minimize the effects of bias. Numerous steps were taken to detect and eliminate sources of cultural, gender, and racial bias. First, the effects of bias were controlled and minimized through the inclusion of minority groups in the normative sample. Second, the examination of reliability and validity information was presented for the different racial, ethnic, and gender groups. A particularly powerful element of content-description validity is the demonstration of excellent internal consistency reliability for the different racial, ethnic, and gender groups. Finally, the use of differential item functioning analysis was used to reduce item bias during item selection. Delta score values were used to remove items that appeared to be biased against targeted groups.
- Internal consistency reliability coefficients exceed .90 for all scales. In addition, evidence for stability and interscorer reliability is provided, and coefficients are in the .80s and .90s. Thus, the LDDI can be used with confidence to yield consistent results.
- Numerous validity studies were conducted to ensure that the LDDI scores have content-description, criterion-prediction, and construct-identification validity. These studies involved extensive item selection and differentiation examinations, which included confirmatory factor analysis, as well as studies that examined the LDDI's relationship to age, academic achievement, group differentiation, gender, and ethnicity, all of which support the validity of the LDDI scores. Factor analysis research also validated the LDDI's factor structure. These studies provide evidence that the LDDI yields valid results that can be used with confidence to identify the presence or absence of learning disabilities in children and adolescents.

Learning Disability Evaluation Scale (LDES)

General Test Information

Author:	Stephen B. McCarney
Publisher:	Hawthorne Educational Services
Address of Publisher:	800 Gray Oak Drive, Columbia, MO 65201
Telephone Number:	1-800-542-1673
Fax Number:	1-800-442-9509
Web Site of Publisher:	http://www.hes-inc.com
Type of Test:	Assessment of learning disabilities
Administration Time:	Approximately 20 minutes
Type of Administration:	Individual
Ages/Grade Levels:	Grades K to 12

Purpose and Description of Test

The LDES is based on the federal definition of learning disabilities in the Individuals with Disabilities Education Improvement Act. It can be completed by instructional personnel and contains eighty-eight items representing the most commonly identified characteristics of children with learning disabilities.

Subtest Information

The LDES was factor-analyzed to create the seven factor clusters (subscales):

- Listening
- Thinking
- Speaking
- Reading
- Writing
- Spelling
- Mathematical Calculations

Strengths of the Test

- The LDES was standardized on 6,160 students, including students identified with learning disabilities. The standardization sample included students from twenty-six states and seventy-one school districts and represented all geographical regions of the United States.
- The LDES provides separate norms for male and female K–1 students.
- The Pre-Referral Learning Problem Checklist provides a means of calling attention to the behavior for the purpose of early intervention before formal assessment of the student.
- The Learning Disability Intervention Manual contains goals and objectives for the student's individualized education program, as well as a complete set of interventions and instructional strategies for the specific learning problems identified by the LDES.
- The Parent's Guide to Learning Disabilities was written for parents to help their child with learning disabilities experience more success at home and at school.
- The LDES Quick Score computer program converts raw scores to standard and percentile scores and makes the scoring of the rating form efficient and convenient.

Slingerland Screening Tests for Identifying Children with Specific Language Disability

General Test Information

Author:	Beth H. Slingerland
Publisher:	Educators Publishing Service
Address of Publisher:	P.O. Box 9031, Cambridge, MA 02139–9031
Telephone Number:	1-800-435-7728
Fax Number:	1-888-440-2665
Web Site of Publisher:	www.epsbooks.com
Type of Test:	Assessment of learning disabilities
Administration Time:	Forms A, B, and C: 60 to 80 minutes; Form D: 110 to 130 minutes
Type of Administration:	Individual
Ages/Grade Levels:	Grades 1 to 6

Purpose and Description of Test

The Slingerland screens elementary school children for indications of specific language disabilities in reading, spelling, handwriting, and speaking. This is not a test of language but rather a test of auditory, visual, and motor skills related to specific academic areas. It is a multiple-item verbally presented paper-and-pencil examination containing eight subtests.

Subtest Information

Each subtest focuses on curriculum-related skills:

- *Far Point Copying.* This subtest requires the student to copy a printed paragraph from far points to probe visual perception and graphomotor responses. It assesses visual-motor skills related to handwriting.
- *Near Point Copying.* This subtest requires the student to copy a printed paragraph from near points in order to probe visual perception and graphomotor responses. It assesses visual-motor skills related to handwriting.
- *Visual Perception Memory.* This subtest requires the student to recall and match printed words, letters, and numbers presented in brief exposure with a delay before responding. It assesses visual memory skills related to reading and spelling.
- *Visual Discrimination.* This subtest requires the student's immediate matching of printed words and eliminates the memory component of visual perception memory. It assesses basic visual discrimination without memory or written response.
- *Visual Kinesthetic Memory.* This subtest requires the student's delayed copying of words, phrases, letters, designs, and number groups presented with brief exposure. It assesses the combination of visual memory and written response, which is necessary for written spelling.
- *Auditory Kinesthetic Memory.* This subtest requires the student to write groups of letters, numbers, and words to dictation after a brief delay with distraction. It combines auditory perception and memory with written response.
- *Initial and Final Sounds.* This subtest requires the student to write the initial phoneme and later to write the final phoneme of groups of spoken words. It assesses auditory discrimination and sequencing related to basic phonics with a written response.
- *Auditory/Visual Integration.* This subtest requires the student's delayed matching of spoken words, letters, or number groups. It assesses visual discrimination related to word recognition.

There are four forms of this test (Forms A, B, C, and D). Some of the forms contain subtests other than those already mentioned:

- *Following Directions.* This subtest requires the student to provide a written response from a series of directions given by the examiner. It assesses auditory memory and attention with a written response.
- *Echolalia.* This subtest requires the student to listen to a word or phrase given by the examiner and to repeat it four or five times. This is an individual auditory test that assesses auditory kinesthetic confusion related to pronunciation.
- *Word Finding.* This subtest requires the child to fill in a missing word from a sentence read by the examiner. This is an individual auditory test that assesses comprehension and the ability to produce a specific word on demand.
- *Storytelling.* This subtest requires the child to retell a story previously read by the examiner. This is an individual auditory test that assesses auditory memory and verbal expression of content material.

Strengths of the Test

- This is a useful test for screening for academic problems.
- The test uses skills related to classroom tasks.
- This is one of the few tests designed for disability screening for treatment purposes.
- The test has the power to predict reading problems.

Structure of Intellect Learning Abilities Test (SOI-LA)

General Test Information

Authors:	Mary Meeker and Robert Meeker
Publisher:	Slosson Educational Publications
Address of Publisher:	P.O. Box 280, East Aurora, NY 14052
Telephone Number:	1-888-756-7766
Fax Number:	1-800-655-3840
Web Site of Publisher:	www.slosson.com
Type of Test:	Assessment of learning disabilities
Administration Time:	2.5 hours
Type of Administration:	Individual or group
Ages/Grade Levels:	Grades 2 to 12 and ages to adult

Purpose and Description of Test

The SOI-LA is used to diagnose learning disabilities, prescribe educational interventions, profile strengths and weaknesses, identify reasons for underachievement, match cognitive style and curriculum materials, and screen for gifted students.

Strengths of the Test

- The SOI-LA is available in two alternate forms, which are ideal for pre- and posttesting. The Divergent Production subtests are particularly useful in assessing creative thinking. The SOI-LA profile shows at a glance which abilities are poorly developed and which are strong and serve as the basis for further intellectual growth.

Chapter 17

Mathematics

Mathematical thinking is a process that begins early in most children. Even before formal education, children are exposed to situations that involve the application of mathematical concepts. As they enter formal schooling, they take the knowledge of what they previously learned and begin to apply it in a more formal manner (Pierangelo & Giuliani, 2006a).

Although most people use the terms *mathematics* and *arithmetic* interchangeably, the two are not the same. *Mathematics* refers to the study of numbers and their relationships to time, space, volume, and geometry. *Arithmetic* refers to the operations or computations performed.

Mathematics involves many different abilities—for example:

- Solving problems
- Recognizing how to interpret results
- Applying mathematics in practical situations
- Using mathematics for prediction
- Estimation
- Performing computational skills
- Understanding measurement
- Creating and reading graphs and charts

All schools, regular education and special education, use some form of mathematical assessment. Schools begin the process of teaching math skills in kindergarten and proceed throughout the child's formal education. Even at the college level, mathematics is often a core requirement. In general, next to reading, mathematics is probably the area most frequently assessed in school systems (Pierangelo & Giuliani, 2006a).

Mathematics can be assessed at the individual or group level. Consequently it is a skill that is stressed and measured by various tests in schools. Mathematics tests often cover a great deal of areas. However, according to Salvia and Ysseldyke (2004), there are three types of classifications involved in diagnostic math tests, each measuring certain mathematical abilities:

Content—consists of numeration, fractions, geometry, and algebra
Operations—consists of counting, computation, and reasoning
Applications—consists of measurement, reading graphs and tables, money and budgeting time, and problem solving

Furthermore, according to the National Council of Supervisors of Mathematics (1978), basic mathematical skills include:

- Arithmetic computation
- Problem solving
- Applying mathematics in everyday situations
- Alertness to the reasonableness of results
- Estimation and approximation
- Geometry
- Measurement
- Reading charts and graphs
- Using mathematics to predict
- Computer literacy

There are fewer diagnostic math tests than diagnostic reading tests. However, math assessment is more clear-cut. Most diagnostic math tests generally sample similar behaviors.

❖ Analysis and Interpretation of Math Skills

According to McLoughlin and Lewis (1994), mathematics is one of the school subjects best suited for error analysis because students respond in writing on most tasks, thereby producing a permanent record of their work. Also, there is usually only one correct answer to mathematics questions and problems, and scoring is unambiguous. Today, the most common use of error analysis in mathematics is assessment of computation skills. Cox (1975) differentiates between systematic computation errors and errors that are random or careless mistakes. With systematic errors, students are consistent in their use of an incorrect number fact, operation, or algorithm.

McLoughlin and Lewis (1990, cited in Pierangelo & Giuliani, 2006a) identified four error types in computational analysis:

- *Incorrect operation.* The student selects the incorrect operation. For example, if the problem requires subtraction, the student adds.
- *Incorrect number fact.* The number fact recalled by the student is inaccurate. For example, the student recalls the product of 9×6 as 52.
- *Incorrect algorithm.* The procedures that the student uses to solve the problem are inappropriate. The student may skip a step, apply the correct steps in the wrong sequence, or use an inaccurate method
- *Random error.* The student's response is incorrect and apparently random. For example, the student writes 100 as the answer to 42×6.

There are other types of errors that can occur in the mathematics process. For example, a student may make a mistake or error in applying the appropriate arithmetical operations. Such an example would be $50 - 12 = 62$. Here, the student used the operation of addition rather than subtraction. The student may understand how to do both operations but consistently gets these types of questions wrong on tests due to the improper use of the sign.

Another problem that the student may encounter is a *slip.* When a slip occurs, it is more likely due to a simple mistake rather than a pattern of problems. For example, if a child computes $20 - 5$ correctly in eight problems but not in the ninth problem, the error is probably due to a simple slip rather than a serious operational or processing problem. One error on one problem is not an error pattern. Error patterns can be assessed by analyzing all correct and incorrect answers. When designing a program plan for a particular child in mathematics, it is critical to establish not only what the nature of the problem is but also the patterns of problems in the child's responses.

Also, handwriting can play an important role in mathematics. Scoring a math test often involves reading numbers written down on an answer sheet by the student. If a student's handwriting is difficult to interpret or impossible to read, this can create serious problems for the evaluator with respect to obtaining valid scores. When a student's handwriting is not clear on a math test, it is important that the evaluator ask the student to help him or her read the answers. By doing so, the evaluator is analyzing the math skills that need to be assessed rather than spending time trying to decode the student's responses.

❖ Assessment of Mathematical Abilities

There are many arithmetic assessment measures used for determining strengths and weaknesses. Listed here are various mathematics tests used in school systems to assess students' abilities.

Comprehensive Mathematical Abilities Test (CMAT)

General Test Information

Authors:	Wayne P. Hresko, Paul L. Schlieve, Shelley R. Herron, Colleen Swain, and Rita J. Sherbenou
Publisher:	PRO-ED
Address of Publisher:	8700 Shoal Creek Boulevard, Austin, TX 78757–6897
Telephone Number:	1-800-897-3202
Fax Number:	1-800-397-7633
Web Site of Publisher:	www.proedinc.com
Type of Test:	Mathematics
Administration Time:	30 minutes to 2 hours
Type of Administration:	Individual
Ages/Grade Levels:	Ages 7–0 to 18–11

Purpose and Description of Test

Based on materials used to teach math in schools and on state and local curriculum guides, the CMAT represents a major advance in the accurate assessment of the mathematics taught today. All items reflect real-world problems using up-to-date, current information and scenarios. As few as two subtests or as many as twelve can be used, depending on the purpose for testing.

Subtest Information

The CMAT has six core subtests (Addition; Subtraction; Multiplication; Division; Problem Solving; and Charts, Tables, and Graphs) and six supplemental subtests (Algebra, Geometry, Rational Numbers, Time, Money, and Measurement).

For most testing purposes, only the core subtests are administered; this takes about forty minutes. The supplemental subtests are used in those relatively few instances where information about higher-level mathematics ability is needed.

- Core Composites
  - *Basic Calculations.* Subtests that comprise this composite are Addition, Subtraction, Multiplication, and Division.
  - *Mathematical Reasoning.* The Problem Solving and Charts, Tables, and Graphs subtests make up this composite.
  - *General Mathematics.* This composite is formed by combining the six core subtests.
- Supplemental Composites
  - *Advanced Calculations.* The subtests in this composite (Rational Numbers, Algebra, and Geometry) are usually given to middle school or older students who are showing poor achievement or to advanced students.
  - *Practical Applications.* This composite measures the ability to solve problems related to time concepts (Time), the use of money (Money), and aspects of measurement (Measurement).
  - *Overall Mathematic Abilities.* The results of all twelve CMAT subtests combine to form this composite.

Strengths of the Test

- Both age-based norms (ages 7 through 18) and fall and spring grade-based norms (grades 3 through 12) are provided, giving the examiner flexibility in meeting state and local education agency guidelines.
- Reliability was determined using standard methods for estimating the internal consistency of the subtests and composites. Reliability estimates are uniformly high, with all composites and most subtest reliability values exceeding or rounding to .90. Coefficients for time sampling and interscorer reliability are also presented.
- The CMAT manual provides clear evidence for validity. Strong evidence of content-description validity, criterion-prediction validity, and construct-identification validity is provided, including correlational research with individual and group mathematics tests, intelligence tests, and measures of academic ability.
- The CMAT was normed on a national sample of over 1,600 students whose demographic characteristics match those of the United States according to the 2000 Census report. The normative group was stratified on the basis of age, gender, race, ethnic group membership, geographical location, community size, and socioeconomic status (as indicated by educational attainment and family income).
- The CMAT reflects the National Council of Teachers of Mathematics 2000 Guidelines.
- The CMAT helps to identify students who are having difficulty, as well as students who are exceeding beyond expectations.

Diagnostic Screening Test-Math–Third Edition (DSTM–3)

General Test Information

Author:	Thomas D. Gnagey
Publisher:	Slosson Educational Publications
Address of Publisher:	P.O. Box 280, East Aurora, NY 14052
Telephone Number:	1-888-756-7766
Fax Number:	1-800-655-3840
Web Site of Publisher:	www.slosson.com
Type of Test:	Mathematics
Administration Time:	5 to 20 minutes
Type of Administration:	Individual or group
Ages/Grade Levels:	Grades 1 to 12

Purpose and Description of Test

On the DSTM, each item taps a separate math concept, with items divided into two testing divisions. The DSTM pinpoints skills and deficits in seventy-two individual math processes.

Subtest Information

Each item on this test taps a separate math concept, with items divided into two testing divisions. The first is the Basic Processes Section, composed of thirty-six items arranged developmentally within four major areas:

- Addition (grades 1 to 5)
- Subtraction (grades 1 to 6)
- Multiplication (grades 3 to 8)
- Division (grades 3 to 9)

The Specialized Section uses thirty-seven to forty-five items to evaluate the student's conceptual and computational skills in five areas commonly taught in most math programs:

- Money (grades 2 to 5)
- Time (grades 1 to 8)
- Percentage (grades 4 to 9)
- U.S. Measurement (grades 4 to 10)
- Metric Measurement (grades 4 to 10)

Strengths of the Test

- Each area yields a separate Grade Equivalent Score and Consolidation Index Score. Nine supplemental areas are also scored in this basic section: Process, Sequencing, Simple Computation, Complex Computation, Special Manipulations, Use of Zero, Decimals, Simple Fractions, and Manipulation in Fractions. These scores yield diagnostically useful indicators for further investigation.
- The Consolidated Index Score estimates how thoroughly each concept area has been mastered up to the related grade equivalent obtained on that section of the subtest. The DSTM pinpoints skills and deficits in seventy-two individual math processes. Each concept is easily keyed to existing texts and workbooks.

KeyMath–Revised-Normative Update (KeyMath-R/NU)

General Test Information

Author: Austin J. Connolly
Publisher: AGS Publishing
Address of Publisher: 4201 Woodland Road, Circle Pines, MN 55014–1796
Telephone Number: 1-800-328-2560, 1-651-287-7220
Fax Number: 1-800-471-8457
Web Site of Publisher: www.agsnet.com
Type of Test: Mathematics
Administration Time: 35 to 50 minutes
Type of Administration: Individual
Ages/Grade Levels: Grades K to 12, ages 5 to 22

Purpose and Description of Test

KeyMath-R/NU assesses critical math skills through thirteen subtests. The test is a measure of understanding and application of important mathematics concepts and skills.

Subtest Information

The test is broken down into three major areas consisting of thirteen subtests:

- *Basic Concepts.* This part has three subtests that investigate basic mathematical concepts and knowledge: numeration, rational numbers, and geometry.
- *Operations.* This part consists of basic computation processes: addition, subtraction, multiplication, division, and mental computation.
- *Applications.* This part focuses on the functional applications use of mathematics necessary to daily life: measurement, time and money, interpretation of data, problem solving, and estimation.

Strengths of the Test

- The age range for the KeyMath-R/NU has been extended to ages 5 to 22 with the normative update.
- Approximately ten years separate the data collection periods for the original KeyMath-R norms and the NU norms. The differences between the two sets of norms vary according to grade level and mathematics domain, but some general trends are apparent. The average level of performance in Basic Concepts and Applications has declined at grades K to 2 and increased at grades 5 to 8, while average performance in Operations has not changed. In all areas, performance in the below-average range has declined, while the above-average performance levels have risen. Details are provided in the NU Manual and the NU ASSIST User's Guide.
- KeyMath-R has NU norms. Based on a national sampling of over 3,000 people, it provides accurate score comparisons for math operations and math applications with the other achievement batteries with which it was co-normed: the Kaufman Test of Educational Achievement and the Peabody Individual Achievement Test-Revised-Normative Update. The examiner gains added flexibility with this co-norming because he or she can substitute a subtest from a different battery if a subtest is spoiled or if additional diagnostic information is desired.
- With two forms, the examiner can retest, pretest, and posttest confidently. In addition, spring and fall norms let the examiner accurately assess a student's performance at the beginning and the end of the school year to meet Title I evaluation requirements.

Slosson-Diagnostic Math Screener (S-DMS)

General Test Information

Authors:	Bradley T. Erford and Rita R. Boykin
Publisher:	Slosson Educational Publications
Address of Publisher:	P.O. Box 280, East Aurora, NY 14052
Telephone Number:	1-888-756-7766
Fax Number:	1-800-655-3840
Web Site of Publisher:	www.slosson.com
Type of Test:	Mathematics
Administration Time:	30 to 50 minutes
Type of Administration:	Individual or group
Ages/Grade Levels:	Ages 6–0 to 13–11

Purpose and Description of Test

The S-DMS combines the power of a diagnostic assessment with the speed and convenience of a screener. Math conceptual development, math problem solving, and math computation skills are assessed in five grade ranges: 1 to 2, 3, 4 to 5.4, 5.5 to 6, and 7 to 8. The administrator can observe the procedures of each student and quickly attain an overall view for an entire class when group administered.

Strengths of the Test

- The S-DMS yields standard scores and both grade and age norms and scores.
- Normed on 1,699 children, internal consistency and test-retest reliabilities of the total scales were in the mid-.90s.
- Convergent validity with other commonly used math diagnostic tests and screeners was excellent at all grade levels.

Stanford Diagnostic Mathematical Test-4 (SDMT-4)

General Test Information

Author:	Written by Harcourt Brace Educational Measurement
Publisher:	Harcourt Assessment (formerly known as the Psychological Corporation and Harcourt Educational)
Address of Publisher:	6277 Sea Harbor Drive, Orlando, FL 32887
Telephone Number:	1-800-211-8378
Fax Number:	1-800-232-1223
Web Site of Publisher:	www.harcourt.com
Type of Test:	Mathematics
Administration Time:	Varies with age according to mathematical ability
Type of Administration:	Individual or group
Ages/Grade Levels:	Grades 1 through 12

Purpose and Description of Test

The SDMT-4 measures competence in the basic concepts and skills that are prerequisite to success in mathematics, while emphasizing problem solving and problem-solving strategies. It identifies specific areas of difficulty for each student so that teachers can plan appropriate intervention. Designed to be group administered, SDMT-4 provides both multiple-choice and optional free-response assessment formats. Students select and apply problem-solving strategies and use their reasoning and communication skills.

Subtest Information

There are no subtests; however, there are six levels of testing on the SDMT-4 that assess concepts, applications, and computation:

- *Red Level:* Grades 1.5 to 2.5
- *Orange Level:* Grades 2.5 to 3.5
- *Green Level:* Grades 3.5 to 4.5
- *Purple Level:* Grades 4.5 to 6.5
- *Brown Level:* Grades 6.5 to 8.9
- *Blue Level:* Grades 9.0 to 12.9

Strengths of the Test

- The free-response component enables teachers to obtain information regarding students' strengths and needs by observing the problem-solving process used in arriving at the result.
- Practice tests are available for grades 1 through 8 to help students become familiar with the types of questions.
- Evaluates students for program placement.
- Determines mathematics strengths and weaknesses for instructional planning.
- Provides special help for students who lack essential mathematics skills.
- Identifies trends in mathematics achievement.
- Provides information about the effectiveness of instructional programs.
- Measures changes occurring over a specific instructional period.

Test of Early Mathematics Ability–Third Edition (TEMA-3)

General Test Information

Authors:	Herbert P. Ginsburg and Arthur J. Baroody
Publisher:	PRO-ED
Address of Publisher:	8700 Shoal Creek Boulevard, Austin, TX 78757–6897
Telephone Number:	1-800-897-3202
Fax Number:	1-800-397-7633
Web Site of Publisher:	www.proedinc.com
Type of Test:	Mathematics or used as a diagnostic instrument
Administration Time:	40 minutes
Type of Administration:	Individual
Ages/Grade Levels:	Ages 3–0 through 8–11

Purpose and Description of Test

The TEMA-3 measures the mathematics performance of children and is also useful with older children who have learning problems in mathematics. The test can be used to measure progress, evaluate programs, screen for readiness, discover the basis for poor school performance in mathematics, identify gifted students, and guide instruction and remediation.

Subtest Information

The TEMA-3 measures informal and formal (school-taught) concepts and skills in the following domains: numbering skills, number-comparison facility, numeral literacy, mastery of number facts, calculation skills, and understanding of concepts.

Strengths of the Test

- The new standardization sample is composed of 1,219 children. The characteristics of the sample approximate those in the 2001 U.S. Census.
- Internal consistency reliabilities are all above .92; immediate and delayed alternative form reliabilities are in the .80s and .90s. In addition, many validity studies are described.
- Several important improvements were made in the TEMA-3. First, a linear equating procedure is used to adjust scores on the two test forms to allow the examiner to use scores on Forms A and B interchangeably. Second, bias studies are now included that show the absence of bias based on gender and ethnicity. Finally, the pictures of animals and money in the Picture Book are now in color to make them more appealing and more realistic in appearance.

Test of Mathematical Abilities–Second Edition (TOMA-2)

General Test Information

Authors:	Virginia Brown, Mary Cronin, and Elizabeth McEntire
Publisher:	PRO-ED
Address of Publisher:	8700 Shoal Creek Boulevard, Austin, TX 78757–6897
Telephone Number:	1-800-897-3202
Fax Number:	1-800-397-7633
Web Site of Publisher:	www.proedinc.com
Type of Test:	Mathematics
Administration Time:	60 to 90 minutes
Type of Administration:	Individual
Ages/Grade Levels:	Ages 8–0 through 18–11

Purpose and Description of Test

The TOMA-2 was developed for use in grades 3 through 12. It measures math performance on the two traditional major skill areas in math (story problems and computation) as well as attitude, vocabulary, and general application of mathematics concepts in real life. This test can be used to monitor progress, evaluate programs, and do research.

Subtest Information

The test consists of four core subtests and one supplemental subtest:

- *Attitude Toward Math* (supplemental subtest). The child is presented with various statements about math attitudes and must respond with "agree," "disagree," or "don't know."
- *Computation.* The student is presented with computational problems consisting of basic operations and involving manipulation of fractions, decimals, money, percentages, and so on.
- *General Information.* The examiner reads the student questions involving basic general knowledge, and the student must reply orally.
- *Story Problems.* The student reads brief story problems that contain extraneous information and must extract the pertinent information required to solve the problems. Work space is provided for calculation.
- *Vocabulary.* The student is presented with mathematical terms and asked to define them briefly as they are used in a mathematical sense.

Strengths of the Test

- Reliability coefficients for the subtests are above .80; those for the quotient mostly exceed .90. Ample evidence of content, criterion-related, and construct validity is provided in the manual.

Chapter 18

Mental Retardation

According to the 2004 Individuals with Disabilities Education Improvement Act (IDEA) (C.F.R. Section 300.8), mental retardation is defined as a "significantly subaverage general intellectual functioning, existing concurrently with deficits in adaptive behavior and manifested during the developmental period, that adversely affects a child's performance."

Another definition, this one from the American Association on Mental Retardation (2002), states that "mental retardation is a disability characterized by significant limitations both in intellectual functioning and in adaptive behavior as expressed in conceptual, social, and practical adaptive skills."

The association adds that this disability originates before age 18 and that there are five assumptions essential to the application of the definition:

- Limitations in functioning must be considered within the context of community environments typical of the individual's age peers and culture.
- Valid assessment considers cultural and linguistic diversity as well as differences in communication, sensory, motor, and behavioral factors.
- Within an individual, limitations often coexist with strengths.
- An important purpose of describing limitations is to develop a profile of needed supports.
- With appropriate personalized supports over a sustained period, the life functioning of the person with mental retardation generally will improve.

These developmental delays will have an adverse affect on a child's ability to learn. As a result, children with mental retardation may take longer to learn to speak, walk, and take care of their personal needs such as dressing or eating. They are likely to have trouble learning in school. They will learn, but it will take them longer. There may be some things they cannot learn (National Dissemination Center for Children with Disabilities, 2004f).

Recent research suggests that the causes of mental retardation are varied. Among the most common suggested causes are genetic conditions (genetic mutations problems during pregnancy), problems in fetal development, problems at birth (such as anoxia), health problems such as measles, and environmental conditions like lead poisoning (Heward, 2006; Friend, 2005; Taylor, Brady, & Richards, 2004).

❖ Prevalence of Mental Retardation

According to Taylor (2006), the number of individuals with mental retardation is generally reported to be around 1 percent of the population. As many as three out of every hundred people in the country have mental retardation (Arc of the United States, 2001). Nearly 613,000 children ages 6 to 21 have some level of mental retardation and need special education (U.S. Department of Education, 2002). In fact, one out of every ten children who need special education has some form of mental retardation.

❖ Diagnosing Mental Retardation

Mental retardation is diagnosed by looking at the results of two factors. First are the results of an intelligence test: Intelligence refers to a general mental capability. It involves the ability to reason, plan, solve problems, think abstractly, comprehend complex ideas, learn quickly, and learn from experience. Intelligence typically is represented by Intelligent Quotient (IQ) scores obtained from standardized tests given by a trained professional (American Association on Mental Retardation, 2005). The second factor refers to results from a scale of adaptive behavior. Grossman (1983) defined adaptive behavior as an "individual's effectiveness in meeting the standards of maturation, learning, personal independence, and/or social responsibility." The American Association on Mental Retardation (2005) provides specific examples of adaptive behavior skills:

Conceptual Skills

- Receptive and expressive language
- Reading and writing
- Money concepts
- Self-directions

Social Skills

- Interpersonal
- Responsibility
- Self-esteem
- Gullibility (likelihood of being tricked or manipulated)
- Naiveté
- Follows rules
- Obeys laws
- Avoids victimization

Practical Skills

- Personal activities of daily living such as eating, dressing, mobility, and toileting
- Instrumental activities of daily living such as preparing meals, taking medication, using the telephone, managing money, using transportation, and doing housekeeping activities

Occupational Skills

- Time management
- Communication
- Listening
- Using judgment

❖ Maintaining a Safe Environment

Providing services to help individuals with mental retardation has led to a new understanding of how we define mental retardation. After the initial diagnosis of mental retardation is made, clinicians look at a person's strengths and weaknesses and at how much support or help the person needs to get along at home, in school, and in the community. This approach gives a realistic picture of each individual and provides a practical road to success in attaining the goals set by the individualized education program team. It also recognizes that the picture can change. As the person grows and learns, his or her ability to get along in the world grows as well and the chances for independence increase in some cases.

❖ Signs of Mental Retardation

According to the National Dissemination Center for Children with Disabilities (2004f), there are many signs of mental retardation. For example, children with mental retardation may:

- Sit up, crawl, or walk later than other children
- Learn to talk later or have trouble speaking
- Find it hard to remember
- Not understand how to pay for purchases
- Have trouble understanding social rules
- Have trouble seeing the consequences of their actions
- Have trouble solving problems
- Have trouble thinking logically

The educational concerns and least restrictive environments for children with mental retardation will vary greatly because of the range of abilities found with students in this category. Higher-functioning children with IQ ranges near 70 may be educated in inclusion settings or special classes with mainstreaming in regular mainstream schools. While participation for more severely impaired students may also take place in a full inclusion program (based on the concept of zero reject), special schools and institutional settings may also be considered for the more severely impaired population.

AAMR Adaptive Behavior Scales–
Residential and Community (ABS-RC:2)

General Test Information

Authors:	Kazuo Nihira, Henry Leland, and Nadine Lambert
Publisher:	PRO-ED
Address of Publisher:	8700 Shoal Creek Boulevard, Austin, TX 78757–6897
Telephone Number:	1-800-897-3202
Fax Number:	1-800-397-7633
Web Site of Publisher:	www.proedinc.com
Type of Test:	Adaptive behavior/mental retardation
Administration Time:	15 to 30 minutes
Type of Administration:	Individual
Ages/Grade Levels:	Ages 18 through 80

Purpose and Description of Test

The ABS-RC:2 is the 1993 revision of the 1969 and 1974 AAMD Adaptive Behavior Scales. The latest version of the adaptive behavior scales is the product of a comprehensive review of the earlier versions of the rating scales relating to persons with mental retardation in the United States and other countries. The scale items that survived this process were selected on the basis of their interrater reliability and their effectiveness in discriminating (1) among institutionalized persons with mental retardation and those in community settings who previously had been classified at different adaptive behavior levels according to the AAMD's Classification in Mental Retardation (Grossman, 1983) and (2) among adaptive behavior levels in public school populations.

Strengths of the Test

- The scale's normative sample consists of more than 4,000 persons from forty-three states with developmental disabilities residing in the community or in residential settings.
- The test has been extensively examined with respect to reliability and validity, and the evidence supporting the scale's technical adequacy is provided in the manual. Internal consistency reliabilities and stability for all scores exceed .80.

AAMR Adaptive Behavior Scales–School–Second Edition (ABS-S:2)

General Test Information

Authors:	Nadine Lambert, Kazuo Nihira, and Henry Leland
Publisher:	PRO-ED
Address of Publisher:	8700 Shoal Creek Boulevard, Austin, TX 78757–6897
Telephone Number:	1-800-897-3202
Fax Number:	1-800-397-7633
Web Site of Publisher:	www.proedinc.com
Type of Test:	Adaptive behavior/mental retardation
Administration Time:	15 to 30 minutes
Type of Administration:	Individual
Ages/Grade Levels:	Ages 3–0 through 18–11

Purpose and Description of Test

Since its initial publication, investigators have shown the usefulness of the ABS-S:2 for assessing the functioning of children being evaluated for evidence of mental retardation and for evaluating adaptive behavior characteristics of children with autism and differentiating children with behavior disorders who require special education assistance from those with behavior problems who can be educated in regular class programs.

Subtest Information

The scale is divided into two parts. Part One focuses on personal independence and is designed to evaluate coping skills considered to be important to independence and responsibility in daily living. The skills within this part are grouped into nine behavior domains: Independent Functioning, Numbers and Time, Physical Development, Prevocational/Vocational Activity, Economic Activity, Self-Direction, Language Development, Responsibility, and Socialization. Part Two contains content related to social adaptation. The behaviors are assigned to seven domains: Social Behavior, Social Engagement, Conformity Disturbing, Interpersonal Behavior, Trustworthiness, Stereotyped and Hyperactive Behavior, and Self-Abusive Behavior.

Strengths of the Test

- The 1993 revision builds on the authors' evidence for the scale's reliability and validity and capitalizes on the scientific evidence available.
- The scale's normative sample consists of more than 2,000 persons from thirty-one states with developmental disabilities attending public schools and more than 1,000 students who have no disabilities.
- The test has been examined extensively with respect to reliability and validity. Internal consistency reliabilities and stability for all scores exceed .80.

Aberrant Behavior Checklist–Residential (ABC-Residential) and Aberrant Behavior Checklist–Community (ABC-Community)

General Test Information

Authors:	Michael G. Aman and Nirbhay N. Singh
Publisher:	Slosson Educational Publications
Address of Publisher:	P.O. Box 280, East Aurora, NY 14052
Telephone Number:	1-888-756-7766
Fax Number:	1-800-655-3840
Web Site of Publisher:	www.slosson.com
Type of Test:	Adaptive behavior/mental retardation (checklist)
Administration Time:	Untimed
Type of Administration:	Individual
Ages/Grade Levels:	Children and adults

Purpose and Description of Test

The ABC is a symptom checklist for assessing problem behaviors of children and adults with mental retardation at home, in residential facilities, and at work training centers. It is also useful for classifying problem behaviors of children and adolescents with mental retardation in educational settings, residential and community-based facilities, and developmental centers.

The ABC-Community item content is the same as for the ABC-Residential, except that home, school, and workplace are listed as the relevant settings. The ABC-Community has been validated and normed for such client and rater pairs as teacher and parent ratings of children in developmental handicapped classes and care provider ratings of adults in group homes. The ABC asks for degree of retardation, the person's medical status, and current medication. Then fifty-eight specific symptoms are rated, and an extensive manual gives comprehensive descriptions for each assessed behavior. The checklist can be completed by parents, special educators, psychologists, direct caregivers, nurses, and others with knowledge of the person being assessed.

Subtest Information

The ABC-Residential was empirically developed by factor analysis on data from 1,000 residents. The fifty-eight items resolve into five subscales:

- Irritability, Agitation
- Lethargy, Social Withdrawal
- Stereotypic Behavior
- Hyperactivity, Noncompliance
- Inappropriate Speech

Strengths of the Test

- Extensive psychometric assessment of the ABC has indicated that its subscales have high internal consistency, adequate reliability, and established validity. Average subscale scores are available for both U.S. and overseas residential facilities and for children and adults living in the community.

Adaptive Behavior Evaluation Scale–Revised (ABES-R)

General Test Information

Author:	Stephen B. McCarney
Publisher:	Hawthorne Educational Services
Address of Publisher:	800 Gray Oak Drive, Columbia, MO 65201
Telephone Number:	1-800-542-1673
Fax Number:	1-800-442-9509
Web Site of Publisher:	http://www.hes-inc.com
Type of Test:	Adaptive behavior/mental retardation
Administration Time:	Approximately 20 minutes
Type of Administration:	Individual
Ages/Grade Levels:	Ages 5–0 through 18–11

Purpose and Description of Test

The ABES-R is based on the definition of adaptive skills adopted by the American Association on Mental Retardation. The School Version can be completed in approximately twenty minutes and contains 104 items easily observed and documented by educational personnel. The Home Version can be completed by a parent or guardian in approximately twenty minutes and contains 104 items representing behaviors exhibited in and around the home environment.

Subtest Information

The ABES-R represents ten adaptive skill areas:

- Communication skills
- Self-care
- Home living
- Social skills
- Community use
- Self-direction
- Health and safety
- Functional academics
- Leisure
- Work skills

Strengths of the Test

- The ABES-R provides separate norms for male and female students ages 5 through 18.
- The Adaptive Behavior Intervention Manual–Revised includes individualized education program goals, objectives, and interventions for all 104 items on the School Version of the scale.
- The ABES-R Quick Score computer program converts raw scores to standard and percentile scores and makes the scoring of both the School and Home Version rating forms efficient and convenient.
- The computer version of the Adaptive Behavior Intervention Manual–Revised provides an individualized printout of goals, objectives, and interventions chosen for each student's specific adaptive skill problem.
- The ABES-R School Version was standardized on 7,124 students. The sample contained students from twenty-four states and represented all geographical regions of the United States.

Adaptive Behavior Inventory (ABI)

General Test Information

Authors:	Linda Brown and James Leigh
Publisher:	PRO-ED
Address of Publisher:	8700 Shoal Creek Boulevard, Austin, TX 78757–6897
Telephone Number:	1-800-897-3202
Fax Number:	1-800-397-7633
Web Site of Publisher:	http://www.proedinc.com
Type of Test:	Adaptive behavior/mental retardation
Administration Time:	Untimed; 15 to 30 minutes
Type of Administration:	Individual
Ages/Grade Levels:	Ages 6–0 to 18–11

Purpose and Description of Test

The ABI evaluates the functional daily living skills of school-aged children and helps identify students believed to be mentally retarded or emotionally disturbed.

Strengths of the Test

- The tests were standardized on 1,296 nondisabled students and 1,076 students with mental retardation in twenty-one states. The demographic characteristics of the normal intelligence standardization group approximate the eight major characteristics reported in the U.S. Census. In addition, the mentally retarded sample is representative across several variables unique to the retarded population in the United States.
- Internal consistency and test-retest reliability are in the .80s and .90s at most ages.
- Evidence of concurrent and construct validity is provided.

Assessment for Persons Profoundly or
Severely Impaired (APPSI)

General Test Information

Authors:	Patricia Connard and Sharon Bradley-Johnson
Publisher:	PRO-ED
Address of Publisher:	8700 Shoal Creek Boulevard, Austin, TX 78757–6897
Telephone Number:	1-800-897-3202
Fax Number:	1-800-397-7633
Web Site of Publisher:	www.proedinc.com
Type of Test:	Adaptive behavior/mental retardation
Administration Time:	30 to 60 minutes
Type of Administration:	Individual
Ages/Grade Levels:	Clients of any age who are preverbal and functioning at a mental age up to 8 months

Purpose and Description of Test

The APPSI provides assessment results relevant to planning effective intervention for individuals functioning at the lowest levels of mental development. It aids in defining individuals' preferred methods of communication, which is useful for planning instruction to enhance the independence of these individuals.

Strengths of the Test

- Helps discover clients' preferences for visual, auditory, and tactile stimuli on the receptive side and also for social interaction and methods of communicative output. The test is aligned with the Piagetian sensorimotor framework of stages I through III.
- The APPSI is not normed, but it was piloted in three states with thirty-two individuals (ages 2 through 24) who have severe and profound impairments. Reliability coefficients for the test range from .76 to .92, indicating a very high level of reliability.

Developmental Assessment for Students with Severe Disabilities–Second Edition (DASH-2)

General Test Information

Authors:	Mary Kay Dykes and Jane Erin
Publisher:	PRO-ED
Address of Publisher:	8700 Shoal Creek Boulevard, Austin, TX 78757–6897
Telephone Number:	1-800-897-3202
Fax Number:	1-800-397-7633
Web Site of Publisher:	www.proedinc.com
Type of Test:	Adaptive behavior/mental retardation
Administration Time:	120 to 180 minutes
Type of Administration:	Individual
Ages/Grade Levels:	No age ranges indicated; rather, it is used for individuals functioning between birth and 6-11 developmentally

Purpose and Description of Test

DASH-2 offers concise information about individuals who are functioning between birth and age 6–11 developmentally. It is sensitive to small changes in skill performance. It identifies these skills as task resistive, needing full assistance, needing partial assistance, needing minimal assistance, or an independent performance.

Subtest Information

The DASH-2 consists of five pinpoint scales that assess performance in the following areas:

- Dressing
- Feeding
- Toileting
- Home routines
- Travel and safety

Strengths of the Test

- Provides multiple examples of behavior at young ages.
- Provides a scoring method to measure the condition under which behavior occurs.
- DASH-2 begins with an individual's areas of strength and builds from there. Therefore, it can function as an initial assessment instrument, a tool for curriculum planning, and a means of monitoring progress. This information can be applied to program planning, communicating with families and other team members, and developing intervention strategies.

Chapter 19

Neuropsychology

According to Merz, Buller, and Launey (1990), "Neuropsychology is the study of how the functions of your brain and nervous system affect the way you think and behave. For some time now, neuropsychology has helped hospital clinicians assess patients who have experienced head injuries to determine how neurological damage affects their patients' thinking skills and behavior. Clinical psychologists have also benefited from neuropsychology because it helps them more accurately assess the causes of some patients' behaviors" (p. 1).

Prior to passage of the 1997 Individuals with Disabilities Education Improvement Act (IDEA 97), schools relied on standard evaluations to assess children for suspected disabilities. These evaluations consisted mostly of intellectual and academic assessments using basic standardized testing. With IDEA 97 and recently the 2004 Individuals with Disabilities Education Improvement Act, the introduction of a multidisciplinary team approach has required schools to consider other and sometimes more in-depth evaluation procedures involving a wider variety of assessment professionals, for example, occupational therapist and psychiatrist.

According to Iannelli (2005), using neuropsychology in schools can help teachers serve children with learning disabilities more effectively because a child who has neurologically related disabilities does not benefit from the same teaching techniques (such as repetition) that a student who learns at a slower rate benefits from.

Merz, Buller, and Launey (1990) feel that neurological assessment is a tool for evaluating how much a child's performance may be influenced by unusual functions of the brain and nervous system. It helps school psychologists systematically measure a child's skills and determine the best learning environment for the child.

According to Tsatsanis and Volkmar (2001), the following cognitive functions are likely to be assessed:

- Sensory perceptual and motor functions
- Attention
- Memory
- Auditory and visual processing

- Language
- Concept formation and problem solving
- Planning and organization
- Speed of processing
- Intelligence
- Academic skills
- Behavior, emotions, and personality

As with any other comprehensive assessment measure, the neuropsychological assessment involves gathering important information on the child that, along with observation, interviews, and assessment, will enable the evaluator to arrive at an appropriate conclusion and series of recommendations. This information will need to be collected from a variety of sources:

- The student's parents through interviews, checklists, and observation
- The student's teacher through work samples, checklists, reports, and anecdotal records
- The student through observation, interview, and assessment

The use of a neuropsychological assessment in the assessment of a student with a suspected disability will add to the knowledge base of that student's disability and provide necessary information on learning style, functional academic abilities, cognitive functioning, perceptual organization, and processing ability.

Behavior Rating Inventory of Executive Function (BRIEF)

General Test Information

Authors:	Gerard A. Gioia, Peter K. Isquith, Steven C. Guy, and Lauren Kenworthy
Publisher:	PAR
Address of Publisher:	16204 North Florida Avenue, Lutz, FL 33549
Telephone Number:	1-800-331-8378, ext. 361
Fax Number:	1-800-727-9329
Web Site of Publisher:	http://www.parinc.com
Type of Test:	Neuropsychology
Administration Time:	10 to 15 minutes
Type of Administration:	Individual
Ages/Grade Levels:	Children and adolescents

Purpose and Description of Test

The BRIEF consists of two rating forms—a parent questionnaire and a teacher questionnaire—designed to assess executive functioning in the home and school environments. Executive functioning refers to how children manage, organize, and respond to what they have learned. In other words, it is the ability to interpret and act on information. It is useful in evaluating children with a wide spectrum of developmental and acquired neurological conditions, such as:

- Learning disabilities
- Low birth weight
- Attention deficit-hyperactivity disorder (ADHD)
- Tourette's disorder
- Traumatic brain injury (TBI)
- Pervasive developmental disorders/autism

Subtest Information

Each BRIEF questionnaire contains eighty-six items in eight nonoverlapping clinical scales and two validity scales. These theoretically and statistically derived scales form two broader indexes: Behavioral Regulation (three scales) and Metacognition (five scales), as well as a Global Executive Composite score.

Strengths of the Test

- High internal consistency (alphas = .80-.98), test-retest reliability (r = .82 for parents and .88 for teachers), and moderate correlations between teacher and parent ratings (r = .32-.34).
- Convergent validity was established with other measures of inattention, impulsivity, and learning skills; divergent validity was demonstrated against measures of emotional and behavioral functioning; Working Memory and Inhibit scales differentiate among ADHD subtypes.
- Normative data are based on child ratings from 1,419 parents and 720 teachers from rural, suburban, and urban areas, reflecting 1999 U.S. Census estimates for socioeconomic status, ethnicity, and gender distribution.
- Separate normative tables for both the parent and teacher forms provide *T*-scores, percentiles, and 90 percent confidence intervals for four developmental age groups (5 to 18 years) by gender of the child.
- The clinical sample included children with developmental disorders or acquired neurological disorders (such as reading disorder, ADHD subtypes, TBI, Tourette's disorder, mental retardation, localized brain lesions, and high-functioning autism).

Brief Test of Head Injury (BTHI)

General Test Information

Authors:	Nancy Helm-Estabrooks and Gillian Hotz
Publisher:	PRO-ED
Address of Publisher:	8700 Shoal Creek Boulevard, Austin, TX 78757–6897
Telephone Number:	1-800-897-3202
Fax Number:	1-800-397-7633
Web Site of Publisher:	http://www.proedinc.com
Type of Test:	Neuropsychology
Administration Time:	25 to 30 minutes
Type of Administration:	Individual
Ages/Grade Levels:	Adolescents and adults

Purpose and Description of Test

The BTHI can quickly probe cognitive, linguistic, and communicative abilities of patients with severe head trauma. It provides useful diagnostic information for immediate treatment and a baseline for charting recovery.

Subtest Information

The BTHI has these item clusters:

- Orientation and Attention
- Following Commands
- Linguistic Organization
- Reading Comprehension
- Naming, Memory
- Visual-Spatial Skills

Strengths of the Test

- Its sensitivity to small performance changes makes the BTHI useful for tracking recovery patterns during the period of spontaneous recovery.
- The internal consistency coefficients were generally high: .65 to .86 for item clusters and .95 for the BTHI Total Score.
- Test-retest (average seventeen days interim) yielded significantly higher retest means. Correlations with the Glasgow Coma Scale at admission (.29) and at the time of BTHI testing (.35) were low. Correlations with the Rancho Los Amigos Scale at the time of BTHI testing were moderately high (.75).

California Verbal Learning Test–Children's Version (CVLT–C)

General Test Information

Authors:	Dean C. Delis, Joel H. Kramer, Edith Kaplan, and Beth A. Ober
Publisher:	Harcourt Assessment (formerly known as the Psychological Corporation and Harcourt Educational)
Address of Publisher:	6277 Sea Harbor Drive, Orlando, FL 32887
Telephone Number:	1-800-211-8378
Fax Number:	1-800-232-1223
Web Site of Publisher:	www.harcourt.com
Type of Test:	Neuropsychology
Administration Time:	15 to 20 minutes, plus a 20-minute interval to accommodate delayed recall measure
Type of Administration:	Individual
Ages/Grade Levels:	Ages 5–0 through 16–11

Purpose and Description of Test

The CVLT–C assesses verbal learning and memory in children and adolescents. It can be used in a variety of settings to identify learning and memory difficulties, isolate deficient learning strategies, and assist in designing remediation programs.

Strengths of the Test

- CVLT–C evaluates children and adolescents who have learning and memory impairments that may have resulted from traumatic brain injury or are evidenced by mild to severe learning disabilities, attention deficit disorders, mental retardation, psychiatric problems, or other neurological disorders. It measures multiple aspects of how verbal learning occurs, or fails to occur, as well as the amount of verbal material learned.
- CVLT–C assesses verbal learning through an everyday memory task in which the child is asked to recall a list. An interference task is given, followed by short-delay free recall and cued recall trials. Free recall, cued recall, and a word recognition trial are also administered after a twenty-minute delay.
- CVLT–C produces a detailed analysis of the child's performance on recall measures, learning characteristics measures, areas of recall errors, and contrast measures.

Cognitive Symptom Checklists (CSC)

General Test Information

Authors:	Christiane O'Hara, Minnie Harrell, Eileen Bellingrath, and Katherine Lisicia
Publisher:	PAR
Address of Publisher:	16204 North Florida Avenue, Lutz, FL 33549
Telephone Number:	1-800-331-8378, ext. 361
Fax Number:	1-800-727-9329
Web Site of Publisher:	http://www.parinc.com
Type of Test:	Neuropsychology
Administration Time:	10 to 20 minutes per checklist
Type of Administration:	Individual
Ages/Grade Levels:	Ages 16 to adult

Purpose and Description of Test

The CSC is a series of five checklists designed to pinpoint the areas where individuals ages 16 years and older who have impaired cognitive functioning may be having difficulties in everyday activities. It can be used as a screening tool to supplement formal neuropsychological or other cognitive testing.

These checklists are designed for use with individuals ages 16 and older. Items are written at a seventh-grade reading level. The client completes the checklists the clinician feels are necessary to determine potential problems in five basic cognitive areas:

- Attention/concentration
- Visual processes
- Executive functions
- Memory
- Language

The client checks each problem he or she experiences and circles those that seem most important for treatment. The clinician inquires about each item that the client checked and uses this information to identify baseline cognitive problem areas, develop treatment plans, provide information to clients and their families, and measure posttreatment progress.

Strengths of the Test

- According to the publisher, "These five checklists provide a framework for clinicians to gather additional information about the nature of specific problems and to assist the client and clinician in prioritizing problems to target for treatment."

Comprehensive Trail-Making Test (CTMT)

General Test Information

Author:	Cecil R. Reynolds
Publisher:	PRO-ED
Address of Publisher:	8700 Shoal Creek Boulevard, Austin, TX 78757–6897
Telephone Number:	1-800-897-3202
Fax Number:	1-800-397-7633
Web Site of Publisher:	www.proedinc.com
Type of Test:	Neuropsychology
Administration Time:	5 to 12 minutes
Type of Administration:	Individual
Ages/Grade Levels:	Ages 11 to 74

Purpose and Description of Test

The CTMT provides clinicians and research workers with a hierarchy of specific as well as global summary measures that operationally define important basic and complex components of executive function. It is an important new psychometric instrument that should be studied intensively and applied widely in clinical as well as basic and applied research settings. Its primary uses are the evaluation and diagnosis of brain injury and other forms of central nervous system compromise. More specific purposes include the detection of frontal lobe deficits; problems with psychomotor speed, visual search, and sequencing; and attention and impairments in set shifting.

The basic task of trail-making is to connect a series of stimuli (numbers, expressed as numerals or in word form, and letters) in a specified order as quickly as possible. The score derived for each trail is the number of seconds required to complete the task. The composite score is obtained by pooling the *T*-scores from the individual trails. The five trails are similar but also different in some significant ways:

- *Trail 1.* The examinee draws a line to connect the numbers 1 through 25 in order. Each numeral is contained in a plain circle.
- *Trail 2.* The examinee draws a line to connect the numbers 1 through 25 in order. Each numeral is contained in a plain circle. Twenty-nine empty distractor circles appear on the same page.
- *Trail 3.* The examinee draws a line to connect the numbers 1 through 25 in order. Each is contained in a plain circle. Thirteen empty distractor circles and nineteen distractor circles containing irrelevant line drawings appear on the same page.
- *Trail 4.* The examinee draws a line to connect the numbers 1 through 20 in order. Eleven of the numbers are presented as arabic numerals (for example, 1, 7), and nine numbers are spelled out (for example, Ten, Four).
- *Trail 5.* The examinee draws a line to connect in alternating sequence the numbers 1 through 13 and the letters A through L. The examinee begins with 1 and then draws a line to A, then proceeds to 2, then B, and so on until all the numbers and letters are connected. Fifteen empty distractor circles appear on the same page.

Strengths of the Test

- The CTMT is standardized on a nationwide sample of 1,664 persons whose demographic characteristics match U.S. 2000 Census data.
- Reliability of scores for each individual trail is high, and the composite score has a reliability coefficient of .90 or higher at all ages.
- The CTMT is extremely sensitive to neurological insult, disease, injury, or dysfunction, including the subtle neuropsychological dysfunction often present in individuals with learning disabilities.
- The Examiner's Manual includes discussion of the test's theoretical and research-based foundation, administration and scoring procedures, and more extensive reliability and validity data.

Continuous Visual Memory Test (CVMT)

General Test Information

Authors:	Donald E. Trahan and Glenn J. Larrabee
Publisher:	PAR
Address of Publisher:	16204 North Florida Avenue, Lutz, FL 33549
Telephone Number:	1-800-331-8378, ext. 361
Fax Number:	1-800-727-9329
Web Site of Publisher:	http://www.parinc.com
Type of Test:	Neuropsychology
Administration Time:	45 to 50 minutes (includes 30-minute delay)
Type of Administration:	Individual
Ages/Grade Levels:	Children to adults

Purpose and Description of Test

The CVMT uses complex, ambiguous designs and a recognition format to measure visual learning and memory. Studies suggest that these features may increase task sensitivity and reduce the confounding influence of verbal encoding strategies. This format also eliminates the motor responses required by drawing tasks and restricts the verbal labeling required by tests that use simplistic geometric figures and common objects.

Subtest Information

The CVMT has three tasks for assessing visual memory:

- The Acquisition Task tests recognition memory by asking the respondents to discriminate new from repeated stimuli using 112 designs presented at two-second intervals.
- The Delayed Recognition Task measures retrieval from long-term storage after a thirty-minute delay, asking respondents to distinguish old stimuli from perceptually similar stimuli.
- A Visual Discrimination Task distinguishes visual discrimination deficits from visual memory problems.

Strengths of the Test

- The clinical sensitivity of the CVMT has been demonstrated in patients who have suffered severe head trauma.
- The new CVMT Manual Supplement provides normative data for 778 American and Canadian children, extending the age range to include ages 7 to 15. Expanded normative data are also provided for older adult respondents, and the authors recommend using these new data for individuals who are 50 years and older. The revised Scoring Form incorporates total score cutoffs for the Delayed Recognition Task by age group.

Digit Vigilance Test (DVT)

General Test Information

Author:	Ronald F. Lewis
Publisher:	PAR
Address of Publisher:	16204 North Florida Avenue, Lutz, FL 33549
Telephone Number:	1-800-331-8378, ext. 361
Fax Number:	1-800-727-9329
Web Site of Publisher:	http://www.parinc.com
Type of Test:	Neuropsychology
Administration Time:	10 minutes (timed)
Type of Administration:	Individual
Ages/Grade Levels:	Ages 20 to 80

Purpose and Description of Test

The DVT is a commonly used test of attention, alertness, and mental processing capacity using a rapid visual tracking task. It is sensitive to subtle changes in neuropsychological status but relatively insensitive to the effects of either repeated administrations or practice. The DVT appears to isolate alertness and vigilance while placing minimal demands on two other components of attention: selectivity and capacity.

The materials consist of a new Professional User's Guide, the Test Booklet, and a set of four color-coordinated Scoring Keys. Respondents (ages 20 to 80 years) are asked to find and cross out either "6" or "9" (alternate administration), which appear randomly within fifty-nine rows of single digits. These rows are printed in red on the first stimulus page and in blue on the second.

Strengths of the Test

- Assesses attention during rapid visual tracking.
- The four scoring keys (one for "6" and one for "9" in each of the colors) allow the test administrator to count and record errors of commission and omission. Administration and scoring can be accomplished by individuals with no formal training under the supervision of a qualified psychologist.

Kaplan Baycrest Neurocognitive Assessment (KBNA)

General Test Information

Authors:	Larry Leach, Edith Kaplan, Dmytro Rewilak, Brian Richards, and Guy B. Proulx
Publisher:	Harcourt Assessment (formerly known as the Psychological Corporation and Harcourt Educational)
Address of Publisher:	6277 Sea Harbor Drive, Orlando, FL 32887
Telephone Number:	1-800-211-8378
Fax Number:	1-800-232-1223
Web Site of Publisher:	www.harcourt.com
Type of Test:	Neuropsychological
Administration Time:	60 minutes
Type of Administration:	Individual
Ages/Grade Levels:	Adults

Purpose and Description of Test

The KBNA assesses cognitive abilities of adults with a comprehensive screening test. It gives important information for a general overview, in-depth diagnosis, or treatment planning and monitoring. The test combines behavioral neurology and traditional neuropsychological approaches to assessment. KBNA evaluates the major areas of cognition:

- Attention/concentration
- Immediate memory—recall
- Delayed memory—recall
- Delayed memory—recognition
- Verbal fluency
- Spatial processing
- Reasoning/conceptual shifting

Strengths of the Test

- KBNA is correlated with the Wechsler Abbreviated Scale of Intelligence, providing valuable clinical information about the effect of general cognitive ability on KBNA subtests. It is also correlated with a variety of commonly used neuropsychological tests, including the California Verbal Learning Test, the California Verbal Learning Test–Second Edition, and the Boston Naming Test.
- KBNA allows examiners to choose among a general overview of cognition by calculating index scores only, a detailed analysis of neurocognitive functioning by also calculating process scores, or a combination of both. The process scores help break down an examinee's performance into component processes, making it easier to identify strengths and weaknesses, reach a diagnosis, plan treatment, and document improvement over time.
- Normative Data Profile Sheets eliminate tables of norms and provide all normative information for each of the seven age groups.

Kaufman Short Neuropsychological Assessment Procedure (K-SNAP)

General Test Information

Authors:	Alan S. Kaufman and Nadeen L. Kaufman
Publisher:	AGS Publishing
Address of Publisher:	4201 Woodland Road, Circle Pines, MN 55014–1796
Telephone Number:	1-800-328-2560, 1-651-287-7220
Fax Number:	1-800-471-8457
Web Site of Publisher:	www.agsnet.com
Type of Test:	Neuropsychology
Administration Time:	30 minutes
Type of Administration:	Individual
Ages/Grade Levels:	Ages 11 through 85+

Purpose and Description of Test

This brief, individually administered measure assesses aspects of the mental functioning of adolescents and adults, ages 11 to over 85 years.

Subtest Information

The four subtests are organized in three levels of cognitive complexity:

- Attention-orientation (Mental Status)
- Simple memory and perceptual skills (Number Recall and Gestalt Closure)
- Complex intellectual functioning and planning ability (Four-Letter Words)

Strengths of the Test

- K-SNAP was developed with the Kaufman Adolescent and Adult Intelligence Test, Kaufman Brief Intelligence Test, and Kaufman Functional Academic Skills Test, and normed on a representative standardization sample of 2,000 people. All items were checked for cultural bias. In addition, several studies support K-SNAP's reliability and validity, using both normal and clinical samples (including neurologically impaired individuals and individuals with Alzheimer's). This assessment procedure can be administered in about 30 minutes by a range of personnel, although score interpretation should be made by appropriately trained professionals.
- The K-SNAP provides standard scores across a wide range of ability levels, including enough easy items to reliably evaluate people with moderate to severe mental retardation or dementia. The K-SNAP's wide age range means examiners can test a person more than once and compare results.

NEPSY

General Test Information

Authors:	Marit Korkman, Ursula Kirk, and Sally Kemp
Publisher:	Harcourt Assessment (formerly known as the Psychological Corporation and Harcourt Educational)
Address of Publisher:	6277 Sea Harbor Drive, Orlando, FL 32887
Telephone Number:	1-800-211-8378
Fax Number:	1-800-232-1223
Web Site of Publisher:	www.harcourt.com
Type of Test:	Neuropsychology
Administration Time:	Core Assessment: ages 3 to 4, 45 minutes; ages 5 to 12: 65 minutes; Full NEPSY: ages 3 to 4, 1 hour; ages 5 to 12: 2 hours
Type of Administration:	Individual
Ages/Grade Levels:	Ages 3–0 through 12–11

Purpose and Description of Test

NEPSY is a child-friendly test that provides a wealth of clinical data useful for planning treatment. When a complete diagnostic picture is needed, NEPSY provides a flexible approach for evaluating attention/executive functions, language, visuospatial processing, sensorimotor functions, and memory and learning in children.

Subtest Information

Using NEPSY's comprehensive subtests, examiners can identify strengths and analyze deficits in five functional domains that facilitate or interfere with a child's learning:

- *Attention and Executive Functions*—assesses inhibition, self-regulation, monitoring, vigilance, selective and sustained attention, maintenance of response set, planning, flexibility in thinking, and figural fluency
- *Language*—assesses phonological processing abilities, receptive language comprehension, expressive naming under confrontation and speeded naming conditions, verbal fluency, and the ability to produce rhythmic oral motor sequences
- *Sensorimotor Functions*—assesses sensory input at the tactile level, fine motor speed for simple and complex movements, the ability to imitate hand positions, rhythmic and sequential movements, and visuomotor precision in controlling pencil use
- *Visuospatial Processing*—assesses the ability to judge position and directionality and the ability to copy two-dimensional geometric figures and reconstruct three-dimensional designs from a model or picture
- *Memory and Learning*—assesses immediate memory for sentences; immediate and delayed memory for faces, names, and list learning; and narrative memory under free and cued recall conditions

Strengths of the Test

- NEPSY subtests were designed to be sensitive to disruptions in various abilities that affect learning. Subtests may be used for assessing children with sensory or motor handicaps, learning problems, attention deficits, traumatic brain injuries, autistic disorders, mental retardation, and genetic syndromes.
- All of the NEPSY subtests were normed together, providing an accurate diagnostic picture of the child. Up-to-date norms are based on a nationally representative sample of more than 1,000 U.S. children, so a child's performance can be compared to others in the appropriate age group.

- NEPSY was designed to be used in a variety of cultural and racial/ethnic groups. Both males and females were sampled, and the performances of different racial/ethnic groups were evaluated through an oversampling procedure. All items were reviewed by a panel of recognized bias experts.
- Each domain has a core set of subtests. A summary standard score, based on the domain's core subtests, can be obtained for each domain. For any domain, examiners can also perform an expanded assessment using the additional subtests from that domain or a selective assessment using additional subtests across domains. In addition to subtest-level scores, on many subtests the subcomponents may also be scored (these are supplemental scores). Qualitative observations made about the child's behavior may be examined in relation to base rates of occurrence in the standardization sample.
- The NEPSY manual reports reliability statistics, including interrater and interscorer agreement, subtest internal consistency, and test-retest stability. Validity data include content and construct validity, as well as studies with children diagnosed with learning disabilities, attention deficit-hyperactivity disorders, traumatic brain injury, autistic disorders, and speech and language impairments.

Quick Neurological Screening Test–Second Edition (QNST-II)

General Test Information

Authors:	Margaret Mutti, Harold Sterling, Nancy A. Martin, and Norma Spalding
Publisher:	Academic Therapy
Address of Publisher:	20 Commercial Boulevard, Novato, CA 94949
Telephone Number:	1-800-422-7249
Fax Number:	1-888-287-9975
Web Site of Publisher:	http://www.academictherapy.com
Type of Test:	Neuropsychology
Administration Time:	Untimed; approximately 20 minutes to administer
Type of Administration:	Individual
Ages/Grade Levels:	Ages 5 through 18

Purpose and Description of Test

The popular QNST has been updated to include the latest research findings concerning the soft neurological signs that may accompany learning disabilities. Current clinical research documents the co-occurrence of learning disabilities and problems of physical development in such areas as manual dexterity, spatial orientation, fine and gross motor movements, visual tracking, and tactile perceptual activities.

Strengths of the Test

- Performance patterns screen for early identification of learning disabilities. Scoring patterns suggest possible avenues of further diagnostic assessment.
- The QNST-II manual explores the importance of such soft neurological signs in educational settings as well as the medical implications. Special education personnel will appreciate knowing whether behaviors seen in the classroom have physiological (organic) or emotional origins. The detailed scoring information will also allow other rehabilitation professionals assistance with planning appropriate remediation.
- According to its publisher, "An optional training video and extensive pictures within the text provide guidance for scoring each task."

Rey Complex Figure Test and Recognition Trial (RCFT)

General Test Information

Authors:	John E. Meyers and Kelly R. Meyers
Publisher:	PAR
Address of Publisher:	16204 North Florida Avenue, Lutz, FL 33549
Telephone Number:	1-800-331-8378, ext. 361
Fax Number:	1-800-727-9329
Web Site of Publisher:	http://www.parinc.com
Type of Test:	Neuropsychology
Administration Time:	Approximately 45 minutes, including a 30-minute delay interval (timed)
Type of Administration:	Individual
Ages/Grade Levels:	Ages 6 to adult

Purpose and Description of Test

The RCFT measures visuospatial ability and visuospatial memory. It standardizes the materials and procedures for administering the Rey complex figure. The Recognition trial measures recognition memory for the elements of the Rey complex figure and assesses the respondent's ability to use cues to retrieve information.

Strengths of the Test

- The normative sample included 601 adults ages 18 to 89 years and 505 children and adolescents ages 6 to 17 years. Demographically corrected normative data for the RCFT copy and memory variables are presented to assist in interpretation as well as in making comparisons among individuals and various patient groups.
- Intercorrelations between the RCFT and other measures, in samples of both normal and brain-damaged subjects, establish the convergent and discriminant validity of the RCFT as a measure of visuospatial constructional ability (Copy trial) and visuospatial memory (Immediate Recall, Delayed Recall, and Recognition trials).
- Results of factor analysis suggest the RCFT captures five domains of neuropsychological functioning: visuospatial recall memory, visuospatial recognition memory, response bias, processing speed, and visuospatial constructional ability.
- It reliably discriminates among brain-damaged, psychiatric, and normal subjects. In addition, the Recognition trial provides incremental diagnostic power compared to using recall trials alone.

Ross Information Processing Assessment–Second Edition (RIPA-2)

General Test Information

Author:	Deborah Ross-Swain
Publisher:	PRO-ED
Address of Publisher:	8700 Shoal Creek Boulevard, Austin, TX 78757–6897
Telephone Number:	1-800-897-3202
Fax Number:	1-800-397-7633
Web Site of Publisher:	www.proedinc.com
Type of Test:	Neuropsychology
Administration Time:	60 minutes
Type of Administration:	Individual
Ages/Grade Levels:	Ages 15 to 90

Purpose and Description of Test

The RIPA-2 enables the examiner to quantify cognitive-linguistic deficits, determine severity levels for each skill area, and develop rehabilitation goals and objectives. It is a revision of the popular Ross Information Processing Assessment. The addition of reliability and validity studies performed on individuals with traumatic brain injury is a major improvement in the test.

Subtest Information

The RIPA-2 provides quantifiable data for profiling ten key areas basic to communicative and cognitive functioning:

- Immediate memory
- Recent memory
- Temporal orientation (recent memory)
- Temporal orientation (remote memory)
- Spatial orientation
- Orientation to environment
- Recall of general information
- Problem solving and abstract reasoning
- Organization
- Auditory processing and retention

Strengths of the Test

- The study sample contained 126 individuals with traumatic brain injury in seventeen states. The sample was representative of traumatic brain injury demographics for gender, ethnicity, and socioeconomic status.
- Internal consistency reliability was investigated, and the mean reliability coefficient for RIPA-2 subtests was .85, with a range of .67 to .91. This indicates that test error was minimal and that the RIPA-2 can be used with confidence. Content, construct, and criterion-related validity were thoroughly studied.
- Correlations between the RIPA-2 and selected subtests of the Woodcock-Johnson Tests of Cognitive Ability show a considerable relationship. The RIPA-2 scores distinguish dramatically between groups known to have cognitive deficits and those known to have normal cognitive skills. The investigations were done by independent researchers working in hospitals, rehabilitation centers, clinics, and private practices. Convincing evidence also is provided to demonstrate that RIPA-2 items are not biased with regard to age or gender.

- New features of the RIPA-2
  - Internal consistency reliability is demonstrated.
  - Criterion-related validity studies demonstrate a considerable relationship with other cognitive batteries.
  - The provision of a factorial analysis has enhanced the construct validity of the test.
  - Studies demonstrating the absence of age and gender bias have been added.
  - A representative study sample of individuals with traumatic brain injury has been included.
  - Standard scores have been included in addition to raw scores and percentiles.
  - Administration procedures have been rewritten for improved clarity.
  - Test items have proven to be unbiased.

Ruff Figural Fluency Test (RFFT)

General Test Information

Author:	Ronald M. Ruff
Publisher:	PAR
Address of Publisher:	16204 North Florida Avenue, Lutz, FL 33549
Telephone Number:	1-800-331-8378, ext. 361
Fax Number:	1-800-727-9329
Web Site of Publisher:	http://www.parinc.com
Type of Test:	Neuropsychology
Administration Time:	5 minutes (60 seconds for each of the five parts)
Type of Administration:	Individual
Ages/Grade Levels:	Adolescents and adults

Purpose and Description of Test

The RFFT was developed to provide clinical information regarding nonverbal capacity for fluid and divergent thinking, ability to flexibly shift cognitive set, planning strategies, and executive ability to coordinate this process. It was designed as a nonverbal analogue to popular verbal fluency tests that require respondents ages 16 to 70 years to generate as many words as possible starting with a specific letter.

Materials include the RFFT Professional Manual and the RFFT Test Booklet. The Test Booklet consists of five sixty-second parts, each with a different stimulus presentation. The task is to draw as many unique designs as possible within a set period of time (sixty seconds) by connecting the dots in different patterns. In each part of the test booklet, the five-dot stimuli are presented in thirty-five contiguous squares, arranged in a grid five by seven squares. Analogous to the different alphabetical letters that are used in verbal fluency tests, the five-dot stimulus configurations are different in three parts of the test. In the other two parts, distractors are added to the dot configurations.

Strengths of the Test

- The updated RFFT Professional Manual provides normative information as well as a review of validity studies and recent research. Demographically corrected normative data based on a sample of 358 healthy, normal respondents are presented for four age groups and three education levels. Performance on the RFFT has been shown to be temporally stable; studies to date support the construct validity of the RFFT as a measure of initiation, planning, and divergent reasoning.

Scales of Cognitive Ability for Traumatic Brain Injury (SCATBI)

General Test Information

Authors:	Brenda B. Adamovich and Jennifer Henderson
Publisher:	PRO-ED
Address of Publisher:	8700 Shoal Creek Boulevard, Austin, TX 78757–6897
Telephone Number:	1-800-897-3202
Fax Number:	1-800-397-7633
Web Site of Publisher:	www.proedinc.com
Type of Test:	Neuropsychology
Administration Time:	30 minutes to 2 hours
Type of Administration:	Individual
Ages/Grade Levels:	Adolescents and adults

Purpose and Description of Test

The SCATBI assesses cognitive and linguistic abilities of adolescent and adult patients with head injuries. Its results can be used to establish the severity of the injury and can be charted to show progress during recovery.

Subtest Information

The SCATB consists of five subtests: Perception/Discrimination, Orientation, Organization, Recall, and Reasoning. Because the subtests use the same standard score scale, direct comparison of performance on the different subtests is possible. Unlike other tests for this population, the SCATBI progresses in difficulty to levels that even some noninjured adults do not typically master. This permits patients who functioned at very high levels prior to injury to be measured with the same instrument as they regain the use of higher-level abilities (such as complex organization and abstract reasoning).

Strengths of the Test

- The SCATBI is time efficient; examiners administer only the scales they think are useful for evaluating a particular patient. The SCATBI was standardized on a sample of head-injured patients and a sample of matched adults with no history of head injury.
- Internal consistency coefficients were high (.90 or higher) for all subtests. Test-retest coefficients from a patient sample ranged from a low of .73 (Reasoning) to a high of .89 (Recall).
- Concurrent validity was supported by correlations between SCATBI scores and levels of the Rancho Los Amigos Scales. Discriminant analysis showed that the five SCATBI scales accurately classified 94 percent of head-injured participants and 79 percent of noninjured participants.

Chapter 20

Occupational Therapy

A ccording to the American Occupational Therapy Association (2005),

> Occupational therapy is skilled treatment that helps individuals achieve independence in all facets of their lives. It gives people the "skills for the job of living" necessary for independent and satisfying lives. Services typically include:
>
> - Customized treatment programs to improve one's ability to perform daily activities
> - Comprehensive home and job site evaluations with adaptation recommendations
> - Performance skills assessments and treatment
> - Adaptive equipment recommendations and usage training
> - Guidance to family members and caregivers

Occupational therapies are important components of the special education process. Many school districts now have occupational therapists as part of their staff. These therapists may help students individually, in small groups, or as consultants. Occupational therapy focuses mainly on fine motor and upper body functions. The services are provided for students with disabilities who exhibit a range of difficulties such as learning disabilities (for example, fine and gross motor problems or perceptual problems), developmental delays (for example, mental retardation, vision or hearing impairment), respiratory problems (for example, cystic fibrosis or asthma), neuromuscular problems (for example, muscular dystrophy, cerebral palsy), muscle skeletal problems (for example, arthritis, orthopedic problems, postural deviations), or traumatic accidents (for example, amputations, brain injuries, burns). In addition to providing therapy for such students, occupational therapists offer many other services, including evaluations, screenings, consultations, education, and training.

Occupational evaluations may be referred to the multidisciplinary team or individualized education program (IEP) committee by any number of school or medical professionals. Parents may also ask for a referral for occupational and physical therapy services for their child. In any case, parental written consent is required for an evaluation.

Assessments that are unique to occupational therapy include:

- Neuromuscular functioning
- Sensory processing
- Manual dexterity
- Leisure-time abilities
- Physical facilities
- Prevocational skills
- Oral motor and feeding problems

Following is a list of problems requiring occupational therapy:

- Perceptual problems (eye-hand coordination)
- Sensory problems (sensitive to sound, visual changes, and odors and overly sensitive to touch)
- Gross motor difficulties (trouble with balance, coordination, moving)
- Fine motor problems (difficulty with coordination, handwriting, using scissors)
- Hardship with daily living activities (cannot dress, feed, or care for self)
- Organizational problems (difficulties with memory, time, spatial concepts)
- Attention span difficulties (difficulties focusing on task, short attention span)
- Interpersonal problems (difficulty with environmental and school-related social situations)

An occupational therapist can conduct the following evaluations:

- Vision
- Abnormal movement patterns
- Range of motion
- Skeletal and joint conditions
- Behavior
- Skin and soft tissue
- Fine motor
- Perceptual
- Gross motor
- Balance and equilibrium
- Activities for daily living
- Equipment analysis

Occupational therapists may act as liaisons between the IEP committee, the teaching staff, medical professionals, outside agencies, and parents. Many pupils in need of occupational therapy have severe medical problems that often require supervision of a family doctor. The occupational therapist should help with the coordination between the school physician and the family doctor. Consequently, the occupational therapist may play an important role in the special education process.

When the IEP team determines that occupational therapy is needed for a student in order to meet his or her annual goals, then occupational therapy should be included in the student's IEP (American Occupational Therapy Association, 2003).

Adolescent/Adult Sensory Profile

General Test Information

Authors:	Catana Brown and Winnie Dunn
Publisher:	Harcourt Assessment (formerly known as the Psychological Corporation and Harcourt Educational)
Address of Publisher:	6277 Sea Harbor Drive, Orlando, FL 32887
Telephone Number:	1-800-211-8378
Fax Number:	1-800-232-1223
Web Site of Publisher:	www.harcourt.com
Type of Test:	Occupational therapy
Administration Time:	20 to 30 minutes
Type of Administration:	Individual
Ages/Grade Levels:	Ages 11 through adult

Purpose and Description of Test

The Adolescent/Adult Sensory Profile enables clients to evaluate themselves through the use of a self-questionnaire. It is a standardized method for professionals to measure sensory processing abilities and profile the effect of sensory processing on functional performance in the daily life of an individual. There are sixty items in the profile. Individuals complete the profile by reporting how frequently they respond in the way described by each item.

Strengths of the Test

- According to its publisher, the Adolescent/Adult Sensory Profile provides a way for professionals to engage in theory-based decision making during assessment and intervention planning.
- The profile yields four scores that correspond to the four quadrants of sensory processing: sensation seeking, sensation avoiding, sensory sensitivity, and low registration.
- It is nonintrusive and easy to administer and score.

Bruininks-Oseretsky Test of Motor Proficiency

General Test Information

Author: Robert Bruininks
Publisher: AGS Publishing
Address of Publisher: 4201 Woodland Road, Circle Pines, MN 55014–1796
Telephone Number: 1-800-328-2560, 1-651-287-7220
Fax Number: 1-800-471-8457
Web Site of Publisher: www.agsnet.com
Type of Test: Motor skills/occupational therapy evaluation
Administration Time: Complete battery: 45 to 60 minutes; short form: 15 to 20 minutes
Type of Administration: Individual
Ages/Grade Levels: Ages 4–6 to 14–5

Purpose and Description of Test

The Bruininks-Oseretsky Test of Motor Proficiency is an individually administered measure of gross and fine motor skills. It is a forty-six-item physical performance and paper-and-pencil assessment measure containing eight subtests. The examiner observes and records the student's performance on certain tasks, and the student is given a booklet in which he or she completes cutting and paper-and-pencil tasks.

Subtest Information

The test consists of eight subtests in three areas:

- *Gross motor development:* Running Speed and Agility, Balance, Bilateral Coordination, Strength (Arm, Shoulder, Abdominal, and Leg)
- *Gross and fine motor development:* Upper-Limb Coordination
- *Fine motor development:* Response Speed, Visual-Motor Control, Upper-Limb and Speed Dexterity

Strengths of the Test

- The test is relatively inexpensive.
- The short form is useful for testing large numbers of students because of its ease of administration and short test time.
- The manual is clearly written.
- The test is an enjoyable one for children.
- The Bruininks-Oseretsky Test thoroughly assesses the motor proficiency of able-bodied students, as well as students with serious motor dysfunctions and developmental handicaps. The test can also be useful in developing and evaluating motor training programs.

Children's Assessment of Participation (CAPE) and Enjoyment and Preferences for Activities of Children (PAC)

General Test Information

Authors:	Gilliam King, Mary Law, Susanne King, Patricia Hurley, Peter Rosenbaum, Steven Hanna, Marilyn Kertoy, and Nancy Young
Publisher:	Harcourt Assessment (formerly known as the Psychological Corporation and Harcourt Educational)
Address of Publisher:	6277 Sea Harbor Drive, Orlando, FL 32887
Telephone Number:	1-800-211-8378
Fax Number:	1-800-232-1223
Web Site of Publisher:	www.harcourt.com
Type of Test:	Occupational therapy evaluation
Administration Time:	CAPE: 30 to 45 minutes; PAC: 15 to 20 minutes
Type of Administration:	Individual
Ages/Grade Levels:	Ages 6 to 21

Purpose and Description of Test

The CAPE is a standard method to explore an individual's day-to-day participation for the purpose of intervention planning or measuring outcomes. The PAC may be used to assess an individual's preference for activities.

Subtest Information

Activity types addressed in both measures include recreational, physical, social, skill based, and self-improvement.

Strengths of the Test

- CAPE and PAC measure both participation and engagement in activities, as well as the child's preferences.
- Both measures may be administered by having the client complete the record form with assistance from the parent or caregiver or by the clinician using the activity and category cards.

FirstSTEp: Screening Test for Evaluating Preschoolers (FirstSTEp)

General Test Information

Author:	Lucy J. Miller
Publisher:	Harcourt Assessment (formerly known as the Psychological Corporation and Harcourt Educational)
Address of Publisher:	6277 Sea Harbor Drive, Orlando, FL 32887
Telephone Number:	1-800-211-8378
Fax Number:	1-800-232-1223
Web Site of Publisher:	www.harcourt.com
Type of Test:	Occupational therapy
Administration Time:	15 minutes
Type of Administration:	Individual
Ages/Grade Levels:	Level 1: ages 2–9 to 3–8; Level 2: ages 3–9 to 4–8; Level 3: ages 4–9 to 6–2

Purpose and Description of Test

This test is designed to identify children who exhibit moderate preacademic problems. The FirstSTEp is a short but comprehensive preschool assessment instrument that evaluates children for mild to moderate developmental delays. The test includes an examiner's manual, item score sheets, and all materials needed for administration.

Subtest Information

The test consists of five performance areas:

- *Foundations Index*—assesses abilities involving basic motor tasks and the awareness of sensations, both of which are fundamental for the development of complex skills
- *Coordination Index*—assesses complex gross, fine, and oral motor abilities
- *Verbal Index*—assesses memory, sequencing, comprehension, association, and expression in a verbal context
- *Nonverbal Index*—assesses memory, sequencing, visualization, and the performance of mental manipulations not requiring spoken language
- *Complex Tasks Index*—measures sensorimotor abilities in conjunction with cognitive abilities

Strengths of the Test

- The publisher presents detailed information in the manual for the administration of each of the five indexes.
- It is a short, carefully developed, and well-standardized test.
- The test can be scored quickly.
- FirstSTEp is sensitive enough to detect even mild developmental delays and can identify children who need in-depth diagnostic testing.
- It addresses the Individuals with Disabilities Education Improvement Act domains of cognition, communication, and motor.
- Reports classify results as Within Acceptable Limits, Caution, or At-Risk.

Infant/Toddler Sensory Profile

General Test Information

Author:	Winnie Dunn
Publisher:	Harcourt Assessment (formerly known as the Psychological Corporation and Harcourt Educational)
Address of Publisher:	6277 Sea Harbor Drive, Orlando, FL 32887
Telephone Number:	1-800-211-8378
Fax Number:	1-800-232-1223
Web Site of Publisher:	www.harcourt.com
Type of Test:	Occupational therapy evaluation
Administration Time:	15 minutes
Type of Administration:	Individual
Ages/Grade Levels:	Birth to 36 months

Purpose and Description of Test

The Infant/Toddler Sensory Profile is a standardized tool to examine sensory processing patterns in infants and toddlers who are at risk or have specific disabilities related to sensory processing abilities.

Subtest Information

The Sensory Profile contains item categories that reflect particular types of sensory processing (for example, auditory processing, visual processing) with quadrant scores based on Dunn's Model of Sensory Processing (Low Registration, Sensory Seeking, Sensory Sensitive, Sensation Avoiding).

Strengths of the Test

- Provides a natural way to include families in the information-gathering process.
- Provides a way for professionals to engage in theory-based decision making during assessment and intervention planning.
- Provides the clinician with information to determine early intervention for an infant's best outcomes.

Miller Function and Participation Scales (M-FUN-PS)

General Test Information

Author:	Lucy J. Miller
Publisher:	Harcourt Assessment (formerly known as the Psychological Corporation and Harcourt Educational)
Address of Publisher:	6277 Sea Harbor Drive, Orlando, FL 32887
Telephone Number:	1-800-211-8378
Fax Number:	1-800-232-1223
Web Site of Publisher:	www.harcourt.com
Type of Test:	Occupational therapy evaluation
Administration Time:	55 to 65 minutes
Type of Administration:	Individual
Ages/Grade Levels:	Ages 2–6 through 7–11

Purpose and Description of Test

The M-FUN-PS assesses a child's functional performance related to school participation. It is designed to assess a child's motor performance in functional tasks needed to participate successfully in classroom and school activities.

Subtest Information

Motor and visual motor performance items are embedded in functional activities. Children are administered items in functional activities that are typical of preschool and primary school environments. Component motor skills are scored throughout each activity.

Strengths of the Test

- This assessment uses the International Classification of Functioning, Disability, and Health as a framework and addresses participation, activity, and body function.

Peabody Developmental Motor Scales–
Second Edition (PDMS-2)

General Test Information

Authors: M. Rhonda Folio and Rebecca R. Fewell
Publisher: PRO-ED
Address of Publisher: 8700 Shoal Creek Boulevard, Austin, TX 78757–6897
Telephone Number: 1-800-897-3202
Fax Number: 1-800-397-7633
Web Site of Publisher: www.proedinc.com
Type of Test: Motor skills/occupational therapy evaluation
Administration Time: Untimed; 20 to 30 minutes
Type of Administration: Individual
Ages/Grade Levels: Birth to 5 years

Purpose and Description of Test

The PDMS-2 is an early childhood motor development program that provides in one package both in-depth assessment and training or remediation of gross and fine motor skills.

Subtest Information

The assessment is composed of six subtests that measure interrelated motor abilities that develop early in life:

- *Reflexes:* This eight-item subtest measures a child's ability to react automatically to environmental events. Because reflexes typically become integrated by the time a child is 12 months old, this subtest is given only to children from birth through 11 months.
- *Stationary:* This thirty-item subtest measures a child's ability to sustain control of his or her body within its center of gravity and retain equilibrium.
- *Locomotion:* This eighty-nine-item subtest measures a child's ability to move from one place to another. The actions measured are crawling, walking, running, hopping, and jumping forward.
- *Object Manipulation:* This twenty-four-item subtest measures a child's ability to manipulate balls. Examples of the actions measured are catching, throwing, and kicking. Because these skills are not apparent until a child has reached the age of 11 months, this subtest is given only to children ages 12 months and older.
- *Grasping:* This twenty-six-item subtest measures a child's ability to use his or her hands. It begins with the ability to hold an object with one hand and progresses up to actions involving the controlled use of the fingers of both hands.
- *Visual-Motor Integration:* This seventy-two-item subtest measures a child's ability to use his or her visual perceptual skills to perform complex eye-hand coordination tasks such as reaching and grasping for an object, building with blocks, and copying designs.

Strengths of the Test

- Psychometrically, the second edition of the PDMS has improved in the following ways:
  - Studies showing the absence of gender and racial bias have been added.
  - Reliability coefficients were computed for subgroups of the normative sample (for example, individuals with motor disabilities, African Americans, Hispanic Americans, females, and males), as well as for the entire normative sample.
  - New validity studies have been conducted; special attention has been devoted to showing that the test is valid for a wide variety of subgroups as well as for the general population.
  - Each item was evaluated using both conventional item analyses to choose "good" statistical items and the new differential item functioning analyses to find biased items.
- The PDMS-2 has also improved or added the following user-friendly components:
  - The new Profile/Summary Forms enable the examiner to record the child's scores and graphically display the child's performance in two formats.
  - The new Examiner Record Booklets contain all of the items to be given to the child.
  - The Peabody Motor Activities Program is the instruction and treatment program for the PDMS-2. It contains units organized developmentally by skill area.
  - The new Peabody Motor Development Chart provides the examiner with a convenient reference for the motor skills measured by the PDMS-2 and the ages at which 50 percent of the normative sample performed the skill.

Perceived Efficacy and Goal Setting System (PEGS)

General Test Information

Authors:	Cherly Missiuna, Nancy Pollock, and Mary Law
Publisher:	Harcourt Assessment (formerly known as the Psychological Corporation and Harcourt Educational)
Address of Publisher:	6277 Sea Harbor Drive, Orlando, FL 32887
Telephone Number:	1-800-211-8378
Fax Number:	1-800-232-1223
Web Site of Publisher:	www.harcourt.com
Type of Test:	Occupational therapy evaluation
Administration Time:	20 to 30 minutes
Type of Administration:	Individual
Ages/Grade Levels:	Ages 5–0 to 10–11

Purpose and Description of Test

The PEGS enables children to participate in goal setting with an innovative measure. The forty-eight PEGS Picture Cards are arranged in pairs that depict children performing twenty-four tasks that a school-aged child typically does every day. In order to determine the child's perception of his or her competence, the child is asked to indicate which picture is more like him or her and whether that picture is a lot or a little like him or her. After viewing twenty-four sets of pictures, the child has the opportunity to state additional tasks that are difficult for him or her to perform. The therapist discusses the tasks with the child and goes through a process of goal setting with the child to establish priorities for intervention.

Strengths of the Test

- PEGS uses colorful picture cards to enable even young children to reflect on their participation in daily activities and select areas for intervention.
- Parent and teacher questionnaires give insight into their perceptions of the child's performance and participation.
- Clinicians can compare responses of the child, parent, and teacher to establish collaborative goals.
- The test can be administered to children diagnosed with attention deficit-hyperactivity disorder, cerebral palsy, autism, developmental coordination disorder, learning disabilities, medical conditions, and other functional motor impairments.
- Activities that are focused on in the self-report measure reflect skills that have normally been acquired by children of this age and are essential for daily living and participation at school.

Quick Neurological Screening Test–Second Edition (QNST-II)

General Test Information

Authors:	Margaret Mutti, Harold Sterling, Nancy A. Martin, and Norma Spalding
Publisher:	Academic Therapy
Address of Publisher:	20 Commercial Boulevard, Novato, CA 94949
Telephone Number:	1-800-422-7249
Fax Number:	1-888-287-9975
Web Site of Publisher:	http://www.academictherapy.com
Type of Test:	Occupational therapy
Administration Time:	Untimed; approximately 20 minutes to administer
Type of Administration:	Individual
Ages/Grade Levels:	Ages 5 to 18

Purpose and Description of Test

The test is designed to assess neurological integration as it relates to learning. It is used for the early screening of learning disabilities. The QNST-II is a screening test that assesses fifteen areas of neurological integration. It requires the examinee to perform a series of motor tasks adapted from neurological pediatric examinations and from neuropsychological and developmental scales. Each of the areas tested involves a motor task similar to those observed in neurological pediatric examinations. The test includes recording forms, an examiner's manual, reproduction sheets, remedial guidelines, and an administration and scoring flip card.

Subtest Information

The following areas of neurological integration are measured by the QNST-II:

- Motor development
- Fine and gross motor control
- Motor planning and sequencing and rhythm
- Visual and spatial perception
- Spatial organization
- Balance and vestibular function
- Attentional disorders

Strengths of the Test

- Performance patterns screen for early identification of learning disabilities. Scoring patterns suggest possible avenues for further diagnostic assessment.
- The QNST-II manual explores the importance of such soft neurological signs in educational settings as well as the medical implications. Special education personnel will appreciate knowing whether behaviors seen in the classroom have physiological or emotional origins. The detailed scoring information also provides other rehabilitation professionals invaluable assistance with planning appropriate remediation.
- According to the publisher, "An optional training video and extensive pictures within the text provide guidance for scoring each task."

Sensory Integration and Praxis Tests (SIPT)

General Test Information

Author:	A. Jean Ayres.
Publisher:	Western Psychological Services
Address of Publisher:	12031 Wilshire Boulevard, Los Angeles, CA 90025–1251
Telephone Number:	1-800-648-8857 (United States and Canada only), 1-310-478-2061
Fax Number:	1-310-478-7838
Web Site of Publisher:	http://www.wpspublish.com
Type of Test:	Occupational therapy
Administration Time:	The entire battery can be given in 2 hours, and any of the individual tests can be administered separately in about 10 minutes.
Type of Administration:	Individual
Ages/Grade Levels:	Ages 4–0 to 8–11

Purpose and Description of Test

The SIPT is an occupational therapy test measuring the sensory integration processes that underlie learning and behavior.

Subtest Information

SIPT measures visual, tactile, and kinesthetic perception as well as motor performance. It is composed of seventeen brief tests:

Space Visualization	Figure-Ground	Standing/Walking Balance
Design Copying	Postural Praxis	Bilateral Motor
Praxis on Verbal Command	Constructional Praxis	Coordination
Motor Accuracy	Sequencing Praxis	Postrotary Nystagmus
Manual Form Perception	Kinesthesia	Oral Praxis
Graphesthesia	Localization of Tactile Stimuli	Finger Identification

Strengths of the Test

- Norms are provided for each test based on a national sample of more than 2,000 children between the ages of 4–0 and 8–11.
- By showing how children organize and respond to sensory input, SIPT helps pinpoint organic problems associated with learning disabilities, emotional disorders, and minimal brain dysfunction.

Sensory Profile

General Test Information

Author:	Winnie Dunn
Publisher:	Harcourt Assessment (formerly known as the Psychological Corporation and Harcourt Educational)
Address of Publisher:	6277 Sea Harbor Drive, Orlando, FL 32887
Telephone Number:	1-800-211-8378
Fax Number:	1-800-232-1223
Web Site of Publisher:	www.harcourt.com
Type of Test:	Occupational therapy evaluation
Administration Time:	20 minutes
Type of Administration:	Individual
Ages/Grade Levels:	Ages 3 to 10

Purpose and Description of Test

The Sensory Profile is a standardized method for professionals to measure a child's sensory processing abilities and profile the effect of sensory processing on functional performance in the daily life of a child.

Subtest Information

The Sensory Profile contains six categories that reflect particular types of sensory processing (for example, auditory processing, visual processing), five modulation categories that reflect various combinations of modulation of input for use in daily life, and three behavioral and emotional response categories.

Strengths of the Test

- Provides a natural way to include families in the information-gathering process
- Provides parents and caregivers with validation of their children's sensory processing issues
- Provides a way for professionals to engage in theory-based decision making during the assessment process and intervention planning

Chapter 21

Personality

According to the *Diagnostic and Statistical Manual of Mental Disorders* (DSM-IV-TR) (American Psychiatric Association, 2000), "A personality disorder is an enduring pattern of inner experience and behavior that deviates markedly from the expectation of the individual's culture, is pervasive and inflexible, has an onset in adolescence or early adulthood, is stable over time, and leads to distress or impairment" (p. 685).

Personality disorders are chronic behavioral and relationship patterns that interfere with a person's life over many years (National Library of Medicine, 2004a).

There are ten distinct personality disorders identified in the DSM-IV:

• *Antisocial Personality Disorder:* To receive this diagnosis, a person must have first had behavior that qualifies for a diagnosis of conduct disorder during childhood (National Library of Medicine, 2004a). Symptoms include lack of regard for the moral or legal standards in the local culture and marked inability to get along with others or abide by societal rules. These individuals are sometimes called psychopaths or sociopaths.

• *Avoidant Personality Disorder:* This disorder is a psychiatric condition characterized by a lifelong pattern of extreme shyness, feelings of inadequacy, and sensitivity to rejection. People with this disorder form relationships with others only if they believe they will not be rejected. They are preoccupied with their own shortcomings. Loss and rejection are so painful that these individuals will choose loneliness rather than risk trying to connect with others (National Library of Medicine, 2004b). Symptoms include marked social inhibition, feelings of inadequacy, and extreme sensitive to criticism.

• *Borderline Personality Disorder:* This condition is characterized by impulsive actions, mood instability, and chaotic relationships (National Library of Medicine, 2004c). Symptoms include lack of one's own identity, with rapid changes in mood, intense and unstable interpersonal relationships, marked impulsively, feelings of emptiness and boredom, and instability in affect and self-image.

- *Dependent Personality Disorder:* This is a chronic condition involving overreliance on others to meet emotional and physical needs (National Library of Medicine, 2004d). Symptoms include an extreme need of other people, to a point where the person is unable to make any decisions or take an independent stand, fear of separation and submissive behavior, and marked lack of decisiveness and self-confidence. People with this disorder do not trust their own ability to make decisions. They may be devastated by separation and loss and may go to great lengths, even suffering abuse, to stay in a relationship.

- *Histrionic Personality Disorder:* This involves a pattern of excessive emotional expression and attention seeking, including an excessive need for approval and inappropriate seductiveness (National Library of Medicine, 2004e). Symptoms include exaggerated and often inappropriate displays of emotional reactions, approaching theatricality, in everyday behavior, and sudden and rapidly shifting emotional expressions.

- *Narcissistic Personality Disorder:* This condition is characterized by an inflated sense of self-importance and an extreme preoccupation with one's self (National Library of Medicine, 2004f). Symptoms include behavior or a fantasy of grandiosity, a lack of empathy, a need to be admired by others, an inability to see the viewpoints of others, and hypersensitivity to the opinions of others. This disorder usually begins by early adulthood and is marked by disregard for the feelings of others, grandiosity, obsessive self-interest, and the pursuit of primarily selfish goals.

- *Obsessive-Compulsive Personality Disorder:* This is a condition characterized by a chronic preoccupation with rules, orderliness, and control. People with this disorder believe that their preoccupations are appropriate. They tend to be high achievers and have a sense of urgency about their actions. They may become extremely upset if others disturb their rigidly ordered routines (National Library of Medicine, 2004g).

- *Paranoid Personality Disorder:* This is a psychiatric condition characterized by extreme distrust and suspicion of others (National Library of Medicine, 2004h). People with this disorder are highly suspicious of others, are usually unable to acknowledge their own negative feelings toward others, and have a marked distrust of others, including the belief, without reason, that others are exploiting, harming, or trying to deceive them. They lack trust, believe others will betray them, see hidden meanings, are unforgiving, and hold grudges.

- *Schizoid Personality Disorder:* This is a psychiatric condition characterized by a lifelong pattern of indifference to others and social isolation (National Library of Medicine, 2004i). The disorder is characterized by a very limited range of emotion, both in expression of and experiencing, and an indifference to social relationships. This disorder may be associated with schizophrenia and shares many of the same risk factors. However, schizoid personality disorder is not as profoundly disabling as schizophrenia, since it is not marked by hallucinations, delusions, or the complete disconnection from reality that occurs in untreated (or treatment-resistant) schizophrenia.

- *Schizotypal Personality Disorder:* This is a psychiatric condition characterized by a pattern of deficiency in interpersonal relationships and disturbances in thought patterns, appearance, and behavior (National Library of Medicine, 2004j). Symptoms include peculiarities of thinking, odd beliefs, and eccentricities of appearance, behavior, interpersonal style, and thought such as belief in psychic phenomena and having magical powers. People with schizotypal personality disorder tend to have odd beliefs and behaviors, but they are not profoundly disconnected from reality and usually do not hallucinate.

Personality tests aim to categorize an individual's temperament according to certain criteria and help determine whether a child or adult has a personality disorder. Personality tests are not meant to be used as diagnostic tools, but rather as tools to give insight into a potential disorder that may be having a negative impact on a child or adult—for example, on a child's performance in school or an adult's adjustment to work, social life, or relationships. Only a trained professional can properly administer and diagnose a personality disorder.

Aggression Questionnaire (AQ)

General Test Information

Authors:	Arnold H. Buss and W. L. Warren
Publisher:	Western Psychological Services
Address of Publisher:	12031 Wilshire Boulevard, Los Angeles, CA 90025–1251
Telephone Number:	1-800-648-8857 (United States and Canada only), 1-310-478-2061
Fax Number:	1-310-478-7838
Web Site of Publisher:	http://www.wpspublish.com
Type of Test:	Psychological/personality
Administration Time:	10 minutes
Type of Administration:	Individual
Ages/Grade Levels:	Ages 9 to adult

Purpose and Description of Test

This self-report inventory makes it possible—and practical—to routinely screen children and adults for aggressive tendencies. The AQ measures an individual's aggressive responses and ability to channel those responses in a safe, constructive manner. Because it takes just ten minutes to complete, the AQ can be administered quickly to large numbers of people.

Written at a third-grade reading level, AQ items describe characteristics related to aggression. The respondent rates each item on a five-point scale ranging from "Not at all like me" to "Completely like me." Because it is brief and easy to read, the scale can be used with virtually anyone, including respondents who have difficulty with more complex verbal measures.

Subtest Information

The AQ is a full revision of the Buss-Durkee Hostility Inventory, a long-time standard for assessing anger and aggression. It consists of just thirty-four items, scored on the following scales:

- Physical Aggression
- Verbal Aggression
- Anger
- Hostility
- Indirect Aggression

Strengths of the Test

- A total score is provided, along with an Inconsistent Responding Index. Standardization is based on a sample of 2,138 individuals, ages 9 to 88, and norms are presented in three age sets: 9 to 18, 19 to 39, and 40 to 88. In addition, norms for the Verbal Aggression and Physical Aggression scales are separated by sex.
- The test can be hand-scored in minutes, or it can be administered and scored online using the AQ Disk, which also allows the examiner to print out a detailed interpretive report on the spot.
- In clinical settings, the AQ's five subscale scores provide a level of detail that is particularly useful for treatment planning and outcome measurement. In correctional settings, the simplicity of the AQ makes it an excellent choice for documenting need for service and focusing rehabilitation efforts. In other institutional settings—schools, businesses, military installations, and geriatric or convalescent hospitals—it can be used for both screening and program evaluation. Brief and inexpensive, the AQ makes large-scale screening of aggression a realistic option.

Children's Apperception Test (CAT)

General Test Information

Authors:	Leopold Bellack and Sonya Sorel Bellack
Publisher:	PAR
Address of Publisher:	16204 North Florida Avenue, Lutz, FL 33549
Telephone Number:	1-800-331-8378, ext. 361
Fax Number:	1-800-727-9329
Web Site of Publisher:	www.parinc.com
Type of Test:	Psychological
Administration Time:	Untimed
Type of Administration:	Individual
Ages/Grade Levels:	Ages 5 to 10

Purpose and Description of Test

This projective technique presents situations of special concern to children. It consists of ten animal pictures in a social context involving the child in conflict, identities, roles, family structures, and interpersonal interaction. This test uses a storytelling technique for personality evaluation. It employs pictures of animal figures in a variety of situations because it is assumed that children will be more comfortable expressing their feelings with pictures of animals than of humans.

Strengths of the Test

- This test is a good indicator of the presence of psychological needs.
- This test is easy to administer.
- This is a popular test within school systems as part of a psychological battery.
- Children who do not produce stories readily can manipulate these forms as a play technique. The CAT-H consists of human figures and situations that parallel the original CAT.

Jesness Inventory–Revised (JI–R)

General Test Information

Author:	Carl F. Jesness
Publisher:	Multi-Health Systems
Address of Publisher:	P.O. Box 950, North Tonawanda, NY 14120–0950
Telephone Number:	1-800-456-3003, 1-416-492-2627
Fax Number:	1-888-540-4484, 1-416-492-3343
Web Site of Publisher:	www.mhs.com
Type of Test:	Psychological/personality
Administration Time:	20 to 30 minutes
Type of Administration:	Individual
Ages/Grade Levels:	Ages 8 to adult

Purpose and Description of Test

The JI–R is a personality assessment classification system for delinquent and conduct-disordered youths and adults.

Subtest Information

- Personality Scales
  - Social Maladjustment
  - Manifest Aggression
  - Value Orientation
  - Withdrawal-Depression
  - Immaturity
  - Social Anxiety
  - Autism
  - Repression
  - Alienation
  - Denial
  - Asocial Index
- Subtype Scales
  - Undersocialized, Active/Undersocialized Aggressive
  - Undersocialized, Passive Undersocialized, Passive
  - Conformist/Immature Conformist
  - Group-Oriented/Cultural Conformist
  - Pragmatist/Manipulator
  - Autonomy-Oriented/Acting-Out, Neurotic
  - Anxious/Introspective, Neurotic
  - Inhibited/Situational Emotional Reaction
  - Adaptive/Cultural Identifier

Strengths of the Test

- The JI–R is easy to understand and has long been recognized as a classic measure for assessing personality and behavior.
- It was standardized on 4,380 North American participants: 3,421 nondelinquents and 959 delinquents.

Novaco Anger Scale and Provocation Inventory (NAS-PI)

General Test Information

Author:	Raymond W. Novaco
Publisher:	Western Psychological Services
Address of Publisher:	12031 Wilshire Boulevard, Los Angeles, CA 90025–1251
Telephone Number:	1-800-648-8857 (United States and Canada only), 1-310-478-2061
Fax Number:	1-310-478-7838
Web Site of Publisher:	http://www.wpspublish.com
Type of Test:	Psychological/anger scale
Administration Time:	25 minutes
Type of Administration:	Individual
Ages/Grade Levels:	Ages 9 to 84; separate norms are provided for preadolescents and adolescents (9 to 18 years) and adults (19 years and older)

Purpose and Description of Test

Initially developed in conjunction with the MacArthur Foundation Network on Mental Health and Law, the NAS-PI helps clinicians and researchers evaluate the role of anger in various psychological and physical conditions.

Subtest Information

The NAS-PI is composed of two parts: the Novaco Anger Scale (sixty items), which tells how an individual experiences anger, and the Provocation Inventory (twenty-five items), which identifies the kinds of situations that induce anger in particular individuals:

- Novaco Anger Scale
  - *Total*—general inclination toward anger reactions, based on Cognitive, Arousal, and Behavior subscales
  - *Cognitive*—anger justification, rumination, hostile attitude, and suspicion
  - *Arousal*—anger intensity, duration, somatic tension, and irritability
  - *Behavior*—impulsive reaction, verbal aggression, physical confrontation, and indirect expression
  - *Anger Regulation*—ability to regulate anger-engendering thoughts, effect self-calming, and engage in constructive behavior when provoked
- Provocation Inventory
  - *Total*—A reflection of five content areas: disrespectful treatment, unfairness, frustration, annoying traits of others, and irritations

Strengths of the Test

- The test has shown good test-retest reliability in nonclinical, clinical, and correctional samples.
- Studies reported in the manual demonstrate that the NAS-PI can distinguish between assaultive and nonassaultive forensic inpatients and predict assaultive behavior in institutions as well as violent behavior in the community following hospital discharge.
- The NAS-PI is an excellent way to assess anger reactivity, anger suppression, and change in anger disposition.

Personality Inventory for Children–Second Edition (PIC-2)

General Test Information

Authors:	David Lachar and Christian P. Gruber
Publisher:	Western Psychological Services
Address of Publisher:	12031 Wilshire Boulevard, Los Angeles, CA 90025–1251
Telephone Number:	1-800-648-8857 (United States and Canada only), 1-310-478-2061
Fax Number:	1-310-478-7838
Web Site of Publisher:	http://www.wpspublish.com
Type of Test:	Personality inventory
Administration Time:	About 40 minutes
Type of Administration:	Individual
Ages/Grade Levels:	Ages 5 to 19

Purpose and Description of Test

The PIC-2 evaluates the emotional, behavioral, cognitive, and interpersonal adjustment of children and teens.

Subtest Information

The PIC-2 consists of various scales and subscales. These include:

- Response Validity Scales
  - Inconsistency
  - Dissimulation
  - Defensiveness

- Adjustment Scales and Subscales

Cognitive Impairment	Poor Achievement	Developmental Delay
Family Dysfunction	Parent Maladjustment	Psychological Discomfort
Depression	Sleeping Disturbance	Impulsivity
Fearlessness	Reality Distortion	Hallucinations and
Social Withdrawal	Isolation	Delusions
Dyscontrol	Noncompliance	Delinquency
Anxiety	Social Skill Deficits	Somatic Concern
Conflict with Peers	Limited Peer Status	

Strengths of the Test

- Updated items
- Expanded content coverage (for example, eating disorders and substance abuse)
- Fourth-grade reading level
- A validated Spanish-language translation
- New scales that are almost parallel to Personality Inventory for Youth (PIY) scales
- Substantially nonoverlapping scales (and subscales)
- A ninety-six-item Behavioral Summary
- Nationally representative norms
- Actuarially constructed interpretive guidelines based on external correlates
- Critical Items Summary Sheet

- Computer scoring
- The publication completes a set of three coordinated instruments: the PIC-2 provides the parent's description of the child, the PIY provides the child's self-report, and the Student Behavior Survey supplies a teacher rating. While each of these instruments has been validated to function independently, together they provide an integrated picture of the child's adjustment at home, at school, and in the community.
- The PIC-2 was standardized on ratings from 2,306 parents of boys and girls in kindergarten through grade 12. Protocols were collected from twenty-three urban, rural, and suburban schools in twelve states. Participating parents represented all socioeconomic levels and all major ethnic groups. In addition, data were collected from a sample of 1,551 parents whose children had been referred for educational or clinical intervention.

Personality Inventory for Youth (PIY)

General Test Information

Authors:	David Lachar and Christian P. Gruber
Publisher:	Western Psychological Services
Address of Publisher:	12031 Wilshire Boulevard, Los Angeles, CA 90025–1251
Telephone Number:	1-800-648-8857 (United States and Canada only), 1-310-478-2061
Fax Number:	1-310-478-7838
Web Site of Publisher:	http://www.wpspublish.com
Type of Test:	Personality inventory
Administration Time:	45 minutes
Type of Administration:	Individual
Ages/Grade Levels:	Grades 4 through 12

Purpose and Description of Test

The PIY assesses psychological problems in fourth through twelfth graders. It answers the need for a multidimensional, psychometrically sound self-report instrument designed specifically for young people. It is a broad survey of behavior, emotion, and social adjustment that focuses on both home and school.

The twenty-four subscales reveal more specific clinical content, making the PIY an excellent diagnostic tool. In addition, four validity scales help determine whether the respondent is uncooperative; is exaggerating, malingering, or responding defensively or carelessly; or does not comprehend adequately.

Written at a third-grade reading level, the PIY can be completed in forty-five minutes. (An audiotape is available for poor readers, and a Spanish Administration Booklet is provided for those who read Spanish only.) The first eighty items can be used as a brief classroom screener to quickly identify students who would show problems if the full inventory were administered.

Subtest Information

The PIY consists of various subtests

- Cognitive Impairment
  - Poor Achievement and Memory
  - Inadequate Abilities
  - Learning Problems
- Family Dysfunction
  - Parent-Child Conflict
  - Parent Maladjustment
  - Marital Discord
- Psychological Discomfort
  - Fear and Worry
  - Depression
  - Sleeping Disturbance
- Impulsivity/Distractibility
  - Brashness
  - Distractibility and Overactivity
  - Impulsivity

- Reality Distortion
  - Feelings of Alienation
  - Hallucinations and Delusions
- Social Withdrawal
  - Social Introversion
  - Isolation
- Delinquency
- Dyscontrol
- Noncompliance
- Somatic Concern
  - Psychosomatic Syndrome
  - Muscular Tension and Anxiety
  - Preoccupation with Disease
- Social Skill Deficits
  - Limited Peer Status
  - Conflict with Peers

Strengths of the Test

- A broad survey of behavior, emotion, and social adjustment, focusing on both home and school.
- Norms based on a sample of 9- to 19-year-olds.
- Third-grade reading level, with an audiocassette for problem readers.
- Student-derived validity scales that alert the examiner to problem denial, exaggeration, and random or incompetent responding.
- Subscales to enhance scale interpretation.
- The option of supplementing the PIY self-report with a parallel parent inventory (the Personality Inventory for Children–Second Edition) and a teacher problem checklist (the Student Behavior Survey).
- Standardized on a nationally representative sample of more than 2,300 students in grades 4 through 12 and developed using a clinical sample of more than 1,100, the PIY gives a reliable and valid measure of child and adolescent psychopathology, based on the respondent's own perceptions.

State-Trait Anger Expression Inventory-2 (STAXI-2)

General Test Information

Author: Charles D. Spielberger
Publisher: PAR
Address of Publisher: 16204 North Florida Avenue, Lutz, FL 33549
Telephone Number: 1-800-331-8378, ext. 361
Fax Number: 1-800-727-9329
Web Site of Publisher: http://www.parinc.com
Type of Test: Psychological
Administration Time: 5 to 10 minutes
Type of Administration: Individual or group
Ages/Grade Levels: Ages 16 and older

Purpose and Description of Test

The STAXI-2 provides easily administered and objectively scored measures of the experience, expression, and control of anger for adolescents and adults age 16 and older. It was developed to assess components of anger and anger expression for a detailed evaluation of normal and abnormal personality and to measure the way these components of anger contribute to medical conditions such as hypertension and coronary heart disease. Recent studies on the nature of anger and its effects on mental and physical health guided the development of STAXI-2. To investigate the effects of anger on mental and physical disorders, the experience of anger must be clearly distinguished from anger expression and control.

Subtest Information

The fifty-seven-item STAXI-2 consists of six scales, five subscales, and an Anger Expression Index that provides an overall measure of total anger expression. The STAXI-2 scales are:

- State Anger
- Trait Anger
- Anger Expression–Out
- Anger Expression–In
- Anger Control–Out
- Anger Control–In
- Anger Expression Index

The STAXI-2 State Anger scale assesses the intensity of anger as an emotional state at a particular time. The Trait Anger scale measures how often angry feelings are experienced over time. The Anger Expression and Anger Control scales assess four relatively independent anger-related traits: (1) expression of anger toward other persons or objects in the environment (Anger Expression–Out), (2) holding in or suppressing angry feelings (Anger Expression–In), (3) controlling angry feelings by preventing the expression of anger toward other persons or objects in the environment (Anger Control–Out), and (4) controlling suppressed angry feelings by calming down or cooling off (Anger Control–In).

Strengths of the Test

- A sixth-grade reading ability is generally required to complete the STAXI-2. Individuals rate themselves on four-point scales that assess both the intensity of their anger at a particular time and the frequency that they experience, express, and control anger.
- The normative sample for the STAXI-2 included more than 1,900 individuals (1,644 normal adults, 276 hospitalized psychiatric patients). Normative tables provide raw-score-to-percentile and raw-score-to-*T*-score conversions for STAXI-2 scale and subscale scores for the total normative sample, as well as by gender for three age groups: 16 to 19 years, 20 to 29 years, and 30 years and older.
- The STAXI-2 can be administered and scored by individuals with limited training. Interpretation requires professional training in psychology, psychiatry, or educational testing.
- The STAXI-2 materials include the professional manual, reusable item booklets, carbonless self-rating sheets, and profile forms. The manual provides directions for administration and scoring, information on the construction and development of the STAXI/STAXI-2, guidelines for interpretation, validation studies, a summary of current research, and an extensive bibliography. A profile form for graphing percentiles or *T*-scores facilitates the interpretation of individual patterns in scale and subscale scores.

Thematic Apperception Test (TAT)

General Test Information

Authors:	Henry A. Murray
Publisher:	PAR
Address of Publisher:	16204 North Florida Avenue, Lutz, FL 33549
Telephone Number:	1-800-331-8378, ext. 361
Fax Number:	1-800-727-9329
Web Site of Publisher:	http://www.parinc.com
Type of Test:	Psychological/personality test
Administration Time:	Variable
Type of Administration:	Individual
Ages/Grade Levels:	Ages 10 and older

Purpose and Description of Test

Created in 1943, the TAT remains a widely used projective test that helps assess an individual's perception of interpersonal relationships. The thirty-one picture cards are used to stimulate stories or descriptions about relationships or social situations and can help identify dominant drives, emotions, sentiments, conflicts, and complexes. The TAT is useful as part of a comprehensive study of personality and in the interpretation of behavior disorders, psychosomatic illnesses, neuroses, and psychoses.

Strengths of the Test

- The test is a good indicator of the presence of psychological needs.
- The test is easy to administer.
- The test is very popular within school systems as part of a psychological battery because of the easy administration and the quality of information that can be obtained.

Chapter 22

Psychological

Psychology is the scientific study of behavior and mental processes. Psychological tests assess and evaluate information that an individual gives to the examiner, which is why the formal name of psychological testing is *psychological assessment.*

Psychological tests are used to measure individual differences (for example, in personality, aptitude, ability, attainment, or intelligence) and can be systematically scored and administered.

They are usually administered and interpreted by a psychologist because academic courses and supervision in psychological testing are an integral part of the doctoral degree in clinical psychology (Richmond, 2005). Psychologists are trained in the administration, scoring, and interpretation of psychological tests. The use of psychological tests in a therapeutic or diagnostic setting should be restricted to licensed psychologists. Other mental health professionals (psychiatrists, social workers, counselors) are usually not trained in the administration, scoring, and interpretation of psychological tests (Psychology Information Online, 2005).

The selection of which psychological tests to use when assessing individuals is very important. According to the Chartered Institute of Personnel and Development (2006), evaluators should ensure they receive satisfactory answers from the test suppliers to the following questions before selecting a test to use:

- Are the norms provided by the supplier for comparative purposes up to date and appropriate for the user's requirements?
- Do the norm results apply to a sufficiently representative mix of occupations, gender, or ethnic groups to allow fair comparison with the user's group?
- Has the test been used effectively in similar circumstances?
- How reliable is the test, and how consistent is it as a measure?
- How valid is the test, and does it identify the attributes or skills that the supplier claims?
- Is the method of test evaluation and scoring appropriate to the purpose for which the test will be used?
- What evidence can suppliers provide that their tests do not unfairly disadvantage certain groups?
- Will the test seem appropriate in the eyes of those taking it, and what have previous reactions been to this test?

If the answers to these questions are not available or are unsatisfactory, then the test should not be used.

Adolescent Psychopathology Scale (APS)

General Test Information

Author:	William M. Reynolds
Publisher:	PRO-ED
Address of Publisher:	8700 Shoal Creek Boulevard, Austin, TX 78757–6897
Telephone Number:	1-800-897-3202
Fax Number:	1-800-397-7633
Web Site of Publisher:	www.proedinc.com
Type of Test:	Psychological
Administration Time:	45 to 60 minutes
Type of Administration:	Individual or group
Ages/Grade Levels:	Ages 12 to 19

Purpose and Description of Test

The APS evaluates specific *Diagnostic and Statistical Manual of Mental Disorders,* Fourth Edition (DSM-IV; American Psychiatric Association, 2000) symptoms found in adolescents and assesses other problems and behaviors that may interfere with an adolescent's psychosocial adaptation and personal competence. The APS is a multidimensional self-report measure of a wide range of psychopathological, personality, and social-emotional problems and competencies. Its 346 items directly evaluate specific DSM-IV symptoms of psychiatric disorders found in adolescents.

Subtest Information

This broad-based instrument is composed of forty scales that measure four broad content domains:

- Twenty clinical disorder scales (twenty DSM-I Axis I disorders)
- Five personality disorder scales
- Eleven psychosocial problem content scales
- Four response-style indicator scales

Strengths of the Test

- The APS also assesses other psychological problems and behaviors that interfere with the adolescent's psychosocial adaptation and personal competence, including substance abuse, suicidal behavior, emotional liability, excessive anger, aggression, alienation, and introversion.
- The APS employs a unique multiple-response format designed to conform to the nature of the specific DSM-IV symptom criteria.
- APS scores represent the severity of disorder-specific symptomatology evaluated across different time periods.

Joseph Picture Self-Concept Scale

General Test Information

Author:	Jack Joseph
Publisher:	Western Psychological Services
Address of Publisher:	12031 Wilshire Boulevard, Los Angeles, CA 90025–1251
Telephone Number:	1-800-648-8857 (United States and Canada only), 1-310-478-2061
Fax Number:	1-310-478-7838
Web Site of Publisher:	http://www.wpspublish.com
Type of Test:	Self-concept scale
Administration Time:	5 to 10 minutes
Type of Administration:	Individual
Ages/Grade Levels:	Ages 3–0 to 13–11

Purpose and Description of Test

The Joseph Picture Self-Concept Scale test quickly identifies children whose negative self-appraisals put them at risk for academic and behavioral difficulties. The scale employs a unique administration format that lets youngsters respond using pictures rather than words. Children are shown pairs of illustrations representing common self-appraisal situations and are asked to choose between a picture representing positive self-concept and another representing negative self-concept. For example, one picture might show a youngster being disciplined and the other a youngster being praised. The examiner asks the child to indicate which of the two illustrated situations happens to him or her more frequently. The child may answer orally or may simply point to his or her choice.

The scale consists of two forms: the Young Child Interview (Form Y), used to assess children ages 3–0 to 7–11, and the Older Child Interview (Form O), designed for children ages 7–0 to 13–11. Each form includes its own Stimulus Booklets—Light-Skin and Dark-Skin versions—which contain picture pairs for both boys and girls. Form Y has twenty-one items and Form O, thirty items. Either form can be completed in five to ten minutes.

Strengths of the Test

- This interview-and-picture response format is particularly useful with preschoolers and older children who may have developmental problems or language difficulties. Because it requires no reading, the Joseph Picture Self-Concept Scale can be used with virtually any child.
- Both forms yield a Total Self-Concept Score as well as clinical indicators of response validity. Standardization is based on a sample of 934 children, from 3 to 13 years old, who were assessed with either the Young Child ($n = 379$) or Older Child ($n = 555$) form.
- In addition to its clinical applications, the Joseph Scale can be used to evaluate psychological and educational interventions, investigate the relationship between self-concept and other traits and behaviors (for example, empathy, school readiness, disruptive behaviors, depression), and monitor changes in self-concept over time.

Mental Status Checklist–Adolescent (MSC-Adolescent)

General Test Information

Authors:	Edward H. Dougherty and John A. Schinka
Publisher:	PAR
Address of Publisher:	16204 North Florida Avenue, Lutz, FL 33549
Telephone Number:	1-800-331-8378, ext. 361
Fax Number:	1-800-727-9329
Web Site of Publisher:	http://www.parinc.com
Type of Test:	Psychological
Administration Time:	Varies
Type of Administration:	Individual
Ages/Grade Levels:	Ages 13–0 to 17–11

Purpose and Description of Test

Designed for use with adolescents ages 13 to 17 years, this checklist consists of 174 items in ten areas typically included in a mental status examination of adolescents, including presenting problems, recreation and reinforcers, personal information, family and peer relationships, physical and behavioral observations, developmental status, academic performance and attitudes, health and habits, legal issues and aggressive behavior, and impressions and recommendations.

Strengths of the Test

- According to its publisher, the MSC is "helpful in assessing adolescent mental status."
- Used to identify problems and establish rapport in order to prepare children for further diagnostic testing.
- Provides written documentation of presenting problems.

Mental Status Checklist–Children (MSC-Children)

General Test Information

Authors:	Edward H. Dougherty and John A. Schinka
Publisher:	PAR
Address of Publisher:	16204 North Florida Avenue, Lutz, FL 33549
Telephone Number:	1-800-331-8378, ext. 361
Fax Number:	1-800-727-9329
Web Site of Publisher:	http://www.parinc.com
Type of Test:	Psychological
Administration Time:	Untimed; 10 to 20 minutes
Type of Administration:	Individual
Ages/Grade Levels:	Ages 5–0 to 12–11

Purpose and Description of Test

Intended for use with children ages 5 to 12 years, the children's version of the Mental Status Checklist consists of 153 items. The ten topic areas, identical to those found in the adolescent version, contain items specific to developmental issues for children. This checklist provides a detailed outline for capturing information from the child, parents, and caregivers.

Strengths of the Test

- According to its publisher, the MSC is "helpful in assessing mental status of children."
- Used to identify problems and establish rapport in order to prepare children for further diagnostic testing.
- Provides written documentation of presenting problems.

Multi-Dimensional Self-Concept Scale (MSCS)

General Test Information

Author:	Bruce Bracken
Publisher:	PRO-ED
Address of Publisher:	8700 Shoal Creek Boulevard, Austin, TX 78757–6897
Telephone Number:	1-800-897-3202
Fax Number:	1-800-397-7633
Web Site of Publisher:	www.proedinc.com
Type of Test:	Self-concept
Administration Time:	20 minutes
Type of Administration:	Individual or group
Ages/Grade Levels:	Youth/adolescents

Purpose and Description of Test

The MSCS assesses global self-concept and six context-dependent self-concept domains that are functionally and theoretically important in the social-emotional adjustment of youth and adolescents.

Subtest Information

The six domains assessed by the MSCS are the most important areas of psychosocial functioning for youth and adolescents:

- Social
- Competence
- Affect
- Academic
- Family
- Physical

Strengths of the Test

- Each MSCS subscale evidences very high reliability (coefficient alpha more than .90), and the Total Scale Score reliability exceeds .97 for the total sample.
- The MSCS correlates strongly with other measures of self-concept and self-esteem and has been shown empirically to identify clients previously identified as being low in self-concept.
- Several concurrent validity studies were conducted during the MSCS development and are presented in the manual.

My Worst Experience Scale (MWES)

General Test Information

Authors:	Irwin A. Hyman, Pamela A. Snook, John M. Berna, Joseph DuCette, and Melinda A. Kohr
Publisher:	Western Psychological Services
Address of Publisher:	12031 Wilshire Boulevard, Los Angeles, CA 90025–1251
Telephone Number:	1-800-648-8857 (United States and Canada only), 1-310-478-2061
Fax Number:	1-310-478-7838
Web Site of Publisher:	http://www.wpspublish.com
Type of Test:	Psychological
Administration Time:	20 to 30 minutes
Type of Administration:	Individual
Ages/Grade Levels:	Ages 9 to 18

Purpose and Description of Test

Most instruments that are used to diagnose posttraumatic stress disorder in children rely on information from adults. Few address developmental issues specific to youth. The MWES lets children and teens speak for themselves. This self-report scale asks them about symptoms that young people typically experience following a traumatic event. In addition, the MWES conforms to standard diagnostic criteria for posttraumatic stress disorder (PTSD).

Subtest Information

The MWES is composed of two sections. Part One asks respondents to indicate which of twenty-one events—including natural disasters, divorce, assault, abuse, loss, and school problems—was their worst experience and to answer six questions about the nature of that experience. (If the event chosen involves school, they can provide more detailed information by completing a supplementary form, the School Trauma and Alienation Survey.) Part Two then asks respondents to indicate the frequency and duration of 105 thoughts, feelings, and behaviors that they may have experienced after the traumatic event.

Strengths of the Test

- The MWES helps identify PTSD in children, whether it is caused by events traditionally viewed as traumatic or those only recently traumatic, such as excessive spanking, bullying, or divorce. In addition, the MWES can be used to monitor symptom change during clinical interventions.
- Easy to administer and score, the test can be given not only to individual children but also to large groups as part of a mental health audit following school tragedies or other disastrous events.

Piers-Harris Children's Self-Concept Scale– Second Edition (Piers-Harris 2)

General Test Information

Authors:	Ellen V. Piers, Dale B. Harris, and David S. Herzberg
Publisher:	Western Psychological Services
Address of Publisher:	12031 Wilshire Boulevard, Los Angeles, CA 90025–1251
Telephone Number:	1-800-648-8857 (United States and Canada only), 1-310-478-2061
Fax Number:	1-310-478-7838
Web Site of Publisher:	http://www.wpspublish.com
Type of Test:	Self-concept
Administration Time:	10 to 15 minutes
Type of Administration:	Individual
Ages/Grade Levels:	Ages 7 to 18

Purpose and Description of Test

The Piers-Harris, one of the most widely used measures of psychological health in children and adolescents, is now available in a revised and updated second edition. Like the original scale, the Piers-Harris 2 quickly identifies youngsters who need further testing or treatment. It is widely used in schools and clinics. It is often administered as routine classroom screening to identify children who might benefit from further evaluation. And it is commonly used in clinical settings to determine specific areas of conflict, typical coping and defense mechanisms, and appropriate intervention techniques.

Subtest Information

The Piers-Harris 2 consists of six subscales:

- Physical Appearance and Attributes
- Intellectual and School Status
- Happiness and Satisfaction
- Freedom from Anxiety
- Behavioral Adjustment
- Popularity

Strengths of the Test

- The revision has a larger, more diverse standardization sample than the previous edition: 1,387 students from districts throughout the United States.
- The age range has been expanded to ages 7 to 18 rather than 8 to 18.
- The length has been reduced from eighty to sixty items. There are no new or reassigned items, so the revision is compatible with the original.

Reynolds Adolescent Adjustment Screening Inventory (RAASI)

General Test Information

Author:	William M. Reynolds
Publisher:	PAR
Address of Publisher:	16204 North Florida Avenue, Lutz, FL 33549
Telephone Number:	1-800-331-8378, ext. 361
Fax Number:	1-800-727-9329
Web Site of Publisher:	http://www.parinc.com
Type of Test:	Psychological
Administration Time:	Approximately 5 minutes
Type of Administration:	Individual or group
Ages/Grade Levels:	Ages 12 to 19

Purpose and Description of Test

The RAASI quickly identifies adolescents who need psychological evaluation and services. These adolescents may exhibit significant adjustment problems in the areas of antisocial behaviors, anger problems, and emotional distress. The RAASI contains thirty-two items derived from the item pool of the Adolescent Psychopathology Scale. It requires only a third-grade reading level.

Strengths of the Test

- Helpful in identifying at-risk adolescents.
- Hand-scorable test booklet.
- Raw-score-to-*T*-score conversions for total standardization sample, gender, age group, and gender-by-age group.
- Normative data derived from 1,827 adolescents.
- Reliability coefficients range from .71 to .88 for the scales and .91 for the total score.
- Test-retest reliability ranges from .83 to .89.

Self-Esteem Index (SEI)

General Test Information

Authors:	Linda Brown and Jacquelyn Alexander
Publisher:	PRO-ED
Address of Publisher:	8700 Shoal Creek Boulevard, Austin, TX 78757–6897
Telephone Number:	1-800-897-3202
Fax Number:	1-800-397-7633
Web Site of Publisher:	www.proedinc.com
Type of Test:	Self-esteem index
Administration Time:	30 minutes
Type of Administration:	Individual or group
Ages/Grade Levels:	Ages 7–0 to 18–11

Purpose and Description of Test

The SEI is a multidimensional measure of the way that individuals perceive and value themselves.

Subtest Information

There are four scales on the SEI:

- Academic Competence
- Family Acceptance
- Peer Popularity
- Personal Security

Overall self-esteem is measured by the Self-Esteem Quotient.

Strengths of the Test

- Evidence of the reliability of the SEI is provided in the form of coefficients alpha computed at each one-year age interval, all of which approach or exceed accepted standards.

Trauma Symptom Inventory (TSI)

General Test Information

Author:	John N. Briere
Publisher:	PAR
Address of Publisher:	16204 North Florida Avenue, Lutz, FL 33549
Telephone Number:	1-800-331-8378, ext. 361
Fax Number:	1-800-727-9329
Web Site of Publisher:	http://www.parinc.com
Type of Test:	Psychological
Administration Time:	20 minutes
Type of Administration:	Individual
Ages/Grade Levels:	Adolescents and adults

Purpose and Description of Test

The TSI, a 100-item test, is designed to evaluate posttraumatic stress and other psychological sequelae of traumatic events, including the effects of rape, spouse abuse, physical assault, combat, major accidents, natural disasters, and the lasting sequelae of childhood abuse.

Subtest Information

It contains ten clinical scales that measure the extent to which the respondent endorses trauma-related symptoms, which can be subsumed under three broad categories of distress (trauma, self, and dysphoria):

- Anxious Arousal
- Dissociation Behavior
- Depression
- Sexual Concerns
- Anger/Irritability
- Dysfunctional Sexual Behavior
- Intrusive Experiences
- Impaired Self-Reference
- Defensive Avoidance
- Tension Reduction

In addition, in contrast to other trauma measures, the TSI contains three validity scales (Response Level, Atypical Response, and Inconsistent Response), which assess the respondent's tendency to deny symptoms that others commonly endorse, overendorse unusual or bizarre symptoms, and respond to items in an inconsistent or random manner.

Trauma Symptom Checklist for Children (TSCC)

General Test Information

Author:	John N. Briere
Publisher:	PRO-ED
Address of Publisher:	8700 Shoal Creek Boulevard, Austin, TX 78757–6897
Telephone Number:	1-800-897-3202
Fax Number:	1-800-397-7633
Web Site of Publisher:	www.proedinc.com
Type of Test:	Psychological
Administration Time:	15 to 20 minutes
Type of Administration:	Individual or group
Ages/Grade Levels:	Ages 8 to 16

Purpose and Description of Test

The TSCC is a self-report measure of posttraumatic stress and related psychological symptomatology in children ages 8 to 16 who have experienced traumatic events (for example, physical or sexual abuse, major loss, natural disaster, witnessing violence). The fifty-four-item TSCC contains two validity scales (Underresponse and Hyperresponse), six clinical scales (Anxiety, Depression, Anger, Posttraumatic Stress, Dissociation, and Sexual Concerns), and eight critical items.

Strengths of the Test

- The TSCC scales are internally consistent (alpha coefficients for clinical scales range from .77 to .89 in the standardization sample) and exhibit reasonable convergent, discriminant, and predictive validity in normative and clinical samples.
- The TSCC was standardized on a group of more than 3,000 inner-city, urban, and suburban children and adolescents from the general population. Data from trauma and child abuse centers are also provided.

Chapter 23

Reading

The assessment of reading abilities and skills should use a variety of approaches in order to provide an understanding of what students know and are able to do. Assessment of reading and writing should reflect integrated activities that evaluate students' ability to think, rethink, construct, and interpret knowledge (Cohen & Spencer, 2003).

Reading is a fundamental way for individuals to exchange information. It is also a means by which much of the information presented in school is learned. As a result, reading is the academic area most associated with academic failure. Reading is a complex process that requires numerous skills for its mastery. Consequently, identifying the skills that lead to success in reading is extremely important.

Reading difficulties are observed among students with learning disabilities more than any other problem area of academic performance. It is the most prevalent type of academic difficulty for students with learning disabilities. It is estimated that as many as 90 percent of students with learning disabilities have reading difficulties, and even the low estimates are approximately 60 percent (Bender, 2001). Most authorities believe that this problem is related to deficient language skills, especially phonological awareness, or the ability to understand that speech flow can be broken into smaller sound units such as words, syllables, and phonemes.

There are numerous reading tests available for assessing a student's ability to read. Choosing which one to use depends on what area needs to be assessed. Different reading tests measure different reading subskills:

• *Oral reading*. A number of tests or parts of tests are designed to assess the accuracy and fluency of a student's ability to read aloud. According to Salvia and Ysseldyke (1998, cited in Pierangelo & Giuliani, 2006a), different oral reading tests record different behaviors as errors or miscues in oral reading.

• *Reading comprehension*. Reading comprehension assesses a student's ability to understand what he or she is reading. Many children can read yet do not understand what they have read. Therefore, an examiner doing a reading assessment must assess not just decoding but also the ability to understand what is being decoded. Diagnostic reading tests often assess six kinds of reading comprehension skills. According to Salvia and Ysseldyke (1998), these are:

Literal comprehension. The student reads the paragraph or story and is asked questions based on it.

Inferential comprehension. The student reads a paragraph or story and must interpret what has been read.

Listening comprehension. The student is read a paragraph or story by the examiner and is then asked questions about the material.

Critical comprehension. The student reads a paragraph or story and then analyzes, evaluates, or makes judgments on what he or she has read.

Affective comprehension. The student reads a paragraph or story, and the examiner evaluates his or her emotional responses to the text.

Lexical comprehension. The student reads a paragraph or story, and the examiner assesses his or her knowledge of vocabulary words.

• *Word attack skills.* When assessing the reading abilities of the student, evaluators often examine the child's word attack and word analysis skills. Word attack skills are those used to derive meaning and pronunciation of a word through context clues, structural analysis, or phonics. In order to assess the word attack skills of the student, the examiner will normally read a word to the student, who must then identify the consonant, vowel, consonant cluster, or digraph that has the same sound as the beginning, middle, or ending letters of the word.

Assessment of Literacy and Language (ALL)

General Test Information

Authors:	Linda J. Lombardino, R. Jane Lieberman, and Jaumeiko C. Brown
Publisher:	Harcourt Assessment (formerly known as the Psychological Corporation and Harcourt Educational)
Address of Publisher:	6277 Sea Harbor Drive, Orlando, FL 32887
Telephone Number:	1-800-211-8378
Fax Number:	1-800-232-1223
Web Site of Publisher:	www.harcourt.com
Type of Test:	Reading; speech and language
Administration Time:	60 minutes or less
Type of Administration:	Individual
Ages/Grade Levels:	Preschool through grade 1

Purpose and Description of Test

The ALL aids in early detection of language disorders that could lead to reading difficulties.

Subtest Information

The ALL consists of language and emergent literacy subtests:

- *Language subtests:* Basic Concepts, Receptive Vocabulary, Word Relationships, Parallel Sentence Production, and Listening Comprehension
- *Emergent literacy subtests:* Rhyme Knowledge, Phonics Knowledge, Sound Categorization, Elision, and Sight Word Recognition

Strengths of the Test

- This assessment identifies children for reading difficulties by evaluating for both language disorder and emergent literacy deficit. Subtest scores with spring and fall detail aid in the selection of specific interventions. ALL subtests match the instructional components of the Reading First and Early Reading First Programs, making it appropriate for programs tied to funding by this national effort.

Diagnostic Assessments of Reading with Trial Teaching Strategies (DARTTS)

General Test Information

Authors:	Florence G. Roswell and Jeanne S. Chall
Publisher:	Riverside Publishing
Address of Publisher:	425 Spring Lake Drive, Itasca, IL 60143–2079
Telephone Number:	1-800-323-9540
Fax Number:	1-630-467-7192
Web Site of Publisher:	www.riverpub.com
Type of Test:	Reading
Administration Time:	50 to 60 minutes
Type of Administration:	Individual or group
Ages/Grade Levels:	Prereading through high school

Purpose and Description of Test

The DARTTS is the link between reading assessment and reading instruction. The program comprises individually administered tests and related diagnostic lessons. The testing component of the program is the Diagnostic Assessments of Reading; the teaching component is designed to be used in conjunction with the testing component to discover the teaching methods and instructional materials that will be most effective with individual students.

Subtest Information

The DARTTS has six tests of reading and language:

- Word Recognition
- Word Analysis
- Oral Reading
- Silent Reading Comprehension
- Spelling
- Word Meaning

Strengths of the Test

- Brief lessons tailored to stages of reading development
- Enhances student awareness of reading achievement
- Reinforces positive student attitudes
- Can be used with individuals or groups
- Multilevel, ungraded format
- Administered and scored simultaneously
- Reveals strengths and weaknesses

Diagnostic Screening Test-Reading–Third Edition (DSTR-3)

General Test Information

Authors:	Thomas D. Gnagey and Patricia A. Gnagey
Publisher:	Slosson Educational Publications
Address of Publisher:	P.O. Box 280, East Aurora, NY 14052
Telephone Number:	1-888-756-7766
Fax Number:	1-800-655-3840
Web Site of Publisher:	www.slosson.com
Type of Test:	Reading
Administration Time:	5 to 10 minutes
Type of Administration:	Individual
Ages/Grade Levels:	Grades 1 to 12

Purpose and Description of Test

The DSTR-3 is a quick, valid method for estimating practical data about a student's reading skills.

Subtest Information

Although there are no subtests on the DSTR-3, four major scores are computed:

- *Word Reading Comfort Level*—the level at which the student knows almost all of the words and reads each without assistance.
- *Word Reading Instructional Level*—the level at which the student knows 85 to 90 percent of the words and so reads easily enough to gradually acquire the new vocabulary and associated skills.
- *Word Reading Frustration Level*—the level at which the student is unable to read many of the words and therefore misses the essence of the passage and finds the task of reading uncomfortable or unpleasant.
- *Comprehension of Passages Level*—the level at which the student is able to understand and remember the facts and subtleties of passages. (Both reading and listening comprehension are tested.)

There are eight diagnostic scores that reflect skills in phonics and word attack proficiencies plus sight vocabulary. A Consolidation Index score is computed for the instructional word reading level.

Strengths of the Test

- An initial pool of 3,221 reading words was obtained by having seventy-one teachers, grades 1 to 12, submit lists of up to one hundred words typically taught for the first time at their grade level. The total number was 12,000 in the 1981 revision project, with approximately equally sized subgroups at each grade level.
- These scores are presented for the phonics and sight subtests for each form. Since the sample of ninety-five students each in grades 2 to 8 (average level reading comprehenders) had essentially identical scores in reading and listening comprehension, the same norms are used for both ($r = .94$).
- Reliability and validity are both quite high for such a short, wide-ranging power test. Seven years of word sample use also validate appropriate contents.
- The DSTR-3 has an eighty-four-word range. An appropriate remedial program can be initiated immediately using the teacher's favorite materials.

Durrell Analysis of Reading Difficulty–Third Edition (DARD-3)

General Test Information

Authors:	Donald D. Durrell and Jane H. Catterson
Publisher:	Harcourt Assessment (formerly known as the Psychological Corporation and Harcourt Educational)
Address of Publisher:	6277 Sea Harbor Drive, Orlando, FL 32887
Telephone Number:	1-800-211-8378
Fax Number:	1-800-232-1223
Web Site of Publisher:	www.harcourt.com
Type of Test:	Reading
Administration Time:	30 to 90 minutes
Type of Administration:	Individual
Ages/Grade Levels:	Grades 1 to 6

Purpose and Description of Test

This test has long served a population of experienced teachers whose primary purpose was to discover and describe weaknesses and faulty habits in children's reading. The kit includes an examiner's manual, student record booklets, tachistoscope, and a subtest presentation booklet containing reading passages.

Subtest Information

The Durrell Analysis consists of nineteen subtests designed to assess a student's reading and listening performance. They are included in the following twelve sections of the test:

- *Identifying Sounds in Words.* The examiner reads lists of words at increasing difficulty levels. The student's score is based on the total number of identifying sounds in words that he or she can recall correctly.
- *Listening Comprehension.* The examiner is directed to read one or two paragraphs aloud to determine the student's ability to comprehend information presented orally.
- *Listening Vocabulary.* The child listens to a series of words and indicate the category to which it belongs.
- *Oral Reading.* The student reads orally and answers questions that require the recall of explicit information.
- *Phonic Spelling of Words.* The examiner reads lists of words at increasing difficulty levels, and the student's score is based on the total number of words he or she spells phonetically correctly.
- *Prereading Phonics Abilities Inventory.* This optional subtest includes syntax matching, naming letters in spoken words, naming phonemes in spoken words, naming lowercase letters, and writing letters from dictation.
- *Silent Reading.* The student reads silently and answers questions that require the recall of explicit information.
- *Sounds in Isolation.* This test assesses the student's mastery of sound-symbol relationships, including letters, blends, digraphs, phonograms, and affixes.
- *Spelling of Words.* The examiner reads lists of words at increasing difficulty levels, and the student's score is based on the total number of words he or she spells correctly.

- *Visual Memory of Words.* The examiner reads visually presented lists of words at increasing difficulty levels, and the student's score is based on the total number of words the student can recall correctly when the word list is presented again.
- *Word Analysis.* The examiner reads lists of words at increasing difficulty levels, and the score is based on the total number of words that the child analyzes correctly.
- *Word Recognition.* The examiner reads lists of words at increasing difficulty levels, and the score is based on the total number of words that the child recognizes correctly.

Strengths of the Test

- The manual for the third edition is improved, providing clearer procedures for testing.
- A continuing strength of the test is its set of behavioral checklists, urging close observation of individual reader characteristics.
- The checklist can help evaluators analyze reading errors.
- The addition of several new subtests makes for a more complete battery for assessment; however, the major focus of the test continues to be on specific skills.

Gates-MacGinitie Reading Tests (GMRT)

General Test Information

Authors:	Walter H. MacGinitie, Ruth K. MacGinitie, Katherine Maria, and Lois G. Dreyer
Publisher:	Riverside Publishing
Address of Publisher:	425 Spring Lake Drive, Itasca, IL 60143–2079
Telephone Number:	1-800-323-9540
Fax Number:	1-630-467-7192
Web Site of Publisher:	www.riverpub.com
Type of Test:	Reading
Administration Time:	60 minutes
Type of Administration:	Individual
Ages/Grade Levels:	Grades K to 12 and adults

Purpose and Description of Test

The GMRT uses scientific research to provide valid and reliable norm-referenced data about K–12 students' and adults' reading ability. It can be used to provide information about students' general level of reading achievement throughout their entire school careers and screen them for placement.

Subtest Information

The subtests on the GMRT are:

- Literacy Concepts
- Oral Language Concepts (Phonological Awareness)
- Letters and Letter/Sound Correspondences
- Listening (Story) Comprehension
- Initial Consonants and Consonant Clusters
- Final Consonants and Consonant Clusters
- Vowels
- Basic Story Words

Strengths of the Test

- Pinpoints students' decoding skill challenges. Levels 1 and 2 allow a detailed analysis of students' decoding skills.
- Measures each important stage along the comprehension continuum, from listening skills to mature reading comprehension.
- Organizes students into appropriate instructional groups using scale scores, grade equivalents, percentile ranks, stanines, or normal curve equivalents.
- Ascertains which students are reading on grade level.
- Identifies students for additional individual diagnosis and special instruction.
- Evaluates the effectiveness of instructional programs; there are two forms for pre- and posttesting.
- Reports student progress to agencies, parents, and teachers.
- Identifies proven instructional techniques based on students' results with guidance from the Linking Testing to Teaching: A Classroom Resource for Reading Assessment and Instruction manuals.

Gates-McKillop-Horowitz Reading Diagnostic Tests

General Test Information

Authors: Arthur I. Gates, Anne S. McKillop, and Elizabeth Horowitz
Publisher: Teachers College Press
Address of Publisher: 1234 Amsterdam Avenue, New York, NY 10027
Telephone Number: 1-800-575-6566
Fax Number: 1-212-678-4149
Web Site of Publisher: www.teacherscollegepress.com
Type of Test: Reading
Administration Time: 40 to 60 minutes
Type of Administration: Individual
Ages/Grade Levels: Grades 1 to 6

Purpose and Description of Test

This is an eleven-part verbal paper-and-pencil test. Not all parts need to be given to all students. Subtests are selected based on the student's reading level and reading difficulties.

Subtest Information

The eleven-part test consists of the following fifteen subtests:

- *Auditory Blending.* The student is required to blend sounds to form a whole word.
- *Auditory Discrimination.* The student is required to listen to a pair of words and determine whether the words are the same or different.
- *Informal Writing.* The student is required to write an original paragraph on a topic of his or her choice.
- *Letter Sounds.* The student is required to give the sound of a printed letter.
- *Naming Capital Letters.* The student is required to name uppercase letters.
- *Naming Lowercase Letter.* The student is required to name lowercase letters.
- *Oral Reading.* The student is required to read seven paragraphs orally. No comprehension is required.
- *Reading Sentences.* The student is required to read four sentences with phonetically regular words.
- *Reading Word.* The student is required to read fifteen one-syllable nonsense words.
- *Recognizing and Blending Common Word Parts.* The student is required to read a list of nonsense words made up of common word parts.
- *Spelling.* The student is required to take an oral spelling test.
- *Syllabication.* The student is required to read a list of nonsense words.
- *Vowels.* The student is required to determine which vowel is associated with a nonsense word presented by the examiner.
- *Words/Flash Presentation.* The student is required to identify words presented by a tachistoscope in half-second intervals.
- *Words/Untimed.* The student is required to read the same word list as presented in Words/Flash Presentation. However, the student is given the opportunity to use word attack skills in an untimed setting.

Strengths of the Test

- It tests many critical reading skills.
- A careful selection of subtests allows every student some successful reading experiences.
- Students can maintain a high level of interest throughout the test because of its varied format and the informal tone of the procedures.

Gilmore Oral Reading Test

General Test Information

Authors:	John V. Gilmore and Eunice C. Gilmore
Publisher:	Harcourt Assessment (formerly known as the Psychological Corporation and Harcourt Educational)
Address of Publisher:	6277 Sea Harbor Drive, Orlando, FL 32887
Telephone Number:	1-800-211-8378
Fax Number:	1-800-232-1223
Web Site of Publisher:	www.harcourt.com
Type of Test:	Reading
Administration Time:	15 to 20 minutes
Type of Administration:	Individual
Ages/Grade Levels:	Grades 1 to 8

Purpose and Description of Test

This test measures three aspects of oral reading competency: pronunciation, comprehension, and reading rate. It is used for diagnosing the reading needs of students identified as having reading problems.

Subtest Information

The test is made up of ten paragraphs in increasing order of difficulty that form a continuous story about episodes in a family group. There are five comprehension questions on each paragraph and a picture that portrays the characters in the story.

Strengths of the Test

- The updated Gilmore is among the most well known and commonly used standardized tests of accuracy in oral reading of meaningful material.
- The test directions are clear and concise.
- No special training is required to administer this test satisfactorily.
- The test provides informal error analysis.

Gray Diagnostic Reading Tests–Second Edition (GDRT-2)

General Test Information

Authors:	Brian R. Bryant, J. Lee Wiederholt, and Diane P. Bryant
Address of Publisher:	8700 Shoal Creek Boulevard, Austin, TX 78757–6897
Telephone Number:	1-800-897-3202
Fax Number:	1-800-397-7633
Web Site of Publisher:	www.proedinc.com
Type of Test:	Reading
Administration Time:	45 to 60 minutes
Type of Administration:	Individual
Ages/Grade Levels:	Ages 6–0 to 13–11

Purpose and Description of Test

The GDRT-2 has been revised and updated to reflect current research in reading. It assesses students who have difficulty reading continuous print and require an evaluation of specific abilities and weaknesses. Two parallel forms are provided to study a student's reading progress over time. Teachers and reading specialists find this test useful and efficient in gauging reading skills progress.

Subtest Information

The GDRT-2 has four core subtests, each measuring an important reading skill:

- Letter/Word Identification
- Phonetic Analysis
- Reading Vocabulary
- Meaningful Reading

The three supplemental subtests (Listening Vocabulary, Rapid Naming, and Phonological Awareness) measure skills that many researchers and clinicians think have important roles in the diagnosis or teaching of developmental readers or children with dyslexia.

Strengths of the Test

- The GDRT-2 was normed in 2001–2002 on a sample of 1,018 students ages 6 through 18. The normative sample was stratified to correspond to key demographic variables (race, gender, and geographical region).
- The reliabilities of the test are high; all average internal consistency reliabilities for the composites are .94 or above.
- Studies showing the absence of culture, gender, race, and disability bias have been added, and several new validity studies have been conducted, including a comparison of the test to the Wechsler Intelligence Scale for Children-III.

Gray Oral Reading Tests–Fourth Edition (GORT-4)

General Test Information

Authors:	J. Lee Wiederholt and Brian R. Bryant
Publisher:	PRO-ED
Address of Publisher:	8700 Shoal Creek Boulevard, Austin, TX 78757–6897
Telephone Number:	1-800-897-3202
Fax Number:	1-800-397-7633
Web Site of Publisher:	www.proedinc.com
Type of Test:	Reading
Administration Time:	15 to 30 minutes
Type of Administration:	Individual
Ages/Grade Levels:	Ages 6–0 through 18–11

Purpose and Description of Test

The widely used and popular Gray Oral Reading Tests–Third Edition has been revised and all new normative data provided. The GORT-4 provides an efficient and objective measure of growth in oral reading and an aid in the diagnosis of oral reading difficulties.

Strengths of the Test

- The GORT-4 was normed on a sample of more than 1,600 students aged 6 through 18. The sample was stratified to correspond to key demographic variables (race, gender, ethnicity, and geographical region).
- The reliabilities of the test are high; all average internal consistency reliabilities are .90 or above. The test-retest study was conducted with all ages for which the test can be administered and illustrates the stability and reliability of the measure. The validity is extensive and includes studies that illustrate that the GORT-4 can be used with confidence to measure change in oral reading over time.
- Several improvements were made in the GORT-4:
  - An easier story to both forms was added, and thus the GORT-4 consists of fourteen rather than thirteen stories.
  - A linear equating procedure was used to adjust scores on the two test forms to allow the examiner to use scores on Forms A and B interchangeably.
  - The publisher included bias studies that show the absence of bias based on gender and ethnicity.
  - Several new validity studies have been conducted, including an examination of the relationship of the Wechsler Intelligence Scale for Children-III to the GORT-4.

Gray Silent Reading Tests (GSRT)

General Test Information

Authors: J. Lee Wiederholt and Ginger Blalock
Publisher: PRO-ED
Address of Publisher: 8700 Shoal Creek Boulevard, Austin, TX 78757–6897
Telephone Number: 1-800-897-3202
Fax Number: 1-800-397-7633
Web Site of Publisher: www.proedinc.com
Type of Test: Reading
Administration Time: Untimed; 15 to 30 minutes
Type of Administration: Individual or group
Ages/Grade Levels: Ages 7 to 25

Purpose and Description of Test

The GSRT, a new addition to the Gray reading test battery, will help examiners quickly and efficiently measure an individual's silent reading comprehension ability. This test consists of two parallel forms, each containing thirteen developmentally sequenced reading passages with five multiple-choice questions.

Strengths of the Test

- The GSRT reliability is sufficiently high to warrant the use of the test in a wide variety of cases. Unlike many other tests of reading, internal consistency is reported for each one-year interval. The test subgroups studied include males, females, European Americans, African Americans, Hispanic Americans, Asian Americans, Native Americans, and those with learning disability, serious emotional disturbance, and attention deficit-hyperactivity disorder. Reliability coefficients alpha are all at or above .97.
- Test-retest, alternate forms–immediate, alternate forms–delayed, and scorer reliability coefficients were uniformly high. Evidence is provided for content-description, criterion-prediction, and construct-identification validity for the GSRT.
- Sources of cultural, racial, and gender bias were eliminated. Convincing evidence is presented in all three instances. Validity data also show that the GSRT can be used with the Gray Oral Reading Tests–Third Edition.

Nelson-Denny Reading Test

General Test Information

Authors:	James I. Brown, Vivian Vick Fishco, and Gerald S. Hanna
Publisher:	Riverside Publishing
Address of Publisher:	425 Spring Lake Drive, Itasca, IL 60143–2079
Telephone Number:	1-800-323-9540
Fax Number:	1-630-467-7192
Web Site of Publisher:	www.riverpub.com
Type of Test:	Reading
Administration Time:	45 minutes
Type of Administration:	Individual
Ages/Grade Levels:	High school and adult

Purpose and Description of Test

The Nelson-Denny Reading Test, Forms G and H, is a reading survey test for high school and college students and adults. A two-part test, it measures vocabulary development, comprehension, and reading rate. Part One (Vocabulary) is a fifteen-minute timed test; Part Two (Comprehension and Rate) is a twenty-minute test. The first minute of the Comprehension test is used to determine reading rate.

Strengths of the Test

- The national standardization and norming of the test was completed during the 1992–1993 school year. Norms are available for high school and two- and four-year colleges. Special norms are available for the extended-time administration and for law enforcement academies. All norms conversion tables are included in the Manual for Scoring and Interpretation. Information about the standardization and other technical data are included in the Technical Report.
- Forms G and H are parallel forms that have been equated and can be used interchangeably as pretests and posttests.
- A unique feature of the 1993 edition is the extended-time administration of the test to meet the needs of special populations, such as students with English as a second language or as a foreign language or returning adults.
- The 1993 edition of the Nelson-Denny Reading Test, Forms G and H, is the current edition of this widely used high school and college test. All test items and reading passages are exclusive to this edition and appear in a test format similar to that used in earlier editions. The basic test format was retained because of its wide acceptance by test users.
- Other changes from previous editions include a reduction in the number of vocabulary items from one hundred to eighty and inclusion of seven rather than eight reading comprehension passages, with a total of thirty-eight rather than thirty-six items. These changes advance a trend in recent Nelson-Denny forms away from speediness and toward measurement of reading power.

Phonics-Based Reading Test (PRT)

General Test Information

Author: Rick Brownell
Publisher: Academic Therapy
Address of Publisher: 20 Commercial Boulevard, Novato, CA 94949
Telephone Number: 1-800-422-7249
Fax Number: 1-888-287-9975
Web Site of Publisher: http://www.academictherapy.com
Type of Test: Reading
Administration Time: 15 minutes
Type of Administration: Individual
Ages/Grade Levels: Ages 6 through 12

Purpose and Description of Test

The PRT provides a quick evaluation of phonics skills that relate to reading.

Subtest Information

There are two distinct parts of the PRT:

- Decoding
- Fluency and Comprehension

Strengths of the Test

- The criterion-referenced interpretation of the student's performance in relation to specific skills gives the teacher or reading specialist valuable information that can be directly tied to instructional objectives.
- The normative sample is nationally stratified, and demographics match the U.S. Census.

Pre-Literacy Skills Screening (PLSS)

General Test Information

Authors:	Linda Crumrine and Helen Lonegan
Publisher:	PRO-ED
Address of Publisher:	8700 Shoal Creek Boulevard, Austin, TX 78757–6897
Telephone Number:	1-800-897-3202
Fax Number:	1-800-397-7633
Web Site of Publisher:	www.proedinc.com
Type of Test:	Reading
Administration Time:	10 to 15 minutes
Type of Administration:	Individual
Ages/Grade Levels:	Students preparing to enter kindergarten

Purpose and Description of Test

The PLSS is a screening test that identifies incoming kindergarten children who may be at risk for literacy failure.

Subtest Information

The PLSS contains nine subtests:

- Rhyme
- Sentence Repetition
- Naming
- Blending
- Sentence Segmentation
- Letter Naming
- Syllable Segmentation
- Deletion
- Multisyllabic Word Repetition

Strengths of the Test

- Interpretation of PLSS results is simple and straightforward.
- Helps in identifying at-risk students by selecting the lowest 20 percent of the students screened.
- Data collected informally with this screening protocol indicate good accuracy in predicting children who will encounter difficulty learning to read.
- School districts using this screening are able to begin intervention in kindergarten.

Slosson Oral Reading Test–Revised (SORT-R3)

General Test Information

Authors:	Richard L. Slosson; revised by Charles L. Nicholson; Supplementary Manual by Sue Larson
Publisher:	Slosson Educational Publications
Address of Publisher:	P.O. Box 280, East Aurora, NY 14052
Telephone Number:	1-888-756-7766
Fax Number:	1-800-655-3840
Web Site of Publisher:	www.slosson.com
Type of Test:	Reading
Administration Time:	3 to 5 minutes
Type of Administration:	Individual
Ages/Grade Levels:	Preschool to adult

Purpose and Description of Test

The SORT-R3 is a multidimensional reading assessment tool that can be used for regular education testing populations and for most special testing populations. It gives a brief measure of reading ability and is most useful in identifying individuals with reading disabilities.

Subtest Information

There are no subtests on the SORT-R3. However, it contains two hundred words in ascending order of difficulty in groups of twenty words. These word groups approximate grade reading levels. Thus, List 1 is equivalent to approximately the first-grade level, List 2 is equivalent to approximately the second-grade level, and so on. The same pattern continues throughout the word lists. The last group is listed as grades 9 to 12. This list contains the most difficult words, with words frequently encountered at the adult level.

Strengths of the Test

- The SORT-R3 is a quick and reliable screening test of reading word recognition.
- The test offers grade and age equivalents and national percentiles, with updated norms, as well as new scoring methodologies such as standard scores, *T*-scores, stanines, and normal curve equivalents.
- The test has been nationally restandardized on more than a thousand subjects across thirty states.
- The SORT-R3 remains a quick estimate of target word recognition for children and adults and can easily be administered.
- The reading lists on the test are available in braille for administration with visually impaired and legally blind students and adult testing populations.
- It provides administration and scoring options for use with individuals with verbal impairments.

Slosson Test of Reading Readiness (STRR)

General Test Information

Authors:	Leslie Anne Perry and Gary J. Vitali
Publisher:	Slosson Educational Publications
Address of Publisher:	P.O. Box 280, East Aurora, NY 14052
Telephone Number:	1-888-756-7766
Fax Number:	1-800-655-3840
Web Site of Publisher:	www.slosson.com
Type of Test:	Reading
Administration Time:	15 minutes
Type of Administration:	Individual
Ages/Grade Levels:	Later kindergarten and first grade

Purpose and Description of Test

The STRR was designed to identify children who are at risk of failure in programs of formal reading instruction. Utility and accountability were key goals in the development of the STRR. It can be used to screen children (toward the end of kindergarten or in first grade) whose emerging competence with reading is problematic and may require additional instruction or assessment. Stimulus items are relevant to contemporary programs of prereading instruction. This test was designed to be administered by teachers, assessment specialists, and paraprofessionals.

Strengths of the Test

- Test administration and scoring are quick and easy. Test results can be reported in a traditional normed referenced format using scaled scores with a mean of 100 and standard deviation of 16. In addition, criterion-referenced pass-fail tables are included by subtest and by total score.
- The STRR manual is comprehensive. Sections covering administration and scoring are clear and concise.
- Test reliability (coefficient alpha) is .96, and test stability (one week, Pearson product moment correlation) is .87.
- Predictive validity studies were performed using several of the country's most widely used standardized tests that target reading.
- The STRR test items cluster on cognitive, auditory, and visual abilities.

Spache Diagnostic Reading Scales (DRS)

General Test Information

Author:	George D. Spache
Publisher:	CTB Macmillan/McGraw-Hill
Address of Publisher:	20 Ryan Ranch Road, Monterey, CA 93940
Telephone Number:	1-800-538-9547
Fax Number:	1-800-282-0266
Web Site of Publisher:	www.ctb.com
Type of Test:	Reading
Administration Time:	60 minutes
Type of Administration:	Individual or group
Ages/Grade Levels:	Grades 1 through 7 and poor readers in grades 8 through 12

Purpose and Description of Test

The DRS consists of a battery of individually administered tests used to estimate the student's instructional, independent, and potential reading levels.

Subtest Information

The DRS contains these subtests:

- *Auditory Comprehension.* The student is required to respond to questions orally about paragraphs read aloud by the examiner.
- *Oral Reading.* The student is required to read paragraphs aloud and answer questions orally.
- *Silent Reading.* The student is required to read a passage silently and respond orally to the examiner's questions.
- *Supplementary Phonics Test.* This subtest measures the student's word attack skills and phonics knowledge.
- *Word Recognition List.* This test contains graded word lists that are used to determine a student's reading ability.

Strengths of the Test

- The latest version of the DRS represents a substantial improvement over the previous version.
- The revised examiner's manual, the training tape cassette, and the guidelines for testing students who speak nonstandard dialects are all positive features.

Standardized Reading Inventory–Second Edition (SRI-2)

General Test Information

Author:	Phyllis Newcomer
Publisher:	PRO-ED
Address of Publisher:	8700 Shoal Creek Boulevard, Austin, TX 78757–6897
Telephone Number:	1-800-897-3202
Fax Number:	1-800-397-7633
Web Site of Publisher:	www.proedinc.com
Type of Test:	Reading
Administration Time:	Untimed; 30 to 90 minutes
Type of Administration:	Individual or group
Ages/Grade Levels:	Grades 1 to 8

Purpose and Description of Test

Designed like an informal reading inventory, each of the two forms consists of ten graded passages, ranging from the lowest reading level (preprimer) to the highest level (eighth grade). Each passage incorporates key words extracted from five popular basal reading series to form a new word list for primary, intermediate, and advanced readers. On each passage, oral and silent reading are assessed before students answer a series of comprehension questions.

Strengths of the Test

- The test was normed on 1,099 children residing in twenty-eight states. The demographics of the sample were stratified using figures reported in the 1997 U.S. Census. Reliability coefficients are high at all age intervals. The averaged r ranged from .88 to .97.
- Criterion-referenced validity studies correlated SRI-2 with the Gray Oral Reading Test–Third Edition, Gray Silent Reading Test–Second Edition, Comprehensive Test of Phonological Processes, and Otis-Lennon School Abilities Test with favorable results.
- Evidence of construct validity is presented showing that the SRI-2 discriminates between good readers and the following groups: poor readers, students with learning disabilities, and students with speech/language disorders. Bias studies demonstrate little item bias in the instrument.
- A major strength is that the examiner can use portions of the complete instrument to identify readers who require in-depth diagnostic assessment. Each piece provides further evidence for the examiner.

Stanford Diagnostic Reading Test–Fourth Edition (SDRT-4)

General Test Information

Authors:	Bjorn Karlsen and Eric F. Gardner
Publisher:	Harcourt Assessment (formerly known as the Psychological Corporation and Harcourt Educational)
Address of Publisher:	6277 Sea Harbor Drive, Orlando, FL 32887
Telephone Number:	1-800-211-8378
Fax Number:	1-800-232-1223
Web Site of Publisher:	www.harcourt.com
Type of Test:	Reading
Administration Time:	85 to 105 minutes
Type of Administration:	Group
Ages/Grade Levels:	Kindergarten to grade 12

Purpose and Description of Test

The SDRT-4 provides group-administered diagnostic assessment of the essential components of reading in order to determine students' strengths and needs. It includes detailed coverage of reading skills, including many easy questions, so teachers can better assess students struggling with reading and plan instruction appropriately.

Subtest Information

The SDRT-4 subtests are Phonetic Analysis, Vocabulary, Comprehension, and Scanning.

Strengths of the Test

- High-quality selections, many written by published children's authors, provide relevant information about students' reading processes and strategies. The results can be used to:
  - Evaluate students for program placement.
  - Determine reading strengths and weaknesses for instructional planning.
  - Provide special help for students who lack essential reading skills.
  - Identify trends in reading achievement at the classroom, school, and district levels.
  - Provide information about the effectiveness of instructional programs.
  - Measure changes occurring over a specific instructional period.

Test of Early Reading Ability–Third Edition (TERA-3)

General Test Information

Authors:	D. Kim Reid, Wayne P. Hresko, and Donald D. Hammill
Publisher:	PRO-ED
Address of Publisher:	8700 Shoal Creek Boulevard, Austin, TX 78757–6897
Telephone Number:	1-800-897-3202
Fax Number:	1-800-397-7633
Web Site of Publisher:	www.proedinc.com
Type of Test:	Reading
Administration Time:	Untimed; 30 minutes
Type of Administration:	Individual
Ages/Grade Levels:	Ages 3–6 through 8–6

Purpose and Description of Test

The TERA-3 is a direct measure of the reading ability of young children. Rather than assessing children's readiness for reading, it assesses their mastery of early developing reading skills.

Subtest Information

This new edition provides three subtests:

- *Alphabet,* measuring knowledge of the alphabet and its uses
- *Conventions,* measuring knowledge of the conventions of print
- *Meaning,* measuring the construction of meaning from print

Strengths of the Test

- All new normative data were collected during 1999 and 2000.
- Characteristics of the normative sample (*n* = 875) relative to socioeconomic factors, gender, disability, and other critical demographics are the same as those projected by the U.S. Bureau of the Census for 2000 and are representative of the current U.S. population.
- The normative information is stratified by age relative to geography, gender, race, residence, and ethnicity.
- Studies showing the absence of gender, racial, disability, and ethnic bias have been added.
- Reliability coefficients have been computed for subgroups of the normative sample (for example, African Americans, Hispanic Americans, females) as well as for the entire normative sample. Reliability is consistently high across all three types of reliability studied. All but two of the thirty-two coefficients reported to approach or exceed .90.
- New validity studies have been conducted; special attention has been devoted to showing that the test is valid for a wide variety of subgroups as well as for a general population.
- New items have been added to make the test more reliable and valid for the upper and lower ages covered by the test.
- All pictures have been drawn in color to present a more appealing look to children.
- Examiners no longer have to prepare their own items that require the use of company logos and labels because these items are now standardized and provided as part of the test kit. Logos and labels from such national companies as McDonald's and Kraft are used to make the TERA-3 colorful and meaningful.
- Age and grade equivalents are provided.

Test of Reading Comprehension–Third Edition (TORC-3)

General Test Information

Authors:	Virginia Brown, Donald Hammill, and J. Lee Wiederholt
Publisher:	PRO-ED
Address of Publisher:	8700 Shoal Creek Boulevard, Austin, TX 78757–6897
Telephone Number:	1-800-897-3202
Fax Number:	1-800-397-7633
Web Site of Publisher:	www.proedinc.com
Type of Test:	Reading
Administration Time:	30 minutes
Type of Administration:	Individual or group
Ages/Grade Levels:	Ages 7–0 through 17–11

Purpose and Description of Test

The TORC-3 uses a constructivist orientation that focuses on holistic, cognitive, and linguistic aspects of reading.

Subtest Information

The test comprises eight subtests grouped under the General Reading Comprehension Core, which yields a Reading Comprehension Quotient (RCQ) that can be compared to measures of abstract thinking, oral language abilities, and achievement, and Diagnostic Supplements. The following subtests are in the General Reading Comprehension Core:

- *General Vocabulary*—measures the reader's understanding of sets of vocabulary items that are all related to the same general concept
- *Syntactic Similarities*—measures the reader's understanding of meaningfully similar but syntactically different sentence structures
- *Paragraph Reading*—measures the reader's ability to answer questions related to story-like paragraphs
- *Sentence Sequencing*—measures the ability to build relationships among sentences, to both each other and a reader-created whole

Four Diagnostic Supplements subtests are used to obtain a more comprehensive evaluation of relative strengths and weaknesses among various kinds of comprehension abilities. Three of the subtests are measures of content-area vocabulary in Mathematics, Social Studies, and Science.

Strengths of the Test

- The TORC-3 was standardized on 1,962 students from nineteen states. Data are provided supporting test-retest and internal consistency reliability. Information on the normative sample of students is provided by geographical region, gender, residence, race, ethnicity, and disabling condition stratified by age and keyed to 1990 Census data. Criterion-related and content validity has been updated and expanded, and test-retest reliability has been reworked to account for age effects. Studies also have been added showing the absence of gender and racial bias.
- Information about the normative sample relative to geographical region, gender, residence, race, ethnicity, and disabling condition is reported.
- The normative information has been stratified by age.
- Research supporting criterion-related validity has been updated and expanded.
- Discussion of content validity has been enhanced, especially that pertaining to the three content-area subtests (Mathematics, Social Studies, and Science).

Test of Silent Word Reading Fluency (TOSWRF)

General Test Information

Authors:	Nancy Mather, Donald D. Hammill, Elizabeth A. Allen, and Rhia Roberts
Publisher:	PRO-ED
Address of Publisher:	8700 Shoal Creek Boulevard, Austin, TX 78757–6897
Telephone Number:	1-800-897-3202
Fax Number:	1-800-397-7633
Web Site of Publisher:	www.proedinc.com
Type of Test:	Reading
Administration Time:	3 minutes for a single form; 10 minutes for both forms
Type of Administration:	Individual or group
Ages/Grade Levels:	Ages 6–6 through 17–11

Purpose and Description of Test

The TOSWRF measures a student's ability to recognize printed words accurately and efficiently. It accurately identifies students who are struggling with reading. It can also be used for monitoring reading progress and as a research tool. Because the test can be administered easily and quickly in a group format, it is an efficient and cost-effective screening method. The TOSWRF is not intended to be the sole measure for making eligibility or placement decisions; rather, it is best used as an initial screening measure to identify poor readers. Once students with poor reading skills have been identified, a more detailed diagnostic assessment can help determine the factors contributing to reading difficulties and the goals for intervention.

Using a testing format originally pioneered by Guilford in his Structure of Intellect studies, the TOSWRF measures a student's current reading skill levels by counting the number of printed words that he or she can identify within three minutes. Students are presented with rows of words, ordered by reading difficulty; no spaces appear between the words (for example, *dimhowfigblue*). Students are given three minutes to draw a line between the boundaries of as many words as possible (for example, *dim/how/fig/blue*). Two equivalent forms (A and B) are provided.

Strengths of the Test

- Identifies students struggling with reading and aids in monitoring student progress as specified by the Reading First initiative.
- Is quick to administer and easy to score.
- Converts raw scores to percentiles, standard scores, and age and grade equivalents.
- Two equivalent forms measure reading fluency.
- Is both valid and reliable for its stated purposes.
- Is appropriate for use with elementary students through high school students.

Test of Word Reading Efficiency (TOWRE)

General Test Information

Authors:	Joseph Torgesen, Richard Wagner, and Carol Rashotte
Publisher:	PRO-ED
Address of Publisher:	8700 Shoal Creek Boulevard, Austin, TX 78757–6897
Telephone Number:	1-800-897-3202
Fax Number:	1-800-397-7633
Web Site of Publisher:	www.proedinc.com
Type of Test:	Reading
Administration Time:	5 to 10 minutes
Type of Administration:	Individual
Ages/Grade Levels:	Ages 6–0 through 24–11

Purpose and Description of Test

The TOWRE is a nationally normed measure of word reading accuracy and fluency. Because it can be administered quickly, it provides an efficient means of monitoring the growth of two kinds of word reading skills that are critical in the development of overall reading ability: the ability to recognize familiar words as whole units, or sight words, and the ability to sound out words quickly.

Subtest Information

The test contains two subtests:

- *Sight Word Efficiency,* which assesses the number of real printed words that can be accurately identified within forty-five seconds
- *Phonetic Decoding Efficiency,* which measures the number of pronounceable printed nonwords that can be accurately decoded within forty-five seconds

Each subtest has two forms (Forms A and B) that are of equivalent difficulty; either one or both forms of each subtest may be given depending on the purposes of the assessment.

Strengths of the Test

- The TOWRE was normed on over 1,500 individuals ranging in age from 6 to 24 years old residing in thirty states. The sample characteristics were stratified by age and keyed to the demographic characteristics reported in the *1997 Statistical Abstract of the United States* (U.S. Census Bureau, 1997). Reliability of the TOWRE was investigated using estimates of content sampling, time sampling, and scorer differences.
- The average alternate forms reliability coefficients (content sampling) all exceed .90. The test-retest (time sampling) coefficients range from .83 to .96. The magnitude of the coefficients reported from all the reliability studies suggests that there is little error in the TOWRE and that examiners can have confidence in the results.
- Extensive evidence of the validity of TOWRE test scores is provided for content-description validity, criterion-prediction validity, and construct-identification validity.

Woodcock Reading Mastery Tests–
Revised-Normative Update (WRMT-R/NU)

General Test Information

Author:	Richard W. Woodcock
Publisher:	AGS Publishing
Address of Publisher:	4201 Woodland Road, Circle Pines, MN 55014–1796
Telephone Number:	1-800-328-2560, 1-651-287-7220
Fax Number:	800-471-8457
Web Site of Publisher:	www.agsnet.com
Type of Test:	Reading
Administration Time:	10 to 30 minutes for each cluster of tests
Type of Administration:	Individual
Ages/Grade Levels:	Kindergarten to grade 16; ages 5–0 through 75

Purpose and Description of Test

The WRMT-R/NU helps assess reading skills of children and adults. It helps identify specific children's strengths and weaknesses in reading skills, ascertain students' difficulties and their root causes in order to plan targeted remediation, and determine the reading strategies so that students with special needs can get help learning to read.

Subtest Information

Two forms, G and H, make it easy to test and retest, or the examiner can combine the results of both forms for a more comprehensive assessment. Form G contains six subtests:

- *Letter Identification.* This test measures a student's skill in naming or pronouncing letters of the alphabet. Uppercase and lowercase letters are used.
- *Passage Comprehension.* The student must read silently a passage that has a word missing and then tell the examiner a word that could appropriately fill in the blank space. The passages are drawn from newspaper articles and textbooks.
- *Visual Auditory Learning.* The student is required to associate unfamiliar visual stimuli (rebuses) with familiar oral words and translate sequences of rebuses into sentences.
- *Word Attack.* This test assesses skill in using phonic and structural analysis to read nonsense words.
- *Word Comprehension.* This section has three parts: Antonyms, Synonyms, and Analogies.
- *Word Identification.* This test measures skill in pronouncing words in isolation.

Form H has four tests of reading achievement with parallel test items to Form G: Word Identification, Word Attack, Word Comprehension (Antonyms, Synonyms, Analogies), and Passage Comprehension.

Strengths of the Test

- Based on a national sampling of over 3,000 people, the WRMT-R provides accurate score comparisons for reading decoding and reading comprehension with the other achievement batteries with which it was co-normed: the Kaufman Test of Educational Achievement/Normative Update and the Peabody Individual Achievement Test–Revised-Normative Update. The examiner gains added flexibility with this co-norming because he or she can substitute a subtest from a different battery if a subtest is spoiled or if additional diagnostic information is desired.
- Reading vocabulary, measured by the Word Comprehension test, may be evaluated in four areas: general reading, science-mathematics, social studies, and humanities. WRMT-R/NU includes practice items and training procedures to help administer the test to younger children.

Chapter 24

Speech and Language

Under the Individuals with Disabilities Education Improvement Act (IDEA; Section 300.8), *speech or language impairment* refers to a communication disorder, such as stuttering, impaired articulation, a language impairment, or a voice impairment, that adversely affects a child's educational performance.

Communication disorders relate to the components of the process affected: speech or language, or both. A speech disorder refers to difficulty producing sounds as well as disorders of voice quality or fluency of speech. A language disorder is difficulty receiving, understanding, and formulating ideas and information. IDEA recognizes that both types of communication disorders can adversely affect a student's educational performance (Turnbull, Turnbull, Shank, & Smith, 2004).

Speech and language disorders refer to problems in communication and related areas such as oral motor function. Speech is the audible, oral output of language. It is the use of the oral channel for exchanging information and knowledge (Shames & Anderson, 2002).

Language is a socially shared, rule-governed code used for communication. It is not limited to oral expression, however; it occurs in written form (or through use of gestures and alternative methods of communication for those who are low verbal or nonverbal) and within the brain in one's thoughts (Morales, 2005). Delays and disorders in language range from simple sound substitutions to the inability to understand or use language or use the oral-motor mechanism for functional speech and feeding.

According to the U.S. Department of Education (2004), more than 1.1 million students between the ages of 6 and 21 were identified as having speech and language impairments. This represents approximately 19 percent of all students having a classification in special education, or about 1.7 percent of all school-aged students. This estimate does not include children who have speech/language problems secondary to other conditions such as deafness. Language disorders may be related to other disabilities such as mental retardation, autism, or cerebral palsy. It is estimated that communication disorders (including speech, language, and hearing disorders) affect one of every ten people in the United States.

This estimate does not include children who have speech or language problems secondary to other conditions, such as deafness. Language disorders may be related to other disabilities,

369

such as mental retardation, autism, or cerebral palsy. It is estimated that communication disorders (including speech, language, and hearing disorders) affect one of every ten people in the United States.

According to Friend (2005), prevalence related to race or ethnicity is difficult to establish because of the many complicating factors that can arise from evaluating students with speech and language disorders (Kim & Kaiser, 2000; Nipold, 2001).

There is some indication of a familial pattern in speech or language impairment, with clinicians noting patterns across generations. Research suggests a possible genetic link, though there are still many problems in identifying such a gene. Sometimes the siblings of an affected child show milder forms of the difficulty, complicating the picture. One of the major stumbling blocks is the definition of the disorder, because the population of children with language impairments is still much more heterogeneous than required to support a search for a gene.

A child's communication is considered delayed when the child is noticeably behind his or her peers in the acquisition of speech or language skills, or both. Sometimes a child will have greater receptive (understanding) than expressive (speaking) language skills, but this is not always the case. A child with a communication problem may present many different symptoms. These may include difficulty following directions, attending to a conversation, pronouncing words, perceiving what was said, expressing oneself, or being understood because of a stutter or a hoarse voice (Brice, 2001).

Speech disorders refer to difficulties producing speech sounds or problems with voice quality. They might be characterized by an interruption in the flow or rhythm of speech, such as stuttering, which is called *dysfluency*. Stuttering has been long thought to be caused by emotional factors, but researchers who have studied adults with persistent stuttering found that these individuals have anatomical irregularities in the areas of the brain that control language and speech (American Academy of Neurology, 2001).

Children with speech disorders may have problems with the way sounds are formed, called *articulation* or *phonological disorders,* or they may be difficulties with the pitch, volume, or quality of the voice. There may be a combination of several problems. People with speech disorders have trouble using some speech sounds, which can also be a symptom of a delay. They may say *see* when they mean *ski* or may have trouble using other sounds like *l* or *r*. Listeners may have trouble understanding what someone with a speech disorder is trying to say. People with voice disorders may have trouble with the way their voices sound.

According to the Child Development Institute (2005), a child with a possible hearing problem may appear to strain to hear, ask to have questions repeated before giving the right answer, demonstrate speech inaccuracies (especially dropping the beginnings and endings of words), or exhibit confusion during discussion. Detection and diagnosis of hearing impairment have become sophisticated. It is possible to detect the presence of hearing loss and evaluate its severity in a newborn infant. Students who speak dialects different from standard English may have communication problems that represent either language differences or, in more severe instances, language disorders.

As a result of the numerous factors that contribute to these disorders, treatment can be complex (Barlow & Gierut, 2002; Forrest, 2002; Forrest, Elbert, & Dinnsen, 2002; Gierut & Champion, 2001; Gierut, 2001; Dodd & Bradford, 2000).

Because all communication disorders carry the potential to isolate individuals from their social and educational surroundings, it is essential to find appropriate timely intervention. While many speech and language patterns can be called "baby talk" and are part of a young child's normal development, they can become problems if they are not outgrown as expected. In this way, an initial delay in speech and language or an initial speech pattern can become a disorder that can cause difficulties in learning. Because of the way the brain develops, it is easier to learn language and communication skills before the age of 5. When children have muscular disorders, hearing problems, or developmental delays, their acquisition of speech, language, and related skills is often affected.

Arizona Articulation Proficiency Scale– Third Revision (Arizona-3)

General Test Information

Author:	Janet Barker Fudala
Publisher:	Western Psychological Services
Address of Publisher:	12031 Wilshire Boulevard, Los Angeles, CA 90025–1251
Telephone Number:	1-800-648-8857 (United States and Canada only), 1-310-478-2061
Fax Number:	1-310-478-7838
Web Site of Publisher:	www.wpspublish.com
Type of Test:	Speech and language
Administration Time:	2 to 10 minutes
Type of Administration:	Individual
Ages/Grade Levels:	Ages 18 months through 18 years; although norms stop at age 18, the Arizona-3 can be used with older individuals as well

Purpose and Description of Test

For decades, speech/language pathologists have relied on the Arizona Articulation Proficiency Scale for a precise, objective, and well-standardized assessment of articulatory skill in children. The third edition of this enduring test, the Arizona-3, is comprehensive, simple, and brief. It covers all major speech sounds in the English language, including initial and final consonants and blends, vowels, and diphthongs. It can be administered to most children in less than three minutes, and it generates a clear-cut total score indicating the severity of articulatory deviation.

To administer the Arizona-3, the examiner shows the child forty-two spiral-bound picture cards, one at a time. The child responds by naming the object depicted on each card. The examiner listens for the particular consonants and vowels being tested and then scores the child's response according to simple, quantitative rules. Because the examiner is not required to judge the severity of distorted sounds, the Arizona-3 provides a more objective measure of articulatory ability than many other instruments.

Strengths of the Test

- The picture cards have been revised, eliminating objectionable content and incorporating more contemporary clothing and activities.
- The Arizona-3 was standardized on a national sample of more than 5,500 children and teens. The sample represents the U.S. population in terms of ethnicity, region, and parental education, and it includes equal numbers of boys and girls.
- The scale is designed for children from 18 months through 18 years of age. Although norms stop at age 18, the Arizona-3 can be used with older individuals as well.
- The Arizona-3 provides three new optional assessment tasks that enhance its clinical usefulness.
- To simplify test interpretation, the improved test booklet includes both Intelligibility Ratings and Severity Ratings.
- This option lists all target words on a single card, so that older examinees can read them rather than naming objects on the picture cards. Teenagers and adults are often more comfortable with this option.
- The Arizona-3 adds several new picture cards that encourage spontaneous speech. These optional cards, which show groups of children engaged in various activities, allow the examiner to collect a sample of continuous speech.

371

Bankson-Bernthal Test of Phonology (BBTOP)

General Test Information

Authors:	Nicholas W. Bankson and John E. Bernthal
Publisher:	PRO-ED
Address of Publisher:	8700 Shoal Creek Boulevard, Austin, TX 78757–6897
Telephone Number:	1-800-897-3202
Fax Number:	1-800-397-7633
Web Site of Publisher:	www.proedinc.com
Type of Test:	Speech and language
Administration Time:	15 to 20 minutes
Type of Administration:	Individual
Ages/Grade Levels:	Ages 3 through 9

Purpose and Description of Test

The BBTOP allows clinicians to assess a child's articulation and phonology from three points of view: a whole word accuracy analysis, a traditional consonant articulation analysis, and a phonological process analysis. Designed for preschool and school-aged children, the BBTOP includes a colorful Picture Book containing eighty pictures, one for each test item, and an easel on which to place the book. The examiner may interpret the results in the way that best describes the child's performance and needs.

Subtest Information

The Word Inventory, based on percentage of words correctly produced, quickly indicates if more in-depth analysis is needed. The Consonant Inventory, a traditional articulation assessment, examines misarticulations by individual segments in initial and final positions. The Phonological Process Inventory probes ten of the most frequently occurring phonological processes: assimilation, gliding, cluster simplification, final consonant deletion, weak syllable deletion, deaffrication, stopping, vocalization, depalatalization, and fronting.

Strengths of the Test

- Elicits sounds in multiple positions.
- Yields normed scores for word accuracy, consonant articulation, and phonological processes.
- Lists common responses from standardization for each target.
- Includes practice exercises for scoring the Phonological Process Inventory.
- Gives clinicians the ability to report either percentile ranks or standard scores ($M = 100$, $SD = 15$).
- Was standardized on 1,000 children.
- Has high reliabilities: internal consistency from .92 to .98, test-retest from .74 to .85, and interrater from .93 to .99 for the three inventories.
- The Record Form makes scoring easy by including examples of all the common phonological processes observed for each target word in the standardization sample.
- Practice phonological process scoring exercises are provided in the manual, with examples drawn from many ages and levels of phonological accuracy.

Bankson Language Test–Second Edition (BLT-2)

General Test Information

Author:	Nicholas W. Bankson
Publisher:	PRO-ED
Address of Publisher:	8700 Shoal Creek Boulevard, Austin, TX 78757–6897
Telephone Number:	1-800-897-3202
Fax Number:	1-800-397-7633
Web Site of Publisher:	www.proedinc.com
Type of Test:	Speech and language
Administration Time:	Untimed; 30 minutes
Type of Administration:	Individual
Ages/Grade Levels:	Ages 3–0 through 6–11

Purpose and Description of Test

The BLT-2 is a valuable assessment instrument for use by speech/language pathologists, special educators, and others. It provides examiners with a measure of children's psycholinguistic skills.

Subtest Information

The selection of subtests for the BLT-2 was predicated on a review of the areas that language interventions frequently test and remediate in younger children. The device is organized into three general categories that assess a variety of areas:

- *Semantic Knowledge*—body parts, nouns, verbs, categories, functions, prepositions, opposites
- *Morphological/Syntactical Rules*—pronouns, verb use/verb tense, verb use (auxiliary, modal, copula), plurals, comparatives and superlatives, negation, and questions
- *Pragmatics*—ritualizing, informing, controlling, and imagining

Strengths of the Test

- The normative sample consisted of more than 1,200 children living in nineteen states. The demographic features of the sample are representative of the U.S. population as a whole on a variety of variables as provided by the *1985 Statistical Abstract of the United States* (U.S. Census Bureau, 1985).
- Evidence of internal consistency reliability is provided in the test manual, and reliability coefficients exceed .90. Support for content, concurrent, and construct validity also is provided.
- A twenty-item short form is available to screen children for language problems.

Children's Communication Checklist-2

General Test Information

Author:	D.V.M. Bishop
Publisher:	Harcourt Assessment (formerly known as the Psychological Corporation and Harcourt Educational)
Address of Publisher:	6277 Sea Harbor Drive, Orlando, FL 32887
Telephone Number:	1-800-211-8378
Fax Number:	1-800-232-1223
Web Site of Publisher:	www.harcourt.com
Type of Test:	Speech and language
Administration Time:	15 minutes or less
Type of Administration:	Individual
Ages/Grade Levels:	Ages 4–0 to 16–11

Purpose and Description of Test

The Children's Communication Checklist-2 screens children and adolescents who are likely to have social language deficits for pragmatics impairments that are not adequately evaluated by existing standardized tests.

Subtest Information

The Checklist-2 consists of ten scales:

- Speech
- Syntax
- Semantics
- Coherence
- Inappropriate Initiation
- Stereotyped Language
- Use of Context
- Nonverbal Communication
- Social Relations
- Interests

Strengths of the Test

- Provides a much-needed assessment that focuses on social language delays and pragmatics impairments.
- The Caregiver questionnaire format provides information not adequately captured by existing standardized assessments, which the clinician can interpret using the normative sample.

Clinical Evaluation of Language Fundamentals-4 (CELF-4) and CELF-4 Spanish Edition

General Test Information

Authors:	Eleanor Semel, Elisabeth H. Wiig, and Wayne A. Secord
Publisher:	Harcourt Assessment (formerly known as the Psychological Corporation and Harcourt Educational)
Address of Publisher:	6277 Sea Harbor Drive, Orlando, FL 32887
Telephone Number:	1-800-211-8378
Fax Number:	1-800-232-1223
Web Site of Publisher:	www.harcourt.com
Type of Test:	Speech and language
Administration Time:	Untimed; 30 to 60 minutes
Type of Administration:	Individual
Ages/Grade Levels:	Ages 6 through 21

Purpose and Description of Test

The CELF-4 evaluates language performance and determines the extent and nature of language disorders, helping the clinician choose the most appropriate solutions.

Subtest Information

Core Subtests make up the Total Language Score to identify the presence and nature of language disorder. Twelve supplementary, optional subtests allow clinicians to diagnose language strengths and weaknesses and choose the most effective intervention techniques.

Strengths of the Test

- The four-level assessment approach allows the clinician to determine if a language problem exists and to then explore language strengths, weaknesses, and the clinical factors behind the language disorder.
- The flexibility of subtest administration allows the option of a shorter testing time while providing highly reliable, accurate results.
- A separately developed Spanish test with separate norms provides a culturally fair language assessment for Spanish speakers.

Clinical Evaluation of Language Fundamentals-4 Screening Test (CELF-4 Screening Test)

General Test Information

Authors:	Eleanor Semel, Elisabeth H. Wiig, and Wayne A. Secord
Publisher:	Harcourt Assessment (formerly known as the Psychological Corporation and Harcourt Educational)
Address of Publisher:	6277 Sea Harbor Drive, Orlando, FL 32887
Telephone Number:	1-800-211-8378
Fax Number:	1-800-232-1223
Web Site of Publisher:	www.harcourt.com
Type of Test:	Speech and language
Administration Time:	15 minutes
Type of Administration:	Individual
Ages/Grade Levels:	Ages 3 through 6

Purpose and Description of Test

The CELF-4 Screening Test helps to quickly identify children who may be at risk for a language disorder

Strengths of the Test

- Very helpful for a quick determinant of receptive, expressive, grammatical, and semantic skills for the risk of language disorder.

Comprehensive Receptive and Expressive Vocabulary Test– Second Edition (CREVT-2)

General Test Information

Authors:	Gerald Wallace and Donald D. Hammill
Publisher:	PRO-ED
Address of Publisher:	8700 Shoal Creek Boulevard, Austin, TX 78757–6897
Telephone Number:	1-800-897-3202
Fax Number:	1-800-397-7633
Web Site of Publisher:	www.proedinc.com
Type of Test:	Speech and language
Administration Time:	20 to 30 minutes
Type of Administration:	Individual
Ages/Grade Levels:	Ages 4–0 to 89–11

Purpose and Description of Test

The CREVT-2 is an innovative, efficient measure of receptive and expressive oral vocabulary. This two-subtest measure is based on current theories of vocabulary development. Two equivalent forms are available, and full-color photos are used on the Receptive Vocabulary subtest.

Subtest Information

There are two subtests in this measure:

- *Receptive Vocabulary.* The format for this sixty-one-item subtest is a variation of the familiar "point-to-the-picture-of-the-word-I-say" technique, featuring the unique use of thematic full-color photographs. The subtest is made up of ten plates, each comprising six pictures.
- *Expressive Vocabulary.* This subtest uses the "define-the-word-I-say" format, the most popular and precise way to measure expressive vocabulary. This format encourages and requires the individual to converse in detail about a particular stimulus word, making the subtest ideal to measure expressive ability.

Strengths of the Test

- Identifies students who are significantly below their peers in oral vocabulary proficiency
- Notes discrepancies between receptive and expressive oral vocabulary
- Documents progress in oral vocabulary development as a consequence of intervention programs
- Measures oral vocabulary in research studies

Comprehensive Test of Phonological Processing (CTOPP)

General Test Information

Authors:	Richard Wagner, Joseph Torgesen, and Carol Rashotte
Publisher:	PRO-ED
Address of Publisher:	8700 Shoal Creek Boulevard, Austin, TX 78757–6897
Telephone Number:	1-800-897-3202
Fax Number:	1-800-397-7633
Web Site of Publisher:	www.proedinc.com
Type of Test:	Speech and language
Administration Time:	30 minutes
Type of Administration:	Individual
Ages/Grade Levels:	Ages 5–0 to 24–11

Purpose and Description of Test

The CTOPP assesses phonological awareness, phonological memory, and rapid naming. In addition, it has four principal uses: to (1) identify individuals who are significantly below their peers in important phonological abilities, (2) determine strengths and weaknesses among developed phonological processes, (3) document an individual's progress in phonological processing as a consequence of special intervention programs, and (4) serve as a measurement device in research studies investigating phonological processing.

Subtest Information

The CTOPP contains the following subtests:

- Elision, Blending Words
- Sound Matching
- Memory for Digits
- Nonword Repetition
- Rapid Color Naming
- Rapid Digit Naming
- Rapid Letter Naming
- Rapid Object Naming
- Blending Nonwords
- Phoneme Reversal
- Segmenting Words
- Segmenting Nonwords

Strengths of the Test

- The CTOPP was normed on over 1,600 individuals ranging in age from 5 through 24 and residing in thirty states. Over half of the norming sample came from children in elementary school (through grade 5), where the CTOPP is expected to have its widest use. The demographic characteristics of the normative sample are representative of the U.S. population as a whole with regard to gender, race, ethnicity, residence, family income, educational attainment of parents, and geographical regions. The sample characteristics were stratified by age and keyed to the demographic characteristics reported in the *1997 Statistical Abstract of the United States* (U.S. Census Bureau, 1997).
- Reliability of the CTOPP was investigated using estimates of content sampling, time sampling, and scorer differences. Most of the average internal consistency or alternate forms of reliability coefficients (content sampling) exceed .80. The test-retest (time sampling) coefficients range from .70 to .92. The magnitude of the coefficients reported from all the reliability studies suggests that there is limited error in the CTOPP and that examiners can have confidence in the results.

Early Language Milestone Scale–Second Edition (ELM Scale-2)

General Test Information

Author:	James Coplan
Publisher:	PRO-ED
Address of Publisher:	8700 Shoal Creek Boulevard, Austin, TX 78757–6897
Telephone Number:	1-800-897-3202
Fax Number:	1-800-397-7633
Web Site of Publisher:	www.proedinc.com
Type of Test:	Speech and language
Administration Time:	1 to 10 minutes
Type of Administration:	Individual
Ages/Grade Levels:	Birth to 36 months

Purpose and Description of Test

The ELM Scale-2 assesses speech and language development from birth to 36 months of age. It is ideally suited to help clinicians implement the mandate to serve the developmental needs of children from birth to age 3; it also can be used with older children with developmental delays whose functional level falls within this range.

Subtest Information

The ELM Scale-2 consists of forty-three items arranged in three divisions:

- Auditory Expressive (which is further subdivided into Content and Intelligibility)
- Auditory Receptive
- Visual

Strengths of the Test

- The ELM Scale-2 may be administered using a pass-fail or a point scoring method. The pass-fail method yields a global pass or fail rating for the test as a whole, whereas the point scoring method yields percentile values, standard score equivalents, and age equivalents for each area of language function (Auditory Expressive, Auditory Receptive, and Visual), as well as a Global Language score. Individuals wishing to update their first edition kits need only purchase the new Examiner's Manual and new Record Forms.

Evaluating Acquired Skills in Communication–Revised (EASIC-R)

General Test Information

Author:	Anita Marcott Riley
Publisher:	PRO-ED
Address of Publisher:	8700 Shoal Creek Boulevard, Austin, TX 78757–6897
Telephone Number:	1-800-897-3202
Fax Number:	1-800-397-7633
Web Site of Publisher:	www.proedinc.com
Type of Test:	Speech and language
Administration Time:	Untimed; 15 to 30 minutes
Type of Administration:	Individual
Ages/Grade Levels:	Ages 3 months to 8 years

Purpose and Description of Test

EASIC-R is an inventory developed to measure spoken language (receptive and expressive) of children with autism who are ages 3 months to 8 years.

Subtest Information

The EASIC-R assesses semantics, syntax, morphology, and pragmatics communication skills at five levels:

- *Pre-Language*—before meaningful speech
- *Receptive I*—understanding simple noun labels, action verbs, and basic concepts
- *Expressive I*—emerging modes of communication
- *Receptive II*—understanding more complex language functions
- *Expressive II*—using a more complex level of communication

Strengths of the Test

- It was field-tested on 200 individuals with autism over a six-year period. Although the materials were developed for persons with autism, the EASIC-R has also been used successfully with others who have developmental language delays.
- Once the assessment is completed, the EASIC-R's results can be displayed on the Skills Profile. This form provides space for displaying the results from up to five assessments, taken over time, and is a means for showing the changes that have occurred from one testing to the next.
- In addition, the results can be portrayed on the Developmental Age Chart, where communication skills are arranged in order from easy to difficult, along with age ranges at which children normally acquire each described skill.
- Finally, 142 Goals and Objectives cards are provided. These cards are directly tied to the skills described in the inventory and can be used in the development of intervention plans.

Examining for Aphasia: Assessment of Aphasia and Related Impairments–Third Edition (EFA-3)

General Test Information

Author:	Jon Eisenson
Publisher:	PRO-ED
Address of Publisher:	8700 Shoal Creek Boulevard, Austin, TX 78757–6897
Telephone Number:	1-800-897-3202
Fax Number:	1-800-397-7633
Web Site of Publisher:	www.proedinc.com
Type of Test:	Speech and language
Administration Time:	30 minutes to 2 hours
Type of Administration:	Individual
Ages/Grade Levels:	Adolescents and adults

Purpose and Description of Test

EFA-3 assesses aphasia and aphasic impairments relative to receptive and evaluative (decoding) and expressive and productive (encoding) impairments. It acknowledges cognitive, personality, and linguistic modifications associated with acquired aphasia.

Subtest Information

The EFA-3's thirty-three subtests help determine areas of strength and weakness for receptive and expressive functions. EFA-3 tests for agnosia (visual, auditory, and tactile); linguistic reception (oral and written) of words, sentences, and paragraphs; and expressive impairments, including simple skills, automatic language, arithmetic computations, and language items that parallel those for receptive tasks. An optional "Tell a Story" test in response to a picture assesses self-organized language content.

Strengths of the Test

- The Profile/Response Form is used to record information on the examinee and his or her test performance as well as to record and profile the EFA-3 subtest and composite scores. Raw scores can be converted to percentiles and plotted on the profile.
- The Examiner Record Booklet includes brief administration directions for experienced EFA-3 examiners and space for observations and clinical impressions.

Expressive One-Word Picture Vocabulary Test (EOWPVT)

General Test Information

Author:	Rick Brownell
Publisher:	Academic Therapy
Address of Publisher:	20 Commercial Boulevard, Novato, CA 94949
Telephone Number:	1-800-422-7249
Fax Number:	1-888-287-9975
Web Site of Publisher:	www.academictherapy.com
Type of Test:	Speech and language
Administration Time:	20 minutes
Type of Administration:	Individual
Ages/Grade Levels:	Ages 2 through 18

Purpose and Description of Test

The test is used to obtain measures of English expressive vocabulary using color pictures in multiple-choice format. To administer the test, the examiner presents a series of illustrations, each depicting an object, action, or concept. The examinee is asked to name each illustration. The test begins at a point at which the examinee is expected to meet with success in naming each illustration. The examiner then presents items that become progressively more difficult. When the examinee is unable to correctly name a number of consecutive illustrations, testing is discontinued.

Strengths of the Test

- This edition of the EOWPVT includes national norms based on a representative sample of more than 2,000 individuals residing in the United States. The test has also been co-normed with the Receptive One-Word Picture Vocabulary Test so that meaningful comparisons can be made easily between an individual's expressive and receptive language.
- Other notable changes to this edition include the addition and replacement of many test items as well as new administration procedures that permit the examiner to prompt or cue examinees so that they will attend to the relevant aspects of each illustration.
- All illustrations have been newly rendered in full color with drawings that are easy to interpret and better hold the examinee's interest.
- Easy to administer and score.
- Co-normed with the Receptive One-Word Picture Vocabulary Test.
- Normative sample is nationally stratified, and demographics match the U.S. Census.

Expressive Vocabulary Test (EVT)

General Test Information

Author: Kathleen T. Williams

Publisher: AGS Publishing

Address of Publisher: 4201 Woodland Road, Circle Pines, MN 55014–1796

Telephone Number: 1-800-328-2560, 1-651-287-7220

Fax Number: 1-800-471-8457

Web Site of Publisher: www.agsnet.com

Type of Test: Speech and language

Administration Time: 15 minutes

Type of Administration: Individual

Ages/Grade Levels: Ages 2–6 to 90+

Purpose and Description of Test

The EVT is an individually administered, norm-referenced test of expressive vocabulary and word retrieval. For the thirty-eight labeling items, the examiner points to a picture or a part of the body and asks a question. On the 152 synonym items, the examiner presents a picture and stimulus words within a carrier phrase. The examinee responds to each item with a one-word answer. All stimulus pictures are in full color, carefully balanced for gender and ethnic representation.

Strengths of the Test

- The EVT reliability analyses indicate a high degree of internal consistency. Split-half reliabilities range from .83 to .97 with a median of .91. Alphas range from .90 to .98 with a median of .95. And test-retest studies with four separate age samples resulted in reliability coefficients ranging from .77 to .90, indicating a strong degree of test stability.
- The EVT and the Peabody Picture Vocabulary Test–Third Edition were standardized on the same population of 2,725 examinees ranging in ages from 2–6 to 90+. This co-norming lets the examiner make direct comparisons of receptive and expressive vocabulary.
- Quick administration and scoring.
- Untimed administration rules.
- Easy-to-follow basal and ceiling rules.
- Full-color stimulus pictures.
- Portable testing easel.
- Item bias analysis.

Goldman-Fristoe Test of Articulation–Second Edition (Goldman-Fristoe-2)

General Test Information

Authors:	Ronald Goldman and Macalyne Fristoe
Publisher:	AGS Publishing
Address of Publisher:	4201 Woodland Road, Circle Pines, MN 55014–1796
Telephone Number:	1-800-328-2560, 1-651-287-7220
Fax Number:	1-800-471-8457
Web Site of Publisher:	www.agsnet.com
Type of Test:	Speech and language
Administration Time:	5 to 15 minutes for Sounds-in-Words Section; varies for other two sections
Type of Administration:	Individual
Ages/Grade Levels:	Ages 2 to 21

Purpose and Description of Test

The Goldman-Fristoe-2 provides information about a child's articulation ability by sampling both spontaneous and imitative sound production. Examinees respond to picture plates and verbal cues from the examiner with single-word answers that demonstrate common speech sounds. Additional sections provide further measures of speech production.

The Goldman-Fristoe-2 can be used to measure articulation of consonant sounds, determine types of misarticulation, and compare individual performance to national, gender-differentiated norms.

Subtest Information

Three sections sample a wide range of articulation skills:

- The Sounds-in-Words section uses pictures to elicit articulation of the major speech sounds when the examinee is prompted by a visual and verbal cue.
- The Sounds-in-Sentences section assesses spontaneous sound production used in connected speech. The examinee is asked to retell a short story based on a picture cue. Target speech sounds are sampled within the context of simple sentences.
- The Stimulability section measures the examinee's ability to correctly produce a previously misarticulated sound when asked to watch and listen to the examiner's production of the sound. The examinee repeats the word or phrase modeled by the examiner.

Strengths of the Test

- New items have been added to sample more speech sounds; thirty-nine consonant sounds and clusters can now be tested with the Goldman-Fristoe-2. Some objectionable or culturally inappropriate items (such as a gun and a Christmas tree) have been removed.
- All artwork has been redrawn and reviewed for cultural bias and fairness.
- The age range for the Goldman-Fristoe-2 has been expanded to include ages 2 through 21. Age-based standard scores include separate normative information for females and males.
- Normative tables are based on a national sample of 2,350 examinees stratified to match the most recent U.S. Census data on gender, race/ethnicity, region, and socioeconomic as determined by mother's education level.

Illinois Test of Psycholinguistic Abilities–Third Edition (ITPA-3)

General Test Information

Authors:	Donald D. Hammill, Nancy Mather, and Rhia Roberts
Publisher:	PRO-ED
Address of Publisher:	8700 Shoal Creek Boulevard, Austin, TX 78757–6897
Telephone Number:	1-800-897-3202
Fax Number:	1-800-397-7633
Web Site of Publisher:	www.proedinc.com
Type of Test:	Speech and language
Administration Time:	45 to 60 minutes
Type of Administration:	Individual
Ages/Grade Levels:	Ages 5–0 to 12–11

Purpose and Description of Test

The ITPA-3 is an effective measure of children's spoken and written language. All of the subtests measure some aspect of language, including oral language, writing, reading, and spelling.

Subtest Information

- Spoken Language
  - *Spoken Analogies.* For example, in response to "Birds fly, fish _____," the child might say "swim."
  - *Spoken Vocabulary.* For example, the examiner may say, "I am thinking of something with a roof," to which the child might respond "house."
  - *Morphological Closure.* For example, the examiner says, "big, bigger, _____," and the child completes the phrase by saying the missing part, "biggest."
  - *Syntactic Sentences.* The examiner says a sentence that is syntactically correct but semantically nonsensical; for example, "Red flowers are smart." The child repeats the sentence.
  - *Sound Deletion.* The examiner asks the child to delete words, syllables, and their phonemes from spoken words. For example, the examiner might ask the student to say "weekend" without the "end."
  - *Rhyming Sequences.* The examiner says a string of rhyming words that increase in length, and then the child is required to repeat them.
- Written Language
  - *Sentence Sequencing.* For example, if the following three sentences were rearranged in B-C-A order, they would make sense: "A. I go to school. B. I get up. C. I get dressed."
  - *Written Vocabulary.* After reading an adjective (for example, "A broken _____"), the child responds by writing a noun that is closely associated with the stimulus word (for example, "vase" or "mirror").
  - *Sight Decoding.* The child pronounces a list of printed words that contain irregular parts (for example, "would," "laugh," "height," "recipe").
  - *Sound Decoding.* The child reads aloud phonically regular names of make-believe animal creatures (for example, Flant, Yang).
  - *Sight Spelling.* For example, if the examiner says, "said," and the child sees "s___d," he or she writes in the missing letters, "ai."
  - *Sound Spelling.* The examiner reads aloud phonically regular nonsense words, and the child writes the word or the missing part.

To enhance the clinical and diagnostic usefulness of the ITPA-3, the subtests can be combined to form ten composites:

- Global Composites
  - *General Language Composite:* Formed by combining the results of all twelve subtests. For most children, this is the best single estimate of linguistic ability because it reflects status on the widest array of spoken and written language abilities.
  - *Spoken Language Composite:* Formed by combining the results of the six subtests that measure aspects of oral language. The subtests assess the semantical, grammatical, and phonological aspects of oral language.
  - *Written Language Composite:* Formed by combining the results of the six subtests that measure different aspects of written language. The subtests assess the semantic, graphophonemic, and orthographic aspects of written language. All subtests that involve graphemes (printed letters) to any degree in reading, writing, or spelling are assigned to this composite.
- Specific Composites
  - *Semantics Composite:* Formed using the results of the two subtests that measure the understanding and use of purposeful speech.
  - *Grammar Composite:* Formed using the two subtests that measure grammar used in speech (one measures morphology and the other syntax).
  - *Phonology Composite:* The two subtests that make up this composite measure competency with speech sounds, including phonemic awareness. One subtest involves deleting parts of words, and the other involves recalling strings of rhyming words.
  - *Comprehension Composite:* The results of the two subtests that measure the ability to comprehend written messages (to read) and express thoughts in graphic form (to write) make up this composite.
  - *Spelling Composite:* The two subtests' results that measure spelling form this composite.
  - *Sight-Symbol Processing Composite:* The two subtests in this composite measure the pronunciation and spelling of irregular words. A part of these words has to be mastered by sight because it does not conform to the most common English spelling rules or patterns (for example, *thumb*).
  - *Sound-Symbol Processing Composite:* The two subtests in this composite measure the pronunciation and spelling of pseudowords (phonetically regular nonwords). These nonwords conform to the standard English phoneme-to-grapheme correspondence rules involved in pronouncing printed words or spelling spoken words.

Strengths of the Test

- All ITPA-3 subtests now measure linguistic abilities, both spoken and written.
- New subtests have been developed that are appropriate for elementary children.
- Evidence is provided to show that the basic principles in the test model are still current.
- New normative information was collected during the years 1999 and 2000.
- The normative sample reflects the population characteristics of the United States for 1999 and projected for the year 2000 relative to ethnicity, race, gender, disability status, geographical region, parental education, rural/urban residence, and family income.
- Internal consistency, stability, and interscorer reliability for all subtests and composites are high enough to allow ITPA-3 scores to be used as the basis for making clinical judgments (r greater than .90).
- Validity evidence shows that all ITPA-3 subtests are useful for measuring both spoken and written language.
- Studies showing the absence of gender, ethnic, and racial bias have been included.
- Evidence is provided to show that the test is reliable and valid for specific gender, ethnic, and racial groups, as well as for a general population.

Kindergarten Language Screening Test (KLST-2)

General Test Information

Authors:	Sharon Gauthier and Charles Madison
Publisher:	PRO-ED
Address of Publisher:	8700 Shoal Creek Boulevard, Austin, TX 78757–6897
Telephone Number:	1-800-897-3202
Fax Number:	1-800-397-7633
Web Site of Publisher:	www.proedinc.com
Type of Test:	Speech and language
Administration Time:	5 minutes
Type of Administration:	Individual
Ages/Grade Levels:	Ages 4–0 through 6–11

Purpose and Description of Test

The KLST-2 is a thorough, quick language screener based on the original KLST, which has a twenty-five-year history of use in the field. This individually administered screening test helps identify children who need further diagnostic testing to determine whether they have language deficits that will accelerate academic failure. It assesses expressive and receptive language competence by screening the child's ability to demonstrate common preschool knowledge, understand questions, follow commands, repeat sentences, compare and contrast common objects, and use spontaneous speech.

Strengths of the Test

- This edition is completely restandardized and updated; some items have been modified, and the test has been normed. This is a user-friendly screening test that employs a number of psycholinguistically relevant tasks.
- The KLST-2 has strong predictive validity.
- The KLST-2 was normed on a sample of 519 children, ages 4–0 through 6–11. Reliability coefficients through four test-retest studies were .82 or above. Criterion-related validity has been demonstrated through three studies that demonstrate correlations with the Preschool Language Scale–Third Edition, the Test of Language Development–Primary: 3, and the Clinical Evaluation of Language Fundamentals–Preschool.

Oral and Written Language Scales (OWLS)

General Test Information

Author:	Elizabeth Carrow-Woolfolk
Publisher:	AGS Publishing
Address of Publisher:	4201 Woodland Road, Circle Pines, MN 55014–1796
Telephone Number:	1-800-328-2560, 1-651-287-7220
Fax Number:	1-800-471-8457
Web Site of Publisher:	www.agsnet.com
Type of Test:	Speech and language
Administration Time:	Listening Comprehension Scale: 5 to 15 minutes; Oral Expression Scale: 10 to 25 minutes
Type of Administration:	Individual
Ages/Grade Levels:	Ages 3–0 through 21–11

Purpose and Description of Test

The OWLS is an individually administered assessment of receptive and expressive language for children and young adults.

Subtest Information

The OWLS consists of the Listening Comprehension Scale (LCS) and the Oral Expression Scale (OES). The LCS is a measure of receptive language. Using a convenient easel, the examiner reads a verbal stimulus aloud. The examinee responds by indicating a picture on the examinee's side of the easel. Correct responses are indicated on the examiner's side of the easel and on the record form. For the OES, the examinee answers a question, completes a sentence, or generates one or more sentences in response to a visual or verbal stimulus. Common correct and incorrect responses are included on the record form.

Strengths of the Test

- Provides a wealth of information about an individual's expressive and receptive language knowledge processing in a short time.
- Offers useful information that helps in the individualized education program process.
- Co-normed LC/OE Scales and WE Scale give a broad-based record of growth for ages 5 to 21.
- Neither scale requires the examinee to read. Descriptive Analysis Worksheet Masters that allow the examiner to categorize responses by item type (lexical, syntactic, pragmatic, and supralinguistic) are provided.
- The LCS easel and the record form contain correct responses for each item for on-the-spot scoring. For the OES, the examiner may do a preliminary tally and then consult the item-by-item scoring rules to determine scores of particular items.
- The manual reports correlations of OWLS scales with other measures of receptive and expressive language as well as with tests of cognitive ability and academic achievement. Also, the score profiles of seven clinical groups are compared with matched control samples.

Peabody Picture Vocabulary Test–Third Edition (PPVT-III)

General Test Information

Authors:	Lloyd M. Dunn and Leota M. Dunn
Publisher:	AGS Publishing
Address of Publisher:	4201 Woodland Road, Circle Pines, MN 55014–1796
Telephone Number:	1-800-328-2560, 1-651-287-7220
Fax Number:	1-800-471-8457
Web Site of Publisher:	www.agsnet.com
Type of Test:	Speech and language
Administration Time:	10 to 15 minutes
Type of Administration:	Individual
Ages/Grade Levels:	Ages 2–6 through 90

Purpose and Description of Test

Like the first two editions, the PPVT-III is a measure of receptive vocabulary for standard English and a screening test of verbal ability. The test is offered in two parallel forms, IIIA and IIIB, for reliable testing and retesting. Items consist of pictures arranged in a multiple-choice format. To administer an item, the evaluator shows a plate in the test easel and says a corresponding stimulus word. The child or adult responds by pointing to one of the pictures to measure receptive vocabulary.

Strengths of the Test

- Wide range of use
- Objective and rapid scoring
- Quick administration time
- Clear black-and-white line drawings
- No reading or writing required of examinee
- New features:
  - National norms extended from ages 2–6 to 90+ years
  - Test items increased to 204 in each form
  - Test items grouped into seventeen sets of twelve in each form
  - Locator tabs identify the seventeen sets of test items
  - Many new illustrations for better gender and ethnic balance
  - Now easier, faster, and more accurate

Phonemic Awareness Skills Screening (PASS)

General Test Information

Author:	Linda Crumrine
Publisher:	PRO-ED
Address of Publisher:	8700 Shoal Creek Boulevard, Austin, TX 78757–6897
Telephone Number:	1-800-897-3202
Fax Number:	1-800-397-7633
Web Site of Publisher:	www.proedinc.com
Type of Test:	Speech and language
Administration Time:	Untimed; 15 minutes
Type of Administration:	Individual
Ages/Grade Levels:	Grades 1 and 2

Purpose and Description of Test

This quick, individual screener is a highly useful diagnostic tool for general and special education teachers. It easily identifies specific weaknesses in the phonological processing ability of first- and second-grade students.

Subtest Information

The PASS contains eight sections:

- Rhyme
- Sentence Segmentation
- Blending
- Syllable Segmentation
- Deletion
- Phoneme Isolation
- Phoneme Segmentation
- Phoneme Substitution

Strengths of the Test

- The manual includes a variety of specific phonological activities and suggestions for using the results to plan instruction. It also contains a rationale, an overview, administration directions, and test plates. The PASS manual explains how to accommodate individual differences, shift the responsibility for learning to the student, and encourage reflective teaching and learning.

Receptive-Expressive Emergent Language Test–Third Edition (REEL-3)

General Test Information

Authors:	Kenneth R. Bzoch, Richard League, and Virginia L. Brown
Publisher:	PRO-ED
Address of Publisher:	8700 Shoal Creek Boulevard, Austin, TX 78757–6897
Telephone Number:	1-800-897-3202
Fax Number:	1-800-397-7633
Web Site of Publisher:	www.proedinc.com
Type of Test:	Speech and language
Administration Time:	20 minutes
Type of Administration:	Individual
Ages/Grade Levels:	Birth through 3 years

Purpose and Description of Test

The REEL-3 is designed to help identify infants and toddlers who have language impairments or other disabilities that affect language development. It is especially useful as an assessment and planning instrument in early childhood intervention programs mandated under P.L. 99–457.

Subtest Information

The REEL-3 has two core subtests, Receptive Language and Expressive Language, and a new supplementary subtest, Inventory of Vocabulary Words. Results are obtained from a caregiver interview.

Strengths of the Test

- The REEL-3 is based on a contemporary linguistic model. It includes current studies relating to a normative base, reliability, and validity. The normative sample includes 1,112 infants and toddlers from around the nation. The demographic characteristics of the sample were matched to those of the United States according to the 2000 Census. The normative sample was stratified on the basis of age, gender, race, ethnic group membership, and geographical location. Standard scores, percentile ranks, and age equivalents are provided.
- The average reliability coefficients for all the test scores are high (exceeding .90). Test-retest studies show that the REEL-3 is stable over time.
- The potential bias of every item on the test on the basis of gender and ethnic group was studied. In all, no items showed bias beyond a negligible effect size. Validity data are reported as well, documenting the test's relationship to the Developmental Assessment of Young Children, the Early Language Milestone Scale–Second Edition, and the Cognitive Abilities Test–Second Edition.

Receptive One-Word Picture Vocabulary Test

General Test Information

Author:	Rick Brownell
Publisher:	Academic Therapy
Address of Publisher:	20 Commercial Boulevard, Novato, CA 94949
Telephone Number:	1-800-422-7249
Fax Number:	1-888-287-9975
Web Site of Publisher:	http://www.academictherapy.com
Type of Test:	Speech and language
Administration Time:	20 minutes
Type of Administration:	Individual
Ages/Grade Levels:	Ages 2 through 18

Purpose and Description of Test

The Receptive One-Word Picture Vocabulary Test helps examiners obtain measures of English receptive vocabulary using color pictures in multiple-choice format.

Strengths of the Test

- Completely revised from earlier editions with new items and new drawings.
- Easy to administer and score.
- Co-normed with the Expressive One-Word Picture Vocabulary Test.
- The normative sample is nationally stratified, and demographics match the U.S. Census.

Ross Information Processing Assessment–Primary (RIPA-P)

General Test Information

Author:	Deborah Ross-Swain
Publisher:	PRO-ED
Address of Publisher:	8700 Shoal Creek Boulevard, Austin, TX 78757–6897
Telephone Number:	1-800-897-3202
Fax Number:	1-800-397-7633
Web Site of Publisher:	www.proedinc.com
Type of Test:	Speech and language
Administration Time:	30 minutes
Type of Administration:	Individual
Ages/Grade Levels:	Ages 5–0 through 12–11

Purpose and Description of Test

The RIPA-P is a valuable tool for speech pathologists in hospitals, clinics, private practice, and public schools, as well as for resource specialists and special education teachers. It helps identify and quantify information processing skill impairments in children ages 5 through 12 who have had a traumatic brain injury, have experienced other neuropathologies that affect information processing such as seizure disorders or anoxia, or exhibit learning disabilities or weaknesses that interfere with learning acquisition or educational achievement.

Subtest Information

Subtests assess memory, spatial and temporal orientation, organization, problem solving, and abstract reasoning. Of the eight subtests, four are suitable for children ages 5 through 12:

- Immediate Memory
- Recent Memory
- Spatial Orientation
- Recall of General Information

The other four subtests are suitable for children ages 8 through 12:

- Temporal Orientation
- Organization
- Problem Solving
- Abstract Reasoning

Strengths of the Test

- RIPA-P is unique in that its norms include children who have learning disabilities, and its eight subtests allow the examiner to assess a wide range of information processing skills, all in a single battery.
- The RIPA-P was standardized on 115 individuals ages 5 through 12. Reliability coefficients were found to be .81 or above, and more than a third of them were over .90.
- Validity studies show that the test discriminates between "normal" children and those who are learning disabled or have neurological problems. Item discrimination coefficients for the RIPA-P range from .39 to .94.

Slosson Articulation Language Test with Phonology (SALT-P)

General Test Information

Author:	Wilma Jean Tade
Publisher:	Slosson Educational Publications
Address of Publisher:	P.O. Box 280, East Aurora, NY 14052
Telephone Number:	1-888-756-7766
Fax Number:	1-800-655-3840
Web Site of Publisher:	www.slosson.com
Type of Test:	Speech and language
Administration Time:	7 to 10 minutes
Type of Administration:	Individual
Ages/Grade Levels:	Ages 3–0 to 5–11

Purpose and Description of Test

The test model of the SALT-P incorporates the assessment of articulation, phonology, and language into a single score that indicates the communicative competency of a child. The child's score is compared to an index of scores that denotes normal performance with respect to chronological age. Test administration and scoring occur simultaneously, employing overlay cutouts onto the color-coded score sheet. The results are recorded on an easily prescored test form. Consonants plus vowels and diphthongs, phonological processes, and language errors are tabulated into the child's total composite score for evaluation and assessment.

Strengths of the Test

- The screening format uses structured conversation centering around attractive stimulus pictures.
- A user-friendly template simplifies scoring through clearly identified cutouts on test pages.
- Step-by-step instructions are provided.
- Designed for use in educational, clinical, private practice, Head Start, and similar preschool programs.
- The articulation section assesses twenty-two initial and eighteen final consonants, ten clusters or blends, and eight vowels and diphthongs. Phonological processes probed are initial and final consonant deletion, fronting, stopping, and cluster reduction. The language subscore reflects errors on thirty-one language behaviors normally acquired between the ages of 3–0 and 5–11.
- The statistical section is included in the manual.

Slosson Phonics and Structural Analysis Test (SP-SAT)

General Test Information

Authors:	Leslie Anne Perry and Bradley T. Erford
Publisher:	Slosson Educational Publications
Address of Publisher:	P.O. Box 280, East Aurora, NY 14052
Telephone Number:	1-888-756-7766
Fax Number:	1-800-655-3840
Web Site of Publisher:	www.slosson.com
Type of Test:	Speech and language
Administration Time:	Untimed
Type of Administration:	Individual or group
Ages/Grade Levels:	Ages 6–0 to 9–11

Purpose and Description of Test

The SP-SAT assesses the language concepts of phonics and structural analysis. Phonics, the study of letter-sound relationships, and structural analysis, the examination of words for meaningful parts, are necessary skills for children to acquire in order to become independent readers. This test was designed for teachers, reading specialists, special education teachers, speech/language pathologists, and others familiar with phonics and structural analysis.

The essential elements of Phonics Clusters assess:

- Consonant blends
- Consonant digraphs
- Short vowels
- Long vowels—final *e* and open syllable
- Long vowels—vowel digraphs
- *R*-controlled vowels
- *A* followed by *l, ll, w,* and *u*
- Diphthongs
- Hard and soft sounds of *c* and *g*
- Silent consonants

Essential elements of structural analysis clusters assess:

- Indicating root words
- Indicating suffixes
- Indicating prefixes
- Forming plurals
- Forming possessives
- Adding suffixes
- Rewriting contractions
- Forming compound words
- Writing abbreviations
- Indicating syllables

Strengths of the Test

- Administration and scoring are quick and easy.
- Overall test-retest reliability was .90, and internal consistency was .96.
- Concurrent validity studies resulted in overall Phonics Index correlations of .75, .68, and .86 with the Woodcock-Johnson-Revised L-W Identification and Word Attack and the Wide Range Achievement Test–Third Edition Reading subtests, respectively.
- Both age and grade norms are provided.

Speech and Language Evaluation Scale (SLES)

General Test Information

Authors:	Diane R. Fressola and Sandra Ciponeri Hoerchler
Publisher:	Hawthorne Educational Services
Address of Publisher:	800 Gray Oak Drive, Columbia, MO 65201
Telephone Number:	1-800-542-1673
Fax Number:	1-800-442-9509
Web Site of Publisher:	www.hes-inc.com
Type of Test:	Speech and language
Administration Time:	Approximately 20 minutes
Type of Administration:	Individual
Ages/Grade Levels:	Ages 4–5 to 18+

Purpose and Description of Test

The SLES is based on the federal definition of *speech impaired* and the speech and language disorders definitions recognized by the American Speech-Language-Hearing Association. It contains sixty-eight items easily observed and documented by educational personnel.

Subtest Information

The SLES consists of Speech and Speech Language subscales. The SLES Speech subscales are Articulation, Voice, and Fluency. The SLES Speech Language subscales are Form, Content, and Pragmatics.

Strengths of the Test

- The SLES was standardized on 4,501 students.
- The standardization sample included students from twenty-seven states and eighty-two school districts and represented all geographical regions of the United States.
- The SLES was factor-analyzed to create the factor clusters (subscales).
- The Pre-Referral Speech and Language Checklist provides a means of calling attention to speech and language difficulties for the purpose of early intervention before formal assessment of the student.

Stuttering Prediction Instrument for Young Children

General Test Information

Author: Glyndon D. Riley

Publisher: PRO-ED

Address of Publisher: 8700 Shoal Creek Boulevard, Austin, TX 78757–6897

Telephone Number: 1-800-897-3202

Fax Number: 1-800-397-7633

Web Site of Publisher: www.proedinc.com

Type of Test: Speech and language

Administration Time: Untimed

Type of Administration: Individual

Ages/Grade Levels: Ages 3 to 8

Purpose and Description of Test

The SPI is designed for children ages 3 to 8 years and assesses a child's history, reactions, part-word repetitions, prolongations, and frequency of stuttered words to assist in measuring severity and predicting chronicity.

Strengths of the Test

- According to its publisher, "This easily administered tool can help you determine whether or not to schedule a child for therapy."

Stuttering Severity Instrument
for Children and Adults–Third Edition (SSI-3)

General Test Information

Author:	Glyndon D. Riley
Publisher:	PRO-ED
Address of Publisher:	8700 Shoal Creek Boulevard, Austin, TX 78757–6897
Telephone Number:	1-800-897-3202
Fax Number:	1-800-397-7633
Web Site of Publisher:	www.proedinc.com
Type of Test:	Speech and language
Administration Time:	Untimed
Type of Administration:	Individual
Ages/Grade Levels:	Ages 2–10 to adult

Purpose and Description of Test

The SSI-3 measures the stuttering severity of children and adults for clinical and research use.

Subtest Information

The SSI-3 Test Record and Frequency Computation Form is divided into four major areas: frequency (converted to scale scores 0 through 18), duration (converted to scale scores 0 through 18), physical concomitants (rated by degree of distractibility 0 through 20), and severity conversion tables for preschool children (ages 2–10 through 5–11), school-aged children (ages 6–1 to 16–11), and adults (ages 17–0 and older).

Strengths of the Test

- The SSI-3 can be used in conjunction with the Stuttering Prediction Instrument for Young Children to evaluate the effects of therapy. The third edition of this widely used test includes the following features: new and updated procedures (for example, percentage stuttered syllables is used to express frequency, duration of the longest stuttering events is timed, and physical concomitants are rated), new normative data are reported (reliability data are provided for research and clinical use, and validity issues are addressed and related data are provided), and picture plates are expanded to simplify speaking samples (new action pictures encourage guided conversation; readings at the fifth-grade, seventh-grade, and adult levels are provided).

Test for Auditory Comprehension of Language–Third Edition (TACL-3)

General Test Information

Author:	Elizabeth Carrow-Woolfolk
Publisher:	PRO-ED
Address of Publisher:	8700 Shoal Creek Boulevard, Austin, TX 78757–6897
Telephone Number:	1-800-897-3202
Fax Number:	1-800-397-7633
Web Site of Publisher:	www.proedinc.com
Type of Test:	Speech and language
Administration Time:	15 to 25 minutes
Type of Administration:	Individual
Ages/Grade Levels:	Ages 3–0 through 9–11

Purpose and Description of Test

The TACL-3 is a popular, individually administered measure of receptive spoken vocabulary, grammar, and syntax. Each item is composed of a word or sentence and a corresponding picture plate that has three full-color drawings. One of the three pictures for each item illustrates the meaning of the word, morpheme, or syntactic structure being tested. The other two pictures illustrate either two semantic or grammatical contrasts to the stimulus or one contrast and one decoy. The examiner reads the stimulus aloud, and the subject is directed to point to the picture that he or she believes best represents the meaning of the word, phrase, or sentence spoken by the examiner. No oral response is required on the part of the subject.

Subtest Information

The test consists of 142 items divided into three subtests that assess a child's ability to understand the following categories of English-language forms:

- *Vocabulary*—the literal and most common meanings of word classes such as nouns, verbs, adjectives, and adverbs and of words that represent basic percepts and concepts
- *Grammatical Morphemes*—the meaning of grammatical morphemes such as prepositions, noun number and case, verb number and tense, noun-verb agreement, derivational suffixes, and the meaning of pronouns, tested within the context of a simple sentence
- *Elaborated Phrases and Sentences*—the understanding of syntactically based word relations and elaborated phrase and sentence constructions, including the modalities of single and combined constructions (interrogative sentences, negative sentences, active and passive voice, direct and indirect object), embedded sentences, and partially and completely conjoined sentences

The test items are ordered according to difficulty within each of the three subtests.

Strengths of the Test

- The TACL-3 was normed on a standardization sample of 1,102 children. The Examiner's Manual includes a comprehensive discussion of the test's theoretical and research-based foundation, item development, standardization, administration and scoring procedures, norms tables, and guidelines for using and interpreting the test's results. Reliability studies were carried out with individuals with normal language abilities and individuals who are language delayed, hearing impaired, aphasic, or mentally retarded.
- The Third Edition has the following new features:
  - New normative data representing the current population have been obtained.
  - Characteristics of the normative sample relative to socioeconomic factors, ethnicity, gender, disability, and other critical variables are the same as those estimated for the year 2000 by the U.S. Bureau of the Census in the *1998 Statistical Abstract of the United States* (1998).
  - The normative information is stratified by age relative to gender, race, ethnicity, and disability.
  - Studies to identify gender, racial, disability, or ethnic bias were conducted, and appropriate modifications were made.
  - Reliability coefficients are computed for subgroups of the normative sample (for example, individuals with speech disabilities, African Americans, European Americans, Hispanic Americans, females) as well as for the entire normative group.
  - New validity studies were conducted, showing that the test is valid for a wide variety of subgroups as well as for the general population.
  - All pictures have been redrawn in color to present a more appealing look to children.
  - Each item on the test was reevaluated using both conventional item analyses to choose "good" items, and the new differential analyses to find and eliminate potentially biased items.
  - The TACL-3 is quick to give and easy to score.

Test for Examining Expressive Morphology (TEEM)

General Test Information

Authors: Kenneth G. Shipley, Terry A. Stone, and Marlene B. Sue
Publisher: PRO-ED
Address of Publisher: 8700 Shoal Creek Boulevard, Austin, TX 78757–6897
Telephone Number: 1-800-897-3202
Fax Number: 1-800-397-7633
Web Site of Publisher: www.proedinc.com
Type of Test: Speech and language
Administration Time: 7 minutes
Type of Administration: Individual
Ages/Grade Levels: Ages 3 through 7

Purpose and Description of Test

The TEEM evaluates expressive morpheme development in children. It samples a variety of morphemes and allomorphic variations through the use of a sentence-complete format with accompanying pictures. The TEEM's fifty-four items assess variations of six major morphemes:

- Present progressives
- Plurals: /z/, /s/, /z/ irregular forms
- Possessives: /z/, /s/, /z/
- Past tenses: /d/, /t/ irregular forms
- Third-person singulars: /z/, /s/, /z/
- Derived adjectives: -er or irregular comparatives; -est or irregular superlatives

Strengths of the Test

- The manual features administration instructions and statistical information regarding validity and reliability.
- A child's performance on individual items can be compared to the ages at which 75 and 90 percent of children master each item. In addition, each child's total score can be compared to the score ranges achieved by children tested in the sample.

Test of Adolescent and Adult Language–Third Edition (TOAL-3)

General Test Information

Authors:	Virginia Brown, Donald Hammill, Stephen Larson, and J. Lee Wiederholt
Publisher:	PRO-ED
Address of Publisher:	8700 Shoal Creek Boulevard, Austin, TX 78757–6897
Telephone Number:	1-800-897-3202
Fax Number:	1-800-397-7633
Web Site of Publisher:	www.proedinc.com
Type of Test:	Speech and language
Administration Time:	60 to 180 minutes
Type of Administration:	Individual
Ages/Grade Levels:	Ages 12–0 to 24–11 years

Purpose and Description of Test

The TOAL-3 is the latest revision of the popular Test of Adolescent Language originally published in 1981 and revised in 1987. A major improvement in the test is the extension of the norms to include 18- through 24-year-old persons enrolled in postsecondary education programs. This improvement required that the name of the test be changed to indicate the presence of the older population in the normative sample.

Subtest Information

The test consists of the following composites:

- *Listening*—assesses the ability to understand the spoken language of other people
- *Speaking*—assesses the ability to express ideas orally
- *Reading*—assesses the ability to comprehend written messages
- *Writing*—assesses the ability to express thoughts in graphic form
- *Spoken Language*—assesses the ability to listen and speak
- *Written Language*—assesses the ability to read and write
- *Vocabulary*—assesses the ability to understand and use words in communication
- *Grammar*—assesses the ability to understand and generate syntactic structures
- *Perceptive Language*—assesses the ability to comprehend both written and spoken language
- *Expressive Language*—assesses the ability to produce written and spoken language

Strengths of the Test

- The test is carefully developed and has a comprehensive system for assessing selected adolescent and adult languages.
- Scores allow for the clear differentiation between groups known to have language problems and those known to have normal language.
- The reliability is high.
- Items do not appear to be biased.
- The TOAL-3 assesses both oral and written language.

Test of Adolescent and Adult Word Finding (TAWF)

General Test Information

Author:	Diane J. German
Publisher:	PRO-ED
Address of Publisher:	8700 Shoal Creek Boulevard, Austin, TX 78757–6897
Telephone Number:	1-800-897-3202
Fax Number:	1-800-397-7633
Web Site of Publisher:	www.proedinc.com
Type of Test:	Speech and language
Administration Time:	20 to 30 minutes
Type of Administration:	Individual
Ages/Grade Levels:	Adolescents and adults

Purpose and Description of Test

The TAWF assesses expressive vocabulary skills.

Subtest Information

The test presents five naming sections:

- Picture Naming: Nouns
- Picture Naming: Verbs
- Sentence Completion Naming
- Description Naming
- Category Naming

It includes a special sixth comprehension section so that the examiner can determine if errors are a result of word-finding problems or due to poor comprehension. The TAWF provides formal and informal analyses of two dimensions of word finding: speed and accuracy.

Strengths of the Test

- TAWF features include age norms for ages 12 to 80, grade norms for grades 7 through 12, nationally standardized on 1,753 individuals (1,200 adolescents, 553 adults), high technical quality, a brief test with 40 items, 107 items for grades 7 through 12, and administration time of twenty to thirty minutes. This brief test takes twenty minutes or less, making it ideal for examiners with limited time or for participants who exhibit severe difficulties.

Test of Early Language Development–Third Edition (TELD-3)

General Test Information

Authors:	Wayne Hresko, D. Kim Reid, and Don Hammill
Publisher:	PRO-ED
Address of Publisher:	8700 Shoal Creek Boulevard, Austin, TX 78757–6897
Telephone Number:	1-800-897-3202
Fax Number:	1-800-397-7633
Web Site of Publisher:	www.proedinc.com
Type of Test:	Speech and language
Administration Time:	20 minutes
Type of Administration:	Individual
Ages/Grade Levels:	Ages 2–0 to 7–11 years

Purpose and Description of Test

The TELD-3 screens children for language deficiency. It is designed for normal children but can be administered to special populations after making proper adjustments in administering the test and establishing different norms. The TELD-3 is a major revision. Like the previous edition, it yields an overall Spoken Language score, and now it includes scores for Receptive Language and Expressive Language subtests.

Subtest Information

The TELD-3 has two subtests: Receptive Language and Expressive Language.

Strengths of the Test

- Normative information is reported with respect to geographical residence, gender, race, ethnicity, education, and socioeconomic status, and it is stratified by age.
- Studies showing the absence of gender, ethnic, disability, and racial bias have been included.
- Pictures are presented in color to make them more attractive to children.
- Standard scores (with a mean of 100 and a standard deviation of 15) and percentiles are provided for subtest and composite scores. Age-equivalent scores are reported for the subtests.
- The TELD-3 was built in accordance with the American Psychological Association's guidelines for test construction.
- The test is quick and easy to administer and score. The attractive pictures and content, along with the untimed nature of the items, allow optimal assessment.
- The kit includes all the manipulatives needed.
- The TELD-3 was built to ensure excellent psychometric qualities:
  - The TELD-3 was standardized on 2,217 children representing thirty-five states. Its normative population is clearly representative of the U.S. population as reported in the *1997 Statistical Abstract of the United States* (U.S. Census Bureau, 1997). In addition, the TELD-3 compares favorably to the projected year 2000 demographic characteristics.
  - Extensive studies of test reliability (coefficient alpha, test-retest, immediate test-retest with equivalent forms, and interscorer) support the use of the TELD-3 with individual students.

- Content-description validity was established through careful selection of items, controlled vocabulary, construct review by a panel of language experts, conventional item analysis, differential item functioning analysis, and form equivalence. Criterion-prediction validity was established by correlating TELD-3 standard scores with a variety of widely recognized measures of language ability (CELF Preschool, Expressive One-Word Picture Vocabulary Test, Preschool Language Scale–Third Edition, Peabody Picture Vocabulary Test–Revised, Receptive One-Word Picture Vocabulary Test–Spanish Bilingual Edition, and Test of Language Development–Primary: 3). Construct-identification validity was established by studying the relationship of the TELD-3 standardized scores with age, IQ, and academic achievement and the ability of the TELD-3's standard scores to differentiate groups with known language problems from those without such problems.
- Given the general concern with potential bias in test items, the TELD-3 was examined to ensure that little or no bias relative to gender, disability, racial, socioeconomic, or ethnic groups existed. The TELD-3 was examined using differential item functioning techniques. Furthermore, a wide range of mainstream and minority populations, including gender, racial, ethnic, linguistic, and disability categories, was included in the normative sample. Finally, reliability and validity information is provided for different mainstream and minority subgroups.

Test of Language Development–Primary: 3 (TOLD-P:3)

General Test Information

Authors:	Phyllis L. Newcomer and Donald D. Hammill
Publisher:	PRO-ED
Address of Publisher:	8700 Shoal Creek Boulevard, Austin, TX 78757–6897
Telephone Number:	1-800-897-3202
Fax Number:	1-800-397-7633
Web Site of Publisher:	www.proedinc.com
Type of Test:	Speech and language
Administration Time:	60 minutes
Type of Administration:	Individual
Ages/Grade Levels:	Ages 4–0 to 8–11

Purpose and Description of Test

The test measures a child's ability to understand word meanings, understand relationships between words, give simple definitions, understand sentences, imitate spoken sentences, and complete sentences. It uses a two-dimensional linguistic model involving linguistic systems (listening and speaking) and linguistic features (phonology, syntax, and semantics). The subtests sample each component of the model.

Subtest Information

The TOLD-P:3 has these subtests:

- Picture Vocabulary (understanding words, semantics)
- Oral Vocabulary (defining word, semantics)
- Grammatic Understanding (understanding sentence structure, syntax)
- Sentence Imitation (generating proper sentences, syntax)
- Grammatic Completion (morphological usage, syntax)
- Relational Vocabulary (understanding similarities, semantics)
- Word Discrimination (noticing sound differences, phonology)
- Word Articulation (saying words correctly, phonology)
- Phonemic Analysis (segmenting words into smaller units, phonology)

Strengths of the Test

- The TOLD-P:3 is well designed in terms of using established psychometric criteria for reliability and criterion-related validity.
- The test is a useful measure for investigating the oral language skills of young children.
- The test is useful in identifying areas in which the child is proficient and areas that require further evaluation.
- Many different language areas can be assessed.
- Children may find the test fun to take because the colored pictures are pleasant to observe.

Test of Oral Structures and Functions (TOSF)

General Test Information

Author:	Gary J. Vitali
Publisher:	Slosson Educational Publications
Address of Publisher:	P.O. Box 280, East Aurora, NY 14052
Telephone Number:	1-888-756-7766
Fax Number:	1-800-655-3840
Web Site of Publisher:	www.slosson.com
Type of Test:	Speech and language
Administration Time:	15 to 20 minutes
Type of Administration:	Individual
Ages/Grade Levels:	Ages 7 to adult

Purpose and Description of Test

The TOSF is one of the most popular standardized tests of oral structures and functions. Both brief and flexible, the systematic standardized format facilitates caseload management decisions. It addresses such questions as: Does this child have an articulation disorder or delay? Does this person have apraxia or dysarthria error patterns? Are there oral dysfunctions that place the patient at risk?

Subtest Information

Descriptive information and expected subtest performance are given for dysarthria, apraxia, Broca's aphasia, velopharyngeal incompetence-insufficiency, and functional disorders.

Strengths of the Test

- Directly facilitates questions regarding diagnosis, prognosis, and placement.
- Useful for identifying children and adults with special needs in the areas of articulation, voice, swallowing, and more.
- Graphic and verbal summaries to facilitate individualized education program or related meetings.
- The TOSF is more than an oral mechanism checklist. It systematically assesses oral structures and motor integrity during verbal and nonverbal oral functioning.
- Effective for such uses as screening, differential diagnosis, caseload management decisions, and pre- or post-treatment assessment.
- Reliability: Interrater .96 internal consistency; coefficient alpha (verbal functioning) .95; (nonverbal functioning) .89; odd-even split-half, .95.

Test of Phonological Awareness–Second Edition (TOPA-2+)

General Test Information

Authors:	Joseph K. Torgensen and Brian R. Bryant
Publisher:	PRO-ED
Address of Publisher:	8700 Shoal Creek Boulevard, Austin, TX 78757–6897
Telephone Number:	1-800-897-3202
Fax Number:	1-800-397-7633
Web Site of Publisher:	www.proedinc.com
Type of Test:	Speech and language
Administration Time:	Kindergarten version, 30 to 45 minutes; Early Elementary version, 15 to 30 minutes
Type of Administration:	Individual or group
Ages/Grade Levels:	Ages 5 to 8

Purpose and Description of Test

The TOPA-2+ has two versions, the Kindergarten version and the Early Elementary version, that measure young children's ability to isolate individual phonemes in spoken words and understand the relationships between letters and phonemes in English. The latter skill was not assessed by the original TOPA and is the reason the "plus" was added to the title. One version, the Kindergarten TOPA-2+, can be administered at any time during the kindergarten year but is likely to be most sensitive to individual differences during the second half of the year. The Early Elementary version, for children in first and second grades, is similar in structure to the Kindergarten version, except that the child must identify final sounds in words, a more difficult task.

Subtest Information

The Kindergarten TOPA-2+ uses two item types to assess phonemic awareness:

- Ten Initial Sound-Same items require children to mark which of three words begins with the same sound as a target word.
- Ten Initial Sound-Different items require children to mark which word in a group of four words begins with a different first sound from the other three.

A child's total score for phonemic awareness is the number correct on each item type added together. The Letter-Sounds subtest requires children to mark which letter, from a set of four, corresponds to a specific phoneme. The subtest has fifteen items, and the child's score for the test is the total number correct.

In the Early Elementary TOPA-2+, the ten Ending Sound-Same items require children to identify which of three words ends with the same sound as a target word, while the ten Ending Sound-Different items ask children to mark which of a group of four words ends in a different sound from the others. As with the kindergarten version, the number correct on both item types is summed to get one total score for phonemic awareness. The Letter-Sounds test for the Early Elementary version requires children to spell simple pseudowords that are given as the names of "funny animals." The words vary from two to five phonemes in length, and they are all single syllable. The child's score is the total number of words spelled correctly.

Strengths of the Test

- The TOPA-2+ was normed on 2,085 students from twenty-six states: 1,035 for the Kindergarten version and 1,050 for the Early Elementary version. The sample is representative of the United States across several key demographic variables (geographical region, gender, race, ethnicity, family income, educational attainment of parents).
- The TOPA-2+ manual provides evidence of internal consistency reliability, test-retest reliability, and interscorer reliability, all of which meet or exceed .80 across all ages. Evidence is also provided for content-descriptive validity, criterion-prediction validity, and construct-identification validity.
- The manual provides evidence that the TOPA-2+ subtests are nonbiased with regard to gender, race, and ethnicity.
- Major improvements in this edition:
  - All new normative data were collected during 2002 and 2003.
  - Characteristics of the normative sample with regard to age, geographical region, gender, race, residence, Hispanic ethnicity, family income, and parents' education are keyed to the 2000 Census data projections and therefore are representative of the current U.S. population.
  - The normative data for geographical region, gender, race, and residence have been stratified by age. Studies showing the absence of culture, gender, race, and disability bias have been added.
  - Reliability coefficients have been computed by age and separately for males, females, European Americans, African Americans, and Hispanic Americans, and those with language and learning disabilities, as well as for the entire normative group.
  - All new validity studies have been conducted; these studies show clearly that the test results are valid for a wide variety of mainstream and minority subgroups, as well as for the general population.
  - Some items from the original scale were changed to less offensive words and pictures.
  - The new letter-sound correspondence subtests add substantially to the predictive accuracy of early screening for reading difficulties.
  - The overall look of the test has been updated and improved.

Test of Word Finding–Second Edition (TWF-2)

General Test Information

Author:	Diane J. German
Publisher:	PRO-ED
Address of Publisher:	8700 Shoal Creek Boulevard, Austin, TX 78757–6897
Telephone Number:	1-800-897-3202
Fax Number:	1-800-397-7633
Web Site of Publisher:	www.proedinc.com
Type of Test:	Speech and language
Administration Time:	20 to 30 minutes
Type of Administration:	Individual
Ages/Grade Levels:	Ages 4–0 to 12–11 years

Purpose and Description of Test

Like the TWF, the TWF-2 is a diagnostic tool for the assessment of children's word finding skills. Three forms are provided: a preprimary form for preschool and kindergarten children, a primary form for the first and second grades, and an intermediate form for the third through sixth grades. These new norms extend the use of the TWF-2 to include preschool-aged children.

Subtest Information

The TWF-2 uses four naming sections to test a student's word finding ability:

- *Picture Naming Nouns*—an assessment of a student's accuracy and speed when naming compound and one- to four-syllable target words
- *Sentence Completion Naming*—an assessment of a student's accuracy when naming target words to complete a sentence read by the examiner
- *Picture Naming Verbs*—an assessment of a student's accuracy when naming pictures depicting verbs in the progressive and past tense forms
- *Picture Naming Categories*—an assessment of a student's accuracy and speed when naming objects and the distinct categories to which they belong

Strengths of the Test

- The TWF-2 was normed on 1,836 students residing in twenty-six states from 1996 to 1999. Characteristics of the sample matched the national population in 1997.
- Test reliability was demonstrated using test-retest, coefficient alpha, interscorer reliability, and item response theory (IRT) goodness-of-fit statistics. In all cases except one (.76), traditional reliability coefficients for typical performing students and students with word finding difficulties exceeded .84.
- Validity was studied extensively. Content validity was represented in test development: TWF-2 content reflected child language literature and research, and IRT and classical methodologies along with differential item function analyses were conducted on select items.
- Concurrent and predictive validity of the TWF-2 were demonstrated by correlating it with commonly used vocabulary tests. Correlations between TWF-2 and other tests of vocabulary showed a considerable relationship. Construct validity was established by demonstrating that the TWF-2 differentiated between groups of children with and without word finding difficulties.

- New features for the TWF-2:
  - All new norms were collected from 1996 through 1999 keyed to the current census data. Norms are completely representative of the U.S. population and stratified by age.
  - Designed for use with children from ages 4–0 to 12–11, the TWF-2 adds two years downward extension to the original TWF.
  - TWF-2 is proven to be unbiased relative to gender and race.
  - Revised naming sections and items include more multisyllabic words, compound words, and progressive and past-tense verb forms.
  - The Word Finding Quotient is provided to represent a student's accuracy and speed in naming.
  - The theoretical model underlying the TWF-2 was expanded to accommodate current thinking on word retrieval.
  - New supplementary analyses, including phonemic cueing, were added to reflect the theoretical model and enhance the differential diagnosis of a student's word finding errors.
  - Item response theory and classical item methodologies were used to choose statistically reliable items, and differential item function analyses were used to find and eliminate biased items.

Woodcock Language Proficiency Battery–Revised (WLPB-R)

General Test Information

Authors:	Richard W. Woodcock and Ana F. Muñoz-Sandoval (Spanish Form)
Publisher:	Riverside Publishing
Address of Publisher:	425 Spring Lake Drive, Itasca, IL 60143–2079
Telephone Number:	1-800-323-9540
Fax Number:	1-630-467-7192
Web Site of Publisher:	www.riverpub.com
Type of Test:	Speech and language
Administration Time:	Varies; typically 20 to 60 minutes
Type of Administration:	Individual
Ages/Grade Levels:	Ages 2.0 to 90.0+

Purpose and Description of Test

The WLPB-R provides an overall measure of language proficiency and greatly expanded measures of oral language, reading, and written language in both English and Spanish. The English Form and Spanish Form are parallel versions, which facilitates comparison between the languages. The tests in the WLPB-R are primarily measures of language skills predictive of success in situations characterized by Cognitive Academic Language Proficiency requirements. The WLPB-R can be used for purposes of eligibility, determination of level of language proficiency, achievement levels, entrance and exit criteria, determination of discrepancies, progress, and reevaluation.

Strengths of the Test

- Cluster reliabilities are in the .90s.
- The Examiner's Manual documents the validity of the WLPB-R as a technically sound measure of language proficiency.
- The English Form is standardized on more than 6,300 subjects in the United States; the Spanish Form is standardized on more than 2,000 native Spanish-speaking subjects.
- The Supplemental Manual for the Spanish Form provides technical information about the development and standardization of the form, scoring criteria for writing samples and handwriting, and a chapter on the use and training of ancillary Spanish examiners.
- When both versions of the WLPB-R have been administered, the Comparative Language Index that allows direct comparison between English and Spanish scores will be obtained. Equated norms allow meaningful interpretation of results in either language.

Chapter 25

Visual Processing

A child having problems in memory and expression will fall behind the rest of the class very quickly. The longer these processing difficulties continue, the greater the chance is for secondary emotional problems to develop (emotional problems resulting from continued frustration with the ability to learn). Perceptual evaluation has a number of purposes:

- To develop a learning profile. This can help the classroom teacher understand the best way to present information to the child and therefore increase his or her chances of success.
- To help determine the child's stronger and weaker modality for learning. Some children are visual learners, some are auditory, and some can learn through any form of input. However, if a child is a strong visual learner in a class where the teacher relies on auditory lectures, then his or her ability to process information may be hampered. The evaluation may provide this information, which is very useful when making practical recommendations to teachers about how to best present information to assist the child in learning.
- To help determine a child's stronger and weaker process areas.
- To help determine if the child's learning process deficits are suitable for a regular class. Along with other information and test results, the child may require a more restrictive educational setting such as a resource room, self-contained class, or special school.

A visual processing, or perceptual, disorder refers to a hindered ability to make sense of information taken in through the eyes. This is different from problems involving sight or sharpness of vision. Difficulties with visual processing affect how visual information is interpreted or processed by the brain (National Center for Learning Disabilities. 2005).

According to the National Center for Learning Disabilities (2005), individuals with visual processing disorders may have these diagnostic symptoms:

- Difficulty in accurately identifying information from pictures, charts, graphs, maps, and other material
- Difficulty copying from board or books

- Easily distracted, especially by competing visual information
- Difficulty finding and retaining important information in reading assignments or tests
- Difficulty finding specific information on a printed page (for example, getting a number out of the phone book)
- Lack of fluidity of movement (for example, getting out of the way of a moving ball, knocking things over)
- Difficulty judging distances (for example, bumping into things, placing objects too close to an edge)
- Misunderstanding or confusing written symbols (for example, +, ×, /, &)
- Difficulty organizing and solving math problems
- Difficulty organizing information from different sources into one cohesive document
- Difficulty reading with speed and precision
- Difficulty remembering directions to a location
- Difficulty sewing or other types of fine motor activities
- Difficulty writing coherent, well-organized essays
- Difficulty writing neatly and quickly
- Difficulty writing within margins or on lines or aligning numbers in math problems

A student with a visual perception problem may see perfectly well the letters *b-a-t* written on the page. What the brain interprets them to be is *t-a-b*. Problems in auditory perception often include difficulties with perceiving sounds that are not attributable to a hearing loss. For example, some students may have trouble understanding whether the word spoken was *king* or *kin, hot* or *hut, fire* or *file*. The result can be misunderstood directions, poor communication, and awkwardness in social situations (Friend, 2005).

The following assessment area skills are most often associated with visual perception:

- *Visual coordination*—the ability to follow and track objects with coordinated eye movements
- *Visual discrimination*—the ability to differentiate visually the forms and symbols in one's environment
- *Visual association*—the ability to organize and associate visually presented material in a meaningful way
- *Visual long-term memory*—the ability to retain and recall general and specific long-term visual information
- *Visual short-term memory*—the ability to retain and recall general and specific short-term auditory information
- *Visual sequential memory*—the ability to recall prior auditory information in correct sequence and detail
- *Visual vocal expression*—the ability to reproduce vocally prior visually presented material or experiences
- *Visual motoric expression (visual motor integration)*—the ability to reproduce motorically prior visually presented material or experiences
- *Visual figure-ground discrimination*—the ability to differentiate relevant stimuli (the figure) from irrelevant stimuli (the background)
- *Visual spatial relationships*—the ability to perceive the relative positions of objects in space
- *Visual form perception (visual constancy)*—the ability to discern the size, shape, and position of visual stimuli

Beery-VMI (Developmental Test of Visual Motor Integration)–Fifth Edition (VMI-5)

General Test Information

Author:	Keith E. Beery
Publisher:	PRO-ED
Address of Publisher:	8700 Shoal Creek Boulevard, Austin, TX 78757–6897
Telephone Number:	1-800-897-3202
Fax Number:	1-800-397-7633
Web Site of Publisher:	www.proedinc.com
Type of Test:	Visual motor processing
Administration Time:	10 to 15 minutes
Type of Administration:	Individual and group
Ages/Grade Levels:	Ages 2 to 18; preschool through grade 12

Purpose and Description of Test

Beery-VMI, now in its fifth edition, offers a convenient and economical way to screen for visual motor deficits that can lead to learning, neuropsychological, and behavior problems. It helps assess the extent to which individuals can integrate their visual motor abilities. The Short Format and Full Format tests present drawings of geometric forms arranged in order of increasing difficulty that the individual is asked to copy.

Strengths of the Test

- The VMI-5 is among the few psychological assessments that provide standard scores as low as age 2.
- The Examiner's Manual provides approximately 600 age-specific norms from birth through age 6. These consist of basic gross motor, fine motor, visual, and visual and fine motor developmental stepping-stones identified by research criteria. Many examiners find the age norm information to be useful in helping parents understand their child's current level of development. The manual also presents teaching suggestions.
- As a culture-free, nonverbal assessment, the VMI-5 is useful with individuals of diverse environmental, educational, and linguistic backgrounds.
- The VMI-5 provides time-efficient screening tools, with the Short and Full Format tests taking only 10 to 15 minutes to complete and the supplemental tests taking only about 5 minutes each.
- The Short and Full Format tests can be administered individually or to groups. (Individual administration is recommended for the supplemental tests.)

Bender Visual-Motor Gestalt Test–
Second Edition (Bender-Gestalt II)

General Test Information

Author:	Lauretta Bender
Publisher:	Western Psychological Services
Address of Publisher:	12031 Wilshire Boulevard, Los Angeles, CA 90025–1251
Telephone Number:	1-800-648-8857 (United States and Canada only), 1-310-478-2061
Fax Number:	1-310-478-7838
Web Site of Publisher:	www.wpspublish.com
Type of Test:	Visual motor processing
Administration Time:	Fourteen stimulus cards: 5 to 10 minutes; visual motor tests: 5 minutes
Type of Administration:	Individual
Ages/Grade Levels:	Ages 3 and older

Purpose and Description of Test

Originally published in 1938 by Lauretta Bender, the Bender Visual-Motor Gestalt Test is one of the most widely used psychological tests in the past half-century. The Bender-Gestalt II updates this classic assessment and continues its tradition as a brief test of visual motor integration that may provide interpretive information about an individual's development and psychological functioning.

Strengths of the Test

- The test is quick and easy to administer.
- The test is one of the oldest and most popular used to assess visual motor abilities.
- The test provides developmental data on a child's perceptual maturity.
- Group administration is a time saver.
- The test is effective as a screening instrument when combined with other tests.
- New recall procedures to assess visual motor memory provide a more comprehensive assessment of visual motor skills.
- Supplemental tests of simple motor and perceptual ability help identify specific visual motor deficits.
- Comprehensive testing observations including physical demeanor, drawing technique, and test-taking behavior and attitude.

Benton Visual Retention Test–Fifth Edition

General Test Information

Author:	Abigail Benton Sivan
Publisher:	Harcourt Assessment (formerly known as the Psychological Corporation and Harcourt Educational)
Address of Publisher:	6277 Sea Harbor Drive, Orlando, FL 32887
Telephone Number:	1-800-211-8378
Fax Number:	1-800-232-1223
Web Site of Publisher:	www.harcourt.com
Type of Test:	Visual motor processing
Administration Time:	15 to 20 minutes
Type of Administration:	Individual
Ages/Grade Levels:	Ages 8 through adult

Purpose and Description of Test

The Benton Visual Retention Test–Fifth Edition assesses visual perception, memory, and visuo-constructive abilities. Each of the three test forms consists of ten designs presented one-by-one. The examinee reproduces the drawings in the Response Booklet-Record Form. The three alternate, equivalent forms of the test allow retesting while minimizing practice effects.

Strengths of the Test

- More than fifty years of proven clinical utility is the hallmark of the Benton Visual Retention Test. This test has proven its sensitivity to reading disabilities, nonverbal learning disabilities, traumatic brain injury, and attention deficit disorder.
- Besides easy administration, the test features updated normative data, expanded scoring examples, and a detailed review of research conducted with the test.
- Interrater scoring is highly reliable (r = .95 to .97).

Comprehensive Test of Visual Functioning Kit (CTVF)

General Test Information

Authors:	Sue Larson, Evelyn Buethe, and Gary J. Vitali
Publisher:	Slosson Educational Publications
Address of Publisher:	P.O. Box 280, East Aurora, NY 14052
Telephone Number:	1-888-756-7766
Fax Number:	1-800-655-3840
Web Site of Publisher:	www.slosson.com
Type of Test:	Visual motor processing
Administration Time:	25 minutes
Type of Administration:	Individual
Ages/Grade Levels:	Ages 8 to adult

Purpose and Description of Test

The CTVF is a brief assessment device for detecting and discriminating visual processing problems.

Subtest Information

The CTVF has nine subtests:

- Visual Acuity
- Visual Tracking
- Figure-Ground
- Visual Closure
- Spatial Orientation
- Perceptual Reasoning
- Visual Motor
- Reading Decoding
- Thematic Maturity

Strengths of the Test

- The CTVF is appropriate with populations manifesting visual and perceptual problems secondary to acute or chronic disorder processes.
- The test was developed on 1,200 individuals. Excellent reliability and validity statistics are included in the manual.
- People of different professional backgrounds can administer it, and no specific training is required.

Developmental Test of Visual Perception–Second Edition (DTVP-2)

General Test Information

Authors:	Don Hammill, Nils Pearson, and Judith Voress
Publisher:	PRO-ED
Address of Publisher:	8700 Shoal Creek Boulevard, Austin, TX 78757–6897
Telephone Number:	1-800-897-3202
Fax Number:	1-800-397-7633
Web Site of Publisher:	www.proedinc.com
Type of Test:	Visual motor processing
Administration Time:	30 minutes to 1 hour
Type of Administration:	Individual
Ages/Grade Levels:	Ages 4 to 10

Purpose and Description of Test

The DTVP-2 is the 1993 revision of Marianne Frostig's popular Developmental Test of Visual Perception (DTVP). The original version of the test was administered to more than 6 million children. The new edition, which includes numerous improvements, measures both visual perception and visual motor integration skills and is based on updated theories of visual perceptual development.

Subtest Information

The tasks are arranged in increasing order of difficulty in eight areas:

- *Eye motor coordination.* This task requires the child to draw lines between increasingly narrow boundaries. These may include straight, curved, or angled lines.
- *Figure-ground.* This task requires the child to distinguish and then outline embedded figures between intersecting shapes.
- *Form constancy.* This task requires the child to discriminate common geometric shapes presented in different shapes, sizes, positions, and textures from other similar shapes.
- *Position in space.* This task requires the child to distinguish between figures in an identical position and those in a reversed rotated position.
- *Spatial relations.* This task requires the child to copy simple forms and patterns by joining dots.
- *Copying.* The child is asked to copy increasingly complex figures from model drawings.
- *Visual closure.* The child is required to view a geometric figure and then select the matching figure from a series of figures that all have missing parts.
- *Visual motor speed.* The child is required to draw special marks in selected geometric designs on a page filled with various designs.

419

Strengths of the Test

- Of all the tests of visual perception and visual motor integration, the DTVP-2 is unique in that its scores are reliable at the .8 or .9 levels for all age groups; its scores are validated by many studies; its norms are based on a large representative sample keyed to the 1990 Census data; it yields scores for both pure visual perception (no motor response) and visual motor integration ability; and it has been proven to be unbiased relative to race, gender, and handedness.
- The DTVP-2 was standardized on 1,972 children from twelve states. Characteristics of the normative sample approximate those provided in the *1990 Statistical Abstract of the United States* (U.S. Census Bureau, 1990) with regard to gender, geographical region, ethnicity, race, and urban/rural residence.
- Internal consistency reliabilities (alphas) and stability reliabilities (test-retest) for all scores exceed .8 at all ages. Criterion-related validity is evidenced by correlating DTVP-2 scores with those from the Developmental Test of Visual-Motor Integration and Motor-Free Visual Perception Test.
- Construct validity is supported by correlations with mental ability tests, achievement tests, and age.

Kent Visual Perceptual Test (KVPT)

General Test Information

Author: Lawrence E. Melamed
Publisher: PAR
Address of Publisher: 16204 North Florida Avenue, Lutz, FL 33549
Telephone Number: 1-800-331-8378, ext. 361
Fax Number: 1-800-727-9329
Web Site of Publisher: www.parinc.com
Type of Test: Visual motor processing
Administration Time: 25 to 30 minutes
Type of Administration: Individual
Ages/Grade Levels: Ages 5–11 years to adult

Purpose and Description of Test

The KVPT is an integrated battery of interrelated tests that demonstrate impairment and distinguish skill levels among three visual processes related to the development of basic reading, early mathematics, and written expression. These tests are particularly effective in individualized neuropsychological assessment and psychoeducational assessment.

Subtest Information

There are three subtests:

- The KVPT-D (Discrimination) requires the individual to select from a set of alternatives the item that matches a standard form. Stimuli are presented in a binder for ease of administration.
- The KVPT-C (Copy) consists of three increasingly difficult subtests that require the individual to reproduce forms of the same type as the KVPT-D items.
- The KVPT-M (Immediate Memory) requires the individual to locate a target form within a set of alternatives immediately following brief exposure to the form. Stimuli are presented in a binder for ease of administration.

Strengths of the Test

- For neuropsychological assessment, the KVPT can be used as the core visual processing battery to characterize visual perceptual deficits and distinguish them from visual memory or visual motor problems. The KVPT can be used to distinguish visual spatial errors or a deficit due to errors in processing the spatial features of forms from errors in reproducing (copying) the forms. The KVPT is sensitive to stroke-related deficits.
- In a school setting, the KVPT can help professionals in school psychology and special education predict early achievement and identify and remediate reading, mathematics, and written expression difficulties due to visual processing (for example, determining that a child with difficulty identifying appropriate mathematical operations has a visual spatial processing deficit). The Professional Manual provides a chapter on clinical interpretation that demonstrates the way appropriate academic interventions can be developed based on a child's KVPT profile.
- All three tests come from a common pool of two-dimensional items based on form perception literature, ensuring both construct validity and comparability in processing difficulty. Although the KVPT was normed with all three tests administered, it is possible to use only one or two of the tests so long as the tests are presented in the following order: KVPT-D, KVPT-C, KVPT-M.

Learning Efficiency Test–Second Edition (LET-II)

General Test Information

Author:	Raymond E. Webster
Publisher:	Academic Therapy
Address of Publisher:	20 Commercial Boulevard, Novato, CA 94949
Telephone Number:	1-800-422-7249
Fax Number:	1-888-287-9975
Web Site of Publisher:	www.academictherapy.com
Type of Test:	Visual and auditory processing
Administration Time:	15 minutes
Type of Administration:	Individual
Ages/Grade Levels:	Ages 4 through adult

Purpose and Description of Test

The LET-II provides a quick and reliable measure of visual and auditory information processing characteristics and is useful in determining information processing deficits that may be related to learning problems. Performance on the test yields information about a person's preferred modality for learning, the impact of verbal interference on memory storage and retrieval, and the kinds of metacognitive strategies used during learning. The test also identifies the presence of global memory deficits, modality-specific memory deficits, or sequential organization deficits that interfere with successful learning. The LET-II has been shown to be useful in identifying learning problems related to characteristics of memory, assessing the effects of physical injury on cognitive functioning, evaluating memory loss in aging adults, and developing specific individualized education programs for atypical learners.

Subtest Information

Strings of two to nine nonrhyming letters are presented visually or orally. Memory is assessed in two modalities (visual and auditory) and in three recall conditions (immediate recall, short-term recall, and long-term recall). The six subtest scores can be collapsed into Modality Scores and a Global Memory Score. Scores can be converted into standard scores and percentiles for comparison with other tests. Sequenced and nonsequenced scores are also obtained.

Strengths of the Test

- The revised edition features new norms expanded to include adults age 75 years and older and an improved record form and scoring system.
- The LET-II manual contains expanded and detailed sections on scoring using pattern analysis, relevant and updated literature on the aptitude-treatment interaction model and modality effects during learning, and several case studies with assessment results characteristic of different diagnosed conditions. It also contains specific remediation activities for use with persons showing various kinds of information processing deficits.

Motor Free Visual Perception Test–Third Edition (MVPT-3)

General Test Information

Authors:	Ronald P. Colarusso and Donald D. Hammill
Publisher:	PRO-ED
Address of Publisher:	8700 Shoal Creek Boulevard, Austin, TX 78757–6897
Telephone Number:	1-800-897-3202
Fax Number:	1-800-397-7633
Web Site of Publisher:	www.proedinc.com
Type of Test:	Visual motor processing
Administration Time:	20 minutes
Type of Administration:	Individual
Ages/Grade Levels:	Ages 4 to 85

Purpose and Description of Test

The MVPT-3 is designed to assess visual perception without reliance on an individual's motor skills; it is particularly useful with those who may have learning, cognitive, motor, or physical disabilities. The MVPT-3 can be used for screening as well as diagnostic and research purposes by teachers, psychologists, educational specialists, rehabilitation therapists, and others who need a quick, highly reliable, and valid measure of overall visual perceptual processing ability in children and adults.

Subtest Information

Tasks include matching, figure-ground, closure, visual memory, and form discrimination. The MVPT-3 measures skills without copying tasks.

Strengths of the Test

- It contains many new, more difficult items at the upper end for older children and adults. Answers are presented in multiple-choice format. Responses may be given verbally or by pointing. Item response times may be interpreted in terms of functional behavioral categories. Clinical population comparisons are also provided.

Slosson Visual-Motor Performance Test (S-VMPT)

General Test Information

Authors:	Richard L. Slosson; revised by Charles L. Nicholson
Publisher:	Slosson Educational Publications
Address of Publisher:	P.O. Box 280, East Aurora, NY 14052
Telephone Number:	1-888-756-7766
Fax Number:	1-800-655-3840
Web Site of Publisher:	www.slosson.com
Type of Test:	Visual motor processing
Administration Time:	10 to 15 minutes
Type of Administration:	Individual or group
Ages/Grade Levels:	Ages 4 to adult

Purpose and Description of Test

The S-VMPT is a test of visual motor integration in which individuals are asked to copy geometric figures, increasing in complexity, without the use of a ruler, compass, or other aids. It measures the ability to interpret and translate visually perceived geometric patterns using hand-motor responses. This test is one of the only measures yielding standard scores and developmental age scores for children and adults. The S-VMPT is designed as a screening test to identify individuals with serious perceptual organizational problems involving eye-hand coordination.

Strengths of the Test

- The record and score forms are designed to facilitate reliability by reducing the number of test stimuli, allowing only two per page. The separate Score Forms have reduced-size stimuli items all on one page with space to write observations, so the examiner can easily tally scores and look at all test items at a single glance and see if there were any patterns to the errors being made.
- Standardization on over 1,000 subjects, including diverse ethnic groups and exceptional children, who were representative of the U.S. population. Internal reliability is .90 and above, and interscorer reliability is .86. Validity with the Bender Gestalt, using the Koppitz method of scoring, indicates the S-VMPT is useful as a brief differential screening instrument for at-risk eye-hand/visual perceptual performance identification.
- Guidelines and examples are included in a comprehensive manual for examiner scoring of test items. Thus, the examiner can practice on examples given in the manual before scoring examinees. The examiner starts by reading the Introductory Remarks on the front cover of the record form to the examinee. The individual is asked to copy as many figures as he or she can. Each geometric pattern is scored 1 or 0 by comparing it with the original figure using the guidelines outlined in the manual.

Test of Gross Motor Development–Second Edition (TGMD-2)

General Test Information

Author:	Dale Ulrich
Publisher:	PRO-ED
Address of Publisher:	8700 Shoal Creek Boulevard, Austin, TX 78757–6897
Telephone Number:	1-800-897-3202
Fax Number:	1-800-397-7633
Web Site of Publisher:	www.proedinc.com
Type of Test:	Visual motor processing
Administration Time:	15 minutes
Type of Administration:	Individual
Ages/Grade Levels:	Ages 3–0 to 10–11

Purpose and Description of Test

The TGMD-2 assesses common motor skills. The primary uses of this test are to identify children who are significantly behind their peers in gross motor skill development, assist in the planning of an instructional program in gross motor skill development, and evaluate the gross motor program. The test is a multiple-item task performance test consisting of two subtests. The examiner records observations in a student record book. The TGMD-2 allows examiners to administer one test relatively quickly and gather data for making important educational decisions.

Subtest Information

The test is divided into two subtests:

- *Locomotion*—measures the run, gallop, hop, leap, horizontal jump, and slide skills that move a child's center of gravity from one point to another
- *Object Control*—measures the ability to strike a stationary ball, stationary dribble, catch, kick, underhand roll, and overhand throw skills that include projecting and receiving objects

Strengths of the Test

- All new normative information is keyed to the projected 2000 Census and stratified by age relative to geography, gender, race, and residence.
- New reliability and validity studies include exploratory and confirmatory factor analyses that empirically support the skills chosen for each subtest.
- Evidence related to content sampling and test-retest time sampling reliability is provided. Reliability coefficients for the Locomotor subtest average .85, the Object Control subtest average .88, and the Gross Motor composite average .91. Standard error of measurement is 1 at every age interval for both subtests and 4 or 5 for the composite score at each age interval. Coefficient alphas for selected subgroups are all above .90 for the subtest and the composite. Time sampling reliability coefficients range from .84 to .96. Content-description, criterion-prediction, and construct-identification validity that further support the use of the TGMD-2 in identifying children who are significantly behind their peers in gross motor development are also provided.
- Using the TGMD-2, the examiner will obtain standard scores, percentile scores, and age equivalents. The test also provides a gross motor quotient if both subtests are completed.

Test of Visual Motor Integration (TVMI)

General Test Information

Authors:	Don Hammill, Nils Pearson, and Judith Voress
Publisher:	PRO-ED
Address of Publisher:	8700 Shoal Creek Boulevard, Austin, TX 78757–6897
Telephone Number:	1-800-897-3202
Fax Number:	1-800-397-7633
Web Site of Publisher:	www.proedinc.com
Type of Test:	Visual motor processing
Administration Time:	Approximately 20 minutes
Type of Administration:	Individual or group
Ages/Grade Levels:	Ages 4–0 to 17–11

Purpose and Description of Test

The TVMI measures visual motor ability in students by asking them to copy a series of increasingly complex geometric figures. The TVMI is unique among visual motor integration tests because it gives the clinician a highly reliable, valid, and unbiased measure for assessing students with wide ranges of visual motor ability.

Strengths of the Test

- The TVMI was normed on a large, representative sample of more than 2,000 students whose demographic characteristics approximate those of the 1990 U.S. Census data.
- Results are reported in standard scores, percentiles, and age equivalents.
- The TVMI is reliable for all ages and is unbiased with regard to gender and race.
- It has internal consistency reliability of .90 or above for all ages and provides numerous examples for practice scoring.

Test of Visual Perceptual Skills–Third Edition (TVPS-3)

General Test Information

Author:	Nancy A. Martin
Publisher:	Academic Therapy
Address of Publisher:	20 Commercial Boulevard, Novato, CA 94949
Telephone Number:	1-800-422-7249
Fax Number:	1-888-287-9975
Web Site of Publisher:	www.academictherapy.com
Type of Test:	Visual motor processing
Administration Time:	45 to 60 minutes
Type of Administration:	Individual or small group
Ages/Grade Levels:	Ages 4 through 18

Purpose and Description of Test

The TVPS-3 provides an in-depth analysis of a person's visual perceptual abilities by presenting black-and-white forms with answer choices in a multiple-choice format; no drawing or motor skills are needed. The test kit contains a manual, test plate (bound), and twenty-five response and scoring forms.

Subtest Information

There are seven subtests on the TVPS-3, each focusing on a particular type of visual perceptual task:

- Discrimination
- Memory
- Spatial Relationships
- Form Constancy
- Sequential Memory
- Figure-Ground
- Closure

Strengths of the Test

- This one test replaces the previous version, which consisted of two separate levels. The multiple-choice format, with no reliance on motor skills, allows the TVPS-3 to be used with a wide variety of students.
- The normative sample is nationally stratified, and demographics match the U.S. Census.

Chapter 26

Written Language

A variety of assessment issues must be addressed in evaluating disorders of written language. These include the characteristics of the dysgraphic writer, such as fine motor and writing speed, attention and concentration, writing organization, spelling, knowledge and use of vocabulary, language expression, and perception of details.

In terms of assessing written language, various characteristics of instruction should be incorporated into the background knowledge and included in the history taking of the student: penmanship instruction; instruction on how to organize and arrange thoughts; and instruction on written language rules, including capitalization, punctuation, grammar, spelling, and sentence structure. The evaluator should determine whether direct instruction has been provided and whether note-taking methods have been taught and practiced.

Spelling is a skill subsumed under written expression. Spelling is one of the academic skills often included in the evaluator's test battery of individual achievement tests used in special education assessment. Spelling, like all other written language skills, is well suited to work sample analysis because a permanent product is produced. Learning to spell is a developmental process, and young children go through a number of stages as they begin to acquire written language skills. Writing begins in the preschool years as young children observe and begin to imitate the act of writing (Pierangelo & Giuliani, 2006a).

According to Pierangelo (2004), there are several questions that should be addressed before analyzing the results of the spelling subtest:

- *Does the child have sufficient mental ability to learn to spell?* This information can be obtained from the school psychologist if an intellectual evaluation was administered. If no such test was administered, a group school abilities index may be present in the child's permanent folder.
- *Are the child's hearing, speech, and vision adequate?* This information can be obtained through the permanent record folder, information in the nurse's office, or informal screening procedures.

- *What is the child's general level of spelling ability according to the teacher's comments and past evaluations or standardized tests?* Teacher comments and observations about the child's spelling history are important to show patterns of disability. Also, standardized tests might show patterns that exist through the years on such tests.

Other information should be obtained from the classroom teacher as well. The teacher can offer some foundational information on the child's patterns:

- The child's attitude toward spelling in the classroom
- The extent to which the child relies on a dictionary in the classroom
- The extent of spelling errors in classroom written work
- Any patterns of procrastination or avoidance of written work
- The student's study habits and methods of work in the classroom
- The history of scores on classroom spelling tests
- Any observable handwriting difficulties
- Any evidence of fatigue as a factor in the child's spelling performance

Children's writing changes as they mature. According to Hallahan, Kauffman, and Lloyd (1999, cited in Gargiulo, 2004, p. 219), "The focus of youngster's writing shifts from (1) the process of writing (handwriting and spelling) to (2) the written product (having written something) to (3) communication with readers (getting across one's message)." Early on, pupils focus on becoming competent in mastering the mechanical aspects of composition—spelling and handwriting; in later grades, they learn to organize and present their ideas in a lucid and logical fashion.

Diagnostic Screening Test-Language–Second Edition (DSTL)

General Test Information

Authors:	Thomas D. Gnagey and Patricia A. Gnagey
Publisher:	Slosson Educational Publications
Address of Publisher:	P.O. Box 280, East Aurora, NY 14052
Telephone Number:	1-888-756-7766
Fax Number:	1-800-655-3840
Web Site of Publisher:	www.slosson.com
Type of Test:	Written language evaluation
Administration Time:	5 to 10 minutes
Type of Administration:	Individual or group
Ages/Grade Levels:	Grades 1 to 12

Purpose and Description of Test

The DSTL was designed as a quick, valid method for estimating overall achievement level in written language and other areas.

Subtest Information

The DSTL provides six major scores:

- Skill Mastery Levels in Grammar
- Punctuation
- Capitalization
- Sentence Structure
- Formal Spelling Rules
- Total

All subtests yield applied versus formal knowledge for twelve scores with 110 items.

Strengths of the Test

- Scoring is simple, converting raw scores to grade equivalent scores to Consolidation Index computation. Percentiles and *T*-scores are also provided for grades 1 through 12. The manual discusses differential subtest pattern analysis, related memory aspects, formal versus applied knowledge, and related aspects.

Diagnostic Screening Test-Spelling–Third Edition (DSTS)

General Test Information

Author:	Thomas D. Gnagey
Publisher:	Slosson Educational Publications
Address of Publisher:	P.O. Box 280, East Aurora, NY 14052
Telephone Number:	1-888-756-7766
Fax Number:	1-800-655-3840
Web Site of Publisher:	www.slosson.com
Type of Test:	Written language evaluation
Administration Time:	5 to 10 minutes
Type of Administration:	Individual or group
Ages/Grade Levels:	Grades 1 to 12

Purpose and Description of Test

The DSTS is designed in a flexible format; it is easy to administer and score and is versatile enough to meet the individual needs and preferences of most examiners. The seventy-eight test words are arranged in developmental sequence. Five diagnostically important problem areas can be explored:

- Sight or phonics orientation for spelling instruction
- Relative efficiency of verbal and written testing procedures
- Analysis of sequential and gross visual memory
- Analysis of sequential and gross auditory memory
- Generally good or poor potential as a speller

A pretest is included to determine an appropriate level of entry.

Strengths of the Test

- Several levels of data interpretation are possible from the results. One is to merely state the grade equivalent level achieved and suggest that spelling instruction begin there. A second level would include a comparison of spelling mastery of strict phonics-proper words with sight words. Then the student's performance can be compared when required to write the words as opposed to spelling them aloud.
- High substantiated validities and reliability studies in the .80s and .90s are included in the manual.

Mather-Woodcock Group Writing Tests (MWGWT)

General Test Information

Authors:	N. Mather and R. Woodcock
Publisher:	Riverside Publishing
Address of Publisher:	425 Spring Lake Drive, Itasca, IL 60143–2079
Telephone Number:	1-800-323-9540
Fax Number:	1-630-467-7192
Web Site of Publisher:	www.riverpub.com
Type of Test:	Written language evaluation
Administration Time:	30 to 60 minutes
Type of Administration:	Individual
Ages/Grade Levels:	Ages 6 through 18

Purpose and Description of Test

The MWGWT is a revised and modified version of the writing test from the Woodcock-Johnson-Revised Achievement Battery. There are three forms of the MWGWT: Basic, Intermediate, and Advanced.

Subtest Information

The MWGWT consists of four subtests:

- *Dictation Spelling*—Requires the student to write spelling words orally presented to him or her
- *Editing*—Requires the student to detect grammatical and spelling errors in the text
- *Writing Samples*—Requires the student to express his or her ideas
- *Writing Fluency*—Requires the student to write simple sentences

Strengths of the Test

- The information obtained by the MWGWT may be used for early identification of problems or weaknesses, measurement of growth in writing skills, instructional planning, and curriculum evaluation.
- The MWGWT provides an alternative to traditional multiple-choice assessments with open-ended, free-response item types.

Slosson Written Expression Test (SWET)

General Test Information

Authors:	Donald B. Hofler, Bradley T. Erford, and William J. Amoriell
Publisher:	Slosson Educational Publications
Address of Publisher:	P.O. Box 280, East Aurora, NY 14052
Telephone Number:	1-888-756-7766
Fax Number:	1-800-655-3840
Web Site of Publisher:	www.slosson.com
Type of Test:	Written language evaluation
Administration Time:	15 minutes
Type of Administration:	Individual or group
Ages/Grade Levels:	Ages 8-0 to 17–11

Purpose and Description of Test

The SWET is a screening test designed to measure children's spontaneous written expression skills. It allows description of the individual child's authentic written expressive skills and a comparison of the child's performance to age peers. The SWET differs from many other writing tests because student responses are analyzed in the context of an authentic composition rather than a close-ended or short-answer format. This format reduces the effects of guessing, which may elevate the child's score, and provides an analysis of the student's genuine writing capabilities.

Subtest Information

The standardized scoring system, featuring specially designed scoring and profile forms, yields subscale scores for spelling, capitalization, punctuation, and two writing maturity measures.

Strengths of the Test

- The SWET's dinosaur, space, and shipwreck themes are highly stimulating picture prompts that help tap students' creative writing skills and are ideal for portfolio- and performance-based assessment approaches. Teachers may desire to evaluate the progress their students make over the course of the school year and decide to administer the three equivalent SWET forms during the beginning, middle, and end of the year.
- The SWET yields a Written Expression total standard score (mean of 100 and standard deviation of 15) and subscale scores (mean 10 and standard deviation of 3), each of which converts easily to percentile ranks. The SWET was standardized on 1,913 children ages 8 to 17. Equivalent form reliabilities and validity comparisons with other tests such as the Woodcock-Johnson Tests of Achievement–Revised and Wide Range Achievement Test–Third Edition warrant use of the SWET as a quick and reliable measure of written expression for children.

Test of Early Written Language–Second Edition (TEWL-2)

General Test Information

Authors:	Wayne Hresko, Shelley Herron, and Pamela Peak
Publisher:	PRO-ED
Address of Publisher:	8700 Shoal Creek Boulevard, Austin, TX 78757–6897
Telephone Number:	1-800-897-3202
Fax Number:	1-800-397-7633
Web Site of Publisher:	www.proedinc.com
Type of Test:	Written language evaluation
Administration Time:	10 to 30 minutes
Type of Administration:	Individual
Ages/Grade Levels:	Ages 3–0 through 10–11

Purpose and Description of Test

The test was developed to assess early writing abilities and covers the five areas of writing transcription, conventions of print, communication, creative expression, and record keeping. The TEWL-2 has forty-two items. The starting items vary by age level. An item is graded as 1 if correct and 0 if incorrect. Each item counts equally, although some require more responses or information than others. It is individually administered.

Subtest Information

The selection of items and the development of the subtests are grounded in the available research literature and other evidence of developing literacy ability. Item types were selected only if recognized experts in the field related them to developing literacy abilities. The TEWL-2 is a companion to the Test of Written Language–Third Edition for extending the assessment range to younger children:

- *Global Writing Quotient.* This composite quotient is formed by combining the standard scores for the Basic Writing Quotient and the Contextual Writing Quotient.
- *Basic Writing Quotient.* Basic Writing is a subtest area that results in a standard score quotient. This quotient is a measure of a child's ability in such areas as spelling, capitalization, punctuation, sentence construction, and metacognitive knowledge. The Basic Writing Subtest may be given independent of the Contextual Writing Subtest.
- *Contextual Writing Quotient.* Contextual Writing is a subtest area that results in a standard score quotient. This quotient is a measure of a child's ability to construct a story when provided with a picture prompt. This subtest measures such areas as story format, cohesion, thematic maturity, ideation, and story structure. Both Form A and Form B consist of fourteen items. A detailed, expanded scoring guide is provided to assist in scoring the Contextual Writing subtest. The subtest may be given independent of the Basic Writing subtest.

Strengths of the Test

- The TEWL-2 is one of several recent efforts to provide assessments for the developmental skills and academic abilities of young children.
- The test is useful in assessing and planning educational activities.
- The test is useful for evaluating educational programs designed to promote the writing skills of young children.
- The test is a good tool to use with other instruments to determine if a child has a mild disability.
- Characteristics of the normative group correspond to those for 1990 Census data relative to gender, geographical region, ethnicity, race, and urban/rural residence.
- Internal consistency reliability coefficients of all scores meet or exceed .90 for all ages, and stability reliability of all scores approximates or exceeds .90.
- Extensive content validity data are presented, and criterion-related validity is evidenced by correlations with the Woodcock-Johnson, the Wechsler Individual Achievement Test, and the Written Language Assessment. Construct-related validity is presented based on correlations with age, cognitive ability, achievement, group discrimination, and the correlation of individual test items with total test scores.

Test of Written Expression (TOWE)

General Test Information

Authors:	Ron McGhee, Brian Bryant, Stephen Larson, and Diane Rivera
Publisher:	PRO-ED
Address of Publisher:	8700 Shoal Creek Boulevard, Austin, TX 78757–6897
Telephone Number:	1-800-897-3202
Fax Number:	1-800-397-7633
Web Site of Publisher:	www.proedinc.com
Type of Test:	Written language evaluation
Administration Time:	60 minutes
Type of Administration:	Individual or group
Ages/Grade Levels:	Ages 6–6 through 14–11

Purpose and Description of Test

The TOWE provides a comprehensive yet efficient norm-referenced assessment of writing achievement. It can be administered conveniently to individuals or groups of students and uses two assessment methods to evaluate a student's writing skills. The first method involves administering a series of seventy-six items that tap different skills associated with writing. The second method requires students to read or hear a prepared story starter and use it as a stimulus for writing an essay: the beginning of the story is provided, and the writer continues the story to its conclusion.

Subtest Information

The TOWE provides two separate assessment methods for measuring a comprehensive set of writing skills:

- Ideation
- Vocabulary
- Grammar
- Capitalization
- Punctuation
- Spelling

Strengths of the Test

- The TOWE provides an excellent source of writing samples that can be used independently in a norm-referenced assessment of writing or as a component of a student's portfolio of written products.
- The scale consists of a normative sample of 1,226 students residing in twenty-one states. The sample is representative of the nation as a whole across gender, race, and geographical region.
- Evidence of validity and reliability (internal consistency, test-retest, interscorer) is provided in the test manual (averaged coefficients are in the .90s).

Test of Written Language–Third Edition (TOWL-3)

General Test Information

Authors:	Donald Hammill and Stephen Larson
Publisher:	PRO-ED
Address of Publisher:	8700 Shoal Creek Boulevard, Austin, TX 78757–6897
Telephone Number:	1-800-897-3202
Fax Number:	1-800-397-7633
Web Site of Publisher:	www.proedinc.com
Type of Test:	Written language evaluation
Administration Time:	60 to 90 minutes
Type of Administration:	Individual or group
Ages/Grade Levels:	Ages 7–6 through 17–11

Purpose and Description of Test

The TOWL-3 is a completely revised edition of the Test of Written Language. It meets the nationally recognized need for a standardized way to document the presence of deficits in this area of literacy.

Subtest Information

The eight subtests of the TOWL-3 measure a student's writing competence through essay analysis (spontaneous) and traditional test (contrived) formats. The TOWL-3 contains the following subtests:
- Spontaneous Formats
  - *Contextual Conventions*—measures capitalization, punctuation, and spelling
  - *Contextual Language*—measures vocabulary, syntax, and grammar
  - *Story Construction*—measures plot, character development, and general composition
- Contrived Formats
  - *Vocabulary*—measures word use
  - *Spelling*—measures ability to form letters into words
  - *Style*—measures punctuation and capitalization
  - *Logical Sentences*—measures ability to write conceptually sound sentences
  - *Sentence Combining*—measures syntax

Strengths of the Test

- The TOWL-3 is shown to be unbiased relative to gender and race and can be administered to individuals or small groups. Because two equivalent forms (A and B) are available, examiners can evaluate student growth in writing using pretesting and posttesting that is not contaminated by memory.
- Internal consistency, test-retest with equivalent forms, and interscorer reliability coefficients approximate .80 at most ages, and many are in the .90s.
- The validity of the TOWL-3 was investigated extensively. Relevant studies are described in the manual, which has a section that provides suggestions for assessing written language informally and gives numerous ideas for teachers to use when remediating writing deficits.
- The TOWL-3 normative sample is representative relative to gender, race, social class, and disability.
- The PRO-SCORE Computer Scoring Systems (an optional component) allows test users to score the TOWL-3 accurately, conveniently, and quickly.

Test of Written Spelling–Fourth Edition (TWS-4)

General Test Information

Authors:	Stephen Larsen, Donald Hammill, and Louisa Moats
Publisher:	PRO-ED
Address of Publisher:	8700 Shoal Creek Boulevard, Austin, TX 78757–6897
Telephone Number:	1-800-897-3202
Fax Number:	1-800-397-7633
Web Site of Publisher:	www.proedinc.com
Type of Test:	Written language evaluation
Administration Time:	20 minutes
Type of Administration:	Individual or group
Ages/Grade Levels:	Grades 1 to 12

Purpose and Description of Test

The revised TWS-4 is a norm-referenced test of spelling administered using a dictated word format. It has two alternate or equivalent forms (A and B), which make it useful in test-teach-test situations. The TWS was developed after a review of 2,000 spelling rules. The words to be spelled are drawn from ten basal spelling programs and popular graded word lists.

The results of the TWS-4 may be used for four purposes: to identify students whose scores are significantly below those of their peers and who might need interventions designed to improve spelling proficiency, determine areas of relative strength and weakness in spelling, document overall progress in spelling as a consequence of intervention programs, and serve as a measure for research efforts designed to investigate spelling.

Subtest Information

The test consists of two subtests: Predictable Words and Unpredictable Words.

Strengths of the Test

- The TWS-4 was standardized on more than 4,000 students. With rare exceptions, internal consistency and test-retest reliability coefficients are greater than .90. Evidence of content, criterion-related, and construct validity is reported in the test manual. The TWS-4 can be administered in twenty minutes to groups or individuals and yields standard scores, percentiles, spelling ages, and grade equivalents.
- The characteristics of the normative sample approximate those for the 2000 U.S. Census. The normative sample has been stratified by age relative to gender, urban or rural residence, geographical region, race, and ethnicity. Studies have been added to show no gender or racial bias, and more study from independent sources has been added supporting reliability and validity.

Word Identification and Spelling Test (WIST)

General Test Information

Authors:	Barbara A. Wilson and Rebecca Felton
Publisher:	PRO-ED
Address of Publisher:	8700 Shoal Creek Boulevard, Austin, TX 78757–6897
Telephone Number:	1-800-897-3202
Fax Number:	1-800-397-7633
Web Site of Publisher:	www.proedinc.com
Type of Test:	Written language evaluation
Administration Time:	40 minutes
Type of Administration:	Individual
Ages/Grade Levels:	Ages 7–0 through 18–11

Purpose and Description of Test

The WIST measures word identification, spelling, and sound-symbol knowledge. It meets teachers' need for detailed information that can be used to identify the areas in which students are having difficulty with reading or spelling and to develop appropriate instructional interventions. It includes both norm-referenced and informal assessments. The WIST specifically targets those aspects of reading that are most important for the identification and treatment of poor and disabled readers.

Subtest Information

The WIST has three subtests that can be used in the norm-referenced or informal assessment. The norm-referenced assessment has two core subtests (Word Identification and Spelling) and one supplemental subtest (Sound-Symbol Knowledge) and a composite score (Fundamental Literacy Index). On the informal assessment, the scores are used for clinical and instructional purposes:

- *Word Identification:* Word Identification measures word reading accuracy, which includes (1) students' sight recognition of familiar words and their ability to apply word attack skills in order to decode unfamiliar words and (2) their sight recognition or orthographic memory of high-frequency words with one or more irregularities.
- *Spelling:* The spelling subtest assesses students' ability to spell words correctly from dictation. It specifically measures students' (1) recall of correct letter sequences for familiar words or the ability to apply sound-symbol relationships and rules of English orthography in order to spell unfamiliar words and (2) their recall of letter order in high-frequency words with one or more irregularities.
- *Sound-Symbol Knowledge:* This subtest assesses a student's ability to associate sounds (phonemes) with specific letters (graphemes).

Three informal procedures provide additional diagnostic information about the student's performance on the test items, sound-symbol skills, and errors peculiar to written words. Information from these analyses will enhance the examiner's interpretation of the child's test performance and help formulate a literacy intervention plan.

Strengths of the Test

- Measures word identification, spelling, and sound-symbol knowledge
- Identifies students who are struggling with reading and spelling
- Has an elementary version (grades 2–5) and a secondary version (grades 6–12)
- Is easy to administer and score
- Is both valid and reliable for its stated purposes
- Includes an extensive yet practical informal assessment system for analyzing student performance that leads to instructional intervention

Writing Process Test (WPT)

General Test Information

Authors:	M. Robin Warden and Thomas A. Hutchinson
Publisher:	PRO-ED
Address of Publisher:	8700 Shoal Creek Boulevard, Austin, TX 78757–6897
Telephone Number:	1-800-897-3202
Fax Number:	1-800-397-7633
Web Site of Publisher:	www.proedinc.com
Type of Test:	Written language evaluation
Administration Time:	45 minutes (plus another 30 minutes if the student revises)
Type of Administration:	Individual or group
Ages/Grade Levels:	Ages 8–0 through 19–9

Purpose and Description of Test

The WPT is a direct measure of writing that requires the student to plan, write, and revise an original composition. It assesses both written product and writing process.

Subtest Information

The test rates the writer's effort on two scales: Development and Fluency. The six Development Scales assess:

- Purpose and Focus
- Audience
- Vocabulary
- Style and Tone
- Support and Development
- Organization and Coherence

The six Fluency Scales assess the following areas:

- Sentence Structure and Variety
- Grammar and Usage
- Capitalization and Punctuation
- Spelling

Strengths of the Test

- Analytical scoring provides diagnostic information that holistic scoring cannot; there are ten four-point scales for precise scoring.
- Uses one score protocol for all grades.
- The score protocol works well for grading most teacher-assigned writing.
- Normed on more than 5,000 students in grades 2 to 12 in class-size groups.
- Internal consistency reliability averaged .84 (interrater averaged .75).

Written Expression Scale (WES)

General Test Information

Author:	Elizabeth Carrow-Woolfolk
Publisher:	AGS Publishing
Address of Publisher:	4201 Woodland Road, Circle Pines, MN 55014–1796
Telephone Number:	1-800-328-2560, 1-651-287-7220
Fax Number:	1-800-471-8457
Web Site of Publisher:	www.agsnet.com
Type of Test:	Written language evaluation
Administration Time:	15 to 25 minutes
Type of Administration:	Individual or small group
Ages/Grade Levels:	Ages 5–0 through 21–11

Purpose and Description of Test

The WES is an assessment of written language for children and young adults. It offers an authentic assessment of written language skills in children and young adults. Its wide age range (5 to 21 years) gives a broad-based record of growth from primary and middle grades through high school and postsecondary years.

Subtest Information

No subtests are on the WES; however, it measures these writing skills:

- Use of conventions (handwriting, spelling, punctuation)
- Use of syntactical forms (modifiers, phrases, sentence structures)
- Ability to communicate meaningfully (relevance, cohesiveness, organization)

Strengths of the Test

- The WES can be administered individually or in small groups. The examiner presents a variety of direct writing prompts, like those tasks found in the classroom, either verbally, with pictures, or in print. Examinees write responses in a booklet.
- The manual features detailed scoring guidelines with samples of actual responses. The record form contains representations of score patterns, a record of item-by-item results, and a summary of score comparisons. Because examinees respond to a developmentally appropriate set of about fifteen items, the examiner is assured of obtaining representative writing samples. The scale has high validity and reliability.
- The ASSIST for the Written Expression Scale is available on one CD-ROM for Windows and Macintosh. The ASSIST provides a score profile, score narrative, suggested exercises, and a descriptive analysis.
- The WEScale correlates .84 to .88 with global scores on achievement batteries (Kaufman Tests of Educational Achievement/Normative Update, Peabody Individual Achievement Test–Revised-Normative Update, and Woodcock Reading Mastery Tests–Revised-Normative Update); .57 and .62 with measures of receptive language (OWLS Listening Comprehension Scale and Peabody Picture Vocabulary Test-R); .66 with the OWLS Oral Expression Scale; and .72 and .67 with measures of verbal intelligence (Wechsler Intelligence Scale for Children–Third Edition [Verbal IQ] and Kaufman Brief Intelligence Test Vocabulary).

Part Three

Overview of the Special Educator as an Educational Evaluator

Chapter 27

Understanding a Student's Behavior During Testing

The evaluation of a student involves many areas of input and observation. A critical period of observation takes place at the time of testing when the special education teacher has a firsthand opportunity to view the child under these types of conditions. It should be noted that the way a child approaches different types of evaluations may be very similar to the style he or she uses in the classroom. There are many behaviors that should be observed when administering tests. Recording these observations will greatly facilitate report writing.

❖ Adjustment to the Testing Situation

- What was the child's initial reaction?
- How did the child react to the examiner?
- Were there any initial signs of overt tension?

How children adjust to the testing situation can vary greatly. Several factors need to be considered when the child first encounters the testing situation:

- Children's initial adjustment to the testing situation can vary greatly. The key to any adjustment period is not necessarily the initial reactions but the duration of the period of maladjustment. Children are usually initially nervous but relax as time goes on with the reassurance of the examiner. Children who maintain a high level of discomfort throughout the sessions may be harboring more serious problems that need to be explored.
- Examiner variables are conditions that may affect test outcome that are directly related to the examiner, such as examiner style, gender, tension, and expectations. These may need to be considered, especially if test results vary greatly from examiner to examiner.
- Overt signs of tension (observable behaviors indicative of underlying tension) may affect the outcome of the test results. Some overt signs of behavior often manifested by children include constant leg motion, little or no eye contact with the examiner, consistent finger or pencil tapping, oppositional behaviors (behaviors that test the limits and guidelines of the examiner), singing or making noises while being tested, or keeping a jacket on or a hat almost

covering his or her face. If this type of tension is extreme, the examiner may want to explore the possibility that the results may be minimal indications of the child's ability.

❖ Reaction Time

- Were responses delayed, blocked, or irregular?
- Was there any indication of negativism?
- Were responses impulsive or well thought out?

The speed with which a child answers questions on a test can indicate several things:

- The child who impulsively answers incorrectly without thinking may have high levels of anxiety that interfere with his or her ability to delay and concentrate.
- The child who is negative or self-defeating (the one who says, "I'm so stupid, I'll never get any of these right") may be exhibiting a very low level of self-confidence or hiding a learning problem.
- The child who blocks or delays may be afraid of reaction or criticism and uses these techniques to ward off what he or she perceives as an ego-deflating situation.

❖ Nature of Responses

- Are some responses nonsensical, immature, or childlike?
- Are they inconsistent?
- Does the subject ask to have questions repeated?
- Is the subject critical of his or her responses?

The types of response a child gives during an evaluation may indicate the following:

- A child who continually asks to have questions repeated may have hearing difficulties. This should always be ruled out first along with visual acuity prior to a testing situation.
- The child who asks to have questions repeated may be having problems processing information and may need more time to understand what is being asked.

❖ Verbalizations

- Is the child verbose?
- Is he or she spontaneous in responding?
- Does he or she have peculiarities of speech?

The verbal interaction with the examiner during an evaluation can be very telling:

- Some children with high levels of anxiety may tend to vent this through constant verbalizations. This may be a factor when these verbalizations begin to interfere and the child has to be constantly reminded to focus on the task at hand.
- Verbal hesitations may be due to immature speech patterns, expressive language problems, poor self-esteem, or lack of understanding of the question due to limited intellectual capacity.

❖ Organizational Approach Used During Testing

- Does the child plan and work systematically?
- Does he or she make false starts?
- Does he or she use trial and error?

The manner in which a child handles individual tasks and organizes his and her approach may indicate the following:

• A child who sizes up a situation and systematically approaches a task using trial and error may have excellent internal organization, the ability to delay, and low levels of tension and anxiety. However, some children with emotional problems may also perform well on short-term tasks because they see it as a challenge and can organize themselves to perform over a relatively short period of time. Their problems in organization and consistency may be revealed when they are asked to perform over an extended period.

• Children with chaotic internal organization may appear as if they know what they are doing, but the overall outcome of a task indicates a great deal of energy input with very low production. It is almost like "spinning wheels," and the energy output is a cover for not knowing what to do.

• Some children may become less organized under the stress of a time constraint. The factor of style under time restrictions is one aspect in determining the child's overall learning style.

• Children with attention deficit-hyperactivity disorder may exhibit a confused sense of organization. However, there are other factors as well as problems in attention that go into the diagnosis of this disorder.

❖ Adaptability During Testing

• Does the child shift from item to item as well as from subtest to subtest with limited to no difficulty?
• Is the child's interest sustained in all types of test items?

The ability of a child (or adult, for that matter) to adapt or shift from one task to another without difficulty is an important factor in determining learning style and may be one predictor for successful outcome of a task. In addition:

• Adaptability in life is one crucial aspect of good adjustment. The ability to shift without expending a great deal of energy offers the person more available resources for the next task. A child who is rigid or does not adapt well is using up much available energy, thus reducing the chances of success on the subsequent task.

• Sustaining interest may also be a direct result of available energy. A child who loses interest quickly may be immature, overwhelmed, or preoccupied. Some of these reactions may be normal for the early ages. However, as the child gets older, such reactions may be symptomatic of other factors, such as learning problems, emotional issues, or limited intellectual capacity.

❖ Effort During Testing

• Is the child cooperative?
• Does he or she give evidence of trying hard?
• Does the child become frustrated easily?

The effort that a child puts into a testing situation may be reflective of the effort exhibited within the classroom and may indicate the following:

• A child who is oppositional or uncooperative may need to control. Always keep in mind that the more controlling a child is, the more out of control he or she feels. Control on the part of a child is aimed at securing predictability in order to deal with a situation even though his or her energy levels may be lowered by conflict and tension. Children who because of tension levels do not adapt well and are easily thrown by new situations or people will try to control a situation or person.

• A child who tries hard to succeed may do so for several reasons. He or she may enjoy success and find the tasks normally challenging. This type of child is usually not thrown by a mistake and can easily move to the next task without difficulty.

Chapter 28

Reporting Assessment Test Results

An important skill for a special education professional is the ability to report test results in such a way that parents walk away with an understanding of the causes, specific areas of strength and weakness, and practical recommendations to alleviate the situation. Many times parents will leave a conference having been "bombarded" with jargon and statistics and understand nothing. Reporting results so that they are understood may be accomplished in the following ways.

❖ Presenting Test Results to Parents

Prior to the official IEP committee meeting, the special educator should meet with the parents to go over the results of testing. This meeting will have several objectives:

- Share the results of testing, scores, and recommendations.
- Inform the parents of their due process rights and provide them with a copy of those rights (this information is usually available from the district office).
- Inform the parents of the process that will be used during the IEP committee meeting and notify the parents who else will be at that meeting.
- Answer any questions that the parent may have about the process. However, the educator should be careful not to reassure the parents as to what may be the classification or placement since that is the role of the IEP committee.

An important skill for special education teachers is their ability to report test results to other professionals or to parents so that they understand the causes, specific areas of strength and weakness, and practical recommendations to alleviate the situation. Many times parents leave a conference having been bombarded with jargon and statistics and understand little or nothing. Reporting results so that they are understood may be accomplished in the following ways:

1. When setting up the appointment with a parent, never begin the explanation of the results over the telephone, even if the parent requests a quick idea of how the child performed. If the parent does request this information, gently say that the type of information that you have is better explained and understood in person. If you sense further anxiety, try to reassure

the parent that you will meet as soon as possible. It is important to visually see the parents so that you can explain areas in which they seem confused or uncomfortable. The face-to-face contact also makes the conference a more personal approach.

2. Make the parents feel comfortable and at ease by setting up a receptive environment. If possible, hold the meeting in a pleasant setting, use a round table (or any other table instead of a desk), and offer some refreshment to ease possible tension.

3. It may be helpful to refresh the parents' memory about the reasons for the evaluation and the symptoms that brought the child to the attention of the team. Explain the tests used, why they were chosen, and what specific types of information you hoped to arrive at by using these measures.

4. Go over the child's strength areas first, no matter how few there may be. You can also report positive classroom comments and any other information that may help set the tone for acceptance of problem areas.

5. Provide a typed outline of the tests and scores for the parents to take with them if the report is not ready. If possible, always try to have the report completed and ready to hand them. It looks more professional and may help alleviate problems that may occur when reports are sent home and the parents read it without a professional present.

6. Explain any statistical terms you may be using, such as *percentiles, stanines,* or *mental ages.* It may be a good idea to define these on the same sheet with the scores so that parents have a key when they later review the scores.

7. Offer the parents a pad and pen so that they can take notes on the meeting. Let them know that they should feel free to call you with any questions or concerns.

8. Put aside a sufficient amount of time for difficult conferences. This is not the type of situation in which you want to run out of time. The parents should leave in a natural manner, not rushed.

9. Take time to explain the differences between symptoms and problems. This explanation can go a long way in alleviating parents' frustration.

10. It is helpful for parents to hear how the problems or deficiencies found were contributing to the symptoms in the classroom and at home. It is reassuring for parents to know that what they were seeing were only symptoms, even though they may have been quite intense, and that the problems have been identified and recommendations are available. Offer as much realistic hope as possible.

11. Be as practical and specific as possible when offering suggestions on how parents can help at home. Offer them printed sheets with step-by-step procedures for any recommendations you make. Parents should not be teachers and should never be given general recommendations that require their interpretation. This may aggravate an already tense situation at home. Offer them supportive materials that they can use with the child. It may be a positive experience for the parent to work with the child, but sometimes, such as when there are low parental frustration levels, this type of interaction may not be a good idea.

12. If the case is going to be reviewed by the committee on special education, take some time to alleviate the parents' fears by explaining the process and what they can expect. Indicate that your report is part of the packet that will be presented and that they are entitled to a copy of all materials. Some school districts charge for these copies, so inform parents if this is the district's policy.

13. Again reassure the parents about the confidentiality of the information gathered. Indicate the individuals on the team who will be seeing the information and the purpose for their review of the facts. Also indicate that in order to send out this information, you need permission from them in the form of a signed release.

❖ Presenting Test Results to the IEP Committee

The responsibilities of the special education teacher on the IEP committee depend on his or her role in the district. Responsibilities when making a presentation will vary, but proper preparation is always crucial. Keep in mind the following aspects:

• Prior to the meeting, meet with the parents and go over your results. Follow the procedures outlined in this chapter.

• Make sure that your report is complete and typed at least one week to ten days before the IEP committee meets. In some districts, the committee requires that the entire packet be forwarded a week in advance.

• Prior to the meeting, outline the important points of the report that you wish to make. Do not go through the report at the committee meeting looking for the issues that you feel need to be discussed. Preparation will make you look more professional.

• Make sure you report the child's strengths as well as weaknesses.

• Although everyone should have copies of your report in front of them, the length of the report may make it impossible for them to filter out the crucial sections in the time allotted for the meeting. Therefore, you may want to develop a one-page summary sheet that clearly outlines what you will be presenting and hand it out as you begin.

• Remember that this is not a conference to review the entire report, so be brief and highlight the important issues. There are several individuals who may need to report results or speak, and the IEP committee may have several meetings that day.

• If you feel that the nature of the case may require more time than that normally set aside by the IEP committee for a review, call the chairperson and request a longer meeting time. Crucial meetings should not have to be ended before all issues have been discussed because of time constraints.

• Be prepared to be questioned about your findings or some aspect of the report by a parent, committee member, lawyer (sometimes brought by the parent), and others. Although this may not happen, you should be ready to answer without being defensive or anxious. Carefully looking over your report and being prepared is the best advice.

Appendix A

Test Publishers

Academic Therapy
20 Commercial Boulevard, Novato, CA 94949
Telephone number: 1-800-422-7249; fax number: 1-888-287-9975; Web site address: www.academictherapy.com

AGS Publishing
4201 Woodland Road, Circle Pines, MN 55014–1796
Telephone numbers: 1-800-328-2560, 1-651-287-7220; fax number: 1-800-471-8457; Web site address: www.agsnet.com

CTB Macmillan/McGraw-Hill
20 Ryan Ranch Road, Monterey, CA 93940
Telephone number: 1-800-538-9547; fax number: 1-800-282-0266; Web site address: www.ctb.com

Curriculum Associates
153 Rangeway Road, North Billerica, MA 01862
Telephone number: 1-800-225-0248; fax number: 1-800-366-1158; Web site address: www.curriculumassociates.com

Educators Publishing Service
P.O. Box 9031, Cambridge, MA 02139–9031
Telephone number: 1-800-435-7728; fax number: 1-888-440-BOOK (2665); Web site address: www.epsbooks.com

Harcourt Assessment
6277 Sea Harbor Drive, Orlando, FL 32887
Telephone number: 1-800-211-8378; fax number: 1-800-232-1223; Web site address: www.harcourt.com

Hawthorne Educational Services
800 Gray Oak Drive, Columbia, MO 65201
Telephone number: 1-800-542-1673; fax number: 1-800-442-9509; Web site address: www.hes-inc.com

Multi-Health Systems
P.O. Box 950, North Tonawanda, NY 14120–0950
Telephone numbers: 1-800-456-3003, 1-416-492-2627; fax numbers: 1-888-540-4484 or 1-416-492-3343; Web site address: www.mhs.com

PAR
16204 North Florida Avenue, Lutz, FL 33549
Telephone number: 1-800-331-8378, ext. 361; fax number: 1-800-727-9329; Web site address: www.parinc.com

Pearson Assessments
5601 Green Valley Drive, Bloomington, MN 55437
Telephone number: 1-800-627-7271; fax number: 1-800-632-9011; Web site address: www.pearsonassessments.com

PRO-ED
8700 Shoal Creek Boulevard, Austin, TX 78757–6897
Telephone number: 1-800-897-3202; fax number: 1-800-397-7633; Web site address: www.proedinc.com

Riverside Publishing
425 Spring Lake Drive, Itasca, IL 60143–2079
Telephone number: 1-800-323-9540; fax number: 1-630-467-7192; Web site address: www.riverpub.com

Slosson Educational Publications
P.O. Box 280, East Aurora, NY 14052
Telephone number: 1-888-756-7766; fax number: 1-800-655-3840; Web site address: www.slosson.com

Stoelting Co.
620 Wheat Lane, Lo Wood Dale, IL 60191
Telephone number: 1-630-860-9700; fax number: 1-630-860-9775; Web site address: www.stoeltingco.com

Teachers College Press
1234 Amsterdam Avenue, New York, NY 10027
Telephone number: 1-800-575-6566; fax number: 1-212-678-4149; Web site address: www.teacherscollegepress.com

Western Psychological Services
12031 Wilshire Boulevard, Los Angeles, CA 90025–1251
Telephone numbers: 1-800-648-8857 (U.S. and Canada only), 1-310-478-2061; fax number: 1-310-478-7838; Web site address: www.wpspublish.com

Referral Forms Commonly Used in the Special Education Process

Unstructured Observation Checklist

Name of Student Observed: **Observer:**
Date of Observation: **Place of Observation:**

Classroom   Playground   Lunchroom   Gym

Behaviors Observed

Impulsivity

Attention to task

Attention span

Conformity to rules

Social interaction with peers

Aggressiveness

Level of teacher assistance required

Frustration levels

Reaction to authority

Verbal interaction

Procrastination

Organizational skills

Developmental motor skills

Classroom Observation Form

Student's Name/ID Number _____

Date of Birth _____ Dominant Language _____

Dates of Observation _____ Length of Observation _____

Observer _____ Position _____

Classroom Observed _____ Location _____

Teacher's Name _____

Subject area being taught _____

TASK-INDIVIDUAL

A. When assigned a task, the student:

❑ Initiates task without need for teacher's verbal encouragement

❑ Requests help in order to start task

❑ Complains before getting started on a task

❑ Demands help in order to start a task

❑ Actively refuses to do task despite teacher's encouragement

❑ Passively retreats from task despite teacher's encouragement

B. While working on task, the student:

❑ Works independently

❑ Performs assigned task without complaint

❑ Needs teacher's verbal encouragement to keep working

❑ Needs teacher in close proximity to keep working

❑ Needs physical contact from teacher to keep working

❑ Seeks constant reassurance to keep working

❑ Is reluctant to have work inspected

❑ Belittles own work

C. At the end of the assigned time, the student:

❑ Completes task

❑ Takes pride in completed task

❑ Goes on to next task

❑ Refuses to complete task

SOCIAL INTERACTION

The student:

❑ Establishes a relationship with one or two peers

❑ Shares materials with peers

Classroom Observation Form *(continued)*

❑ Respects property of peers

❑ Gives help to peers when needed

❑ Accepts help from peers when needed

❑ Establishes a relationship with most peers

❑ Teases or ridicules peers

❑ Expresses prejudiced attitudes toward peers

❑ Physically provokes peers

❑ Physically hurts peers

❑ Seeks to be attacked by peers

❑ Participates appropriately in group activities

❑ Postpones own needs for group objectives

❑ Withdraws from group

❑ Is overly assertive in group

❑ Disrupts group activities (for example, by calling out, using provocative language)

❑ Exhibits aggressive behavior within group not amenable to teacher intervention

RELATIONSHIP TO TEACHER

The student:

❑ Tries to meet teacher's expectations

❑ Functions adequately without constant teacher encouragement

❑ Interacts with teacher in nondemanding manner

❑ Responds to teacher without haggling

❑ Tests limits, tries to see how much teacher will allow

❑ Seeks special treatment from teacher

❑ Responds to teacher's criticism without fear

❑ Responds to teacher's criticism without verbal anger

❑ Responds to teacher's criticism without physical outbursts (for example, temper tantrums)

❑ Defies teacher's requirement

❑ Scorns or ridicules teacher's support

❑ Responds with anger when demands are thwarted by teacher

❑ Blames and accuses teacher ("doesn't help," "doesn't like me")

❑ Abuses teacher verbally (no apparent cause)

❑ Abuses teacher physically (no apparent cause)

❑ Requires close and constant supervision because behavioral controls are so limited

COMMENTS

Referral to the Child Study Team

Student Name:	**Date of Referral:**
Grade Level:	**Date of Birth:**
Teacher Name:	**Chronological Age:**
Parents' Names:	**Phone:**

Please answer the following questions using behavioral terms.

What symptoms is the child exhibiting that are of concern at this time?

What have you tried that has worked?

What have you tried that does not seem to work toward alleviating these symptoms?

What are the child's current academic levels of functioning?

Any observable behavioral or physical limitations?

What is the child's social behavior like?

Current performance estimates (below, on, or above grade level)

Reading: Math: Spelling:

Have the parents been contacted? yes _____ no _____ If no, why not?

Further comments?

Parent Intake Form

Name of Client:

Address:

Phone:

Date of Birth:

Age:

Siblings:

  Brothers (names and ages):

  Sisters (names and ages):

Mother's Name: **Father's name:**

Mother's occupation: **Father's occupation:**

Referred by:

Grade:

School:

Developmental History

Length of pregnancy:

Type of delivery:

Complications:

Long hospital stays:

Falls or injuries:

Allergies:

Medication:

Early milestones (walking, talking, and toilet training):

Traumatic experiences:

Previous psychological evaluations or treatment (Please explain reasons and dates):

Any previous psychiatric hospitalizations?

Sleep disturbances:

Parent Intake Form *(continued)*

Eating disturbances:

Last vision and hearing exams and results:

Excessively high fevers:

Childhood illnesses:

Academic History
Preschool experience:

Kindergarten experience (adjustment, comments):

First grade through sixth grade (teacher's comments, traumatic experiences, strength areas, comments):

Subjects that presented the most difficulty:

Subjects that were the least difficult:

Most recent report card grades (if applicable):

Social History
Groups or organizations:

Social involvement as perceived by parent:

Hobbies or interests:

Initial Referral to the MDT from the School Staff

To:

From: **School:**   **Date:**

Name/Title:

The following student is being referred for suspicion of a disability:

Student Name: **Sex:**   **Grade:**   **Ethnicity:**

Parent/Guardian Name:

Address:

City: **State:**   **Zip:**

Telephone: **Date of Birth:**

Current Program Placement:

Teacher (Elementary):   **Guidance Counselor (Secondary):**

Reasons for Referral: Describe the specific reason and/or needs that indicate the suspicion of a disability. Specify why referral is considered appropriate and necessary.

Describe recent attempts to remediate the pupil's performance prior to referral, including regular education interventions such as remedial reading and math, teaching modifications, behavior modifications, speech improvement, and parent conferences, and the results of those interventions.

Do you have a signed Parent Assessment Plan? Yes _____ No _____ (If yes, send copy attached)

Is there an attendance problem?   Yes _____ No _____

Language spoken at home?

Did student repeat a grade?   Yes _____ No _____ If yes, when?

Is an interpreter needed?   Yes _____ No _____ Deaf:

Is a bilingual assessment needed?   Yes _____ No _____ If yes, what language?

Is student eligible to receive ESL (English as a Second Language) services? Yes _____ No _____

If yes, how many years receiving ESL services? _____ If yes, determine how the student's educational, cultural, and experiential background were considered to determine if these factors are contributing to the student's learning or behavior problems.

Initial Referral to the MDT from the School Staff *(continued)*

TEST SCORES WITHIN LAST YEAR
(Standardized Achievement, Regents Competency, etc.)

TEST NAME	AREA MEASURED	PERCENTILE SCORE	COMMENT

Has school staff informed parent/guardian of referral to CSE? Yes _____ No_____

By whom?

What was the reaction of the parent/guardian to the referral?

To Be Completed by School Nurse—Medical Report Summary

Any medication?   Yes _____ No _____   If yes, specify:

Health problems?   Yes _____ No _____   If yes, specify:

Scoliosis screening: Positive _____ Negative _____

Date of last physical: **Vision results:**   **Hearing results:**

Relevant medical information:

Nurse teacher signature:

Principal's signature:

To Be Completed by the Appropriate Administrator

Date received: **Signature:**

Chairperson:

Date Notice and Consent Sent to Parent/Guardian:

Parent Consent for Initial Evaluation Received:

Date Agreement to Withdraw Referral Received:

Projected Eligibility Meeting Date:

If eligible, projected date of implementation of services:

Projected Eligibility Board of Education meeting date:

Glossary

abduction movement of limb outward, away from body.

ability grouping the grouping of children based on their achievement in an area of study.

affective reactions psychotic reactions marked by extreme mood swings.

accelerated learning an educational process that allows students to progress through the curriculum at an increased pace.

achievement the level of a child's accomplishment on a test of knowledge or skill.

active movements movements a child does without help.

adaptive behavior an individual's social competence and ability to cope with the demands of the environment.

adaptive equipment devices used to position or to teach special skills.

adaptive physical education specially designed physical education program for children with disabilities who cannot, as a result of their disability, benefit from the normal school program. This is an individually designed program of games, sports, and developmental activities that are individually suited to the needs, interests, capabilities, and limitations of each child with a disability.

advocate an individual, either a parent or professional, who attempts to establish or improve services for exceptional children.

age norms standards based on the average performance of individuals in different age groups.

aging out the date on which the child with a disability will no longer be eligible for tuition-free educational services.

agnosia an inability to recognize objects and their meaning, usually resulting from damage to the brain.

albinism a congenital condition marked by severe deficiency in or total lack of pigmentation.

amblyopia a dimness of sight without any indication of change in the eye's structure.

amniocentesis a medical procedure done during the early stages of pregnancy for the purpose of identifying certain genetic disorders in the fetus.

amplification device any device that increases the volume of sound.

anecdotal record a procedure for recording and analyzing observations of a child's behavior; an objective, narrative description.

annual goals yearly activities or achievements to be completed or attained by the child with a disability that are documented on the individualized education program.

annual review an annual review of a child with a disability's classification and educational program. The purpose of this review, which includes the parent and sometimes the student, is to recommend the continuation, modification, or termination of classification, placement, or individualized education program needs and related services for the upcoming year.

anomaly some irregularity in development or a deviation from the standard.

anoxia a lack of oxygen.

anxiety a general uneasiness of the mind characterized by irrational fears, panic, tension, and physical symptoms, including palpitations, excessive sweating, and increased pulse rate.

aphasia the inability to acquire meaningful spoken language by the age of three, usually resulting from damage or disease to the brain.

approved private school a private school that has met state and federal guidelines for providing appropriate services for a child with a disability and as a result appears on a state-approved list from which public schools may enter into contract for services.

apraxia pertains to problems with voluntary or purposeful muscular movement with no evidence of motor impairment.

articulation the production of distinct language sounds by the vocal chords.

assessment the process of gathering information about children in order to make educational decisions.

associated reactions increase of stiffness in spastic arms and legs resulting from effort.

astigmatism a visual defect resulting in blurred vision caused by uneven curvature of the cornea or lens; usually corrected by lenses.

asymmetrical one side of the body different from the other—unequal or dissimilar.

at risk usually refers to infants or children with a high potential for experiencing future medical or learning problems.

ataxia a form of cerebral palsy in which the individual suffers from a loss of muscle coordination, especially movements relating to balance and position.

ataxic no balance, jerky.

athetoid child with uncontrolled and continuously unwanted movements.

athetosis a form of cerebral palsy characterized by involuntary, jerky, purposeless, and repetitive movements of the extremities, head, and tongue.

atrophy the degeneration of tissue.

Attention Deficit-Hyperactivity Disorder (ADHD) a psychiatric classification used to describe individuals who exhibit poor attention, distractibility, impulsivity, and hyperactivity.

audiogram a graphic representation of the results of a hearing test.

audiologist a specialist trained in the evaluation and remediation of auditory disorders.

automatic movements necessary movements done without thought or effort.

balance not falling over; ability to keep a steady position.

baseline data an objective measure used to compare and evaluate the results obtained during some implementation of an instructional procedure.

baseline measure the level or frequency of behavior prior to the implementation of an instructional procedure that will later be evaluated.

behavior modification the techniques used to change behavior by applying principles of reinforcement learning.

bilateral motor skill and performance in purposeful movement that requires interaction between both sides of the body in a smooth manner.

bilingual the ability to speak two languages.

binocular vision vision using both eyes working together to perceive a single image.

blind, legally visual acuity measured at 20/200 in the better eye with best correction of glasses or contact lenses. Vision measured at 20/200 means the individual must be 20 feet from something to be able to see what the normal eye can see at 200 feet.

career education instruction that focuses on the application of skills and content-area information necessary to cope with the problems of daily life, independent living, and vocational areas of interest.

cataract a condition of the eye in which the crystalline lens becomes cloudy or opaque; as a result, a reduction or loss of vision occurs.

categorical resource room an auxiliary pull-out program that offers supportive services to exceptional children with the same disability.

catheter a tube inserted into the body to allow injections or withdrawal of fluids or to maintain an opening in a passageway.

cerebral palsy an abnormal succession of human movement or motor functioning resulting from a defect in, insult to, or disease of the central nervous system.

change in placement with reference to a child with a disability, any change of educational setting from or to a public school, local special school, or state-approved school.

change in program with reference to a child with a disability, any change in any component of a child's individualized education program.

circumduction swinging the limb away from the body to clear the foot.

clonus shaky movements of spastic muscle.

cognition the understanding of information.

compensatory movement a form of movement that is atypical in relation to normal patterns of movement.

compulsion a persistent, repetitive act that the individual cannot consciously control.

conductive hearing loss a hearing loss resulting from obstructions in the outer or middle ear or some malformations that interfere in the conduction of sound waves to the inner ear; may be corrected medically or surgically.

confabulation the act of replacing memory loss by fantasy or by some reality that is not true for the occasion.

congenital a condition present at birth.

consultant teacher a supportive service for a child with a disability in which the services are provided by a specialist in the classroom.

contracture permanently tight muscle or joint.

coordination combination of muscle in movement.

CPSE (Committee on Preschool Special Education) the multidisciplinary team that oversees the identification, monitoring, review, and status of disabled preschool children under the age of five.

cretinism a congenital condition associated with a thyroid deficiency that can result in stunted physical growth and mental retardation.

criterion-referenced tests tests in which the child is evaluated on his or her own performance to a set of criteria and not in comparison to others.

crossing the midline skill and performance in crossing the vertical midline of the body.

cyanosis a lack of oxygen in the blood characterized by a blue discoloration of the skin.

cystic fibrosis an inherited disorder affecting pancreas, salivary, mucous, and sweat glands that causes severe, long-term respiratory difficulties.

declassification the process in which a child with a disability is no longer considered in need of special education services. This requires a meeting of the district's IEP committee and can be requested by the parent, school, or child if he or she is over the age of eighteen.

defense mechanisms the unconscious means by which an individual protects him- or herself against impulses or emotions that are uncomfortable or threatening.

deficit a level of performance that is less than expected for a child.

deformity body or limb fixed in an abnormal position.

delusion a groundless, irrational belief or thought, usually of grandeur or of persecution; usually a characteristic of paranoia.

denial a defense mechanism in which the individual refuses to admit the reality of some unpleasant event, situation, or emotion.

depersonalization a nonspecific syndrome in which the individual senses that he or she has lost his or her personal identity—that he or she is different, strange, or not real.

desensitization a technique used in reinforcement theory in which there is a weakening of a response, usually an emotional response.

diagnosis the specific disorder identified as a result of some evaluation.

diplegia paralysis that affects either or both arms and both legs.

displacement the disguising of the goal or intention of a motive by substituting another in its place.

distractibility difficulty in maintaining attention.

distractible unable to concentrate.

Down syndrome a medical abnormality caused by a chromosomal anomaly that often results in moderate to severe mental retardation. The child with Down syndrome exhibits certain physical characteristics, such as a large tongue, heart problems, poor muscle tone, and broad, flat bridge of the nose.

due process the legal steps and processes outlined in educational law that protect the rights of children with disabilities.

dyscalculia a serious learning disability in which the child has an inability to calculate, apply, solve, or identify mathematical functions.

dysfluency difficulty in the production of fluent speech, as in stuttering.

dysgraphia a serious learning disability in which the child has an inability or loss of ability to write.

dyslexia a severe type of learning disability in which a child's ability to read is greatly impaired.

dysorthographia a serious learning disability that affects a child's ability to spell.

echolalia the repetition of what other people say as if echoing them.

electroencephalogram (EEG) a graphic representation of the electrical output of the brain.

encopresis a lack of bowel control that may also have psychological causes.

endogenous originating from within.

enrichment providing a child with extra and more sophisticated learning experiences than those normally presented in the curriculum.

enureusis a lack of bladder control that may also have psychological causes.

equilibrium balance.

equilibrium reactions automatic patterns of body movements that enable restoration and maintenance of balance against gravity.

etiology the cause of a problem.

exceptional children children whose school performance shows significant discrepancy between ability and achievement and as a result require special instruction, assistance, or equipment.

exogenous originating from external causes.

extension straightening of the trunk and limbs.

eye-hand coordination eye is used as a tool for directing the hand to perform efficiently.

facilitation making it possible for the child to move.

fetal alcohol syndrome a condition usually found in the infants of alcoholic mothers; low birth weight, severe retardation, and cardiac, limb, and other physical defects may be present.

field of vision the area of space visible with both eyes while looking straight ahead; measured in degrees.

figure-ground perception ability to see foreground against the background.

fine motor small muscle movements, use of hands and fingers.

flexion bending—for example, of elbows, hips, or knees.

floppy loose, fluid movements.

fluctuating tone changing from one degree of tension to another—for example, from a low to a high tone.

form constancy ability to perceive an object as possessing invariant properties such as shape, size, color, and brightness.

Free Appropriate Public Education (FAPE) used in Public Law 94–142 to mean special education and related services that are provided at public expense and conform to the state requirements and the child's individualized education program.

gait pattern description of walking pattern, including swing to gait (walking with crutches or walker by moving crutches forward and swinging body up to crutches) and swing through walking with crutches (by moving crutches forward and swinging body in front of the crutches).

genu valgus knock-kneed.

genu varum bowlegged.

glaucoma an eye disease characterized by excessively high pressure inside the eyeball. If untreated, the condition can result in total blindness.

grand mal seizure the most serious and severe form of an epileptic seizure in which the individual exhibits violent convulsions, loses consciousness, and becomes rigid.

gross motor coordinated movements of all parts of the body for performance.

group home a residential living arrangement for handicapped adults, especially the mentally retarded, along with several nondisabled supervisors.

guarding techniques techniques used to help students maintain balance including contact guarding (student requires hands-on contact to maintain balance) and guarded supervision (an individual is close to the student to provide physical support if balance is lost while sitting, standing, or walking).

habilitation an educational approach used with exceptional children that is directed toward the development of the necessary skills required for successful adulthood.

hallucination an imaginary visual image that the person regards as an actual sensory experience.

head control ability to control the position of the head.

hemiplegia paralysis involving the extremities on the same side of the body.

hemophilia an inherited deficiency in the blood clotting factor that can result in serious internal bleeding.

hertz a unit of sound frequency used to measure pitch.

homebound instruction a special education service in which teaching is provided by a specially trained instructor to students unable to attend school. A parent or guardian must always be present at the time of instruction. In some cases, the instruction may take place on a neutral site, that is, not in the home or school.

hydrocephalus a condition present at birth or developing soon afterward from excess cerebrospinal fluid in the brain and results in an enlargement of the head and mental retardation; sometimes prevented by the surgical placement of a shunt, which allows the proper drainage of the built-up fluids.

hyperactivity excessive physical and muscular activity characterized by extreme inattention, excessive restlessness, and mobility; usually associated with attention deficit disorder or learning disabilities.

hyperopia farsightedness; a condition causing difficulty with seeing near objects.

hypertonicity increased muscle tone.

hypotonicity an inability to maintain muscle tone or muscle tension or resistance to stretch.

impartial hearing officer an independent individual assigned by the district's board of education or commissioner of education to hear an appeal and render a decision. These individuals can in no way be connected to the school district, may have to be certified (depending on state regulations), are trained, and usually must update their skills regularly.

impulsivity non-goal-oriented activity that is exhibited by individuals who lack careful thought and reflection prior to a behavior.

inclusion educating the child with a disability in the general education classroom with his or her nondisabled peers.

independent evaluation a full and comprehensive individual evaluation conducted by an outside professional or agency not involved in the education of the child.

individual psychological evaluation a full and comprehensive evaluation by a state-certified school psychologist (if the child is evaluated within the school district) or a licensed psychologist for the purpose of educational planning.

individualized education program (IEP) a written educational plan that outlines the current levels of performance of a child with a disability, related services, educational goals, and modifications; developed by a team of the child's parents, teachers, and supportive staff.

individualized education program committee the multidisciplinary district team that oversees the identification, monitoring, review, and status of all children with disabilities residing within the school district; also referred to as the committee on special education (CSE).

inhibition positions and movements that stop muscle tightness.

insulin a protein hormone produced by the pancreas that regulates carbohydrate metabolism.

intellectualization a defense mechanism in which the individual exhibits anxious or moody deliberation, usually about abstract matters.

interdisciplinary team the collective efforts of individuals from a variety of disciplines in assessing the needs of a child.

intervention preventive, remedial, compensatory, or survival services made on behalf of an individual with a disability.

involuntary movements unintended movements.

iris the opaque, colored portion of the eye.

itinerant teacher a teacher hired by a school district to help in the education of a child with a disability. The teacher is employed by an outside agency and may be responsible for several children in several districts.

juvenile diabetes a disease with onset in childhood characterized by an inadequate secretion or use of insulin resulting in excessive sugar in the blood and urine. This condition is usually controlled by diet or medication, or both; however, in certain cases, control may be difficult, and if untreated, serious complications may arise, such as visual impairments, limb amputation, coma, and death.

kyphosis increased rounding of the upper back.

learning disability refers to children with average or above-average potential intelligence who are experiencing a severe discrepancy between their ability and achievement.

least restrictive environment the principle under IDEA that children with disabilities must be educated with their nondisabled peers to the maximum extent appropriate.

lordosis sway back or increased curve in the back.

magical thinking primitive and prelogical thinking in which the child creates an outcome to meet his or her fantasy rather than the reality.

mainstreaming the practice of educating exceptional children in the regular classroom.

manual muscle test test of isolated muscle strength: normal, 100 percent; good, 80 percent; fair, 50 percent; poor, 20 percent; zero, 0 percent.

meningitis an inflammation of the membranes covering the brain and spinal cord; if untreated, can result in serious complications.

meningocele a type of spina bifida in which there is protrusion of the covering of the spinal cord through an opening in the vertebrae.

mental age the level of intellectual functioning based on the average for children of the same chronological age.

mental retardation refers to a disability in which the individual's intellectual level is measured within the subaverage range and there are marked impairments in social competence.

microcephaly a disorder involving the cranial cavity characterized by the development of a small head. Retardation usually occurs from the lack of space for brain development.

mobility movement of a body muscle or body part or movement of the whole body from one place to another.

monoplegia paralysis of a single limb.

motivation making the student want to move or perform.

motor patterns ways in which the body and limbs work together to make movement. Also known as praxis.

multiple sclerosis a progressive deterioration of the protective sheath surrounding the nerves, leading to a degeneration and failure of the body's central nervous system.

muscular dystrophy a group of diseases that eventually weakens and destroys muscle tissue, leading to a progressive deterioration of the body.

myopia nearsightedness; a condition that results in blurred vision for objects at a distance.

native language the primary language used by an individual.

neologisms made-up words that have meaning only to the child or adult.

neonatal the time usually associated with the period between the onset of labor and six weeks following birth.

neurological impairment an impairment in the functioning of the central nervous system.

noncategorical resource room a resource room in a regular school that provides services to children with all types of classified disabilities. The children with these disabilities are able to be maintained in a regular classroom.

norm-referenced tests tests used to compare a child's performance to the performance of others on the same measure.

nystagmus a rapid, rhythmic, and involuntary movement of the eyes; may result in difficulty reading or fixating on objects.

obsessions repetitive and persistent ideas that intrude into a person's thoughts.

occupational therapist a professional who programs or delivers instructional activities and materials to assist children and adults with disabilities in participating in useful daily activities.

occupational therapy the evaluation and provision of services for children with disabilities in order to develop or maintain adaptive skills designed to achieve maximal physical and mental functioning of the individual in his or her daily life tasks.

ocular mobility the eye's ability to move.

ophthalmologist a medical doctor trained to deal with diseases and conditions of the eye.

optic nerve the nerve in the eye that carries impulses to the brain.

optician a specialist trained to grind lenses according to a prescription.

optometrist a professional trained to examine eyes for defects and prescribe corrective lenses.

organic factors usually associated with the central nervous system that cause a handicapping condition.

organization a student's ability to organize self in approach to and performance of activities.

orthosis a brace

ossicles the three small lobes of the ear that transmit sound waves to the eardrum: the malleus, incus, and stapes.

ostenogenesis imperfecta a hereditary condition that affects the growth of bones and causes them to break easily; also known as brittle bone disease.

otitis media middle ear infection.

otolaryngologist a medical doctor specializing in diseases of the ear and throat.

otologist a medical doctor specializing in the diseases of the ear.

otosclerosis a bony growth in the middle ear that develops around the base of the stapes, impeding its movement and causing hearing loss.

panic attacks a serious episode of anxiety in which the individual experiences a variety of symptoms, including palpitations, dizziness, nausea, chest pains, trembling, fear of dying, and fear of losing control. These symptoms are not the result of any medical cause.

paralysis an impairment to or a loss of voluntary movement or sensation.

paranoia a personality disorder in which the individual exhibits extreme suspiciousness of the motives of others.

paraplegia a paralysis usually involving the lower half of the body, including both legs, as a result of injury or disease of the spinal cord.

paraprofessional teacher assistant or aide in a special education setting.

passive anything that is done to the student without his or her help or cooperation.

pathological due to or involving abnormality.

perception the organization of sensation from useful functioning.

perinatal occurring at or immediately following birth.

perseveration unnecessary repetition of speech or movement.

petit mal seizures a mild form of epilepsy characterized by dizziness and momentary lapse of consciousness.

phenylketonuria (PKU) an inherited metabolic disease that usually results in severe retardation; if detected at birth, a special diet can reduce the serious complications associated with the condition.

phobia an intense irrational fear, usually acquired through conditioning to an unpleasant object or event.

photophobia an extreme sensitivity of the eyes to light; common in albino children.

physical therapist a professional trained to assist and help individuals with disabilities maintain and develop muscular and orthopedic capability and to make correct and useful movements.

physical therapy treatment of motor disabilities by a specialist under the supervision of a physician.

position in space child's ability to understand the relationship of and object to self.

positioning ways of placing an individual that will help normalize postural tone and facilitate normal patterns of movement and that may involve the use of adaptive equipment.

positive reinforcement any stimulus or event that occurs after a behavior has been exhibited that affects the possibility of that behavior's occurring in the future.

postnatal occurring after birth.

postural balance skill and performance in developing and maintaining body posture while sitting, standing, or engaging in an activity.

praxis ability to think through a new task that requires movement. Also known as motor planning.

prenatal occurring before birth.

preschool program a special education program for children with disabilities who are between the ages of three to five years.

projection the disguising of a source of conflict by displacing one's own motives to someone else.

projective tests methods psychologists and psychiatrists use to study personality dynamics through a series of structured or ambiguous stimuli.

pronation turning of the hand with palm down.

prone lying on the stomach.

prosthesis an artificial device used to replace a missing body part.

psychomotor seizure epileptic seizure in which the individual exhibits many automatic seizure activities of which he or she is not aware.

psychosis a serious mental disorder in which the individual has difficulty differentiating between fantasy and reality.

pupil the opening in the middle of the iris that expands and contracts to let in light.

pupil personnel team a group of professionals from the same school who meet on a regular basis to discuss children's problems and offer suggestions or a direction for resolution.

Pupils with Special Educational Needs (PSEN) students defined as having math and reading achievement lower than the 23rd percentile and requiring remediation. These students are not considered disabled but are entitled to assistance to elevate their academic levels.

quadriplegia paralysis involving all four limbs.

range of motion joint motion.

rationalization the interpretation of one's own behavior so as to conceal the motive it expresses by assigning the behavior to another motive.

reaction formation a complete disguise of a motive that is expressed in a form directly opposite to its original intent.

reflex stereotypic posture and movement that occurs in relation to specific eliciting stimuli and outside conscious control.

related services auxiliary services provided to children with disabilities, including speech pathology, audiology, psychological services, physical therapy, occupational therapy, counseling services, and art therapy.

remediation an educational program designed to teach children to overcome some deficit or disability through education and training.

repression the psychological process involved in not permitting memories and motives to enter consciousness although they are operating at an unconscious level.

resource room a special education placement provided to children with disabilities for part of the school day. It is intended to serve children's special needs so that they can be maintained within the least restrictive educational setting.

retina the back portion of the eye containing nerve fibers that connect to the optic nerve on which the image is focused.

retinitis pigmentosa a degenerative eye disease in which the retina gradually atrophies, causing a narrowing of the field of vision.

retrolental fibroplasia an eye disorder resulting from excessive oxygen in incubators of premature babies.

Rh incompatibility a blood condition in which the fetus has Rh-positive blood and the mother has Rh-negative blood, leading to a buildup of antibodies that attack the fetus; if untreated, can result in birth defects.

rheumatic fever a disease characterized by acute inflammation of the joints, fever, skin rash, nosebleeds, and abdominal pain; often damages the heart by scarring its tissues and valves.

righting reactions ability to right head and body when positions are abnormal or uncomfortable.

right/left discrimination skill and performance in differentiating right from left.

rigidity very stiff movements and postures.

rigidity cerebral palsy a type of cerebral palsy characterized by minimal muscle elasticity and little or no stretch reflex, which creates stiffness.

Rorschach Test an unstructured psychological test in which the individual is asked to project responses to a series of ten ink blots.

rotation movement of the trunk; the shoulders move opposite to the hips.

rubella a communicable disease that is usually of concern only when developed by women during the early stages of pregnancy. If contracted at that time, there is a high probability of severe handicaps of the offspring. Also referred to as german measles.

school phobia a form of separation anxiety in which the child's concerns and anxieties are centered around school issues and as a result he or she has an extreme fear about coming to school.

sclera the tough white outer layer of the eyeball that protects as well as holds contents in place.

scoliosis a weakness of the muscles that results in a serious abnormal curvature of the spine; may be corrected with surgery or a brace.

screening the process of examining groups of children in hopes of identifying potential high-risk children.

Section 504 refers to Section 504 of the Rehabilitation Act of 1973 in which guarantees are provided for the civil rights of children with disabilities and adults. It also applies to the provision of services for children whose disability is not severe enough to warrant classification but could benefit from supportive services and classroom modifications.

self-contained class a special classroom for exceptional children usually located within a regular school building.

semicircular canals the three canals within the middle ear that are responsible for maintaining balance.

sensation feeling.

sensorineural hearing loss a hearing disorder resulting from damage to or dysfunction of the cochlea.

sensory-motor experience the feeling of one's own movements.

sequencing the ordering of visual patterns in time and space.

sheltered workshop a transitional or long-term work environment for individuals with disabilities who cannot, or who are preparing for, work in a regular setting. Within this setting, these individuals can learn to perform meaningful, productive tasks and receive payment.

shunt a tube inserted into the body to drain fluid from one part to another. This procedure is common in cases of hydrocephalus to remove excessive cerebrospinal fluid from the head and redirect it to the heart or intestines.

spasm sudden tightness of muscles.

spasticity a type of cerebral palsy characterized by tense, contracted muscles, resulting in muscular incoordination.

spatial relations the ability to perceive the position of two or more objects in relation to self and others.

special class a class consisting of children with the same disability or different disabilities who have been grouped together as a result of similar educational needs and levels for the purpose of being provided special educational services.

spina bifida occulta a type of spina bifida characterized by a protrusion of the spinal cord and membranes. This form of the condition does not always cause serious disability.

stair climbing methods of climbing, including mark stepping (ascending or descending stairs one step at a time) and alternating steps (step over step).

stereognosis the identification of forms and nature of object through the sense of touch.

strabismus crossed eyes.

subluxation a partial dislocation where joint surfaces remain in contact with one another.

supination turning of hand with palm up.

supine lying on the back.

suppression the act of consciously inhibiting an impulse, effect, or idea, as in the deliberate act of forgetting something so as not to have to think about it.

surrogate parent any person appointed to act on the parent's or guardian's behalf when a child's parents are not known or are unavailable or when the child is the ward of the state.

symmetrical both sides equal.

symptom any sign, physical or mental, that stands for something else. Symptoms are usually generated from the tension of conflicts. The more serious the problem or conflict is, the more frequent and intense is the symptom.

syndrome a group of symptoms.

tactile pertaining to the sense of touch of the skin.

tandem walking walks in a forward progression placing heel to toe.

Thematic Apperception Test a structured psychological test in which the individual is asked to project his or her feelings onto a series of drawings or photos.

token economy a system of reinforcing various behaviors through the delivery of tokens—for example, stars, points, candy, chips.

tone firmness of muscles.

total communication the approach to the education of deaf students that combines oral speech, sign language, and finger spelling.

transitional support services temporary special education services, according to a child's individualized education program, provided to students who are no longer classified as disabled and may be transferring to a regular program, or to a child with a disability who may be moving to a program or service in a less restrictive environment.

tremor a type of cerebral palsy characterized by consistent, strong, uncontrolled movements.

triennial review a full and comprehensive reexamination of a child with a disability held every three years. This reexamination may include educational, psychological, and medical or any other evaluation deemed necessary by the committee on special education in order to determine the child's continuing eligibility for special education.

triplegia paralysis of three of the body's limbs.

underachiever a term generally used in reference to a child's lack of academic achievement in school. It is important that the school identify the underlying causes of such underachievement since it may be a symptom of a more serious problem.

Usher's syndrome an inherited combination of visual and hearing impairments.

vestibular system a sensory system that responds to the position of the head in relation to gravity and accelerated and decelerated movements.

visual acuity sharpness or clearness of vision.

visual memory ability to recall visual stimuli in terms of form, detail, position, and other significant features on both a short- and long-term basis.

visual-motor integration the ability to combine visual input with purposeful voluntary movement of other body parts involved in the activity.

vitreous humor the jelly-like fluid that fills most of the interior of the eyeball.

vocational rehabilitation a well-designed program designed to help disabled adults obtain and hold a job.

voluntary movements movements done with attention and concentration.

Wechsler Scales of Intelligence a series of individual intelligence tests measuring global intelligence through a variety of subtests.

References

20 U.S.C. 1414(c). *Individuals with Disabilities Education Improvement Act of 2004—Public Law 108-446*. Washington DC: U.S. Department of Education.

American Academy of Neurology. (2001). *Study ties stuttering to anatomical differences in the brain*. Retrieved August 1, 2005, from http://www.sciencedaily.com/releases/2001/07/010730075359.htm.

American Academy of Pediatrics (2000). Clinical practice guideline: Diagnosis and evaluation of the child with attention-deficit/hyperactivity disorder. *Pediatrics, 105,* 5, 1158-1170.

American Association on Mental Retardation (2002). *Adaptive behavior.* Retrieved November 30, 2005, from http://aamr.org.

American Association on Mental Retardation (2005). *Mental retardation.* Retrieved November 30, 2005, from http://aamr.org/.

American Occupational Therapy Association. (2003). *Occupational therapy in educational settings under the Individuals with Disabilities Education Act.* Bethesda, MD: American Occupational Therapy Association.

American Occupational Therapy Association. (2005). *Consumer information: What is occupational therapy?* Retrieved March 6, 2006, from http://www.aota.org/featured/area6/index.asp.

American Psychiatric Association. (1987). *Diagnostic and statistical manual of mental disorders-III* (3rd ed. rev.). Washington, DC: American Psychiatric Association.

American Psychiatric Association. (1994). *Diagnostic and Statistical Manual of Mental Disorders* (4th ed.). Washington, DC: American Psychiatric Association.

American Psychiatric Association. (2000). *Diagnostic and statistical manual of mental disorders* (4th ed., text rev.). Washington, DC: American Psychiatric Association.

Anxiety Disorders Association of America. (2002). *Anxiety in children.* Retrieved March 12, 2006, from www.adaa.org.

Arc of the United States. (2001). *Mental retardation.* Silver Spring, MD: Arc.

Atkinson, R. (2001). *Achievement versus aptitude tests in college admissions.* Retrieved March 12, 2006, from http://www.ucop.edu/pres/speeches/achieve.htm.

479

Auditory Verbal Center (2006). *Auditory processing*. Retrieved March 6, 2006, from http://www. avc-atlanta.org/.

Autism Society of America (2006). *Diagnosing autism*. Retrieved March 15, 2006, from http://www. autism-society.org/site/PageServer?pagename=autismdiagnosis.

Barlow, J. A., & Gierut, J. A. (2002). Minimal pair approaches to phonological remediation. *Seminars in Speech and Language, 23*(1), 57–67.

Bender, W. (2001). *Learning disabilities: Characteristics, identification, and teaching strategies*. Needham Heights, MA: Allyn and Bacon.

Brice, A. (2001). *Children with communication disorders* [ERIC Digest E 617] (ERIC Document No. ED459549).

Burnette, J. (2000). Assessment of Culturally and Linguistically Diverse Students for Special Education Eligibility. *The ERIC Clearinghouse on Disabilities and Gifted Education (ERIC EC). ERIC EC Digest #E604*. Washington, DC.

C.F.R. 300.7(c)(3)). *Individuals with Disabilities Education Improvement Act of 2004: Public Law 108-446*. Washington, DC: U.S. Department of Education.

C.F.R. 300.7(c)(5)). *Individuals with Disabilities Education Improvement Act of 2004: Public Law 108-446*. Washington, DC: U.S. Department of Education.

C.F.R. Section 300.8. *Individuals with Disabilities Education Improvement Act of 2004: Public Law 108-446*. Washington, DC: U.S. Department of Education.

C.F.R. Section 300.301(a). *Individuals with Disabilities Education Improvement Act of 2004: Public Law 108-446*. Washington, DC: U.S. Department of Education.

C.F.R. Section 300.304(b)(4). *Individuals with Disabilities Education Improvement Act of 2004: Public Law 108-446*. Washington, DC: U.S. Department of Education.

C.F.R. Section 300.304(b)(6)(7). *Individuals with Disabilities Education Improvement Act of 2004: Public Law 108-446*. Washington, DC: U.S. Department of Education.

C.F.R. Section 300.307. *Individuals with Disabilities Education Improvement Act of 2004: Public Law 108-446*. Washington, DC: U.S. Department of Education.

C.F.R. Section 300.308. *Individuals with Disabilities Education Improvement Act of 2004-Public Law 108-446*. Washington, DC: U.S. Department of Education.

Calderon, R., & Naidu S. (2000). Further support for the benefits of early identification and intervention for children with hearing loss. *The Volta Review, 100(5)*, 53–84.

California Department of Education (2001). *Handbook on developing early childhood special education programs and services*. Special Education Division: California Department of Education.

Chartered Institute of Personnel Development. (2006). *Psychological testing*. Retrieved May 20, 2006, from, http://www.cipd.co.uk/subjects/recruitmen/tests/psytest.htm.

Child Development Institute. (2005). *Children with communication disorders*. Retrieved August 1, 2005, from http://www.childdevelopmentinfo.com/.

Cohen, L. G., & Spencer, L. J. (2003). *Assessment of children and youth with special needs* (2nd ed.). Needham Heights, MA: Allyn and Bacon.

Council of State Directors. (2001). *The 1999-2000 state of the states gifted and talented education report*. Longmont, CO: Council of State Directors.

Cox, L. S. (1975). Diagnosing and remediating systematic errors in addition and subtraction computations. *The Arithmetic Teacher, 22*, 151-157.

Dodd, B., & Bradford, A. (2000). A comparison of three therapy methods for children with different types of developmental phonological disorder. *International Journal of Language and Communication Disorders, 35*, 189–209.

Easterbrooks, S. (1999). Improving practices for students with hearing impairments. *Exceptional Children, 65, 537 554.*

Education Commission of the States. (2004, June). *State gifted and talented definitions.* Retrieved March 2, 2006, from http://www.ecs.org/clearinghouse/52/28/5228.htm.

Flores, J., Lopez, E., & DeLeon, J. (2000). *Technical assistance document for assessment and evaluation of preschool children who are culturally and linguistically diverse.* Santa Fe: New Mexico State Department of Education, Special Education Office.

Forrest, K. (2002). Are oral-motor exercises useful in the treatment of phonological/articulatory disorders? *Seminars in Speech and Language, 23,* 15–25.

Forrest, K., Elbert, M., & Dinnsen, D. (2002). The effect of substitution patterns on phonological treatment outcomes. *Clinical Linguistics and Phonetics, 14,* 519–531.

French, J. L. (1964). *The Pictorial Test of Intelligence.* Boston: Houghton Mifflin.

Friend, M. (2005). *Special education: Contemporary perspectives for school professionals.* Needham Heights, MA: Allyn and Bacon.

Friend, M., & Bursuck, W. (2006). *Including students with special needs.* Needham Heights, MA: Allyn and Bacon.

Gargiulo, R. (2004). *Special education in contemporary society: An introduction to exceptionality.* Belmont, CA: Thompson.

Gertner, A. B. (2005). *Auditory processing disorder facts. Department of Communication Disorders and Deafness.* Kean State University, New Jersey. Retrieved March 3, 2006, from www.apdfacts.com.

Gierut, J. A. (2001). Complexity in phonological treatment: Clinical factors. *Language, Speech and Hearing Services in Schools, 32*(4), 229–241.

Gierut, J. A., & Champion, A. H. (2001). Syllable onsets II: Three-element clusters in phonological treatment. *Journal of Speech, Language and Hearing Research, 44,* 886–904.

Grossman, H. (1983). *Classification in mental retardation* (Rev. ed.). Washington, DC: American Association on Mental Retardation.

Hallahan, D., Kauffman, J., & Lloyd, J. (1999). *Introduction to learning disabilities* (2nd ed.). Needham Heights, MA: Allyn and Bacon.

Hammill, D. (1998). *Detroit Test of Learning Aptitude: Examiner's manual.* Austin, TX: PRO-ED.

Hardman, M. L., Drew, C. J., & Egan, M. W. (2005). *Human exceptionality: School, community, and family* (8th ed.). Needham Heights, MA: Allyn and Bacon.

Heward, W. L. (2006). *Exceptional children: An introduction to special education* (8th ed.). Upper Saddle River, NJ: Pearson.

Holden-Pitt, L., & Diaz, J. (1998). Thirty years of the annual survey of deaf and hard-of-hearing children and youth: A glance over the decades. *American Annals of the Deaf, 142*(2), 72–76.

Huefner, D. S. (2000). The risks and opportunities of the IEP requirements under IDEA '97. *Journal of Special Education, 33,* 195–204.

IDEA. (2004). (20 U.S.C. 1414(b) (1)-(3), 1412 (a)(6)(B). *Individuals with Disabilities Education Improvement Act of 2004: Public Law 108-446.* Washington DC: U.S. Department of Education.

IDEA. (2004). Part C [20 U.S.C. §1432(5)(A)(ii)] *Individuals with Disabilities Education Improvement Act of 2004: Public Law 108-446.* Washington DC: U.S. Department of Education.

Iannelli, V. (2005). *Neuropsychological assessment in schools: What you need to know.* Retrieved March 12, 2006, from http://pediatrics.about.com/cs/mentalhealth.

Jacob K. Javits Gifted and Talented Students Education Act of 1988, reauthorized in 1994. *Public Law 108-382, Title XIV,* 1988, p. 388.

Jensen, M. (2005). *Introduction to emotional and behavioral disorders.* Upper Saddle River, NJ: Pearson.

Kaland, M., & Salvatore, K. (2003). *Psychology of hearing loss.* Retrieved September 5, 2005, from www.professional.asha.org/news/020319.cfm.

Kaufman Children's Center (2004). *Receptive language disorders—Signs and symptoms.* Retrieved August 1, 2005, from http://www.kidspeech.com/index.php.

Kim, O. H., & Kaiser, A. P. (2000). Language characteristics of children with ADHD [electronic version]. *Communication Disorders Quarterly, 21,* 154–165.

Kuntz, S., & Hesslar, A. (1998). *Bridging the gap between theory and practice: Fostering active learning through the case method* (p. 23). Annual Meeting of the Association of American Colleges and Universities.

Marland, S. (1972). *Education of the gifted and talented (Report to Congress).* Washington, DC: U.S. Government Printing Office.

McLean, M. (2000). *Conducting child assessments.* Champaign: University of Illinois at Urbana-Champaign.

McLoughlin, J. A., & Lewis, R. B. (1994). *Assessing special students.* Columbus, OH: Merrill.

Merz, W., Buller, M., & Launey, M. (1990). Neuropsychological assessment in schools. *Practical Assessment, Research & Evaluation, 2*(4). Retrieved March 12, 2006, from http://PAREonline.net/getvn.asp?v=2&n=4.

Moores, D. F. (2001). *Educating the deaf: Psychology, principles, and practices* (5th ed.). Boston: Houghton-Mifflin.

Morales, S. (2005). Overview of speech and language impairments. Retrieved August 1, 2005, from http://www.childspeech.net/u_i.html.

National Center for Learning Disabilities. (2005). *Visual and auditory processing disorders.* Retrieved September 10, 2005, from http://www.ldonline.org/ld_indepth/process_deficit/visual_auditory.html.

National Council of Supervisors of Mathematics. (1978). Position statement on basic skills. *Mathematics Teacher, 71,* 147–152.

National Dissemination Center for Children with Disabilities (2004a). *Deafness and hearing loss.* Fact sheet 3 (FS3). Retrieved March 3, 2006, from http://www.nichcy.org/pubs/factshe/fs3txt.htm.

National Dissemination Center for Children with Disabilities. (2004b). *Autism and pervasive developmental disorder.* Retrieved on March 3, 2006, from http://www.nichcy.org/pubs/factshe/fs1txt.htm.

National Dissemination Center for Children with Disabilities. (2004c). *Deafness and hearing loss.* Retrieved March 3, 2006, from http://www.nichcy.org/pubs/factshe/fs3txt.htm.

National Dissemination Center for Children with Disabilities. (2004d). *Emotional disturbance.* Retrieved March 3, 2006, from http://www.nichcy.org/pubs/factshe/fs5txt.htm.

National Dissemination Center for Children with Disabilities. (2004e). *Learning disabilities.* Retrieved March 3, 2006, from http://www.nichcy.org/pubs/factshe/fs7txt.htm.

National Dissemination Center for Children with Disabilities. (2004f). *Mental retardation.* Retrieved March 3, 2006, from http://www.nichcy.org/pubs/factshe/fs8txt.htm.

National Dissemination Center for Children with Disabilities. (2004g). *Speech and language impairments.* Retrieved March 3, 2006, from http://www.nichcy.org/pubs/factshe/fs11txt.htm.

National Dissemination Center for Children with Disabilities. (1999). *Questions and answers about IDEA.* Retrieved March 3, 2006, from www.nichcy.org/pubs/newsdig/nd21txt.htm.

National Dissemination Center for Children with Disabilities. (2005). *Finding help for young children with disabilities (birth to 5)*. Retrieved May 19, 2006, from http://www.nichcy.org/pubs/parent/pa2txt.htm.

National Institute on Deafness and Other Communication Disorders. (2004). *Auditory processing disorder in children*. NIH Pub 01-4949. Washington, DC: National Institute on Deafness and Other Communication Disorders.

National Institute of Mental Health (2000). *Depression*. NIH Publication No. 00-3561: Washington, DC.

National Library of Medicine. (2004a). *Antisocial personality disorder*. Retrieved November 30, 2005, from http://www.nlm.nih.gov/medlineplus/ency/article/000921.htm.

National Library of Medicine. (2004b). *Avoidant personality disorder*. Retrieved November 30, 2005, from http://www.nlm.nih.gov/medlineplus/ency/article/000940.htm.

National Library of Medicine. (2004c). *Borderline personality disorder*. Retrieved November 30, 2005, from http://www.nlm.nih.gov/medlineplus/ency/article/000935.htm.

National Library of Medicine. (2004d). *Dependent personality disorder*. Retrieved November 30, 2005, from http://www.nlm.nih.gov/medlineplus/ency/article/000941.htm.

National Library of Medicine. (2004e). *Histrionic personality disorder*. Retrieved November 30, 2005, from http://www.nlm.nih.gov/medlineplus/ency/article/0001531.htm.

National Library of Medicine. (2004f). *Narcissistic personality disorder*. Retrieved November 30, 2005, from http://www.nlm.nih.gov/medlineplus/ency/article/000934.htm.

National Library of Medicine. (2004g). *Obsessive-compulsive personality disorder*. Retrieved November 30, 2005, from http://www.nlm.nih.gov/medlineplus/ency/article/000942.htm.

National Library of Medicine. (2004h). *Paranoid personality disorder*. Retrieved November 30, 2005, from http://www.nlm.nih.gov/medlineplus/ency/article/000938.htm.

National Library of Medicine. (2004i). *Schizoid personality disorder*. Retrieved November 30, 2005, from http://www.nlm.nih.gov/medlineplus/ency/article/000920.htm.

National Library of Medicine. (2004j). *Schizotypal personality disorder*. Retrieved November 30, 2005, from http://www.nlm.nih.gov/medlineplus/ency/article/0001525.htm.

Nipold, M. A. (2001). Stuttering and phonology: Is there an interaction? *American Journal of Speech-Language Pathology, 11,* 99–110.

OSEP Letter to Michel Williams. (1994, March 14). *21 Individuals with Disabilities Education Law Report* 73.

Pierangelo, R. (2004). *The special educator's survival guide*. San Francisco: Jossey-Bass.

Pierangelo, R., & Giuliani, G. (2006a). *Assessment in special education: A practical approach* (2nd ed.). Needham Heights, MA: Allyn and Bacon.

Pierangelo, R., & Giuliani, G. (2006b). *Learning disabilities: A practical approach to foundations, assessment, diagnosis, and teaching*. Needham Heights, MA: Allyn and Bacon.

Psychology Information Online. (2005). *Psychological testing*. Retrieved March 2, 2006, from, http://www.psychologyinfo.com/treatment/testing.html. Public Law 108–446. (2004). *Individuals with Disabilities Education Improvement Act of 2004*. Washington, DC: U.S. Department of Education.

Richmond, R. L. (2005). *A guide to psychology and its practice*. Retrieved November 30, 2005, from http://www.guidetopsychology.com/testing.htm.

Salvia, J., & Ysseldyke, J. E. (1998). *Assessment* (8th ed.). Boston: Houghton-Mifflin.

Salvia, J., & Ysseldyke, J. E. (2004). *Assessment in special and inclusive education* (9th ed.). Boston: Houghton Mifflin.

Schirmer, B. R. (2000). *Language and literacy development in children who are deaf* (2nd ed.). Needham Heights, MA: Allyn and Bacon.

Shackelford, J. (2006, Feb.). *State and jurisdictional eligibility definitions for infants and toddlers with disabilities under IDEA* (NECTAC Notes No.20). Chapel Hill: The University of North Carolina, FPG Child Development Institute, National Early Childhood Technical Assistance Center.

Shames, G. H., & Anderson, N. B. (2002). *Human communication disorders: An introduction.* Needham Heights, MA: Allyn and Bacon.

Smith, T. E., Polloway, E., Patton, J. R., & Dowdy, C. A. (2004). *Teaching students with special needs in inclusive settings* (4th ed.). Needham Heights, MA: Allyn and Bacon.

Strock, M. (2004). *Autism spectrum disorders* (Pervasive Developmental Disorders). NIH Publication No. NIH-04-5511. Bethesda, MD: National Institute of Mental Health, National Institutes of Health, U.S. Department of Health and Human Services.

Taylor, R. (2006). *Assessment of exceptional students* (7th ed.). Needham Heights, MA: Allyn and Bacon.

Taylor, R. L., Brady, M., & Richards, S. B. (2004). *Mental retardation: Historical perspectives, current practices, and future directions.* Needham Heights, MA: Allyn and Bacon.

Tsatsanis, K. D., & Volkmar, F. R. (2001). *Unraveling the neuropsychological assessment.* Retrieved March 1, 2006, from http://www.aspennj.org/neuro.html.

Turnbull, R., Turnbull, A., Shank, M., & Smith, S. J. (2004). *Exceptional lives: Special education in today's schools* (4th ed.). Upper Saddle River, NJ: Prentice Hall.

U.S. Census Bureau. (1985). *1985 statistical abstract of the United States.* Washington, DC: U.S. Government Printing Office.

U.S. Census Bureau. (1990). *1990 statistical abstract of the United States.* Washington, DC: U.S. Government Printing Office.

U.S. Census Bureau. (1996). *1996 statistical abstract of the United States.* Washington, DC: U.S. Government Printing Office.

U.S. Census Bureau. (1997). *1997 statistical abstract of the United States.* Washington, DC: U.S. Government Printing Office.

U.S. Census Bureau. (2000). *2000 statistical abstract of the United States.* Washington, DC: U.S. Government Printing Office

U.S. Census Bureau. (2001). *Statistical abstract of the United States.* Washington, DC: U.S. Government Printing Office.

U.S. Department of Education. (2002). *Twenty-fourth annual report to Congress.* Washington, DC: U.S. Department of Education.

U.S. Department of Education. (2003). *Identifying and treating attention deficit hyperactivity disorder: A resource for school and home.* Publication No. HS97017002. Washington, DC: U.S. Department of Education.

U.S. Department of Education. (2004). *Twenty-sixth annual report to Congress on the implementation of the Individuals with Disabilities Education Act.* Washington, DC: U.S. Department of Education.

U.S. Department of Health and Human Services. (1999). *Mental health: A report of the surgeon general.* Rockville, MD: U.S. Department of Health and Human Services.

U.S. Department of Health and Human Services. (2005). *Children and adolescents with conduct disorder.* Retrieved March 1, 2006, from http://www.mentalhealth.samhsa.gov/publications/allpubs/CA-0010/default.asp.

Venn, J. J. (2000). *Assessing students with special needs* (2nd ed.). Upper Saddle River, NJ: Merrill.